SINO-SOVIET DIALOGUE ON THE PROBLEM OF WAR

SINO-SOVIET DIALOGUE ON THE PROBLEM OF WAR

by

JOHN YIN

MARTINUS NIJHOFF / THE HAGUE / 1971

PRINTED IN THE NETHERLANDS

PREFACE

The author has spent upwards of ten years in working on this book. His objective is to clarify the military aspect of the Moscow-Peking dialogue which has not yet received its deserved treatment. The apogee of that dialogue seems to have been passed toward the end of the rule of Khrushchev. Yet the Vietnam war spawns fresh contention. Our coverage will span the development from 1956 to the present. The beginning of the dispute with regard to the origins of war in general is taken up in the first two chapters. The next three chapters discuss the several types of war with the frame of reference set in what now appears to be a quondam era. But the principle differences between the disputants are just as outstanding today as they were then.

The penultimate chapter is somewhat wide in scope in order to deal with the larger and more intensely bitter polemics evolving after Khrushchev left office. There have been many new and startling views held by both sides since then, views splitting them poles apart. Ominously at issue now is the question of Sino-Soviet peaceful coexistence. Our work, obviously, cannot wait until that question is answered to be finished. The final chapter concludes our study.

To write of subjects as dynamic as this one is a challenge because they are current affairs. Due to the swift change of events, no sooner is our typescript put to press than it needs a revision. Undeterred, however, by the march of time which always frustrates writers of topical issues, the author has decided to share the results of his research with like-minded students in the area of communist politics.

Laurentian University   J. Yin
Sudbury, Canada

ACKNOWLEDGEMENT

From the research work to the final draft, the author has been helped along by scores of individuals. At one time or another, he approached the reference librarians of the following institutions for strategical sources: University of Southern California, University of California at Berkeley, New York Public Library, the Library of Congress in the American capital, Laurentian University, University of Guelph, Harvard-Yenching Library at Harvard University. Their willingness to make available the information the author required was of overriding importance in his work. Fortunately, because the author himself has received some library education, he did not get lost easily in the huge libraries and often obtained what he desired in the shortest possible time. For critical advices on the subject-matter, he is indebted to Prof. G. Totten, who read all but the last two chapters and offered many valuable comments. Finally, thanks must also go to Mrs. Lorraine Moreau, the Department secretary, for typing nearly the entire manuscript.

TABLE OF CONTENTS

CHAPTER I

INTRODUCTION

The dispute between Soviet Russia and the People's Republic of China concerning the problem of war can properly be dated from the Twentieth Congress of the Communist Party of the Soviet Union (CPSU),[1] although their latent schism harks back a few years earlier.[2] It is possible that the current argument just manifests an old divergence. Yet what has transpired from the records of the recent debate clearly goes beyond the former Sino-Soviet differences. Characterizing the post-1956 development are the ideological struggles in the midst of which any previous hard feeling has gone unnoticed. Only at a few times in the dialogue, for example, did Peking refer to the policy of the Comintern which once dictated the subordination of the Chinese Marxists to the leadership of the Kuomintang, a policy obscuring the identity of the Communist Party and almost annihilating its members altogether.[3]

[1] Rodger Swearingen, "The Russo-Chinese alliance," *Current History*, 43 (October, 1962), 231; Charles B. MacLane, "The Moscow-Peking alliance; the first decade," *ibid.*, 37 (December, 1959), 330; John Gittings, "Cooperation and conflict in Sino-Soviet relations," *International Affairs* (London), 40 (January, 1964), 66; Allen S. Whiting, "'Contradiction' in the Moscow-Peking axis," *Journal of Politics*, 20 (February, 1958), 143–44; A. Kashin, "New Soviet polemics with communist China," Institut zur Erforschung der UdSSR, *Bulletin*, 7 (August, 1960), 36; Richard Harris, "Sino-Soviet dispute," *Political Quarterly*, 35 (July-September, 1964), 334. The Chinese themselves dated their argument with the Soviets from the Twentieth Congress of the CPSU, *see* William Henry Chamberlain, "The quarrel of the communist giants," *Russian Review*, 23 (July, 1964), 218.

[2] An Indian communist, H. Konar, told the Calcutta District Council of the Communist Party of India that the Chinese informed him that their difference with the Soviets started soon after Stalin's death. The Chinese did not like the Soviet leadership's handling of the Beriya case. The way Stalin was denigrated they regarded as obnoxious. The Soviet attitude toward Yugoslavian revisionism they considered cringing; *see* "Inside reports of the dispute," *Link*, October 16, 1960, pp. 13–17. According to one author, the "Chinese communists and the Soviets have respectively designated 1959 and 1960 as the beginning of their increasing difference," *see* Peter Tang, "Sino-Soviet tension," *Current History*, 45 (October, 1963), 224.

[3] Rodger Swearingen, "The political and ideological relationships between the Chinese Communist Party and the Soviet Union" (unpublished Master's thesis, University of Southern California, 1948), chap. vii; B. Schwartz, "On the originality of Mao Tse-tung," *Foreign Affairs* 34 (October, 1955), 67, 76. The following books give a very detailed account of the triangular relations of the CPSU, the Chinese Communist Party (CCP), and the Kuomintang: Harold

In his address to the Twentieth Congress on February 15, 1956, Nikita Khrushchev, First Secretary of the Central Committee of the CPSU, accentuated three points: the avoidability of war, peaceful coexistence, and the parliamentary road to socialism. In effect, there is only one issue involved, for the second and third points may be regarded as corollaries to the first point.[4] Should all nations in the world live together as friends and should a political community change its system through the due process of law which parliamentarianism implies, the military would lose its reason for being. Therefore, all that Khrushchev dwelt upon in his four hours' oration on that February day boiled down to the single tenet of avoidability of armed conflict in the present epoch. What actually consumed so much time was his elaboration of the alleged new line which invalidated Lenin's theory of imperialist war. Certainly such a bold departure, savoring of the "sacrilegious," was a matter of no small order; and it was fitting and proper for him to defend it with great care. Hence he had to go into some detail in reviewing the contemporary situation which required fresh approaches in comparing the problems faced by Lenin with those faced by him, and in appealing to men of reason to work for peace. Humanity, he warned, has reached a point of no return: we face either coexistence or coextinction. There can never be a third way.[5] Since the keynote of the speech was a plea for no war, the marked assumption was that the Soviet Union ought to shoulder the responsibility to adjust the policies of its satellite nations so that peace might be secured through the mounting strength of the communist bloc.[6] Any other course would augur ill for the whole world, not only the West alone.

Isaacs, *The Tragedy of the Chinese Revolution* (rev. ed.; Stanford, Calif.: Stanford University press, 1957), chap. 1–3; Conrad Brandt, *Stalin's Failure in China, 1924–1927* (Cambridge, Mass.: Harvard University press, 1958), pp. 11–38. M. F. Iur'ev, *Revoliutsiya, 1925–1927 gg. v Kitae* (The revolution in China, 1925–1927) (Moskva: Izd-vo "Nauka," 1968); A. I. Chrepanov, *Severnyi pokhod natsional'no-revoliutsionnoi armii Kitaya* (The Northern Expedition of the national revolutionary army of China) (Moskva: Izd-vo "Nauka," 1968).

[4] The "central issue" of the Peking-Moscow dialogue, wrote Leonard Schapiro, "is the devastating effects of a modern nuclear war on all contestants, whether capitalist or socialist," *see* "The Sino-Soviet dispute and the Twenty-Second Congress," *India Quarterly*, 18 (January-March, 1962), 5; the same view was held by Neal Stanford in his "Moscow-Peiping feud grows," *Foreign Policy Bulletin*, 40 (October 1, 1960), 11. However, P. Royle said that the war issue was only attendant on the basic precept of historical determinism; *see* his "Historical inevitability and the Sino-Soviet debate," *Political Quarterly*, 34 (July-September, 1963), 292.

[5] N. V. Pukhovskii, *O mire i voine* (On peace and war) (Moskva: Izd-vo "Mysl'," 1965), p. 137. The Chinese felt that "there is a 'middle way' somewhere between hot war and a detente," *see* Donald S. Zagoria, "The future of Sino-Soviet relations," *Asian Survey*, 1 (April, 1961), 8.

[6] One of the grievances of the Chinese was Khrushchev's failure to consult Peking befo re deciding upon de-Stalinization; *see* George F. Hudson, Richard Lowenthal, and Roderic k

To the guest visitors in the audience, including China's then number two man, Marshal Chu Teh, the implied assertion of Soviet hegemony did not appear presumptive, since it was Russia which represented the mightiest industrial and military complex of the bloc. No other socialist country could remotely approach her in world prestige and influence. Indeed, only a year later at the Moscow Conference of the Ruling Communist Parties, we heard Mao openly acknowledge the Kremlin as the bloc's elder brother. However, with reference to the revision of Lenin's theory of war, Mao was not convinced. At first, he bothered not to refute the Russian statesman probably in the belief that as long as the revisionist principles were not translated into diplomacy, nothing should be taken seriously. After the Twentieth Congress, however, Khrushchev vigorously worked toward improving East-West relations through handshaking with political figures, capitalist and neutralist alike. Perhaps it was his journey to the United States that exhausted the patience of the Chinese.[7] To Mao it was a grave mistake for Khrushchev to pay homage to China's archenemy. Exasperating him still further was the trust apparently placed in President Eisenhower by the Russian Premier, who said the American statesman was desirous of peace. Even more conducive to Mao's anger were the closer relations between Russia and Indonesia and India, as a result of the personal diplomacy of Khrushchev at the very time China was having difficulties with both latter nations.[8] The hesitancy of Moscow to back up, by threatened use of force, the claim held by Peking on Taiwan was perhaps no less important in prompting Peking to challenge Moscow's leadership.[9] The shelling of the offshore islands was all that the Chinese could do in the face of the American stand to defend the stronghold of the Chinese Nationalists. All this experience did not fail to compel Mao to arrive at the conclusion that Khrushchev's action was implementing his

MacFarquhar (eds.), *The Sino-Soviet Dispute: Documented and Analyzed* (New York: Praeger, 1961), p. 1. Hereafter this book will be cited as *Sino-Soviet Dispute. See* also Rodger Swearingen, *Current History*, 43 (October, 1962), 230–231.

[7] Foreign Minister Ch'en Yi lamented such a trip; *see* A. Kashin, "Contradictions between Moscow and Peiping," Institut zur Erforschung der UdSSR, *Bulletin*, 6 (December, 1959), 22; *ibid.*, 7 (August, 1960), 36; Obata Misao, "The Sino-Soviet dispute," *Japan Quarterly*, 8 (January-March, 1961), 31.

[8] K. Alexandrov, "China's independent policy," Institut zur Erforschung der UdSSR, *Bulletin*, 7 (May, 1960), 30.

[9] John Gittings, *International Affairs* (London), 40 (January, 1964), 70, 72; John S. Reshetar, "Sino-Soviet relations," *Western Political Quarterly*, 14 (September, 1961, supplement), 74; Obata Misao, *Japan Quarterly*, 8 (January-March, 1961), 31; "The Sino-Soviet conflict," *Royal Central Asian Journal*, 50 (January, 1963), 61.

policy of coexistence. Hence Peking decided to make an issue of it in its dialogue with Moscow.[10]

In order to call a halt to Khrushchev's detente Mao thought it important to fire his polemic shot before anything concrete might be worked out by the Russian and Western leaders to the detriment of China's interests[11] and the interests of the world proletarians, as he saw them.[12] The occasion for his charge was appropriately Lenin's ninetieth birthday anniversary. The several treatises marking the celebration which were printed in the *Jen-min jih-pao* (People's daily) in the middle of 1960 all centered on the accusation that the Russians were betraying that great leader. From then on until the end of 1964, both sides poured forth a large quantity of literature attacking each other's position and defending their own.[13] Immediately after the retirement of Khrushchev, the verbal engagement seemed to be subsiding, as if the protagonists had become weary.[14] Yet the contest remained an indecisive one;[15] neither party would yield its policy orientation.[16]

[10] Donald S. Zagoria, *Sino-Soviet Conflict, 1956–1961* (Princeton, N. J.: Princeton University Press, 1962), p. 238; Richard Lowenthal, "Shifts and rifts in the Russo-Chinese alliance," *Problems of Communism*, 8 (January-February, 1959), 23–3; J. D. B. Miller, "A Commonwealth for communists," *Australian Outlook*, 17 (April, 1963), 91.

[11] Edward Crankshaw, "Cold war of communisms," *New York Times Magazine*, May 26, 1963; pp. 89–90; Donald S. Zagoria, *Asian Survey*, 1 (April, 1961), 4; John Gittings, *International Affairs* (London), 40 (January, 1964), 68. Richard Hugh suggested that detente would restrain China from military adventures; *see* his "Duel of communism's big two," *New York Times Magazine*, April 1, 1962, p. 118.

[12] Donald S. Zagoria, *Asian Survey*, 1 (April, 1961), 4.

[13] The last known exchange of letters took place in 1963. "Otkrytoe pis'mo Tsentral'nogo Komiteta Kommunisticheskoi Partii Sovetskogo Soiuza partiinym organizatsiyam, vsem kommunistam Sovetskogo Soiuza" (An open letter from the Central Committee of the CPSU to the party apparatus and party members of the CPSU), *Pravda*, July 14, 1963. It also appears in *Peking Review*, 30 (July 26, 1963), 27–46. "A proposal concerning the general line of the international communist movement, letter of the CCP in reply to the letter dated March 30, 1963 of the CPSU," dated June 14, 1963, *Peking Review*, 25 (June 21, 1963), 6–33; *ibid.*, 30 (July 26, 1963), 10–26.

[14] Joseph Kun remarked at the Sixth International Symposium of the Institut zur Erforschung der UdSSR, Munich (May 31–June 2, 1966) that the "primary issues of Sino-Soviet conflict have remained since Khrushchev's displacement," *see* R. Eugene Parta and Robert Farrell, "Vietnam and the Sino-Soviet dispute," *Analysis of Current Developments in the Soviet Union*, 37 (1965–66), 6; A. Kashin, "Moscow claims leadership and unity of world communist movements," *ibid.*, 35 (1965–66), 1, 3, 6.

[15] One student made an interesting remark: "The ideological quarrel between communism and anti-communism is a religious war like that between Islam and Christendom, between catholics and protestants. History teaches us that religious wars are never 'won' or 'lost.' They are never wholly or finally 'settled.' They cool down and fade away until they are no longer matters of life and death," *see* Walter Lippmann, "Dealing with the Soviet Unilon," *Newsweek*, 62 (July 22, 1963), 17.

[16] "I know very well that this split in communism between … them is definite. And they cannot find, I am convinced, compromise on an ideological basis," said M. Djilas in an interview upon his arrival in the United States on October 13, 1968, *New York Times*, November 27, 1968, p. 10.

Since 1965, charges continued to rage after a brief lull. Even though the substance of these charges revealed new grounds of discord, the basic ideological contention differs very little. What both sides have tried to do simply is to reassert their former stands by referring back to certain previously issued documents upon which debate had already taken place. For example, on August 22, 1966, the 11th Plenum of the 8th Central Committee of the CCP, in refuting the Soviets, endorsed again its letter of June 14, 1963 to the CPSU.[17] On the Russian side, the 1957 Declaration and 1960 Statement were recited to defend its concept on the problem of war.[18] However, the post-Khrushchev dialogue has had new dimensions as a result of the war in southeast Asia and is being conducted in a much broader perspective. In a sense, the Sino-Soviet verbal war has escalated along a wide front and outgrown its original local character.

After having sketched the background of the dispute, we shall now set forth the various problems at issue. In negating Khrushchev's avoidability doctrine, the Chinese criticized that it was necessary for him to make a differentiation of the kinds of war first and then set out to discuss their inevitability.[19] The argument for the preclusion of all possibilities of sword-crossing was regarded as too sweeping. His theoretical stand being threatened by the relentless Chinese onslaught, Khrushchev had to modify it considerably, so much so that the apple of discord turned on the bloc's policy toward the West.[20] The Russians felt that since the bloc was getting stronger, it became unnecessary to be impetuous in its foreign policy; the Chinese, on the contrary, argued that now that the bloc had grown powerful, it could afford to be daring. Perhaps because of this tough stance, the Soviets have described the

---

[17] *China after Mao* (Princeton, N. J.: Princeton University press, 1966), p. 283.

[18] N. V. Tropkin, "Strategiya i taktika leninizma" (The strategy and tactics of Leninism), in *V. I. Lenin – velikii teoretik* (V. I. Lenin, a great theorist) (Moskva: Gos. izd-vo polit. lit-ry, 1966), pp. 214–15.

[19] In this regard, the Chinese are truly Leninist. Lenin once wrote that it was impossible to oppose war in general and that one must analyze each military engagement dialectically before expressing his view, *see* "Sotsializm i voina" (Socialism and war), July-August, 1915, *Sochineniya* (Collected works; 5th ed.) (Moskva: Gos. izd-vo polit. lit-ry, 1958–66), vol. 26, p. 311; also in his *O voine, armii i voennoi nauke* (On war, army and military science; 2nd ed.) (Moskva: Voen. izd-vo, 1965), p. 255. Elsewhere Lenin stated: "We Marxists are not unconditional opponents of all wars," in "Voina i revoliutsiya" (War and revolution), May, 1917, first published in April, 1929, *O voine, armii i voennoi nauke* (On war, army and military science; 2nd ed.), p. 362. "To deny war in its entirety without concrete analysis of the historical milieux would amount to a monstrous theorem, erroneous practice and crypto-opportunism," wrote Lenin, *see* his "K peresmotru partiinoi programmy" (Toward review of the party program), October, 1917, *ibid.*, p. 436.

[20] Michael Lindsay, "Is cleavage between Russia and China inevitable?" *Annals of the American Academy of Political and Social Science*, 336 (July, 1961), 57; Merle Fainsod, *How Russia Is Ruled* (rev. ed.; Cambridge, Mass.: Harvard University press, 1964), p. 601.

Chinese as "terribly revolutionary."[21] Reading the Russian polemics, one is led to believe that Peking is really a world-warmonger.[22] The Russian charge has, however, been discerned by many students as unwarranted, because the Chinese were much milder than merely meets the eye.[23] On the other hand, the Peking theorists make one think that the Soviet leadership has abandoned its goal of world communism, or at least planned to postpone it indefinitely. This is also a misrepresentation, for the Soviets have never disavowed that grand commitment.[24] After all, the two communist nations have the identical objective of building up global socialism.[25] To achieve this, the Russians think that they have to wait and the Chinese that they can hardly wait.[26] In a sense, both are realistic: the former, because they believe that too precipitate a course of action would lead to war which they have no need for;[27] the latter, because they believe time is on the side of the enemy. Peking feels the West was getting stronger by availing itself

[21] D. Shelyagin, "Oruzhie srazheniya kommunisticheskikh partiyakh" (The fighting weapon of communist parties), *Sovestkaya Rossiya*, 6 (June 10, 1960), 5.

[22] In his address at Varn (Romania) on May 16, 1962 to the World Peace Conference, Khrushchev stated that people do not think of death, but life, they think of how to better their living and how to raise their children. "We shall work to prevent destructive war," he declared. In the whole speech, China was implicitly accused as warmongering, *see* his *Predotvratit' voinu, otstoyat' mir!* (Prevent war and defend peace!) (Moskva: Gos. izd-vo polit. lit-ry, 1963), p. 75. *See* also Tang Tsou, "Mao Tse-tung and peaceful co-existence," *Orbis*, 8 (Spring, 1954), 36–7, 39; Alexandre Metaxas, "Moscow vs Peking: reasons for the rift," *Nation*, 194 (April 14, 1962), 332.

[23] "In attacking Khrushchev's ideological innovation and the new strategy, the Chinese were not calling for general war or arguing that general war was inevitable, an interpretation prevalent in the West," wrote Donald S. Zagoria, *Sino-Soviet Conflict, 1956–1961*, p. 300. Richard Lowenthal said: "Every one of the Chinese documents in question quoted with approval the sentence of the 1957 Moscow Declaration (based in turn on the resolution of the Twentieth Congress of the CPSU) that owing to the growth of the forces of peace, it is now realistically possible to prevent war," *Sino-Soviet Dispute*, p. 13. The same observation is expressed by the following authors: Victor Zorza, "Choice before world's Marxists," *Guardian*, January 7, 1963, p. 7; Tang Tsou, *Orbis*, 8 (Spring, 1964), 45; Madhu Limaye, "The Sino-Russian conflict within international communism," *United Asia*, 12 (1960), 501; Peter Tang, "Moscow and Peking: the question of war and peace," *Orbis*, 5 (Spring, 1961), 28; Allen S. Whiting, *Journal of Politics*, 20 (February, 1958), 131; Brian Crozier, "The struggle for the third world," *International Affairs* (London), 40 (July, 1964), 446.

[24] Addressing the Third Congress of the Romanian Workers' Party, Khrushchev stated: "More precisely speaking of who will bury whom, it is the working class which, as Karl Marx put it, is the grave-digger of capitalism. And I, being a member of the communist party of the great and mighty working class, do not exclude myself from among the grave-diggers of capitalism,'' *see* his *On Peaceful Coexistence* (Moscow: Foreign languages publishing house, 1961), p. 233.

[25] "Otkrytoe pis'mo Tsentral'nogo Komiteta Kommunisticheskoi Partii Sovetskogo Soiuza partiinym organizatsiyam, vsem kommunistam Sovetskogo Soiuza" (An open letter from the Central Committee of the CPSU to the party apparatus and party members of the CPSU), *Pravda*, July 14, 1963.

[26] Alexander Metaxas, "The Soviet Union and foreign policy," *Listener*, 44 (September 8, 1960), 370; K. Alexandrov, Institut zur Erforschung der UdSSR, *Bulletin*, 7 (May, 1960), 32.

[27] Pukhovskii, *op. cit.*, p. 138.

of the detente, whereas at the present time it was much weaker than the bloc.[28]

The issue of the causes of war figures large in the dispute between the Russians and the Chinese. Whether the avoidability concept holds true depends mainly on the theories of the origins of war. If capitalism is the father of militarism, as suggested by Lenin and pre-First World War socialists, it would be futile to try to rule out arms except by doing away with capitalism.[29] Conversely, should war be a matter of policy, there is then a definite possibility for its control. In that case, war proves amenable to statecraft. Provided there exists the will to proscribe armed struggle, peace can prevail. It is the author's intent to relate Peking's and Moscow's views on the origins of war to their respective policy stands. The basic concern of both countries to universalize Marxism-Leninism may appreciably limit their range of differences. Yet one still has to study how the disputants have sought to assimilate their views on the best available means to achieve the professed objective. Moreover, no matter how successful they have been in working out an ideological compromise, any similar outlook on the roots of war and its prevention depends first upon an identical understanding of Marxism-Leninism, and second, upon an identical strategic consideration. With a view to estimating the likelihood of these two contingencies, we propose to investigate the categories of war, and the situations under which armed struggles have arisen in the views of the disputants.

There has been a common impression in the West that Peking wants to bring about world communism through violent revolution and that Moscow is not so rigid. Supposing that assumption holds true, could this be attributed to Peking's policy of forcing Marxism-Leninism upon others? If a case can be made of China's conviction in the certitude of

[28] K'ang Sheng, "On the current international situation," speech to the Warsaw Treaty Conference, *Peking Review*, 6 (February 5, 1960), 6–9, also in *Sino-Soviet Dispute*, pp. 72–7. The Chinese and Albanian media accused Khrushchev of believing naively in the peace gestures of Eisenhower and Kennedy, *see* William Griffith, *Albania and the Sino-Soviet Rift* (Cambridge, Mass.: MIT press, 1963), p. 119. The Russians in general did not take issue with the Chinese as to the warlike nature of the West. The "New Program," adopted at the Twenty-Second Congress of the CPSU on October 21, 1961 has the following to say: "The imperialist camp is making preparations for the most heinous crime against mankind, a world thermonuclear war," *see* "Novaya programma" (New program), *Pravda*, November 2, 1961; *Izvestiya* of the same date. The statement also appears in *Soviet Communism: Programs and Rules* (edited by J. F. Triska; San Francisco: Chandler publishing company, 1962), pp. 64–5.

[29] The point was originally brought out by the 1907 Stuttgart conference of socialists, *see* Lenin, "Voinstvuiushchii militarizm i anti-militaristskaya taktika sotsial-demokratii" (Militarism and anti-militarist tactic of Social-Democracy), *O voine, armii i voennoi nauke* (On war, army and military science; 2nd. ed), pp. 181–88. For an identical view as held by the present Chinese, *see* Chao Shin, "Lung-tuan tzu-pen ti chün-shih li-yun" (Monopoly profit as a result of militarism), *Shih-chieh-chih-shih* (World knowledge), 8 (April 25, 1966), pp. 18–20.

world war, it seems imperative to look into her rationale, apart from such ready answers as the power hunger of the Chinese leaders. It may be presumed that hostility as a psychological phenomenon indicates more than the sheer urge to struggle; it stems also from a sense of insecurity which in turn is conditioned by a distrust of others. We shall view Mao's thought as communicated through the accessible media to see on what ground he adhered to a policy of no compromise. It cannot be said that Mao regards world war a sure matter because he has a propensity toward aggression. Circumspect research needs to be done before a fair inference can be drawn respecting China's basic attitude toward world conflict. On the other hand, the theory of the avoidability of war held by the Soviets manifests an important change in Leninism. The ideological bases, therefore, require cautious study. Have the Soviets openly flouted Lenin's teaching? What reasons are suggested for the alleged non-inevitability of world war? In taking up these problems, this work will have to examine the meaning of the so-called epoch and the attendant correlation of forces because these have a direct bearing on the possibilities of inter-camp armed struggle.

Is it likely for a capitalist regime to collapse of itself? Khrushchev's non-inevitability doctrine has been interpreted by the Chinese as referring to civil war no less than to world war, and is denounced as un-Leninist. What was the contention Peking advanced to justify its outlook that a class struggle is allegedly raging inside bourgeois nations and forcing the capitalist regime to collapse? It is also important to examine how Khrushchev has later turned around to uphold the inevitability of civil war, while he pretended not to alter his original stand. Finally, the import of civil war in the global strategy of Peking and Moscow can better be evaluated by taking account of another variety of war, namely, local war and war of national liberation.

The problem of those wars became a bone of contention between Mao and his Soviet counterpart. As champions of the cause of the supposed victims of imperialism, both men underwrote the armed revolt of any colony or independent yet weak nation for its survival and equality. However, on account of his unwillingness to coexist with imperialist-capitalism, a system which he denounced as "cannibalistic," Mao can afford to pursue a course to aid the colony undergoing revolution. On the Russian part, the problem gets complicated. While supporting the colonial insurrection, the Soviets professed a policy of peaceful coexistence between states with different systems. Clearly there is a discrepancy, for if the Soviets set out to abet a colony to break away from the imperialists by giving it aid and comfort, their coexistence pledge is less than plausible. The dilemma of the Soviets is this: imperialists must be treated at once as enemies in their relations to the dependencies and as friends in their relations to the socialist nations so that both capitalist and socialist régimes may live as neighbors and cooperate in solving world problems. It seems that the policies pursued by Russia and China have reflected their respective international standings, for the broad contacts Russia has with the outside world incline her toward conciliation, whereas the relative isolation of China conduces her toward a hard line.[30] To help the revolts against the colonial powers would not embarrass Mao in front of the capitalist statesmen, for he sought not to visit and shake hands with them, and would serve to boost his prestige with the victimized peoples. This course, if followed by the Soviets, would conceivably detract from their detente. In our work we shall endeavor to compare the Sino-Soviet views on the question of the capitalist nations at war with their dependencies and of the proper reaction to any West-initiated war of local magnitude.

The writer contrives to build on the hypothesis that Peking deems war inevitable prior to the universal triumph of communism. Following Lenin, the Chinese elites maintain that the ordeal of arms has been characteristic of international relations whenever and wherever capitalism obtains. War cannot be precluded, they felt, except by precluding capitalism in the first place and cannot be regarded as a gloomy matter after all.[31] The East bloc will sooner or later be invaded by the imperialist bloc because, Peking thought, the latter can never be trusted, no matter how meek it appears at times. Furthermore, since capitalists have already fought with the working people, civil war is being started, and it is the obligation of the people to answer it in kind. As to the colonies' attempt to liberate themselves from imperialist rule, the Chinese stand has been that communist nations are bound to come to their aid. Coexistence would dull the revolutionary spirit of the proletarians and their class and national allies. In opposition to Peking, Moscow feels that war can be eliminated by such means as treaties of disarmament between East and West, that capitalist states have already become so weakened that they can no longer unleash war,[32] that

---

[30] Axel Heyst, "The Moscow-Peking tangle," *Contemporary Review*, 204 (August, 1963), 78.
[31] Lin Piao said: "In diametrical opposition to the Khrushchev revisionists, the Marxist-Leninists and revolutionary people never take a gloomy view of war," in his "Long live the victory of people's war," *China after Mao*, p. 256.
[32] Pukhovskii, *op. cit.*, p. 190. *See* also M. D. Kammapi, "Druzhba i bratstvo vsekh narodov SSSR, neterpimost' k natsional'noi i rasovoi nepriyazni (Friendship and fraternity

local war would easily grow into general conflict and must be avoided,[33] and finally that in the present epoch socialism as a system has made world war both unnecessary and unwise.[34]

The Vietnam conflict opens a new phase in the Sino-Soviet dialogue on the issue of war. Starting from an argument as to the extent of aiding Hanoi, the dialogue comes to touch on the gravest problem. China wants to plunge Russia into the war, while Russia makes it clear that "only an absolute necessity may compel her to fight a war and that this necessity has to be the straight menace to the existence of the world socialist system."[35] The Vietnam crisis does not pose such a menace as the Chinese choose to believe. On account of the vast scope of the charges and countercharges, we shall endeavor to analyze the dialogue in broader than military terms.

of the peoples in the Soviet Union, intolerance toward national and race enmity), in M. G. Zhuravkov and O. P. Tsalikova (eds.), *Nravstvennye printsipy stroitelya kommunizma* (Moral principles of the builders of communism) (Moskva: Izd-vo "Mysl'," 1965), p. 280.

[33] Troplin, "Strategiya i taktika leninizma" (The strategy and tactics of Leninism), in *V. I. Lenin – velikii teoretik* (V. I. Lenin, a great theorist), p. 196.

[34] M. S. Shifman, *Voina i ekonomika* (War and economy) (Moskva: Voen. izd-vo, 1964), p. 204. *See* also A. Sudarikov, *Klassy i klassovaya bor'ba, sotsial'nye revoliutsii* (Classes and class struggle, socialist revolutions) (Moskva: Gos. izd-vo polit. lit-ry, 1966), p. 54; *Materialy XXII s'ezda KPSS* (Documentary materials of the 22nd Party Congress) (Moskva: Gospolitizdat, 1961), p. 348.

[35] Pukhovskii, *op. cit.*, p. 147.

THE CAUSES OF WAR

The Materialist Concept of War

Marxism-Leninism teaches that a prevailing model of ideology is conditioned by the economic development of a given community. All human relations mirror the process of turning out concrete articles necessary for daily life. When the latter changes, the former will also change. It is said to be the historic law that a new style of production brings in its trail a revolutionary adjustment of the institutions. The web of social living can be explained by reference to the way the material goods are made and shared. Since war is a troubled human relationship and belongs in the superstructure, it derives its root from the economic base. Lenin did an extensive research on the problem of capitalism and war and arrived at the inference that the two are inseparable.[1] From this view no communist can diverge without stultifying the whole concept of class struggle and revolutionary dialectics. Within the framework of our study we may be wondering how the former number one communist in Russia, Khrushchev, could assert that the teaching of Lenin on the inevitabliity of war under capitalism no longer held. Has Khrushchev gainsaid the economic origins of war? His declared revision was criticized mordantly by Peking. But what is Peking's idea on the issue? In this section an analysis will be made of Lenin's conception of imperialist war, a war embedded in the alleged predatory capitalist economy, and of the problem whether Khrushchev has really repudiated that conception. If he still believed in Lenin's inevitability

---

[1] Lenin, "Voinstvuiushchii militarizm i anti-militaristskaya taktika sotsial-demokratii" (Militarism and anti-military tactics of Social Democracy), July, 1908, *O voine, armii i voennoi nauke* (On war, army and military science; 1st ed.), vol. 1, p. 300. Khrushchev said: "Predacious wars are natural attributes of imperialism and monopoly capitalism," *Predotvratit' voinu, otstoyat' mir!* (Prevent war and defend peace!), p. 38.

theory, then there is no doubt that he considered capitalism the breeding ground of war. We shall first look into Lenin's position, and next
the positions of Peking and Moscow. In this way, we hope to find out
where lies the difference, if any, between Moscow and Peking regarding
the economic parentage of armed conflict.

First of all, let us clarify the concept of war for it has been used by
the communists in diverse ways. The broadest meaning of the term is
sociological. V. I. Gorev, who was a Czarist officer and served in the
early twenties as an instructor in a Soviet military academy, wrote that
war is a social phenomenon and the inevitable accompaniment of
humanity.[2] Such a definition is not accepted by communist writers.
It is their belief that the discord in man's world stems from animosity
between the exploiters and exploited and that the divided society will
give way finally to a working people's commonwealth. It is necessary,
therefore, to regard war not as inherent in the social body. Lenin
declared that war is a form of class conflict;[3] and in the age of imperialism the whole world is the battlefield, the enslaving of men by men
being the motivation. Thus understood, war begins with the advent of
class community and ends with its disappearance. In a similar vein,
Mao wrote that "war is the highest form of collision between classes
and political factions."[4] Both communist leaders used the term "war"
to denote antagonism, contention or rivalry. However, there is a narrow-
er import of war used by both men to imply military engagement. The
books *Imperialism, the Highest Stage of Capitalist Development* (Lenin)[5]
and *On Guerrilla Warfare* (Mao)[6] employed the words *voina* and *chan-
cheng* (war) respectively in the ordinary sense; it means nothing more
than armed contest between two organized formations. As Marshal
Sokolovskii, *et al.* defined it, war is a struggle, but not all struggles are
war. The two concepts should be differentiated, they advised.[7] Criti-

---

[2] "Voina kak sotsial'noe yavlenie" (War as a social phenomenon), *Voina i voennoe iskusstvo v svete istoricheskogo materializma* (War and military art in the light of historical materialism), p. 24.

[3] Lenin, *Sochineniya* (Collected works; 4th ed.), vol. 21, p. 271; vol. 30, p. 149.

[4] Mao, "Chung-kuo ko-ming chan-cheng ti chan-lüeh wen-t'i" (The strategical problems of the Chinese revolutionary war), November ,1936, *Mao Tse-tung hsüan-chi* (Selected works), 1951, vol. 1, p. 100.

[5] The work was written by Lenin during January–July, 1916. This is the book in which he set forth his theory of the imperialist war, and appears in his *Sochineniya* (Collected works; 4th ed.), vol. 22, pp. 173–290. An excerpt can be found in *idem, O voine, armii i voennoi nauke* (On war, army and military science; 1st ed.), vol. 1, pp. 462–83.

[6] This highly technical book, setting forth the tactics and operation against the regular troops, was written in December, 1936. It is published by: New York: Praeger, 1961. Now it is in *Mao Tse-tung hsüan-chi* (Selected works), 1952, vol. 2.

[7] *Voennaya strategiya* (Military strategy; 2nd ed.), p. 215.

cizing some Western writers, especially the late British military historian Liddel-Hart, for abusing the word "war," the Soviets stated: "They appear entangled with the notions of war, policy and class struggle; in reality, war does not mean economic pressure, propaganda, diplomacy, subversive activities." The latter may turn into a military encounter; but "to subsume under the category of war the non-violent media" is wrong.[8] The Russian authors obviously disapproved of Lenin's broad usage of *voina* (war). Their remark was also aimed at the Chinese who, in the authors' words, "treated the peaceful rivalry as war and thus inevitably came to an absurd conclusion that war is a constant factor in human society."[9] In this work we shall use "war" in the common acceptation (as did all the Chinese and Russians in the dispute), meaning the "armed conflict between two parties."

Beginning of the Dispute: Revision of Lenin's Theory of War

The point which began the Sino-Soviet dialogue on war concerns the question of whether war is avoidable. Khrushchev's argument on the matter could be summarized as follows. He commenced his speech to the Twentieth Congress (February 15, 1956) by saying that Marxism-Leninism lays down that wars are inevitable as long as there is imperialism. This results because, he explained, imperialism once made up a world system and met with no counter forces. Now such forces come into being and are potent enough to curb the imperialists. "War is not fatally inevitable," he declared.[10] We should note that the war he talked of is the imperialist war which Lenin deemed unavoidable – a point which will be shortly clarified. Khrushchev then must have in mind the theory of war as propounded by Lenin in his book *Imperialism*. There Lenin found the key to imperialist war in the capitalist economy.

That Khrushchev has been aware of the relationship of economy and war is beyond a doubt. Yet, he states: "People usually take one aspect of the question and examine only the economic basis of war under imperialism. It is not enough. Whether there is to be war largely depends upon political forces."[11] From this statement it is clear that he recognized the political as well as the economic provenance of war. Less clear, however, is whether he grasped the implication of each basis.

---

[8] *Ibid.*, pp. 217–18.
[9] *Ibid.*, p. 218.
[10] "Otchetnyi doklad Tsentral'nogo Komiteta Kommunisticheskoi Partii Sovetskogo Soiuza XX s'ezdu Partii, doklad pervogo sekretarya TsK KPSS t. N. S. Khrushcheva" (Khrushchev's report to the Twentieth Congress of the CPSU), *Pravda*, February 15, 1956.
[11] *Ibid.*

In reality there are two bases of war: economic and political. Both can be found in Lenin's writings; one was elaborated into a theory, while the other was not. The avoidability problem must be analyzed from these two positions. In spite of Khrushchev's vague notion of the double origins of war, he was hopelessly confused. After explaining away his refutation of Lenin's inevitability theory, he conceded: "Certainly, the Leninist precept that, so long as imperialism exists the economic basis giving rise to war will also be preserved, remains in force."[12] The marked inconsistency demonstrates his failure in distinguishing the two causes of war. Lenin's concept of imperialist war, it should be noted, derives from an economic anatomy of international relations of his era. But in Lenin's works there has been another kind of war; it is initiated by the imperialists, but has political roots. That there have been two sources of war is not questioned by the Russians (Khrushchev included) who, however, made little effort to clarify the problem.[13] Since each source has its peculiar manifestations, its remedies are different. In his Twentieth Congress speech, Khrushchev strove to apply a political perventive, viz., a correlation of forces between East and West, for the economic causes of war (imperialist war). Such a poor scholarship of Leninism springs from an ignorance of the nature of imperialism as it was understood by early socialists.

Lenin's Theory of Imperialism and Imperialist War

In spite of the Soviet claim,[14] Lenin was not the first to relate imperialism to war. John Hobson, on whom Lenin depended so much for his concept of imperialism, had previously established the framework of reference in his book on capitalist economy.[15] In addition, Otto Bauer[16] and Rudolf Hilferding[17] also provided Lenin with a mine of information on the theory of commodity and marketing. Before Lenin wrote *Imperialism*, it was a staple argument among the socialists that Euro-

---

[12] *Ibid.*

[13] Sokolovskii and his associates made a passing mention of imperialist and inter-bloc wars; *Voennaya strategiya* (Military strategy; 2nd ed.), p. 234.

[14] L. Leont'ev, *Leninskaya teoriya imperializma* (Lenin's theory of imperialism) (Moskva: Moskovskii rabochii, 1954), pp. 3–13.

[15] John Hobson, *Imperialism* (London: Allen & Unwin, 1939); I. A. Gladkov, "O leninskom metode nauchnogo tvorchestva" (On Lenin's method of scientific creativity), in *V. I. Lenin – velikii teoretik* (V. I. Lenin, a great theorist), p. 469.

[16] *Die Nationalitätenfrage und die Sozialdemokratie* (The nationality problems and social democracy) (Wien: Verlag der Wiener Volksbuchhandlung, 1924), chap. 1.

[17] *Das Finanzkapital; eine Studie über die jüngste Entwicklung des Kapitalismus* (The finance capital; a study of the latest development of capitalism) (Berlin: Diez, 1947), pp. 40–45.

pean industrialists had gone abroad to find outlets for their produce. Regarding the possibility that such adventures would spearhead territorial expansion and give birth to war between states, only Rosa Luxemburg among the socialists manifested some concern. In her work on capitalism, she visualized the armed confrontation among the industrial powers and foresaw the disappearance of imperialism as a result of the confrontation. Historical determinism, she asserted, has assured the ascendancy of socialism.[18] Sharing her optimism, Lenin, of all his contemporaries, developed most fully the same concept. In a competitive capitalism, he wrote, the process of vanquishing small by large business went on inexorably, for price collusion and control of distribution became a powerful weapon in the commercial war.[19] Eventually there emerged titanic monopolies in manufacture, insurance, banking and trade. However, with the formation and growth of chain companies, economic situations worsened on account of two related developments. First, under capitalism over-production was the rule; the excessive supply of merchandise ended in periodical slumps. Second, the impoverishment of the workers shrank the sales market still more. These circumstances forced the entrepreneurs to seek foreign exploitation. To Lenin it signaled the overgrowing of monopoly capitalism into imperialism.[20]

The realm for the factory tycoons was the less industrialized parts of the globe where natural resources remained untapped and demands for finished products were high. At first the domestically unsold goods were exported and cheap materials brought in. But when this proved uneconomical, a resourse was made to taking capital to, and establishing plants in, the colonies.[21] The melange of financial and business exploitation was considered by Lenin the most effective way to sustain monopolist regimes. Due to the uneven development of industrial capitalism among the peoples of the world, some countries were ahead

[18] Rosa Luxemburg, *Die Akkumulation des Kapitals; ein Beitrag zur ökonomischen Erklärung des Imperialismus* (The accumulation of capital; an economic explanation of imperialism) (Berlin: Vorwärts P. Singer, 1913), pp. 210–15.
[19] Lenin, "K peresmotru partiinoi programmy" (Toward review of the party program), October, 1917, *O voine, armii i voennoi nauke* (On war, army and military science; 2nd ed.), p. 437; *idem, Sochineniya* (Collected works; 4th ed.), vol. 22, pp. 173–75.
[20] L. Leont'ev, *loc. cit.*
[21] Lenin wrote that the "productive forces and capacities outgrow the bourgeois national framework," in "Proekt rezoliutsii levykh sotsial-demokratov k pervoi mezhdunarodnoi sotsialisticheskoi konferentsii" (Project of the resolutions of left Social-Democrats to be submitted to the first international socialist conference), *Sochineniya* (Collected works; 5th ed.), vol. 26, p. 282; also in *O voine, armii i voennoi nauke* (On war, army and military science; 2nd ed.), p. 247.

of others in appropriating the colonies.[22] On the eve of the First World War, nearly all the masterless areas of the globe were pre-empted, nothing being left for the newcomers like Germany and Japan. They could not obtain any overseas territory except by forcibly displacing others. Hence war broke out.[23] The first world conflict was always referred to by the communists as the imperialist war.[24] It had as its genesis the exploitative capitalism which assumed the imperialist form. Thus, class struggles within a nation lead to struggles between nations. Imperialist war was inevitable, Lenin posited.

Two Kinds of War

Imperialist war for Lenin was the armed scramble for colonies among the several capitalist regimes;[25] its prime cause was economic in nature. He envisaged another kind of war in which the alleged hostile encirclers waged to stifle the Soviet system.[26] Khrushchev's Twentieth Congress speech leaves no doubt about his awareness of the two types of war. The fact that he invoked the peace forces to support his non-inevitability theory indicates his loose thinking on the matter. It stands to reason that if imperialist war originates in exploitation of one class by another, or one nation by another, its preventive should be a change or revolution in the economic system. Khrushchev's insistence on the balance of forces to preclude war is patently irrelevant here. It was Stalin who seemed to grasp the point. "With the abolition of imperialism not only does the 'inevitability' of war cease to be a problem, even the necessity for preventing it is gone," he wrote.[27] Without Stalin's logic, Khrushchev sought to prescribe a political pill for an economic disease. The correlation of strength could only apply to capitalist-socialist, not to imperialist, wars. Properly speaking the only way to stave off imperial-

---

[22] *Idem*, "O lozunge soedinenykh shtatov evropy" (On the slogan of the United States of Europe), August, 1915, *ibid.*, p. 272.

[23] *Idem*, "Voina i revoliutsiya" (War and revolution), May, 1917, *ibid.*, pp. 367–69.

[24] For example, Frunze, *Izbrannye proizvedeniya* (Collected works), vol. 1, p. 4; *Germanskii militarizm i imperializm* (German militarism and imperialism) (Moskva: Gos. izd-vo polit. lit-ry, l1965), pp. 2–10; N. V. Pukhovskii, *op. cit.*, pp. 11–15. *Mirovaya ekonomika* (World economy) (Moskva: Gos. izd-vo polit. lit-ry, 1965), chap. 1.

[25] Lenin, "Sed'maya (aprel'skaya) vserossiiskaya konferentsiya RSDRP(B)" (The Seventh (April) All-Russian Conference of the RSDRP (B)), April, 1917, *O voine, armii i voennoi nauke* (On war, army and military science; 2nd ed.), pp. 359–60.

[26] In the essay "O lozunge 'razoruzheniya'" (On the slogan of disarmament), Lenin wrote (October, 1916) that socialist states had to wage war against bourgeois states; *ibid.*, p. 321; also in his *Sochineniya* (Collected works; 5th ed.), vol. 30, p. 151.

[27] Stalin, *Economic Problems of Socialism in the Soviet Union* (New York: International publishers, 1952), p. 7. In Russian it is in: *Ekonomicheskie problemy sotsializma v SSSR* (Moskva: Gos. izd-vo polit. lit-ry, 1952), p. 7.

ist war is to abrogate imperialism; and to do the latter, one must liquidate the colonial system. Because imperialism and colonialism, in Lenin's view, are two sides of a coin, with the disappearance of the one, the other follows.

Khrushchev's speech which we cited, and the various pronouncements of the Soviet Government or world communist bodies have shown the same confusion of the two kinds of war mentioned above. Particularly noticeable is the speech, for it is there that he sought to have his cake and eat it, too. In one breath he upheld the validity of Lenin's argument that as long as imperialism exists, war is inevitable, and in the next breath, he argued that imperialist war is not "fatally inevitable."[28] Such a vacillation appears in all the important policy statements subsequently issued. For example, on November 22, 1957, the Declaration of the Ruling Communist Parties expressed at once a belief in the inevitability of war as suggested by Lenin, and in the non-inevitability due to changed circumstances.[29] In truth, there are involved two wars: imperialist war is inevitable, interbloc war not inevitable. In term of genesis, one is economic, the other is political. The communists should have pointed this out in order to avoid confusion and to improve logic.

Economic Causes and the Nature of Imperialists

Is it likely that the nature of imperialism will change and thus remove the cause of war? The communists have argued that imperialists are innately warlike and that their resort to arms is an involuntary act.[30] In an article on the "Problems of war and peace in present-day conditions," Frantsev (President of the Higher Party School in Moscow) charged that the "contemporary revisionists and reformists shut their eyes to the aggressive character of imperialism and proclaim that im-

---

[28] The very expression of not fatally inevitable seems to betray Khrushchev's uncertainty on the matter. It may be that the word "fatally" should not be taken seriously, as suggested by Frederic S. Burin, *American Political Science Review*, 57 (June, 1963), p. 343, note 47. See also V. A. Siderkin, "Vozmozhnost' i deistvitel'nost' (possibility and reality), in M. M. Rozental' and G. M. Shtraks (eds.), *Kategorii materialisticheskoi dialektiki* (Categories of materialist dialectics) Moskva: Gos. izd-vo polit. lit-ry, 1956), p. 267. The author repeated the sentence that "under modern conditions, there is no fatally inevitable war."

[29] "Deklaratsiya soveshchaniya predstavitelei kommunisticheskikh i rabochikh partii sotsialistichekikh stran" (Declaration of the conference of the representatives of the communist and workers' parties of the socialist countries), *Pravda*, November 22, 1957.

[30] "Zayavlenie soveshchaniya predstavitelei kommunisticheskikh i rabochikh partii" (Statement of the conference of the representatives of the communist and workers' parties), *ibid.*, December 6, 1960; also in *Izvestiya*, December 7, 1960.

perialism has changed."[31] He likened imperialism to a toothless wolf, suggesting that imperialism, however weak, always remains vicious. The same metaphor was used by Kozlov (late Presidium member of the CPSU), who warned that imperialism's "selfishness has not changed and will not change."[32] Frantsev sought to dispel the inconsistency of the belligerence of imperialism and the avoidability of war by asserting that "this is the peculiarity of the present-day international situation."[33] It was assumed that imperialists could not do what they desire to because of the counterpoise of the socialist strength. Reporting to the partisan meeting on the Moscow Conference, which ended on December 6, 1960, Khrushchev iterated the relation of imperialism to war with his usual assurance that the latter could be headed off.[34] On this occasion, he brought out an additional concept, persuasive of the economic causes of war. He declared : "Wars arose with the division of society into classes. This means that the breeding ground of wars will be completely abolished only when society is free from class antagonism."[35] It is implied that human avarice has sown the seeds of arms and that there must be imperialist wars prior to the universality of communism.

Khrushchev's view thus far analyzed shows that he embraced military fatalism. True, he held to Lenin's inevitability stand just as fast as to his own opposite stand. The contradiction was just explained. In an effort to find supportive evidence for his position, he advanced the theory of a balance of forces. In addition, he set out to examine the nature of imperialism, hoping to find that it is not invariably aggressive. At Bucharest (June 21, 1960) he called into question the concept of monolithic imperialism. As he perceived it, imperialist countries were compounded of diverse groups, peaceful or otherwise. It was his conviction that there have been good imperialists and that to catalogue all imperialists as warlike went too far.[36] He acknowledged the belligerence of capitalists leading to hostility, but assumed that "history will

[31] Iu. Frantsev, "Problemy voiny i mira v sovremennikh usloviyakh" (The problems of war and peace in present-day conditions), *Pravda*, August 7, 1960.

[32] F. R. Kozlov, "43-ya godovshchina velikoi oktyabr'skoi sotsialisticheskoi revoliutsii" (The 43rd anniversary of the great October Socialist Revolution), *ibid.*, November 6, 1960.

[33] Iu. Frantsev, "Problemy voiny i mira ...," *ibid.*, August 7, 1960.

[34] "Za novye pobedy mirovoi kommunisticheskogo dvizheniya" (For new victories of the world communist movement), *ibid.*, January 7, 1961; "Marksizm-leninizm, znamya nashikh pobed" (Marxism-Leninism is the standard of our victories), *Izvestiya*, January 8, 1961.

[35] *Ibid.*; also in *Kommunist* 1 (January, 1961), 11.

[36] "Rech' t. N. S. Khrushcheva na III s'ezde Rumynskii Rabochei Partii" (Khrushchev's speech to the Third Congress of the Romanian Workers' Party), *Izvestiya*, June 23, 1960; *Pravda*, June 22, 1960.

possibly witness such a time when capitalism is preserved only in a small number of states, maybe, states, for instance, as small as a button on a coat." He went on asking his audience: If that happens, would one have to consult Lenin and point to the inevitability theory?[37] From what has been discussed, we may sum up by saying: (1) that since the Soviets have manifested their faith in Lenin's concept of imperialist war over and over again, the economic causes of armed conflict will remain; (2) that their doctrine of non-inevitability is truly meant for a war other than the imperialist variety; and (3) that imperialist war will not disappear, unless imperialism does.

The Chinese Stand

While the Russians were oscillating in their attempt to revise Lenin's inevitability theory, the Chinese proved more consistent.[38] They have concentrated their criticism on the non-inevitability of war due to changed circumstances. Throughout Peking's polemic media runs the red herring that Lenin's theory is still sound. At no time did they refer to the repeated statements of the Soviets holding the same view. Thus they spread the false impression that Khrushchev had irrevocably jettisoned the inevitability doctrine. The article "Long Live Leninism" reads like a running comment on the book *Imperialism*.[39] "We believe in the absolute correctness of Lenin's thinking: war is an inevitable outcome of the system of exploitation, and the source of modern wars is the imperialist system."[40] Following Lenin, the article ascribed the bellicosity of imperialists to their propensity to live off the labor of others. Enslaving the toilers at home, they were driven to oppress peoples abroad, because foreign aggression is the exploitative policy itself extended. It is argued that wars are waged by the imperialists due to "their insatiable appetite for more wealth."[41] As to the outlook on the abolition of war, the Chinese did not concur with the Twenty-First Congress that "even before the complete victory of socialism on earth

[37] *Ibid.*

[38] "The Chinese argued their case mainly on ideological grounds. It had at least the virtue of being logical and consistent, however unpalatable its implications," wrote John Gittings, *International Affairs* (London), 40 (January, 1964), 74.

[39] George F. Kennan observed that "the Chinese simply parrot, faithfully and unimaginatively, the sort of things Lenin was saying in 1910. It is clear that they have learned nothing and forgotten nothing since that time. With the Russians it is different." *See* his article previously cited, *Saturday Evening Post*, 236 (October 5, 1963), 38.

[40] *Sino-Soviet Dispute*, p. 98. *See* also Yu Chao-li, "On imperialism as a source of war in modern times; and the path of people's struggle for peace," *Peking Review*, 15 (April 12, 1960), 17–24, translation of "lun t'i-kuo chu-i ...," *Hung-ch'i*, 7 (April 1, 1960), 1–12.

[41] *Sino-Soviet Dispute*, p. 83.

... there is a real possibility of excluding world war from human society."[42] The article ends by saying that "so long as capitalist imperialism exists ... the sources and possibility of war will remain."[43] Appearing before the Eighth Congress of the Chinese Communist Party, Liu Shao-ch'i stated: "In the imperialist nations the rich cliques never cease their external adventures in order to get richer yet."[44]

The economic roots of war have long been propounded by Mao Tsetung. In the work "On protracted war" (May, 1938) it was argued that, due to the fierce struggle for the control of the means of production, men have shed streams of blood. Speaking of the Sino-Japanese conflict then going on, he was of the opinion that it had its springhead in the financial crisis after the imperialist war, a communist term for the First World War.[45] The probability that Mao had read Lenin's work *Imperialism* is illustrated by some of his *ad hoc* remarks, especially those found in "The Chinese Revolution and the Chinese Communist Party" (December, 1939). Mao repeated many of Lenin's precepts such as: War is caused by the trampling of the peasantry by the landlords; revolutionary war is the "true" locomotive of history; each war pushes human society a little ahead; a revolutionary party is the guarantee of victories.[46] To him concentration of money is the key to all the armed conquests of the capitalists. "Economic motives lie behind the various wars against China: the 1840 Opium War, the 1857 Anglo-French invasion, the 1884 Sino-French War, the 1894 Sino-Japanese War, and the 1900 Allied attack," he wrote.[47] In short, war is the very core of imperialism.[48] It will be noted that Mao's concepts which seemed drawn

---

[42] "Dal'neishee ukreplenie mirovoi sotsialisticheskoi sistemy" (Further strengthening of the world socialist system), *Pravda*, January 28, 1959; F. R. Kozlov, "43-ya godovshchina...," *ibid.*, November 7, 1960.

[43] *Sino-Soviet Dispute*, p. 83.

[44] *Jen-min shou-ts'e* (People's handbook) (Peking: Tai kung Pao, 1957), p. 22. Liu addressed the congress on September 15, 1956.

[45] *Mao Tse-tung hsüan-chi* (Selected works), 1952, vol. 2, p. 437.

[46] *Ibid.*, p. 595.

[47] *Ibid.*, p. 598.

[48] "The outbreak of the world imperialist war is due to the attempt of the capitalist nations to solve the new economic crisis they face," wrote Mao in his "Mu ch'ien hsing-shih ho tang ti jin-wu" (The current situation and the responsibility of the Party), October 10, 1939, *ibid.*, p. 513. "The ruling class always resorts to war to solve difficult problems," Mao told his followers, in his "Lun chih chiu chan" (On protracted war), May, 1938, *ibid.*, p. 410. It is fore cast by Mao that "war will disappear only when human society progresses to such a stage where there exists no class, no state ..." in his "Chung-kuo ko-ming chan-cheng ti chan-lüeh wen-t'i" (The strategical problems of the Chinese revolutionary war), November, 1936, *ibid.*, vol. 1, p. 172. He further suggested that imperialism and war are identical; *ibid.*, vol. 2, p. 602. This last point is exactly what Lenin once stated; *see* Lenin, "Voennaya programma proletarskoi revoliutsii" (Military program of the proletarian revolution), September, 1916, *O voine, armii i voennoi nauke* (On war, army and military science; 2nd ed.), p. 305.

from Lenin provided the guideline for the Chinese theorists in their dispute with the Russians, it seems therefore natural that it was Lenin from whom they profusely cited to defend their position.

As to the nature of imperialism, there is a great similarity between the Chinese and Russian arguments. K'ang Sheng, formerly an alternate, now a full member of the Politburo, spoke at the Warsaw Conference (February 5, 1960) in favor of a wary stand toward the West, whose warlike character he said remained unaltered.[49] In September, 1959, when Khrushchev visited the United States, Yu Chao-li (a writer for the Politburo) charged that he was light-hearted enough to believe in a butcher turning into a Buddha.[50] Writing in *Hung-ch'i* (April 1, 1960), he declared: "It is absolutely impermissible for us to mistake certain tactical changes on the part of imperialism for changes in the very nature of imperialism."[51]

It is the Chinese conviction that for imperialists to be oriented toward peace is simply as preposterous as for wolves to turn into sheep.[52] The truth, alleged an editorial in *Jen-min jih-pao*, is that the face of imperialism and reaction will never differ.[53] After proclaiming Peking's peace policy, *Jen-min shou-ts'e* cautioned that in spite of it, the "imperialists can continue their encroachment, intensify world tension, and oppress other peoples."[54] The article "Long Live Leninism" argued that a change of conditions could not effect a change in the substance of bourgeois politics.[55] From this statement it appears that Peking was somewhat aware of the anomaly of suggesting political means to prevent economically caused war. The real check for the latter, Peking believed, is not the balance of forces between East and West, but the extirpation of the "imperialist system and the exploiting classes."[56] Until then,

[49] "On the current international situation," *Peking Review*, 6 (February 5, 1960), 6–9; *Sino-Soviet Dispute*, pp. 72–77.

[50] "The Chinese people's great victory in the fight against imperialism," *Peking Review*, 38 (September 22, 1959), 6–11, translation of "Chung-kuo jen-min fan-tui t'i-kuo chu-i tou-cheng ti wei ta sheng -li," *Hung-ch'i*, 18 (September 16, 1959), 9–16.

[51] Yu Chao-li, "On imperialism as a source of war . . .," *Peking Review*, 15 (April 12, 1960), 17–18. Translation of "Lun t'i-kuo chu-i . . .," *Hung-ch'i*, 7 (April 1, 1960), 15–16; also in *NCNA*, March 30, 1960.

[52] At the World Peace Conference in Stockholm, December 16–19, 1961, the Albanian delegate, M. Misha, pointed out that the wolf of imperialism cannot change into a sheep. Even if it disguises itself as a sheep, it has the aim of making it more convenient for itself to eat sheep; *NCNA*, December 19, 1961.

[53] "Fa yang mo-ssu-k'o hsüan-yen ho mo-ssu-k'o shen-ming ti ko-ming ching-shen" (Carry forward the revolutionary spirit of the Moscow declaration and the Moscow statement), *Jen-min jih-pao* (People's daily), November 15, 1962.

[54] *Jen-min shou-ts'e* (People's handbook), 1957, p. 58.

[55] *Sion-Soviet Dispute*, p. 95.

[56] *Ibid.*, p. 79. For similar views in Lenin's teaching, *see* his "O zadachakh proletariata v dannoi revoliutsii" (The tasks of the proletariat in the revolution), April, 1917, *O voine, armii*

wars will surely crop up. Peking claimed to have seen the war clouds
being gathered because the "domain of the imperialists has shrunk
more and more, so that they collide with one another," and because
West German and Japanese imperialists are now fiercely competing for
sales markets.[57] That Peking upheld Lenin's analysis of imperialist war
has seemed to make its view more consistent, since it never pretended
to invalidate Leninism. In fact, the thought of the Chinese is not appreciably divergent from that taken by the Soviets, for both claimed
to put faith in the inevitability of imperialist aggression. Wars are said
to incubate in the alleged exploitative economy of capitalism. We must
add that Moscow also regarded avoidable wars which, as we shall discuss
presently, are political in origin.

VIEWS ON POLITICAL CAUSES

The Legacy of Lenin

Properly construed, imperialist war means armed colonization and its
consequent fight between the powers involved. The term of imperialist
aggression applies only to the incursion and pacification by the Europeans of areas not yet "civilized." It bespeaks a relationship of super-
ordination or subordination. Currently, the communists have made
massive use or rather misuse of the term to indicate the alleged design
of the West on the East, and thus put themselves on the same footing
as the colonies. Be that as it may, both China and Russia have found it
convenient to look at the democracies as imperialist. The uncritical
semantics, nevertheless, betray their lack of an understanding of the
kind of imperialism and imperialist war Lenin wrote about. It is true
that the late Russian leader was at times obsessed by the economic
genesis of war and proceeded to theorize on the matter. The fact that
he produced the book *Imperialism* in the midst of the First World War
(January–June, 1916) and before the advent of a socialist state made
him focus on the inter-imperialist conflict and on the economic causation
thereof.

No matter how cogent Lenin's arguments in the book, war is a

i voennoi nauke (On war, army and military science; 2nd ed.), p. 336; "O lozunge 'razoruzheniya'" (On the slogan of disarmament), October, 1916, *ibid.*, p. 315; "Sotsializm i voina"
(Socialism and war), July–August, 1915, *ibid.*, p. 269; "Revoliutsionnaya armiya i revoliutsionnoe pravitel'stvo" (Revolutionary army and revolutionary government), July, 1905, *ibid.*,
p. 92; "Evropeiskii kapital i samoderzhanie" (European capital and autocracy), April, 1906,
ibid., p. 71; "Padenie Port-Artura" (Fall of Port Arthur), January, 1905, *ibid.*, p. 55.
[57] *Sino-Soviet Dispute*, p. 85.

complex phenomenon and can rarely be accounted for by one reason alone.[58] Although Lenin himself was not prepared to ascribe wars to personal ambitions outside the social economic matrix,[59] some Soviet writers have done so. Rotstein (a sociologist), for one, suggested that the following military contests were of little meaning because they could not be understood in economic terms: the Chinese Generals' war in the nineteen twenties, the wars of the Roses in England from 1455 to 1485, and the Triumvirate bloodshed of ancient Rome.[60] Those wars are devoid of dialectico-materialist import and for the purpose of satisfying power lust. Thus, the communists have sometimes searched for other roots of armed struggle than those implied in imperialism. Such incidents, however, like individual volition are of little significance in the Marxist-Leninist exegesis of the universe.[61] Hence Rotstein's argument is followed by very few soviet writers.[62] Among the Chinese, no such argument ever appeared, because their unanimous conviction has been that war is dialectically determined. It is fought by the oppressed against the oppressors, with individual soldiers marching to the rhythm of history.[63]

No sooner had the Soviet regime come into existence than foreign intervention began. Along with the counterrevolution of non-Red armies, the military pressure of fourteen nations posed a serious threat to Russia. In April 1919, Admiral Kolchak undertook an offensive toward the Volga and broke through the defense line held by the Fifth Army on the eastern front. The end of the same month saw the smashing of the Red resistance in the regions of Bugurushlan and Bugulymy.

[58] Quincy Wright, *Causes of War* (London: Longmans, 1935), pp. 1–10. "It is probable that no great war was ever due to a single cause. Wars are rather the result of a group of causes," Authur Porrit (ed.), *The Causes of War* (New York: Macmillan, 1932), p. xviii. *See* also Dean G. Pruitt, and Richard C. Snyder (eds.), *Theory and Research on the Causes of War* (Englewood Cliffs, N. J.: Prentice-Hall, 1969), pp. 49–94.

[59] "Kriege werden nicht aus blosser Feindschaft geführt" (Wars are not simply caused by personal enmity), wrote Lenin; *see* his *Clausewitz' Werk "Vom Kriege": Auszüge und Randglossen* (Clausewitz's book on war: extracts and annotations) (Berlin: Verlag des Ministerium für National Verteidigung, 1957), p. 39.

[60] F. Rotstein, "Voina kak sotsial'noe yavlenie" (War as a social phenomenon), *Bol'shava sovetskaya entsiklopediya* (The great Soviet encyclopedia) (1st ed.; Moskva: Aktsionernoe obshchestvo "Sovetskaya entsiklopediya," 1927–47), vol. 12, col. 575.

[61] V. I. Lenin, "shto takoe 'druzya naroda' i kak oni voiuiut protiv sotsial-demokratov?" ("What are the 'people's friends' and how do they fight the Social Democrats?") in Lenin, *Sochineniya* (collected works; 5th ed.) vol. 1, pp. 165–167 at 165; also in Marx, Engels, Lenin, *o dialektischeskom materializme* (On dialectical materialism) (Moskva: Gos. izd-vo polit. lit-ry, 1966), p. 158.

[62] Some Russians regarded the Wars of the Roses as senseless acts of slaughter; for example, "Alaya i bylaya roza" (Wars of the Roses), *Bol'shaya sovetskaya entsiklopediya* (The great Soviet encyclopedia) (2nd ed.; Moskva: Gos. nauchnoe izd-vo, 1949–57), vol. 2, p. 33.

[63] Lenin, *Sochineniya* (Collected works; 4th ed.), vol. 21, p. 271; vol. 30, p. 149.

The Soviets now admit that was the darkest moment for them.[64] It was
at this juncture that Lenin made the well-known remark on the death
struggle between his nation and its encirclers.[65] To him the incompatibility of the two types of regime was axiomatic. Unable to cohabitate
on the same planet, they must fight to the bitter end, he forecast.[66]
Here we found a type of war other than that conceived in the book
Imperialism. The hostile action taken by one side against another ought
to be comprehended in non-economic terms, for it is hard enough to
believe that the capitalist attempt to destroy Soviet Russia was for
colonial exploitation. Harder still is it to assume that Soviet Russia,
once attacking the West, was likewise animated by any economic
considerations. However, Lenin did not try to develop a theory on it
comparable to that on the imperialist war.[67] Nowhere in his works can
one find a systematic treatment based on a frame of reference with
supportive documents.[68] Yet his concept may not be dismissed as un-
important on that score. Conversely, any adequate appreciation of
his stand on war must reckon with what may be called politically
motivated struggle. The war between the socialist and capitalist states
has its causes which are non-economic in nature. Khrushchev's balance
of forces as a condition of peace relates to this kind of war alone, not to
imperialist war.

The Imbalance of Forces as a Cause of War

In his addresses to the three Party Congresses (20th, 21st and 22nd)
held in 1956, 1959 and 1961 respectively, Khrushchev sought to buttress
his doctrine of non-inevitability of war by pointing to the preponderance

---

[64] Frunze, *Izbrannye proizvedeniya* (Selected works), vol. 1, pp. 11–12. *See* also N. V.
Tropkin, *op. cit.*, p. 211.

[65] *Infra*, chap. VI, p. 160, note 74. An exhaustive analysis of Lenin's expedient of
peaceful coexistence can be found in P. Fedenko, Institut zur Erforschung der UdSSR,
Bulletin, 10 (March, 1963), 27–36.

[66] Mao's thought was patterned on this precept; *see* K. Pavlov, *ibid.*, 9 (April, 1962), 3–4.

[67] Frederic S. Burin, *American Political Science Review*, 53 (June, 1963), 334–36.

[68] Some fragmentary references can be found in his "O luzunge 'razoruzhenie'" (On the
slogan of disarmament), October, 1916, *O voine, armii i voennoi nauke* (On war, army and
military science; 2nd ed.), p. 312; "Voennaya programma proletarskoi revoliutsii" (Military
program of the proletarian revolution), originally written in German, September, 1916, *ibid.*,
p. 303; "O lozunge soedinennykh shtatov evropy" (On the slogan of the United States of
Europe), August, 1915, *ibid.*, p. 273. The war between socialist and capitalist countries was
adumbrated by Engels, *see* Marx and Engels, *Sochineniya*, 2nd ed., vol. 35, pp. 296–98, 303,
as cited by the editors in Lenin, *O voine, armii i voennoi nauke* (On war, army and military
science; 2nd ed.), p. 761, note 155. Further references can be located in N. Schatagin, "W. I.
Lenin über den Aufbau und die Festigung der Sowjetischen bewaffneten Kräfte" (Lenin on
the building and strengthening of the Soviet armed forces), in *W. I. Lenin als Militärwissenschaftler* (Lenin as a military scientist) (Berlin: Verlag des Ministerium für National Verteidigung, 1956), p. 28.

of bloc strength in general, and Soviet strength in particular. The assumption was that war would break out if there existed a disparity between the opposing forces. Should one side be able to calculate on an easy victory, it would initiate a fight. Therefore, the sure way to forestall an attack is to strike an equilibrium of the power relationship. Contrary to Lenin's view, Khrushchev imputed the outbreak of the First World War to the poor organization of anti-war elements.[69] By asserting that in the present epoch the communist bloc has guaranteed peace, he presaged that even before the final triumph of socialism war could be precluded entirely.[70] As anti-war forces he counted the following: (1) people under socialism numbering many hundreds of millions; (2) the labor movement in the enemy camp; (3) the moral and material stamina of the bloc; (4) the peace zone of the world.[71] Such massive strength, he added, was to be compared with the weakness of the peace forces on the morrow of the Second World War when the Soviet Union and the Mongolian People's Republic were the only lands of socialism. Unable to ward off the menace of arms at that time, they are now joined by fraternal peoples to preserve peace. However, reading his speech to the Twentieth Congress alongside the one to the Twenty-First Congress, one observed that his tone was not so assuring in the second as in the first texts. While 1956 saw him refer to the superiority of socialist forces in general as if they were already sufficient to avoid war, the 1961 Congress was told that those forces were merely crystallizing.[72] Worth noting is that they are now laid down as conditions upon which hinges the non-inevitability of war in the future.

The conditions are: (1) the Soviet Union becomes the first and foremost industrial power; (2) the industry of the Chinese People's Republic waxes mighty; (3) taken together, "all the socialist countries will produce more than half the world's industrial output."[73] When these become true, the "real possibilities will be created for doing away with war as a tool to solve international issues."[74] It implies that there would, however, be war, if, for example, the Soviets were unable to overtake the most advanced nation in the West.[75] MacFarquhar suggested that the "new formulation [of the Twenty-First Congress] was more opti-

---

[69] "Otchetnyi doklad Tsentral'nogo Komiteta...," *Pravda*, February 15, 1956.
[70] "Dal'neishee ukreplenie mirovoi...," *ibid.*, January 28, 1959.
[71] "Otchetnyi doklad Tsentral'nogo Komiteta...," *ibid.*, February 15, 1956.
[72] "Dal'neishee ukreplenie mirovoi...," *ibid.*, January 28, 1959.
[73] *Ibid.*
[74] *Ibid.*
[75] K. Alexandrov, Institut zur Erforschung der UdSSR, *Bulletin*, 7 (May, 1960), 23.

mistic than the old" one contained in the four anti-war forces above-mentioned. This, he argued, was designed to pave the way to better relations with the West at a time when Harold Macmillan journeyed to Moscow and Anastas Mikoyan to the United States.[76] Khrushchev, however, figured that it would have to take another twelve[77] or even twenty years[78] until those conditions were realized. Actually he was repeating the truism that weakness will entice aggressors. There was, too, the desire on his part to please Peking which held that the total elimination of war from human life could not be realized prior to universal socialism.[79] By postponing the deadline of no war a few more years, the Russian leader hoped the Chinese would soften their criticism of his peace offensive.[80]

General observations to the contrary notwithstanding, in the essay "On protracted war," Mao has long ago stated that wars could be averted.[81] Similar statements by other Chinese communists can be multiplied to dispel, to some extent, the military fatalism generally imputed to them. For example, the "firmness of the stand of socialist countries would foil the enemy's war plan," declared an editorial of *Jen-min jih-pao*.[82] Marshal Chu Teh discussed the safeguards of peace through the supremacy of socialism in every field of human endeavor.[83] It was Chou En-lai who repeated Mao's statement made at the Moscow Conference (November 22, 1957) that "every one can see that our socialist camp has definitely gained an upper hand," and that the imperialist camp has been barred from plunging the world into a holocaust.[84] Finally, *Hung-ch'i* editorialized: "The stronger the socialist camp ... the greater will be the safeguard for world peace."[85] All these pronouncements indicated the accord between Moscow and Peking on wars being amenable to some control. Since the causes of this kind of war are not economic, as is true with imperialist war, a solution could

[76] *Sino-Soviet Dispute*, p. 41.

[77] "Dal'neishee ukreplenie mirovoi...," *Pravda*, January 28, 1959.

[78] "Novaya programma" (New program), *ibid.*, November 2, 1961; also in *Izvestiya* of the same date.

[79] Zagoria, *Sino-Soviet Conflict, 1956–1961*, p. 238.

[80] Frantsev held that the East has been surpassing the West percentage-wise in industrial produce; *see* his "Problemy voiny i mira...," *Pravda*, August 7, 1960.

[81] *Mao Tse-tung hsüan-chi* (Selected works), 1952, vol. 2, p. 438.

[82] The editorial was reproduced in *Jen-min shou-ts'e* (People's handbook, 1957), p. 367.

[83] The Marshall was addressing the Twentieth Congress of the CPSU on February 15, 1956, *NCNA*, February 15, 1956; also in *Jen-min shou-ts'e* (People's handbook, 1957), p. 368.

[84] Chou's nationwide policy speech, *NCNA*, February 10, 1958.

[85] "A basic summing-up of experience gained in the victory of the Chinese people's revolution," in *Sino-Soviet Dispute*, pp. 162–67. Translation of "Chung-kuo jen-min ko-ming sheng-li ching yen ti chih-pen tsung-chieh," *Hung-ch'i*, 20–21 (November 1, 1960), 1–13.

be found in the balance of forces. The professed resolve to seek peace, however insincere, conveys at least their idea that war between blocs is a matter of policy subject to control, not one of historical necessity.[86]

Armaments as a Cause of War[87]

The assumption on which the whole idea of disarmament is based has been: (1) war is caused by military hardware; (2) statesmanship can exert a decisive influence on the course of history; (3) the war in question is one between capitalist and socialist states, because Lenin's imperialist war is inevitable anyway.[88] Aside from the good or bad faith with which the various proposals of disarmament were advanced by the Soviet Union in many world bodies, the fact remains that in matters of ideology, they are far from believing in the omnipotence of Mars. The concept of disarmament, however, seems not in tune with that of the balance of strength in at least one aspect. Both Mao and Khrushchev maintained that by increasing the bloc military and industrial power, war could be excluded. The argument is clearly for more arms, while disarmament is directed at the opposite. The logical inference is that since both the largest and smallest quantity of weapons would lead to peace, war is the result of more or less of them in the possession of the belligerents. To put the idea in a different way, a balance of forces is hard to achieve if uncertain amounts of means are at stake. Hence either to have none or to have plenty of them is believed conducive to peace.

On September 18, 1959, in his address to the General Assembly of the United Nations, Khrushchev assured his audience that "if all the armed forces were abolished, world problems would be solved peaceably."[89]

[86] *Jen-min shou-ts'e* (People's handbook, 1957), p. 58. "The resolution of the Eighth Session of the Chinese Communist Party on the political report [of Liu Shao-ch'i on behalf of the Central Committee] September 27, 1956 ... Resolution, no. 4: opposition to war as an agent to solve international problems." Khrushchev also pointed to the possibility of bringing war under control in these words: "We on our part must do all we can to exclude war as a means to settle outstanding questions," *Pravda*, October 1, 1959. He made the statement in Peking.

[87] It should be pointed out that Lenin did not consider arms as the cause of war, because he attributed war to the capitalist system. Hence disarmament, he felt, did not lead to peace, but worked against the interest of the proletariat. "There is no single particle of truth in disarmament," he declared, "O lozunge 'razoruzheniya'" (On the slogan of disarmament), October, 1916, *O voine, armii i voennoi nauke* (On war, army and military science; 2nd ed.), p. 312. He also taught that "nothing is so baneful to the communist cause as saying that people are desirous of peace," in "Zadachi proletariata v nashei revoliutsii" (The tasks of the proletariat in our revolution), April, 1917, *ibid.*, p. 338.

[88] K. Grigor'ev, "Put' k miru cherez razoruzhenie" (The path to peace is through disarmament), *Mezhdunarodnaya zhizn'* (International life), 12 (November, 1960), 76–80.

[89] *Voennaya strategiya* (Military strategy; 2nd ed.), p. 220; Khrushchev, *On Peaceful Co-existence*, pp. 100–125.

The same stand was afterwards restated by the Warsaw Alliance Declaration, which blamed the arms race for the danger of war. Like Khrushchev in the world body, the Alliance called for "general and complete disarmament," the program of which was prepared by the Soviet delegate. What was emphasized in the text of the document concerned the solution of both "ideological and political disputes between states" through pacific media.[90] Written large are the words "preventing war." To enforce the plea for disarmament, Khrushchev tirelessly repeated it on numerous occasions. For example, his report to the Supreme Soviet on January 14, 1960[91] and his address to the Third Congress of the Romanian Workers' Party on June 21, 1960, all centered on the basic assumption that war stems from the presence of arms.[92] In the first-mentioned speech there was pronounced a decision to cut back the military personnel of soviet Russia from an alleged three and a half to two and a half million men. But he added: "The fire power of our forces was effectively retained." Later in the year, the Moscow meeting of world communist leaders discussed the implementation of the disarmament proposal and came out with a suggestion for a cessation of the weapons race and nuclear tests, dismantling of bases on foreign soil and doing away with the military blocs, conclusion of a peace treaty with Germany, and demilitarization of the western part of Berlin.[93] As was made clear by the Warsaw Alliance Declaration of February 4, 1960, the noblest task for the communists is to uproot the main sources of war, viz., arms rivalry.[94]

With some reservations, the Peking regime had concurred with the Soviets on the problem of the probability of war resulting from the possession of armaments. The elimination of the arms is the prelude to comity of nations, they held. The observer K'ang Sheng at the February 1960 Warsaw Conference gave China's blessing to universal disarmament as embodied in the various proposals of the Soviet Union.[95] China

---

[90] "Kommiunike o soveshchanii politicheskogo konsul'tativnogo komiteta gosudarstv, uchastnikov varshavskogo dogovora o druzhbe, sotrudnichestve i vzaimnoi pomoshchi" (Communique of the Political Consultative Conference of the Warsaw Treaty Organization), *Pravda*, February 5, 1960.

[91] "Razoruzhenie – put' k uprocheniiu mira i obespecheniiu druzhby mezhdu narodami" (Disarmament is the key to peace and international comity), *Pravda*, January 15, 1960.

[92] Khrushchev, *On Peaceful Coexistence*, pp. 232–34.

[93] "Zayavlenie soveshchaniya predstavitelei kommunisticheskikh i rabochikh partii" (Declaration of the conference of the representatives of communist and workers' parties), *Pravda*, December 6, 1960; *Izvestiya*, December 7, 1960.

[94] "Kommiunike o soveshchanii...," *Pravda*, February 5, 1960.

[95] *Sino-Soviet Dispute*, p. 74; Zagoria, *Sino-Soviet Conflict, 1956–1961*, p. 296.

claimed over and over again that she had reduced her armed forces.[96] Although the Chinese talked of the prevention of war through military curtailment, they viewed the whole problem differently from the Russians. Peking warned the latter of the impracticality of disarmament due less to procedural quagmire than to a lack of sincerity on the part of the West.[97] It is interesting to note that the Warsaw Pact in its February 1960 meeting declared: "The situation now proves more favorable than ever before for a fruitful disarmament parley."[98] The next day (February 6, 1960) an editorial in *Jen-min jih-pao* refuted that assertion by writing that the situation was getting worse because the arms drive in the imperialist camp had been stepped up.[99] At Bucharest, P'eng Chen, who was then Mayor of Peking and headed the Chinese delegation, specifically charged the United States with poisoning international relations by a feverish push for military preparedness.[100] Such slogans as "detente," "disarmament," or "elimination of war" from the life of mankind were not mentioned by him at all, although they were made the cardinal planks of the entire conference.

Peking's distrust of the West was responsible for its opposition to the unilateral decision to disarm.[101] P'eng Chen states his government's objection in this way: "Any international disarmament ... which is arrived at without the formal participation of the Chinese People's Republic cannot have any binding force on China."[102] That the observer was merely relaying to his audience the official policy of Peking is

[96] China praised the disarmament pledge in the "Communique of the Warsaw Powers" of May 14, 1955, *Jen-min shou-ts'e* (People's handbook, 1957), p. 375.

[97] K'ang told the Warsaw Conference (February 4, 1960) that "certain procedural agreements had been reached on disarmament" between East and West. But he attributed this, not to the good will of the latter, but rather to the repeated struggle of socialist forces and national liberation forces throughout the world. "On the current international situation." *Peking Review*, 6 (February 5, 1960), 6–9; *Sino-Soviet Dispute*, pp. 72–7. Chou En-lai once observed that any agreement on technical arms control was impossible because such agreement must emanate from concurrence on matters of principle; Edgar Snow, "Red China's leaders talk peace on their terms," *Look*, 25 (January, 1961), 93. Since concurrence on matters of principle is impossible, war is unavoidable; Fu Chung, "Mao Tse-tung chün-shih p'ien-cheng fa ti wei-ta sheng-li" (The great victory of Mao Tse-tung's military dialectics), *Jen-min jih-pao*, October 6–7, 1960.

[98] "Kommiunike o soveshchanii...," *Pravda*, February 5, 1960.

[99] "A decisive force to safeguard peace," *Peking Review*, 6 (February 16, 1960), 10; *Jen-min jih-pao*, February 6, 1960.

[100] *Pravda*, June 22, 1960 (without giving any designative title to his speech); *NCNA*, June 22, 1960.

[101] Even the test-ban treaty, which met the Chinese approval, was said to work to the advantage of the United States because "it will enable the United States to perfect, by means of underground testing, tactical nuclear weapons for use against communist-led national liberation movement in the underdeveloped areas," Harold C. Hinton, "Peculiar partnership," *Commonweal*, 79 (October 18, 1963), 93.

[102] *Pravda*, June 22, 1960; *NCNA*, June 22, 1960.

indicated by the fact that early in the year Mao issued a public declaration of which P'eng's statement was a replica.[103] Peking wanted
Moscow to know that the West's proposal of peace was simply a "trick
to lull the bloc."[104] Facing a hostile camp the communist nations ought
to possess fuller rather than emptier magazines, Peking felt.[105] Thus,
the alleged arms cut of the Soviets, according to Mao's way of thinking,
would increase, instead of decrease, the chances of war. In reply,
Khrushchev stated in his report to the Supreme Soviet on January 14,
1960, that in spite of the shrinkage of the size, the strength of the Soviet
forces had gone up and really kept the West from wielding its sword.[106]
Zagoria commented aptly that disarmament, including the test-ban
would have divested China of an opportunity to become a nuclear
power.[107] She might, he went on, be driven to a dilemma of either
having to defy world public opinion when she was developing her nuclear
arsenal, or to subject herself to the superiority of the Soviet Union, a
dilemma she solved in favour of the former, as witnessed by a series of
nuclear tests including the latest on October 14, 1970. Furthermore,
China's reluctance to accept any disarmament, suggested MacFarquhar,
is based on the consideration that so long as the United States does not
withdraw from the Taiwan Strait and southeast Asia, the causes of war
abide.[108] In short, wars can be prevented by international agreements,
provided that the imperialist powers are trustworthy and show signs
of lessening animosity toward the socialist countries.[109] Should there
be a disarmament treaty, the Chinese also believed in the necessity of a
supervisory system to keep it from being violated by the imperialists.[110]

Lack of Diplomatic Communications as a Cause of War
War between states is planned and provoked by men who are responsible for government policy and act for the whole community. Sovereignties engage in war only as a result of the conflict on policy matters. If
it cannot be adjusted through diplomacy, one side may resort to arms.

---

[103] *Peking Review*, 4 (January 26, 1960), 19. A resolution was passed to that effect by the
Standing Committee of the National People's Congress on January 21, 1960.
[104] *Ibid.*, 6 (February 9, 1960), 6–9.
[105] John Boynton, "Sino-Soviet dispute and international congresses," *World Today*, 19
(August, 1963), 324.
[106] "Razoruzhenie – put' k uprocheniiu...," *Pravda*, January 15, 1960.
[107] Zagoria, *The Sino-Soviet Conflict, 1956–1961*, p. 293.
[108] *Sino-Soviet Dispute*, p. 61.
[109] The Chinese, however, believed that such development was unlikely; "A betrayal of
the Soviet people," *Peking Review*, 32 (August 9, 1963), 10–11. Translation of "Che shih tui
su-lien jen-min ti pei-p'an," *Jen-min jih-pao*, August 3, 1963.
[110] *Jen-min shou-ts'e* (People's handbook, 1957), p. 378; *NCNA*, January 1, 1956.

But differences between nations do not necessarily entail violence for their settlement. Statesmen can play a crucial role in cultivating a climate favorable for a reasonable solution. To keep their lines of communication open is likely to avoid headlong collision.[111] The once popular personal diplomacy conducted by the Soviet leaders was grounded on the valid assumption that misunderstanding can be dispelled by tête-à-tête of chiefs of state and that such meetings may make it possible to find out where one's opponent stands. What Otto Kuusinen (an old Bolshevik and until his death in 1963 a Presidium member of the CPSU) called "truly democratic foreign policy" seemed calculated to have the highest decision-makers acquainted with one another. He felt that a compromise could be worked out after the Soviet rulers have had wide "personal contacts with both statesmen and public leaders of bourgeois countries."[112] The Warsaw statement of February 5, 1960 emphasized the "intercourse between officialdoms, public figures and organizations," and the "exchanges of achievements in the fields of culture, science and technology."[113] Lack of communications, it is postulated, would lead to tension and war.

May 16, 1960 saw the miscarriage of the ready-to-be-held summit conference; the avowed desire of Khrushchev to seek a detente compelled him to think of meeting with the next president of the United States due to be elected in the following fall. The unflagging penchant of the Russian leader for a rendezvous with foreign personages was not appreciated by the Chinese, who thought little of this kind of effort.[114] Khrushchev's visits to both India and Indonesia were totally boycotted in Peking's news media; and upon his arrival at the airport of the Chinese capital on September 30, 1959, he was not welcomed by Mao in person.[115] In response to the Chinese attitude, he found it necessary to suggest that although not all bourgeoisie could pronounce the words "peaceful coexistence," the President of the United States proved worth reasoning with.[116] Peking was then advised that since the West has shown its willingness to talk, "we on our part must do all we can

---

[111] Khrushchev told Gardner Couls, a newspaper publisher in Des Moines, Iowa, that there must and should be periodical summit meetings to exchange views and stands; *Predotvratit' voinu, otstoyat' mir!* (Prevent war and defend peace!), p. 42.

[112] "Pretvorenie v zhizn' idei Lenina" (To implement Lenin's idea), *Pravda*, April 23, 1960.

[113] "Kommiunike o soveshchanii...." *ibid.*, February 5, 1960.

[114] Michael Harrington, "China-Soviet conflict?" *Commonweal*, 71 (January 8, 1960), 413. "To Mao, meetings between Soviet and Western officials constitute dangerous traffic with an irreconcilable enemy," *see* R. Hilsman, "How real is the break between Russia and China?" State Department, *Bulletin*, 47 (November 26, 1962), 808.

[115] Michael Harrington, *Commonweal*, 71 (January 8, 1960), 411.

[116] *Pravda*, October 1, 1959. The speech was delivered on September 30, 1959.

to exclude war as a means of settling disputed questions." This piece of counsel was what Mao would not take, for he has always cast a doubtful eye on the peaceful intent of the imperialists. Liu Shao-ch'i, in his report to the Eighth Congress of the Chinese Communist Party (September 15, 1956), declared that "even granted that peoples themselves do not like war, the reactionaries do."[117] All the rulers of the capitalist countries have been warmongers to Peking. Writing in 1965, Lin Piao asked "what kind of logic" lies behind the thought of "Khrushchev revisionists" that the "imperialists like John Kennedy and Lyndon Johnson [are] sensible"?[118] Liao Ch'eng-chih, Chairman of the Chinese Committee for Afro-Asian Solidarity, ridiculed the idea of having two or a few great leaders "to decide the fate of all nations."[119] Marshal Chu Teh spoke to the Eighth Congress of the Chinese Communist Party (September 17, 1956), saying that the communists must not relax, war being in the offing.[120]

The stand of Peking seems that war may be caused by a lack of dialogue between leaders and that state visits by them can improve the international climate. But the problem, it felt, is how to find good imperialists. Since all rulers in the capitalist world are said to be tyrants at home and extortioners abroad, it is no use dealing with them. The style of personal conference is sneered at by Mao as a folly, because it would not win friendship from the governing clique in the West. Concerning this demeanor of Mao, Khrushchev pointed out to him that communist leaders also could be impractical and even mistaken.[121] The import of this remark is that it is by traveling abroad and familiarizing oneself with other leaders that one can learn enough to form right

[117] *Jen-min shou-ts'e* (People's handbook, 1957), p. 10.

[118] *China after Mao*, p. 255.

[119] Speech of Liao at the World Peace Conference which met in Stockholm, December 16–19, 1961, *Peking Review*, 51 (December 22, 1961), 12–14.

[120] *Jen-min shou-ts'e* (People's handbook, 1957), p. 368.

[121] Khrushchev strongly hinted that the socialists could wage unjust wars. Perhaps because of this clearly un-Leninist concept, it was found necessary to reassert Lenin's teaching that socialist countries alone can wage just wars. The reassertion was made by two other theorists, A. Arzumanyan and V. Korionov, "Noveishie otkroveniya revizionizma" (The latest revelations of revisionism) *Pravda*, September 2, 1960. Their stand was a refutation of the concept that socialist countries can initiate unjust wars as suggested by Edward Kardelj in his book *Socialism and War* (London: Methuen, 1961). The Chinese are cocksure of their just cause: The class nature of our state precludes us from taking an aggressive action against others," *see* Chang Hsiang-shan, "Hsüeh-hsi Mao chu-hsi lun chih-min t'i pan chih-min t'i kuo-chia min-tsu min-chu ko-ming wen-t'i ti i-hsieh t'i-hui" (Study Chairman Mao's theory of national democratic revolution in the colonies and semi-colonies), *Chung-kuo ch'ing-nien* (Chinese youth), 9 (May 1, 1960), 10–14. This self-infallibility plus Mao's thought that being provocative on the part of the socialist countries is not aggressive toward the capitalists makes the Peking regime a danger to world peace; *see* Michael Lindsay, *Annals of the American Academy of Political and Social Science*, 336 (July, 1961), 48.

concepts. "We must think realistically and understand the contemporary world correctly," he argued.[122] War can flare up if the socialist nations venture to probe the camps of their opponents. The Russian leader must be understood as saying here that a statesman's lack of self-restraint can set the world aflame. It is important to observe that he disapproved of reckless actions merely under the assumption that one is stronger than his adversary. "We should not think that if we are so powerful we must test by force the stability of the capitalist regime. This would be wrong," he remonstrated.[123] In the address to the party gathering on January 6, 1961, he again stressed the personal factor in the problem of global politics. Here he averred that the present generation is more intelligent than its predecessor, since many problems which proved too much for the latter have now been brought under control.[124]

VIEWS ON PSYCHOLOGICAL CAUSES

The Problem of Accidental War

Being a social phenomenon, war reflects human relations. It cannot happen fortuitously. In the preceding pages we strove to present the various views on the causes of war in economic or political terms. Men appeal to arms, both Moscow and Peking agreed, for certain objectives. In making up his mind to fight, an aggressor has to calculate that he could get away with it and incur no catastrophe. For two reasons there appears no possibility of accidental war in their views. Armed struggle is given birth by defective institutions such as private property, in the first place; and any military action is premeditated, in the second place.[125] In terms of dialectical materialism, an account for war without reference to the system of production and distribution of goods is mistaken. Upon this common ground, the leaders of China and Russia have built. However, with the unfolding of their dialogue, there emerged a dissonance which was initially collateral to the issue of the balance of forces, but turned out to be an independent point of controversy. It is strange that neither side fully realized that it had joined a new battle which could have a far-reaching impact on communist ideology.

[122] *Pravda*, October 1, 1959.

[123] *Ibid.*

[124] "Marksizm-leninizm...," *Izvestiya*, January 8, 1961; "Za novye pobedy...." *Pravda*, January 7, 1961; *Kommunist*, 1 (January, 1961), 31.

[125] Lenin, "Iz 'Otkrytogo pis'ma Borisu Suvarinu'" (From an open letter to Boris Souvarine), December, 1916, *O voine, armii i voennoi nauke* (On war, army and military science; 2nd ed.), p. 321.

The problem could be stated thus. As presented above, the Soviet leader predicated peace on the correlation of strength between East and West in favor of the East. The Chinese Government concurred at the Moscow Conference of the Ruling Communist Parties (November 22, 1957) in a declaration of its own subscribing to all the policy matters, the correlation concept being included. This agreement soon soured. With Khrushchev's detente speeded up, Mao felt irritated by his lack of interest in helping China liberate Taiwan and in getting the United States out of Asia. The article "Long Live Leninism" openly challenged the Russian leader's hypothesis of the likelihood of peace in the face of the West's stubborn policy.[126] In rebuttal to Peking's criticism, Khrushchev asserted that as thermonuclear arms piled up, war could be set off only by men who are bereft of reason. The implication seems clear; the causes of war could be sought outside the economic and political nexus. Social institutions, however rapacious, are not the sole reason for arms, although they may be the most conspicuous ones. Khrushchev's statement posits that war can be engaged in for no sound consideration whatever. It could be a manifestation of an abnormal psychology and have little to do with the way people make a living in a given society. This is a far cry from the earlier strictly materialist exegesis of the communists.

Irrationality as a Cause of War

Both the Soviets and the Chinese have much in common regarding the possibility of wars being brought about by irrationality. It is their argument that the capitalists want to start wars despite the knowledge that they cannot benefit from them. On the contrary, wars could only bring them indescribable calamities. Addressing the Twenty-First Congress (January 27, 1959) Khrushchev declared that as long as capitalism remains ,"there will be some people ... who, contrary to reason, may want to plunge the world into a hopeless war." It went against rationale, he said, because by their act they would only hurry up the downfall of their way of life.[127] It is to be noted that he made no indiscriminate charge of the lack of judgment on the part of the capitalists, the word "some" being consciously chosen.[128] At Bucharest (June 21, 1960) an effort was made by him to differentiate the unreason-

[126] *Sino-Soviet Dispute*, pp. 90–93. On January 18, 1961, the Chinese Communist Party adopted a resolution in support of the Declaration of the Moscow Conference (December 6, 1961); "the West must not be trusted," the party resolution advised, *ibid.*, p. 222.
[127] "Dal'neishee ukreplenie mirovoi...," *Pravda*, January 28, 1959.
[128] K. Alexandrov, Institut zur Erforschung der UdSSR, *Bulletin*, 7 (May, 1960), 33.

able from the reasonable statesmen. Into the former category he entered President Eisenhower, who had assumed personal responsibility for
the U–2 flights, while into the latter, President Charles de Gaulle,
Prime Minister Harold Macmillan, and the future successor to President
Eisenhower.[129] He felt "there were two schools in the West: a school
of the insane, belligerent, and aggressive, and a school of the sober-
minded and conciliatory."[130] In order to justify his view, he found it
necessary to cite Lenin, who "pointed to the need of establishing contacts with those circles of the bourgeoisie which gravitate toward
pacificsm, 'be it even of the palest hue.'"[131] However, the war likely
to be started by maddened creatures was not to be discounted, for there
were such perverted men for whom war would be expedient.[132]

The Chinese should have minimized the personal factor in war, since
they held that capitalism as a system tends to breed wolves, not
lambs.[133] Nonetheless, they seem not to have a mind so one-tracked as
to deny the role of the supervenient. On January 22, 1941, through his
spokesman, Mao told a reporter that "war may be caused by the injudicious thinking of statesmen."[134] He felt that "since it is only a matter
of time before many countries witness their respective revolutions," the
ruling class, if sensible enough at all, might as well surrender their arms
and let the proletariat take over, instead of putting up a forlorn resistance.[135] Insofar as Maoism goes, the argument does not appear
illogical. In the current dialogue with Moscow, Mao's precept has been
followed by his men. Foreign Minister Ch'en Yi, in reviewing China's
diplomacy, suggested that rationality could prevent war. As usual, he
reproached the American Government for lack of that quality in its
policy.[136] Frenzy, he stated, could propel men to the warpath. The very
thought that there were two schools in the West as suggested by

---

[129] "Rech' t. N. S. Khrushcheva na III s'ezde...," (Khrushchev's speech to the Third
Congress of the Romanian Workers' Party), *Pravda*, June 22, 1960; *Izvestiya*, June 23, 1960.

[130] "Marksizm-leninizm...," *ibid.*, January 8, 1961; "Za novye pobedy...," *Pravda*,
January 7, 1961; *Kommunist*, 1 (January, 1961), 35.

[131] *Ibid.*

[132] A. Belyakov, and F. Burlatskii, "Leniniskaya teoriya sotsialisticheskoi revoliutsii i
sovremenost'" (Lenin's theory of socialist revolution in present conditions), *Kommunist*, 13
(September, 1960), 24.

[133] Shih Tung-hsiang, "Refuting the fallacy that the nature of imperialism has changed,"
Peking Review, 25 (June 21, 1960), 11–13. Translation of "P'o t'i-kuo chu-i pen-hsing i pien ti
miu-lun," *Hung-ch'i*, 12 (June 16, 1960), 1–4.

[134] "Chung-kuo ko-ming wei-yuan-hui fa-yen-jen tui hsin-hua-she ch'i-che ti t'an-hua"
(A spokesman of the Chinese Revolutionary Committee talked with a reporter of the New
China News Agency), *Mao Tse-tung hsüan-chi* (Selected works), 1952, vol. 2, p. 751.

[135] *Ibid.*

[136] "The current world situation and our foreign policy," *Jen-min shou-ts'e* (People's
handbook, 1957), p. 117.

Khrushchev in 1960 had been previously entertained by the Chinese. Ch'en Yi as early as 1956 already had that idea in the speech just mentioned, for he referred to the enlightened as well as the lunatic Americans.[137] More noticeable was a statement made by Chou En-lai. Reporting to the Third Plenum of the People's Congress (June 28, 1956), he said: "Recently, statesmen in Great Britain and France indicated that except crazy men, nobody likes war. That is correct."[138] With regard to the leaders in Washington, he emphasized that "only a part of them want to fight."[139] It will be recalled that it was shortly before this time that the ambassadorial talks between the United States and China were inaugurated in Warsaw. Very revealing is Chou's view: "If there is no formal diplomatic relation, inter-governmental contacts are helpful."[140] As to the cause of war, he told the People's Congress that "it is the product of the delirium of men."[141]

It seems that the factor of mental derangement figured even larger in the Chinese media than in the Russian. At first, Moscow spoke generally of some maniacs who were fond of war regardless of whether it would stand them in good stead. It was Moscow's belief, however, that those men had been sobered by Soviet nuclear potency. On the other hand, Peking stressed the foolhardiness of the maniacs. Liu Ch'ang-sheng, the late chairman of Chinese Trade Unions, declared before the World Federation of Trade Unions (June 5, 1960) that there were two distinct problems at issue: the possibility of warding off a conflict, and the desperation of the enemy who might try, nonetheless, to deliver the blow.[142] The two, he went on, were to be treated separately, for it is unsure if the enemy would behave well. *Hung-ch'i* wrote that nuclear danger cannot bring the warmongers to their senses. To mitigate vigilance under the assumption of any sort of deterrence would court disaster.[143] It should be noted that the Chinese position had previously been taken by Khrushchev, who declared that "one

---

[137] *Ibid.*

[138] "The contemporary international situation, our diplomacy and the problem of the liberation of Taiwan," *ibid.*, p. 183.

[139] *Ibid.*, p. 184.

[140] *Ibid.*

[141] *Ibid.*

[142] "On the question of war and peace," *Peking Review*, 24 (June 14, 1960), 13–14; *Sino-Soviet Dispute* pp. 123–26.

[143] "Hsiang kung-ch'an chu-i chin-chün ti hao-chiao" (The clarion-call of armed march toward communism), *Hung-ch'i*, 4 (February 16, 1959), 1–8. It is a "subjectivist logic divorced from reality to hold that the mutually-suicidal character of nuclear war may make imperialists unwilling to start one," Chung Hsin-ching, "Two sources of war threatening world peace," *Peking Review*, 25 (June 21, 1960), 22–7. Translation of "Wei-hsieh shih-chieh ho-ping ti liang-ko chan-cheng tse-yüan t'i," *Hung-ch'i*, 11 (June 1, 1960), 8–15.

could not vouch for a madman."[144] But it was Peking which dramatized this point.[145] Zagoria observed that the "Chinese generally dismissed the idea of 'sober circles' in the Western ruling classes."[146] To this writer, however, it was the Albanians, not the Chinese, who treated the factor of irrationality as insignificant. For example, on April 23, 1960, Lenin's ninetieth birthday anniversary, Ramiz Alia, Albanian Polit-buro candidate member, denounced the Yugoslav revisionists for thinking that war originated from the insanity of people like the Hitlers rather than from the property of capitalist regimes.[147]

War-scares as a Cause of War

L. L. Bernard wrote that fear and distrust provided a favorable climate for war.[148] In the Peking-Moscow dispute, one party has shown much greater concern than the other over the problem of war-scares. The detente of Khrushchev premised itself on the proposition that to spread war-scares would produce a smell of gunpowder.[149] The Warsaw de-claration of February 5, 1960 observed the "noticeable relaxation of international tension" paving the way for a non-aggression pact be-tween East and West.[150] A few months earlier the Russian leader sought to calm down his Peking comrades when he told them that President Eisenhower and other statesmen were men of peace and that it behooved the communists not to militate against good will.[151] His exhortation was clearly designed to expel any jingoistic atmosphere. In effect, Peking was admonished to be patient, for socialism was said

[144] "Rech' t. N. S. Khrushcheva" (Khrushchev's speech [in Krasnodar District]), *Pravda*, October 16, 1958; also a feature article entitled "Izbavit' chelovechestvo ot ugrozy atomnoi voiny" (To save mankind from atomic war) stated that the Western powers never wanted to stop experimenting with new bombs. Later on, the article said that they cannot ignore for long the demand of the mass people for peace; *see*, E. Litoshko and B. Strel'nikov (*Pravda* correspondents in New York), "Mir – glavnaya zadacha OON" (Peace is the main task of the UN), *ibid.*, October 24, 1958. They wrote that the Western aggressive circles did not let peace prevail in the world.

[145] John S. Reshetar, *Western Political Quarterly*, 14 (September, 1961, supplement), 74.

[146] Zagoria, *The Sino-Soviet Conflict, 1956–1961*, p. 358.

[147] As quoted in William Griffith, *Albania and the Sino-Soviet Rift*, p. 36.

[148] *War and Its Causes* (Chicago: Regnery, 1944), p. 281. See also Dean G. Pruitt, and Richard C. Snyder (eds.), *Theory and Research on the Causes of War*, p. 22.

[149] K. Pavlov, Institut zur Erforschung der UdSSR, *Bulletin*, 9 (March, 1962), 4.

[150] "Kommiunike o soveshchanii....," *Pravda*, February 5, 1960.

[151] *Ibid.*, October 1, 1959; *see* also Michael Lindsay, *Annals of the American Academy of Political and Social Science*, 336 (July, 1961), 59. Rejecting the view once held by Khrushchev, the Chinese said: "Lenin and Stalin never suggested that the inner contradictions of imperial-ism would enable imperialism to change its nature ... Facts have proved ... that it is nothing but wishful thinking to regard Eisenhower, Herter and their ilk as forming the sensi-ble group of the American ruling clique and to place hope on diplomatic negotiation with them," Shih Tung-hsiang, "Refuting the fallacy...," *Peking Review*, 25 (June 21, 1960), 11–13. Translation of "Po t'i-kuo chu-i...," *Hung-ch'i*, 12 (June 16, 1960), 1–4.

<dedation for war

to be on its way up; Kuusinen asserted, the "second half of our century will bring complete liberation to the oppressed and dependent nations."[152] It was claimed by Frantsev, that the dark clouds have been receding, because the imperialists dared not risk an invasion of the socialist countries.[153] He believed that the rapid growth of Soviet production has assured the regime's invincibility.[154] Khrushchev, in an effort to exorcise Mars, once resorted to soothsaying in alleging that the time was near when the capitalist countries would find themselves in a predominantly communist world.[155] The old fear of capitalist encirclement[156] should be entertained no longer; to the Supreme Soviet, which met on October 31, 1959, he enumerated some of the signs of thaw in the cold war including the nuclear test talks, the foreign ministers' conferences, the various exchanges of visits, all of "positive significance."[157]

To instill a sense of security into the people, the communist leaders found it necessary to cease military agitation. "The ending of war propaganda, subversive appeals, and attempts to threaten the use of force would be of great significance for smoothing of diplomacy and for ridding of suspicions," said the Warsaw declaration (February 5, 1960).[158] It made the claim that the socialist nations had all carried out such policies. It seems noteworthy that on several occasions when the international atmosphere deteriorated, Khrushchev stepped forward in an attempt to restore some measure of moderation. On August 24, 1958, for example, the day after the Chinese shelled the off-shore islands in Taiwan Strait, he delivered a speech in which he minimized the possibility of war. The crisis was dismissed in these words: "It seems to me that there is no cloud from which thunder could roll."[159] Again, during the Middle-East crisis in July 1958, the Russian Govern-

[152] "Pretvorenie v zhizn'...," *Pravda*, April 23, 1960.
[153] "Problemy voiny i mira...," *ibid.*, August 7, 1960.
[154] *Ibid.*
[155] "Rech' t. N. S. Khrushcheva na III s'ezde...," (Khrushchev's speech to the Third Congress of the Romanian Workers' Party), *ibid.*, June 22, 1960; *Izvestiya*, June 23, 1960.
[156] This concept was most strongly emphasized by Stalin; see his "Beseda s inostrannymi rabochimi delegatsiyami" (Interview with foreign workers' delegation), *Sochineniya* (Collected works), vol. 10, p. 234; also his *Mastering Bolshevism* (New York: Workers' library publishers, 1937), pp. 26–7.
[157] "O mezhdunarodnom polozhenii i vneshnei politike Sovetskogo Soiuza" (International situation and foreign policy of the Soviet Union), *Pravda*, November 1, 1959. The speech was delivered on October 31, 1959.
[158] "Kommiunike o soveshshanii...," *ibid.*, February 5, 1960.
[159] "Rech' t. N. S. Khrushcheva na torzhestvennom zasedanii smolenskogo obkoma KPSS i oblastnogo soveta deputatov trudyashchikhsya, posvyashchennom vrucheniiu oblasti ordena Lenina 13 avgusta 1958 goda" (Khrushchev's speech at a mass meeting in the district of Smolensk), *ibid.*, August 24, 1958.

ment, though manifesting its concern, called for reason and calmness because, it stated, both the United States and England, on the one hand, and the Soviet Union, on the other, have nuclear arms.[160] "You can be confident that we shall do everything to insure that there will be no war in the Middle-East," Khrushchev told a reception in Moscow after he had a talk with Nasser, the then President of Egypt.[161] Having visited Peking late in September 1959, where he was faced with a group of militant leaders, Khrushchev felt it even more compelled to harp on the theme of peace through rationality. On October 6, 1959, he told his Vladivostok audience that the "United States and the Soviet Union could not confront each other like two cocks ready to lay hold and peck."[162] The Chinese communists, however, were not interested in Khrushchev's detente.[163] They thought that the more the East clamored for peace, the more the West became overweening.[164] The journal *Chieh-fang chün-pao* (Liberation army paper) suggested that the bloc's strength made it needless to beg for disarmament.[165]

Human Greed as a Cause of War

Communists regard bourgeois cupidity as the source of social evils like war. Even the religious wars of the past are not considered an exception and are said to have been fought for the sordid purpose of seizing property, appropriation of lands, and taking of hostages.[166] The hypocrisy of the warriors made them more "sinful" before "God" in whose name they took the field. War, thus, is simply an "art of acquiring," the communists agreed with Aristotle.[167] In primitive society, the chieftain led his men to fight to expand his domain[168] During the slave

[160] "Reshitel'no povernut' rul' sobytii s puti voiny na put' mira!" (The wheel is decisively turning from the path of war to the path of peace), *ibid.*, July 21, 1958.

[161] "Priem v poso'stve Pol'skii Narodnoi Respubliki, rech' t. N. S. Khrushcheva" (Khrushchev's speech at the reception of the Polish Embassy on the 14th anniversary of national renascence), *ibid.*, July 23, 1958.

[162] "T. N. S. Khrushchev v primor'e, mnogotysyachnyi miting trudyashchikhsya Vladivostoka" (Khrushchev's speech at a mass meeting in Vladivostok), *ibid.*, October 7, 1959.

[163] Harrison E. Salisbury, "U.S. and USSR: the dangers ahead," *Foreign Policy Bulletin*, 39 (June 15, 1960), 150.

[164] *Jen-min jih-pao*, July 17, 1958.

[165] July 25, 1958; "Ai-sen-ho-wei-erh ti ch'i-chih chiu-shih hai-tao ti ch'i-chih" (The banner of Eisenhower is the banner of pirates), *Jen-min jih-pao*, July 21, 1958; "T'uan-chieh chiu-shih li-lian" (Solidarity is strength), *ibid.*; "The world cannot look on with folded arms," *Peking Review*, 22 (July 29, 1958), 5–6, translation of "Pu-neng hsiu-shou pang-kuan," *Jen-min jih-pao*, July 20, 1958.

[166] Rotstein, "Voina kak sotsial'noe yavlenie" (War as a social phenomenon), *Bol'shaya sovetskaya entsiklopediya* (The great Soviet encyclopedia; 1st ed.), vol. 12, col. 555.

[167] *Ibid.*

[168] Engels, *Der Ursprung der Familie, des Privateigentums und des Staates* (The origin of family, private property, and state) (Hotting-Zürich: Verlag der Schweizerischen Volksbuch-

era, people grabbed arms to secure beasts of burden; and the feudal lords dug up the hatchet to gratify their rapacity.[169] When the capitalist epoch dawned, the avarice of the bourgeoisie knew no bounds. The universal scuffle for resources, inexpensive labor and sales markets started a new round of war to which Lenin, *inter alios*, gave the epithet "imperialist." Since all armed struggles are for private property, to abolish the latter is to achieve peace. In other words, should the means of production be socialized, the incentive of exploitation, the taproot of war, vanishes. Invariably the communists regard proprietorship the sole divisive agent of an otherwise agreeable people and arms the tool to secure wealth.[170]

In the Twentieth Congress, Khrushchev drove the point home by way of a rhetorical question: "Is there a single reason why a socialist state should want war?" He replied that in the Soviet Union there has been no class or group that is "interested in war as a means of enrichment." Meanwhile, he told his partisans of the absence of related causes of war. The Soviets have no motivation for being voracious, he went on, for they get whatever is needed for their life. Neither "territory," nor "natural endowment," nor "markets for our goods" are in short supply. "We have enough and more to spare of all those," he added. Then, he proceeded to say that an imperialist war is "for the sake of the selfish interests of a handful of multi-millionaires."[171] The greediness of one people, and the ungreediness of another spells the orientation toward war and peace. In their Warsaw declaration (February 5, 1960) the communists sought to explain the alleged stiff resistance of the West to the "consolidation of peace" by charging that some "influential forces, over there, do not see the light behind the profits they are receiving from the manufacture of armaments in the event of war."[172]

Using a metaphor to attribute war to the bourgeois thirst for money, Yu Chao-li, in an article entitled "Peaceful competition: an inevitable trend," contended that to keep the United States away from war is

handlung, 1884), pp. 128–29. In English, the source appears in *Handbook of Marxism*, selected by Emile Burns (New York: International publishers [n.d.], p. 331.

[169] S. F. Kechk'yan, "Eksploatatorskie gosudarstva i sistemy prava" (The exploitative states and systems of law), in *Teoriya gosudarstva i prava* (The theory of state and law) (Moskva: Gos. izd-vo iuridicheskoi lit-ry, 1959), p. 175. F. D. Khrustov, "Voina" (War), *Bol'shaya sovetskaya entsiklopediya* (The great Soviet encyclopedia; 2nd ed.), vol. 8, p. 576.

[170] Rotstein, "Voina kak sotsial'noe yavlenie" (War as a social phenomenon), *ibid.*, 1st ed., vol. 12, col. 556; also I. Nizhechek, "Politika i voina" (Policy and war), *Voina i revoliutsiya* (War and revolution) (January–February, 1933), p. 38.

[171] "Otchetnyi doklad Tsentral'nogo Komiteta...," *Pravda*, February 15, 1956.

[172] "Kommiunike o soveshchanii...," *ibid.*, February 5, 1960.

simply as fallacious as "to keep a cat away from fish."[173] It is as unlikely to find a cat which is allergic to fish as it is to know of a peace-
loving imperialist. The assertion that the insatiable traits of the bourgeoisie cannot change was also made by Kuusinen. In his *Pravda* article
on Lenin's birthday anniversary, he stated that "those groups of monopoly capitalists by no means want to give up the profits they get from
the policy of militarization and of the arms race."[174] The groups referred
to are said to consist of the "big shots of NATO and leaders of the
Pentagon."[175] They were charged with determination "to seize others'
territory and to plunder the peoples therein."[176]

The Imperialists' Lack of Fear as a Cause of War

In March, 1954, the then Chairman of the Council of Ministers, G. M.
Malenkov, ventured to presage the annihilation of "world socialist as
well as capitalist system in an all-out nuclear exchange."[177] Feeling
repentant for such an observation which was maligned as "theoretically
insolvent and politically mean" by Konstantinov (an academician),[178]
the Chairman had to recant it with the amendment that war would
destroy the capitalist system alone.[179] The amendment found itself
stated back by Khrushchev and many other Soviets. His Twentieth
Congress speech minced no words in warning of a total disaster befalling
the human race, for any future war would spare neither of the two
systems. Belyakov and Burlatskii, noted Soviet publicists, sounded the
alarm: "A thermonuclear conflict would result in a complete destruction
of the main centers of civilization."[180] The possibility of mutual
ruination was iterated in Soviet media.[181] It was hoped that a sense of

---

[173] Yu Chao-li, "Peaceful competition: an inevitable trend," *Peking Review*, 33 (August 16, 1959), 6–8. Translation of "Ho-ping ching-sai shih ta shih so ch'ü," *Hung-ch'i*, 16 (August 16, 1959), 24–7.

[174] "Pretvorenie v zhizn'...," *Pravda*, April 23, 1960.

[175] *Ibid.*

[176] "Marksizm-leninizm...," *Izvestiya*, January 8, 1961; "Za novye pobedy...," *Pravda*, January 7, 1961; *Kommunist*, 1 (January, 1961), 35.

[177] "Rech' t. G. M. Malenkova na sobranii izbiratelei leningradskogo izbiratel'nogo okruga g. Moskvy 12 marta 1954 g." (Malenkov's election-campaign speech in the Leningrad constituency, Moscow, March 12, 1954), *ibid.*, March 13, 1954.

[178] F. Konstantinov, "I. V. Stalin i voprosy kommunisticheskogo stroitel'stva" (J. V. Stalin and the problem of building of communism), *ibid.*, March 5, 1955.

[179] "Rech' predsedatelya Soveta Ministrov SSSR deputatov, G. M. Maelnkova" (Malenkov's speech to the Supreme Soviet), *ibid.*, April 27, 1954.

[180] A. Belyakov and F. Burlatskii, "Leninskaya teoriya sotsialisticheskoi revoliutsii i sovremennost'" (Lenin's theory of socialist revolution in present conditions), *Kommunist*, 13 (September, 1960), 20.

[181] For example: "Razoruzhenie – put' k uprocheniiu ...," *Pravda*, January 15, 1960; "O mezhdunarodnom polozhenii...," *ibid.*, November 1, 1959; Khrushchev's speech to the

fear may disincline men to war. However, since the peace motive of the socialist camp was taken for granted on account of the alleged lack of class exploitation, the Soviets harped only on the capitalist want of fear as a cause of war. The imperialists, they assured, need not be afraid of a Russian attack,[182] but they ought to bear the consequence if they initiate the fight.

Among the Communist elite, both ideas of mutual destrucion and destruction of the enemy camp alone have coexisted, with the latter idea, however, growing dominant. Thus, the Moscow declaration mentioned the perdition of imperialism;[183] the Warsaw proclamation, the ending of the Western camp;[184] Khrushchev's report to the party conference, destruction of the bourgeois regimes only;[185] the Moscow statement, the burial of capitalism;[186] and "Long Live Leninism," the utter sacrifice, not of mankind, but the warmongers."[187] These assertions all mean exactly what they literally convey. But interpreted in causative terms, they also connote that the lack of fear on the part of the enemy would start wars. The Chinese were quite articulate about it, for they felt that the terror of arms was one thing, the warlike instinct of the enemy, another.To their way of analysis, the imperialists were fearless and had been planning aggression.[188] No matter how destructive, weapons will fail to strike fear into them.[189] The Russians seemed to have more cofidence in the imperialists heeding the language of thermonuclear power. Justifying their view, they dug out a little episode from NadyezhdaKrupskaya's reminiscence of Lenin, her husband. The late Soviet ruler was once told by an engineer that an invention had been in the making which would "mow down a large army from a distance."[190] As she recollected, Lenin was excited and said that war would become impossible. Kuusinen wrote: "Such are the dialectics of military-engineering; a new weapon intended for war begins to exert

World Peace Conference on July 10, 1962, *Predotvratit' voinu, otstoyat' mir!* (Prevent war and defend peace!), p. 246.

[182] "Otchetnyi doklad Tsentral'nogo Komiteta...," *Pravda*, February 15, 1956.

[183] "Deklaratsiya soveshchaniya predstavitelei ...," *ibid.*, November 22, 1957.

[184] "Kommiunike o soveshchanii...," *ibid.*, February 5, 1960.

[185] "Marsizm-leninizm...," *Izvestiya*, January 8, 1961; "Za novye pobedy...," *Pravda*, January 7, 1961; *Kommunist*, 1 (January, 1961), 34–35.

[186] "Zayavlenie soveshchaniya predstavitelei...," *Pravda*, December 6, 1960.

[187] *Sino-Soviet Dispute*, p. 93.

[188] The resolution adopted on January 18, 1961 by the Ninth Plenary Seseion of the Eighth Central Committee of the Chinese Communist Party, *ibid.*, p. 222.

[189] Chung Hsin-ching, "Two sources of war...," *Peking Review*, 25 (June 21, 1960), 22–27. Translation of "Wei-shieh shih-chieh...," *Hung-ch'i*, 11 (June 1, 1960), 8–15.

[190] N. K. Krupskaya, *O Lenine* (On Lenin) (Moskva: Gospolitizdat, 1960), pp. 40–41.

an influence in favor of peace."[191] Mutual fear of calamity, in other words, would restrain adversaries from taking up arms.

There appears the basic difference in the disputants' belief as to whether the enemy could be deterred. The problem of fear in relation to war was not seen by Peking in the same light as by the Russians. The latter seemed convinced of the postulation that it is only when the enemy does not fear and is given to fight his opponent that war will arise. On the other hand, Peking held that the deterrence produces no horror in the enemy's mind or brings the enemy to his senses. He has no fear at all so long as you have in possession something which he is after. It is sure, Peking believed, that he would even run the risk of certain death to strike you in order to achieve his objective.[192] His greed banishes his rationality. The fact that Moscow has thought otherwise is demonstrated by Khrushchev's repeated references to Hitler. "Even the crazy Hitler, if he had believed that the war would end in his shooting a bullet into his head, would not have taken such a bestial decision on war."[193] On another occasion, he iterated the same view in a way showing his belief in the corrigibility of the late German despot. This is how he put it: "If Hitler had had an inkling that his reckless gamble would end in the way it did, then in all probability he would have thought twice before starting the war."[194] Besides the fear of brutal force there is the fear of "just retribution," as Kuusinen suggested. He argued that if it had occurred to the "Nazi ringleaders that there existed an international court of justice which would hang them, as it did in Nüremberg, they could have been restrained."[195] In sum, the Russians felt that the lack of fear is the cause of war and that to strike fear into the enemy would debar him from action. The Chinese, on the other hand, believed in the hypothesis, but disbelieved in the

---

[191] "Pretvorenie v zhizn'...," *Pravda*, April 23, 1960.

[192] The imperialist instinct of aggression is said to be involuntary, for it has been conditioned by the time-worn exploitative tradition of class society. "The various contradictions inherent in the imperialist system cause it [imperialism] to adopt the policy of armaments expansion and war preparations and to engage in aggression and plunder," wrote Chung Hsinching, "Two sources of war...," *Peking Review*, 25 (June 21, 1960), 22–7. Translation of "Wei-sheh shih-chieh...," *Hung-ch'i*, 11 (June 1, 1960), 8–15. Lenin said: "Even the capitalists have involuntarily gone to war because they themselves have little control of their action which is moulded by fifty years' development," in "Zadachi proletariata v nashei revoliutsii" (The tasks of the proletariat in our revolution), April, 1917, *O voine, armii i voennoi nauke* (On war, army and military science; 2nd ed.), p. 338.

[193] *Sino-Soviet Dispute*, p. 137.

[194] "Marksizm-leninizm...," *Izvestiya*, January 8, 1961; *Kommunist*, 1 (January, 1961), 27; "Za novye pobedy...," *Pravda*, January 7, 1961.

[195] "Pretvorenie v zhizn'...," *Pravda*, April 23, 1960.

inference.[196] According to them, the enemy is fear-proof, so to say. It is in vain to rely upon deterrent media in order to make the enemy afraid of fighting. He will fight at any rate.[197]

Other Psychological Causes of War

From the polemic literature one can glean several other causes of war suggested by both disputants. Since war is a hostile act undertaken by one group against another, it must be preceded by a reciprocity of enmity.[198] One of the two sides will behave violently when the enmity goes beyond the possibility of assuagement. It is felt by Peking and Moscow that the alleged bellicose policy of the West toward their bloc stems from the capitalist aversion to their system. Khrushchev asserted that the statesmen in America "are so blinded by hatred for communism" that they dared to make such provocation as the 1959 U–2 flights.[199] He served the warning that if the Government of the United States "continues overflights, that will, of course, have the most serious consequence for the sake of peace."[200] The statement connotes that hatred may lead to war. Khrushchev's detente policy seems to be predicated on the assumption of the desirability of non-hatred of each other's system. On September 30, 1959, he said to Mao that the capitalists cherish their way of life as much as the communists cherish theirs.[201] To bear malice toward a different regime would not help the cause of peace. The Chinese, however, did not appear convinced. Yet, on occasions Peking also has warned of international tension being engendered by the "antipathy toward communism" on the part of the United States.[202] But it chose to be mute on the organized hate-America campaign of its own.

Another cause of war connected with the mental process is revenge-

---

[196] Chao Shin, "Lung-tuan tsu-pen ti chün-shih li-yun" (Monopoly profit as a result of militarism), *Shih-chieh chih-shih* (World knowledge), 8 (April 25, 1966), 18–20.

[197] After all, the Soviets have said that they could not vouch for the madman. But they stated that "should the bellicose imperialist maniacs venture, regardless of anything, to unleash a war, imperialism dooms itself to destruction, for the people will not tolerate a system that brings them so much suffering and exacts so many sacrifices," in "Deklaratsiya soveshchaniya predstavitelei...," *Pravda*, November 22, 1957.

[198] Lenin, *Clausewitz' Werk "Vom Kriege": Auszüge und Randglossen* (Clausewitz's book on war: extracts and annotations), p. 18.

[199] "Rech' t. N. S. Khrushcheva na III s'ezde...," (Khrushchev's speech to the Third Congress of the Romanian Workers' Party), *Pravda*, June 22, 1960; *Izvestiya*, June 23, 1960.

[200] *Ibid.*

[201] *Pravda*, October 1, 1959.

[202] Ch'en Yi, "Current world situation and our diplomacy," *Jen-min shou-ts'e* (People's handbook, 1957), p. 115. The speech was given to the Eighth Plenary Session of the Chinese Communist Party, on September 25, 1956.

seeking. This charge has been made by the Soviets with exclusive reference to the Federal Republic of Germany and Japan. It is asserted that the militarists in both countries, with the abetment of the NATO signatories, are making preparations against the socialist peoples in both East and West.[203] The Moscow statement (December 6, 1960) pointed out that the "West German retaliatory elements openly declare their intention to revise the border arrangement fixed after the Second World War."[204] Such alleged elements proved impotent, in view of the Moscow-Bonn Non-Violence Treaty recently concluded.

Still another cause of war is entirely out of the control of the policy makers. Marshal Sokolovskii and his associates suggested no less than four possibilities: (1) error of radar detection which produces wrong interpretations of objects; (2) misunderstanding of orders; (3) mental aberration of American pilots who are flying planes loaded with atomic bombs; (4) disrepair of electronic devices in the nuclear-missile systems.[205] We also heard Khrushchev mention the probability of accidentally "pushing the wrong button" to trigger off a nuclear war.[206] The armed collisions not attributed to capitalism as a system are largely ignored by the Chinese theorists.[207] Finally, there is the problem of preventive attack. William McDougall spoke of it as the "most powerful of all the latent psychological reasons of war."[208] Even though believing in their deterrent strength, the Soviets also take cognizance of the preventive war which might be unleashed by the west.[209] But the danger is said to be minimized by the big land mass of the Soviet state which neutralizes the advantage of any surprise onslaught.[210] Apparently, due to the alleged peace policy, the Soviet military writers have rarely propounded a preventive war of their own.[211]

---

[203] "Pretvorenie v zhizn'...," *Pravda*, April 23, 1960.

[204] "Zayavlenie soveshchaniya predstavitelei...," *ibid.*, December 6, 1960.

[205] *Voennaya strategiya* (Military strategy; 2nd ed.), pp. 235, 264.

[206] In a speech to the World Peace Conference, July 10, 1962, *Predotvratit' voinu, otstoyat' mir!* (Prevent war and defend peace!), pp. 247–48.

[207] "Significantly the Chinese have raised no objection to the Soviet-American 'hot-line' agreement whose sole effect is to diminish an unintentional thermonuclear war," wrote Harold C. Hinton, *Commonweal*, 79 (October 18, 1963), 91. The Chinese, however, never took the agreement seriously.

[208] *Janus: the concept of war* (London: Kegan Paul [n.d.]), pp. 50–51.

[209] *Voennaya strategiya* (Military strategy; 2nd ed.), p. 351.

[210] *Ibid.*, pp. 347–64; Frunze, *Izbrannye proizvedeniya* (Selected works), vol. 1, p. 30.

[211] "The surprise attack not only can be delivered by the West on the Soviet Union, but also can be done otherwise," in *Marksizm-leninizm o voine i armii* (Marxism-Leninism on war and army) (edited by P. A. Sidorov and A. D. Aristov; 1st ed.; Moskva: Voen. izd-vo, 1956), p. 267.

CHAPTER III

WORLD WAR

THE CONTROVERSY REGARDING THE "NEW EPOCH"

Definition

Although the concept of a "world war" has been a topic of debate between the theorists of Moscow and Peking, nowhere in their polemical literature has there appeared a definition of it. It may be referred to as a war which is neither local or civil, nor national liberatory. But this merely begs the question, for those latter concepts have not been fixed either. Before suggesting our definition, it may be useful to take a quick look at what ideas have been formed by the communists with respect thereto. *Jen-min jih-pao* has spoken of a "major" or "general war";[1] *Pravda*, of a "war against the socialist camp."[2] The appellation of "new world war" (or simply "world war") has also been used to specify the nuclear variety.[3] In addition, the communists have used "imperialist war" and "world war" interchangeably. This is a poor usage, for the first term, as conceptualized by Lenin, is simply a war among the colonial powers.[4] Also denoting world war is the phrase "imperialist military gamble,"[5] or "predatory war,"[6] often seen in propaganda organs. Further, the communists have referred to the "war between

---

[1] "A-la-pai jen chien-chüeh yao mei-ing ch'in-lüeh chün k'un-tan" (The Arabs persistently demand the ouster of Anglo-American troops from the region of Middle-East), *Jen-min jih-pao*, August 18, 1958. Engels mentioned "Allgemein Weltkrieg" (general world war) in contrast with "Lokalisierter Krieg" (localized war), see "Engels an Julie Bebel" (March 12, 1887), in Marx and Engels, *Werke* (Berlin: Dietz, 1967), vol. 36, p. 628.

[2] "Dal'neishee ukreplenie mirovoi...," *Pravda*, January 28, 1959.

[3] "Marksizm-leninizm...," *Izvestiya*, January 8, 1961; "Za novye pobedy...," *Pravda*, January 7, 1961; *Kommunist*, 1 (January, 1961), 35.

[4] "Deklaratsiya soveshchaniya predstavitelei...," *Pravda*, November 22, 1957.

[5] "Rech't. N. S. Khrushcheva na III s'ezde...," (Khrushchev's speech to the Third Congress of the Romanian Workers' Party), *ibid.*, June 22, 1960; *Izvestiya*, June 23, 1960..

[6] Khrushchev, *Predotvratit' voine, otstoyat' mir!* (Prevent war and defend peace!), p. 38

states,"[7] or "international war,"[8] or "inter-state war,"[9] all intimating world armed conflict. From these expressions several points stand out. In the first place, world war has its definite ideological implications and, in this sense, is unprecedented. In the second place, the battle front is drawn between East and West, each representing an alliance. In the third place, the dimension of conflict is truly universal, for no country can stay out of it. In the last place, the war will be thermonuclear. We may, thus, call "world war" a military competition between the socialist and capitalist states which will be carried out with the newest weapons and "will involve millions upon millions of men."[10]

A Change of Epoch

The problem of world war relates to the issue of the change of epoch, viz., whether we have entered an era no longer the one wherein Lenin flourished.[11] Khrushchev told the Twentieth Congress that there was a period when wars and revolutions were the order of the day and when socialism was only an idea but not concrete reality. That was the epoch of the unchallengeable sway of capitalism, with peace the exception, war the rule of human life. However, this situation has gone. He stressed the anti-war forces consequent to the maturity of the socialist regime and came to the conclusion that the present epoch is one of transition from capitalism to socialism, one in which armed struggle has to give way to a competition in economic and cultural activities.[12] The socialist countries, he stated, have become a decisive factor in determining the mighty problems of peace and war. Since the imperialists alone cannot settle the destiny of mankind, there will be a possibility of universal harmony which is central to socialism.[13] The eighty-one-party statement (December 6, 1960) contended that "whatever efforts imperialism makes, it will fail to stop the march of history," and that

---

[7] "Marksizm-leninizm...," *Izvestiya*, January 8, 1961; "Za novye pobedy...," *Pravda*, January 7, 1961; *Kommunist*, 1 (January, 1961), 17.

[8] Khrushchev, *Predotvratit' voinu, otstoyat' mir!* (Prevent war and defend peace!), p. 38; F. Konstantinov and Kh. Momdzhyan, "Dialektika i sovremennye usloviya" (Dialectics and present-day conditions), *Kommunist*, 10 (July, 1960), 35–38.

[9] *Voennaya strategiya* (Military strategy; 2nd ed.), p. 346.

[10] *Ibid.*

[11] Although Lenin was convinced that his was the epoch of imperialism, he also confessed that "we really do not know how long the epoch will last," in "Referat na temu 'proletariat i voina'" (Concerning the topic "proletariat and war"), October, 1914, *O voine, armii i voennoi nauke* (On war, army and military science; 2nd ed.), p. 227. He advised that to understand the meaning of epoch one ought to know which class dominates therein, "Pod chuzhim flagom" (Under the foreign flag), January, 1915, *ibid.*, p. 330.

[12] "Otchetnyi doklad Tsentral'nogo Komiteta...," *Pravda*, February 15, 1956.

[13] "Deklaratsiya soveshchaniya predstavitelei ...,"*ibid.*, November 22, 1957.

a "fresh stage has set in in the development of the general crisis of capitalism."[14]

At Bucharest (June 21, 1960), Khrushchev minced no words in disproving Lenin's theory of the inevitability of war as being anachronistic. Were Lenin alive today, he said, he would have himself updated that theory. "One cannot mechanically repeat ... what Vladimir Il'ych stated many decades ago."[15] Since his death in 1924, he went on, there have come to pass numerous changes of which he had not had the dimmest vision. Now a new array of conditions calling for a fresh outlook has compelled one to refute Lenin and conclude that war is not inevitable. All the Russian writings on the premise for the new epoch were rebuked by Chinese leaders whose thought is elaborated in the noted article "Long Live Leninism." Avowedly loyal to the late Soviet ruler, they treated as immutable his legacy that "war is an inevitable outcome of the system of exploitation" and that its fountainhead is imperialism.[16] They are convinced that the contemporary era is not new at all. It is what it once was when Marx and Lenin lived.[17] "The formulation of revolutionary Marxists that ours is the epoch of imperialism and proletarian revolution remains irrefutable."[18]

To the Russian criticism that they failed to reckon with the real milieux surrounding them,[19] the Chinese retorted that they analysed the problem of war with great profundity and did not let "passing political changes" blind them.[20] In bitter terms, they bemoaned the Soviets as having strayed away from the right course. They recalled that Lenin always taught one the necessity of examining historical development in the light of the class struggle.[21] The future of socialism,

[14] "Zayavlenie soveshchaniya predstavitelei...," *ibid.*, December 6, 1960.
[15] "Rech' t. N. S. Khrushcheva na III s'edze...," (Khrushchev's speech to the Third Congress of the Romanian Workers' Party), *ibid.*, June 22, 1960; *Izvestiya*, June 23, 1960.
[16] *Sino-Soviet Dispute*, p. 98.
[17] For a pertinent comment by a Western scholar, *see* George F. Kennan, *Saturday Evening Post*, 236 (October 5, 1963), 38.
[18] *Sino-Soviet Dispute*, p. 98. The idea receives full treatment in Yu Chao-li, "On imperialism as a source of war...," *Peking Review*, 15 (April 12, 1960), 17–24. Translation of "Lun t'i-kuo chu-i...," *Hung-ch'i*, 7 (April 1, 1960), 1–12.
[19] B. Ponomarev, "Leninizm – nashie znamya i vsepobezhdaiushchee oruzhie" (Leninism is our victorious standard and invincible weapon), *Pravda*, April 23, 1963.
[20] *Sino-Soviet Dispute*, p. 89.
[21] For Lenin's teaching to analyze concrete historical situations in view of class struggle, *see* his "Partizanskaya voina" (On partisan war), September, 1906, first published in *Proletarian*, 5 (September 30, 1906), now in *Sochineniya* (Collected works; 5th ed.), vol. 14, pp. 1–12; also in *O voine, armii i voennoi nauke* (On war, army and military science; 2nd ed.), p. 150. Other references are: "Karikature na marksizm i ob 'imperialisticheskom ekonomizme'" (On the caricature of Marxism and imperialist economy), August–October, 1916, *ibid.*, p. 297; 'Iz 'otkrytogo mis'ma Borisu Suvarinu'" (From an open letter to Boris Souvarine), October,

Peking admitted, has grown brighter since Lenin, but imperialism still breathes and is ready to swoop upon the people's democracy. In addition, the proletariat is heard groaning under the yoke of its masters.[22] Thus, to hold that the international balance of forces has heralded a new era in which the "revolution will fade away" is utterly un-Leninist.[23] A charge was hurled at Belgrade and meant for Moscow that those who tried to write the assignment of collaboration with the imperialists in the communist workbook, instead of the assignment of war and revolution, must be christened renegade.[24] A rebuttal was not slow in coming from Yugoslavia. Edward Kardelj, that nation's Vice-President of Federal Executive Council, stated that it was commonsense that war has become less likely now that the peace forces have grown so preponderant. "Whoever fails to make a factual analysis of this sort as a starting point, yet still talks about the inevitability of war, is indeed afraid of imperialism and has no faith in his own forces."[25] It will be recalled that back in 1949 Mao described the present epoch as one of imperialism, an imperialism which, even senescent, is not yet gone.[26] On account of this obstinacy Peking was dubbed "adventurist" and "ultra-revolutionary."[27] Its "morbid dogmatism," one Soviet professor wrote, echoes only the "gross theoretical and political blunders of its leadership."[28] Marshal Sokolovskii and his colleagues told the Chinese to do more homework on Marxism-Leninism before they came back to take up the subject of war in the new epoch.[29]

1916, *ibid.*, p. 320. Lenin stated clearly: "One must distinguish wars first before he says that he opposes this or that war," in "Referat na temu 'proletariat i voina'" (Concerning the topic 'proletariat and war'), October, 1914, *ibid.*, p. 223.

[22] Lenin said that capitalism is terror to the proletariat; "Voennaya programma proletarskoi revoliutsii" (Military program of the proletarian revolution), September, 1916, *ibid.*, p. 305; "O lozunge 'razoruzheniya'" (On the slogan of disarmament), October, 1916, *ibid.*, p. 313.

[23] *Sino-Soviet Dispute*, p. 90.

[24] *Ibid.*, p. 87; William Henry Chamberlain, *Russian Review*, 23 (July, 1964), 219.

[25] *Socialism and War* (London: Methuen, 1961), p. 36.

[26] *Selected Works* (New York ed.), vol. 5, p. 407; Ai Ssu-ch'i, *Chin i-pu hsüeh-hsi 'chang-wu wu-ch'an chieh-chi shih-chieh kuan'* (To further our learning how to master proletarian Weltanschauung) (Hong Kong; Hsin-ho... publishing house, 1961), pp. 1–56. When Mao stated that we are in the epoch of imperialism, he literally followed the teaching of Lenin who dated the epoch from 1914, *see* Lenin, "Pod chuzhim flagom" (Under foreign flag), January, 1915, *O voine, armii i voennoi nauke* (On war, army and military science; 2nd ed.), p. 231; "Voennaya programma proletarskoi revoliutsii" (Military program of the proletarian revolution), September, 1916, *ibid.*, p. 305. Khrushchev suggested, however, that we are not in the imperialist epoch, ours being the epoch of socialism or at least that of the transition from imperialism to socialism.

[27] Kuusinen, "Pretvorenie v zhizn'...," *Pravda*, April 23, 1960.

[28] Iu. A. Krasin, *Filosofskie nauki* (Philosophical sciences), 5 (1963), 3.

[29] *Voennaya strategiya* (Military strategy; 2nd ed.), p. 223.

Science and War

Aside from the growing stature of the socialist system in the modern world, the new epoch is marked by a technological advance in what Marx called "manslaughter industry."[30] The development of mass destructive arms is considered the turning point in relations between states. World political leaders must come to agree upon a course of action so that a nuclear hecatomb can be staved off.[31] It is because of this practical thinking that the Soviets have proceeded to adopt the policy of peaceful coexistence.[32] There is said to be no alternative to a global suicide in which millions of people will be sacrificed in a few moments.[33] As is known now, the Russians have never dismissed the possibility that a future war would affect them, although sometimes they referred to the ruination of capitalism alone. In early 1962, Khrushchev wrote President Kennedy that the outcome of a war would be quickly settled by missile strikes "before vast armies can be mobilized and thrown into battle."[34] A year earlier, he told the Supreme Soviet of the changed face of armed conflicts which knew no precedent in history because they "begin in the heart of the belligerent states ... during the first minutes."[35] When interviewed by Gardner Couls of *The Des Moines Register* (Iowa) on April 20, 1962, Khrushchev claimed that among the contemporary statesmen he was the one most fearful of nuclear encounters.[36]

The manifest basis of Khrushchev's fear is that wars in the days ahead cannot remain conventional, and that an apparently small crisis could become bigger until it assumes a global scope.[37] With a world polarized into "gigantic military pacts" each in possession of scientific resources, according to Marshal Sokolovskii *et al.*, all new techniques

---

[30] *Voina i voennoe iskusstvo v svete istoricheskogo materializma* (War and military art in the light of historical materialism), p. 173.

[31] "Otchetnyi doklad Tsentral'nogo Komiteta...," *Pravda*, February 15, 1956.

[32] George F. Kennan, *Saturday Evening Post*, 236 (October 5, 1963), 40.

[33] Khrushchev, *Predotvratit' voinu, otstoyat' mir!* (Prevent war and defend peace!), pp. 37, 38, 109, 160, 186, 211, 243.

[34] "Poslanie predsedatelya Soveta Ministrov SSSR, N. S. Khrushcheva, Prezidentu SSHA, Dzhony Kennedi" (A letter from the Chairman of the Council of Ministers, N. S. Khrushchev, to the President of the United States, John F. Kennedy), *Pravda*, February 24, 1962; *Izvestiya* of the same date. In English, the source is in: State Department, *Bulletin*, 47 (October–December, 1962), 741–43.

[35] "Razoruzhenie – put' k uprocheniiu mira...," *Pravda*, January 15, 1960.

[36] Khrushchev, *Predotvratit' voinu, otstoyat' mir!* (Prevent war and defend peace!), p. 37.

[37] It will be recalled that during the First World War Lenin set forth the slogan of turning the international war into civil war. Now Khrushchev urged that civil war must not be turned into international war, "Marksizm-leninizm...," *Izvestiya*, January 8, 1961; "Za novye pobedy...," *Pravda*, January 7, 1961; *Kommunist*, 1 (January, 1961), 29.

would invariably be harnessed for battle.[38] In view of the almost
certainty of the employment of nuclear arms and because of their
incredible devastation, Khrushchev declared that "mankind has arrived
at a stage when the prevention of world war has become the 'problem
of all problems.'"[39] "The working class," he said, "cannot allow the
historically doomed forces to bring down with them hundreds of millions
into their graves."[40] It was his belief that arms innovation plus the
overall strength of the communist nations called for a diplomacy of
detente, the keynote of the new epoch. Gone was the cold war à la
Stalin. Since coexistence required for its success the condition that the
Soviet Union assume an accommodating demeanor toward the West,
the Chinese did not take kindly to it. In an attempt to negate Russia's
detente, Peking asserted that the progress in science detracts nothing
from Marxism-Leninism.[41] "The present world situation has obviously
undergone tremendous changes since Lenin's life time, but these changes
have not proved the obsoleteness of Leninism," they said.[42]

Marx taught that one ought to view "new discoveries" as well as
social phenomena from the vantage ground of class antagonisms and
proletarian internationalism, Peking stated.[43] The Soviets were taken
to task for disheartening the workpeople by exaggerating the role of
weapons. *Chieh-fang chün-pao* (Liberation army paper) assailed those
in the military circle who were enchanted by the atomic myth.[44] True
to Lenin's precept that "scientific development further demonstrates
the veracity of Marxism,"[45] the Chinese leadership believed that modern
technology itself not only failed to falsify Leninism, but further proved
its infallibility.[46] An assertion was made that the imperialists found in
the nuclear device an effective means to embitter their oppression of the
workmen in both the metropolises and the colonies.[47] This certainly
created new dangers for the peace-lovers and made it evermore pressing
to foster a revolutionary fervor among the proletarians. The detente

---

[38] *Voennaya strategiya* (Military strategy; 2nd ed.), p. 234.
[39] "Marksizm-leninizm...," *Izvestiya*, January 8, 1961; "Za novye pobedy...," *Pravda*,
January 7, 1961; *Kommunist*, 1 (January, 1961), 21–25.
[40] *Ibid.*
[41] K. S. Karol, "Fidel, Mao and Nikita," *New Statesman*, 65 (March 22, 1963), 414; 66
(September 20, 1963), 346.
[42] *Sino-Soviet Dispute*, p. 86.
[43] *Ibid.*, p. 91.
[44] August 1, 1958.
[45] Lenin, "Krakh II internatsionala" (Collapse of the Second International), May–June,
1915, *O voine, armii i voennoi nauke* (On war, army and military science; 2nd ed.), p. 242.
[46] *Sino-Soviet Dispute*, p. 86.
[47] *Ibid.*, p. 92.

policy tended to diminish that ferver.[48] Moreover, modern technology
further widens the cleavage between the exploitative and the exploited
in the capitalist society, due to the accelerating cummulation of wealth,
on the one hand, and impoverishment of the common people, on the
other.[49] Hence there set in an increasing erosion within the bourgeois
body politic.[50] Such process would speed up the collapse of monopoly,
Peking argued. It is mendacious to conclude that the piling up of knowledge in physics has devaluated Marxism-Leninism. The Chinese also
claimed that material inventions are to be availed for the advancement
of the progressive cause, implying that the age of steam belongs to
capitalism, the age of electricity to socialism, and the age of atomic
energy to communism. There is no evidence whatever that unprecedented discoveries have depreciated the dialectic truth. Finally, the Chinese
thought that the imperialists would not resort to nuclear weapons in
order to start a world war as the Soviets always supposed they would.[51]
In putting down internal rebellion, they would almost certainly not
resort to such extreme arms. Therefore, future war may not be invariably nuclear.

Socialism and War

We have mentioned the dread with which the Soviets viewed future
armed conflict. In general it is held that human civilization would be
set back should that happen and that the communist nations can no
more avoid disaster than the capitalist nations. Even those who cheered
the annihilation of capitalism alone never ventured to add that socialism could inevitably emerge intact. Belyakov and Burlatskii examined
the relation between war and socialism in a much publicized article.
They held that the problem was "much more complicated than some
people imagine."[52] A prevalent concept, they observed, has been that
armed struggles always result in a victory of the progressive people,
for it is the fate of history. On the whole, the theory is sound, they
believed, for no one can gainsay the dialectic law. Upon thorough analysis, however, there is more to be said about the matter. They found

---

[48] *Ibid.*, p. 91.

[49] *Ibid.*, p. 92.

[50] Lenin saw in his days a moribund bourgeois body politic, "Iz 'otkrytogo pis'ma Borisu
Suvarisu'" (From an open letter to Boris Souvarine), December, 1916, *O voine, armii i voennoi
nauke* (On war, army and military science; 2nd ed.), p. 320.

[51] Liu Ch'ang-sheng addressed the meeting of the World Federation of Trade Unions on
June 22, 1960, *Sino-Soviet Dispute*, p. 126; also "Long live Leninism," *ibid.*, p. 88.

[52] A. Belyakov and F. Burlatskii, "Leninskaya teoriya...," *Kommunist*, 13 (September,
1960), 20.

that wars were not an unmixed blessing, for their effect on society for the most part is negative. "Wars have always been tremendous disasters for the mass of people, causing the workers starvation and destruction in the rear and death and dismemberment at the front."[53] Under these circumstances, the "liberation movement of the masses and the conditions of its development" are often hindered. It is wars which inevitably play havoc with the "productive forces of the community and thereby impede their advance."[54]

The authors were not alone in their realistic assessment of wars; many Russians, including Lenin himself, have taken the same view. The flower of society, once mourned Gorev, was ravished in gunfire.[55] "Doubtless," wrote Lenin, "war exacerbates the calamity of the mass of people beyond words."[56] On many occasions, he seemed quite tender-hearted in regretting that "killing is indeed murder..., even if done for the sake of communism."[57] When the Czarist government rushed troops to Manchuria in 1889 to fight the Chinese, he lamented that such intervention would take away young men from their beloved ones, beside causing onerous taxation and, thus, threatening the livelihood of countless toilers.[58] Khrushchev felt the same way, for he realized that it is the proletarians who do the actual fighting in any war.[59] Two more reasons were set forth to downgrade the role of Mars. During war time, the reactionary forces are well intrenched because of the stringent measures taken to meet the crisis, and war itself increases their political power. The upshot is that the proletarian revolution will be decelerated.[60] This is the first reason. The second reason pertains to the relation between capitalism and war. In addressing the party conference early in 1961, Khrushchev voiced the view that world war was not the sole cause of the capitalist crisis. Anyone seeking to explain the economic predicament of the West by the scourge of war alone sadly mis-

---

[53] *Ibid.*, p. 21.

[54] *Ibid.*, pp. 19–25.

[55] V. I. Gorev, "Voina kak sotsial'noe yavlenie" (War as a social phenomenon), *Voina i voennoe iskusstvo s svete istoricheslogo materializma* (War and military art in the light of historical materialism), p. 31.

[56] Lenin, *O voine, armii i voennoi nauke* (On war, army and military science; 1st ed.), vol. 2, p. 428.

[57] *Idem, Sochineniya* (Collected works; 4th ed.), vol. 35, p. 191.

[58] *Ibid.*, p. 15.

[59] Iu. Frantsev, "Problemy voiny i mira...," *Pravda*, August 7, 1960; "Marksizm-leninizm...," *Izvestiya*, January 8, 1961; "Za novye pobedy...," *Pravda*, January 7, 1961; *Kommunist*, 1 (January, 1961), pp. 12–15.

[60] A. Belyakov and F. Burlatskii, "Leninskaya teoriya...," *Kommunist*, 13 (September, 1960), 17. "A destructive war would only make difficult the process of construction of a new society," Iu. Frantsev, "Problemy voiny i mira...," *Pravda*, August 7, 1960.

understands the nature of monopoly capitalism. The real problem is not war but the "internal contradictions and class struggle" in the capitalist community.[61] Besides, he cast doubt on the possibility of building up socialism on the radioactive rubble of nuclear war.[62] In a nutshell, world war turns out to be a liability to the proletarians and actually is not needed for their success.[63]

While the Warsaw Treaty Alliance was declaring (February 5, 1960) that "war in general can no longer be an agent to solve international disputes,"[64] the Government of China openly extolled sword-crossing. Upon the ruins of a major war, it asserted, there would grow a socialist civilization infinitely higher than ever before.[65] The Chinese stand was refuted by the Russians, who emphasized the destructiveness of war.[66]

[61] "Marksizm-leninizm...," *Izvestiya*, January 8, 1961; "Za novye pobedy...," *Pravda*, January 7, 1961; *Kommunist*, 1 (January, 1961), 24. S. Vygodskii, *et. al.*, *Istoriya diplomatii*, vol. 3: *Diplomatiya na pervom etape obshchego krizisa kapitalisticheskoi sistemy* (A history of diplomacy, vol. 3: diplomacy in the first stage of general crisis of capitalist system; 2nd ed.) (Moskva: Gos. izd-vo polit. lit-ry, 1965), 65–70.

[62] "Ukrepim edinstvo kommunisticheskogo dvizheniya vo imya torzhestva mira i sotsializma" (Let us strengthen the unity of communist movement for the sake of peace and socialism), *Pravda*, January 7, 1963.

[63] Khrushchev's speech in a Bulgarian village on March 18, 1962, *Predotvratit' voiny, otstoyat' mir!* (Prevent war and defend peace!), p. 88. There he held out the slogan "work, not war."

[64] "Kommiunike o soveshchanii...," *Pravda*, February 5, 1960.

[65] This ominous position warrants a full quotation from the Chinese document. "It is certain that if the United States or other imperialists refuse to reach an agreement on the banning of atomic and nuclear weapons and should dare to fly in the face of the will of all humanity by launching a war using atomic and nuclear weapons, the result will be the very speedy destruction of these monsters, encircled by the peoples of the world, and the result will certainly not be the annihilation of mankind. We consistently oppose the launching of criminal wars by imperialism, because imperialist war would impose enormous sacrifices upon the peoples of various countries (including the peoples of the United States and other imperialist countries). But should the imperialists impose such sacrifices on the peoples of various countries, we believe that, just as the experience of the Russian revolution and the Chinese revolution shows, those sacrifices would be repaid. On the debris of a dead imperialism, the victorious people would create very swiftly a civilization thousands of times higher than the capitalist system and a truly beautiful future for themselves," in "Long live Leninism," *Peking Review*, 17 (April 26, 1960), 12. This statement was also echoed by a writer, pen-named "Observer," in an editorial, *Jen-min jih-pao*, December 10, 1961. Lenin did not seem happy about the destructive aspect of wars, although he stated that wars could not be viewed sentimentally, "Revoluitsionnaya armiya i revoliutsionnoe pravitel'stvo" (Revolutionary army and revolutionary government), July, 1905, *O voine, armii i voennoi nauke* (On war, army and military science; 2nd ed.), p. 135. The nearest statement which indicates Lenin's favorable attitude toward the ruinous consequence of wars is: "The more ruinous the wars, the more perfect means will be found to heal the wound inflicted hereby," in "Zadachi proletariata v nashei revoliutsii" (The tasks of the proletariat in our revolution), April, 1917, *ibid.*, p. 340. For Engels' praise of war, *see* Marx and Engels, *Sochineniya* (Collected works; 2nd ed.), vol. 21, p. 361 as quoted in *ibid.*, pp. 506–7. It is this bellicose position of the Chinese that has created "a widespread impression that they would welcome a world war," Harold C. Hinton, *Commonweal*, 79 (October 18, 1963), 91.

[66] Khrushchev, *On Peaceful Coexistence*, p. 232. A. Belyakov and F. Burlatskii, "Leninskaya teoriya...," *Konmmuist*, 13 (September, 1960), 15. The Chinese praise of nuclear wars was specifically bemoaned by the Soviets in "Otkrytoe pis'mo Tsentral'nogo Komiteta KPSS

After being told by Peking that as a result of the First World War, there arose the greatest socialist state in the West, and as a result of the Second World War, the greatest socialist state in the East,[67] Khrushchev questioned: "Can it be inferred from this that international conflict is an indispensable condition for the furtherance of the general crisis of capitalism?"[68] He thought it absurd to have socialism indebted to Mars.[69] Peking's militancy indeed has its Maoist tradition. In a tract "The Chinese revolution and the Chinese Communist Party" (December, 1939), Mao stated that after each war society marches forward some distance.[70] Elsewhere he taught that "we have to wage war to end war,"[71] and that "we must hate the enemy and kill him in war."[72] It is to be noted that in Mao's writings very few references can be identified to show his aversion of war.[73] He seemed never to think that war could stifle a revolution,[74] a view which Lenin felt compelled to take when he ordered the signing of the treaty of Brest-Litovsk in

partinym organizatsiyam, vsem kommunistam Sovetskogo Soiuza" (An open letter from the. Central Committee of the CPSU to the party appparatus, and party members of the CPSU). *Pravda*, July 14, 1963.

[67] Mao's work "On the correct handling of contradictions among the people" reproduced in *Jen-min shou-t'se* (People's handbook, 1958), p. 19; *China after Mao*, p. 261. A few Soviets also considered war helping socialism; *see Voennaya strategiya* (Military strategy; 2nd ed.), p. 223, where it is written that due to the two world wars socialism thrives.

[68] "Marksizm-leninizm...," *Izvestiya*, January 8, 1961; "Za novye pobedy...," *Pravda*, January 7, 1961; *Kommunist*, 1 (January, 1961), 22.

[69] Lenin, however, minced no words in saying that socialism must be given a push by rifles, not by parliamentary tongues, "Mezhdunarodnyi sotsialisticheskii kongress v Shtutgarte" (International socialist congress in Stuttgart), August–September, 1907, *O voine, armii i voennoi nauke* (On war, army and military science; 2nd ed.), p. 172.

[70] The Chinese title reads: "Chung-kuo ko-ming yü chung-kuo kung-ch'an-tang," in *Mao Tse-tung hsüan-chi* (Selected works), 1925, vol. 2, p. 595; also Chang-chiang jih-pao, *Chung-kuo ko-ming chi-pen wen-t'i hsüeh-hsi t'i-kang*. (The fundamental problems of the Chinese revolution, an outline study) (2nd ed.; Hung-ko: Chung-nan Jen-min ch'u pan she, 1957), pp. 50–60. According to the Albanian paper *Zeri i popullit* (early in October, 1963) "Khrushchev claimed that the Chinese views on war and peace were more akin to those of Genghis Khan than to Marx," *see* Victor Zorza, "China charges Mr. K. with racism," *Guardian*, October 22, 1963, p. 13.

[71] Mao, "Lun chih chiu chan" (On protracted war), *Mao Tse-tung hsüan-chi*(Selected works), 1952, vol. 2, pp. 438, 444–45. For the similar view of Lenin's, *see* his "O lozunge 'razoruzheniya'" (On the slogan of disarmament), October, 1916, *O voine, armii i voennoi nauke* (On war, army and military science; 2nd ed.), p. 315.

[72] Mao, "Tsai yen-an wen-i tso-t'an-hui shong ti t'an-hua" (A talk at the literary round-table in Yenan), May 2, 1942, *Mao Tse-tung hsüan-chi* (Selected works), 1952, vol. 2, p. 872.

[73] *Idem*, "Lun lien-ho cheng-fu" (On coalition government), April 24, 1945. Here he wrote that war is a matter of hardship for the people; *ibid.*, 1953, vol. 3, p. 1054.

[74] On the contrary, "revolution can only thrive in war," wrote Mao, "Chung-kuo chieh-chi tou-cheng ti fen-hsi" (An analysis of the inter-class struggle of China), March, 1926, *ibid.*, 1951, vol. 1, p. 6.

March, 1918.[75] Thus, the recipe for a new epoch of cooperation and coexistence is not in Mao's cookbook.[76]

THE DISPUTE ON AVOIDABILITY

Peking's Militancy

Whether world war can be averted has been debated between Moscow and Peking and has produced great confusion. The issue gets entangled first through distortion of each other's view, particularly the distortion of Peking's by Moscow, and second by the somewhat equivocal stand of China.[77] There has been a common observation in the West, thanks to Soviet propaganda perhaps, that Mao was calling for a general war.[78] He was frequently branded "ultra-left,"[79] bent upon setting the world afire. The major block to peace, the Russians felt, was to make use of force to settle international problems and that if Peking should realize the futility of such attempt, mankind would be better off.[80] The Soviet media make one believe that China's truculence is blamable for the nuclear danger.[81] On the other hand, China herself is also culpable for the wrong impression spread by her opponents.[82] Mao's theorists have

---

[75] Lenin, "Doklad o voine i mire" (Report on war and peace), March 7, 1918, *Sochineniya* (Collected works), (3rd ed.; Moskva: Gosizdat, 1932), vol. 22, pp. 324, 327. Even in April 1917, i.e., a year before the Brest-Litovsk Treaty, Lenin reported to the Seventh Party Congress that the "dragging on of the war would endanger the already achieved revolution," in "Sed'maya (aprel'skaya) vserossiiskaya konferentsiya RSDRP (B)" (The Seventh (April), All-Russian Conference of the RSDRP (B)), April, 1917, *O voine, armii i voennoi nauke* (On war, army and military science; 2nd ed.), pp. 349, 359. *See* also Michael Berchin, and Eliahu Ben-Horin, *The Red Army* (1st ed.; New York: Norton, 1942), p. 126; Merle Fainsod, *How Russia Is Ruled* (rev. ed.; Cambridge, Mass.: Harvard University press, 1964), p. 90.

[76] "We are in a new epoch of war and revolution. We shall witness many revolutions in the world," said Mao in "Mu-ch'ien k'ang-jih chan-cheng chung ti chi-ko chan-lüeh wen-t'i" (Several strategical problems facing us in the current anti-Japanese war), May 11, 1940, *Mao Tse-tung hsüan-chi* (Selected works), 1952, vol. 2, p. 735.

[77] Chou En-lai is typical of evasive talkers. On December 30, 1963, he told the French people through the French Government owned television that world war, i.e., inter-camp war, was not inevitable. Immediately he added that the risk of war remained because of the alleged American policy of "war and aggression," *New York Times*, December 31, 1963, p. 1. It is written that "while pointing to the possibility of preventing a new world war, we must also call attention to the possibility that imperialism may unleash a world war. Only by pointing to both possibilities, pursuing correct policies and preparing for both eventualities can we effectively mobilize the masses," in "Two different lines on the question of war and peace – comment on the open letter of the Central Committee of the CPSU by the Editorial Departments of *Renmin ribao* and *Hongqui*," *Peking Review*, 47 (November 22, 1963), 10.

[78] Zagoria, *The Sino-Soviet Conflict, 1956–1961*, p. 300. He said rightly that such an observation was erroneous.

[79] Iu. A. Krasin, *Filosofskie nauki* (Philosophical sciences), 5 (1963), 7.

[80] Kuusinen, "Pretvorenie v zhizn'...," *Pravda*, April 23, 1960.

[81] For China's being charged as dangerous to world peace by socialist countries other than the Soviet Union, *see* Victor Zorza, "Mr. K. fails to move against China," *Guardian*, October 30, 1963, pp. 1, 9.

[82] *Supra*, p. 54, note 65.

nearly always written that war is inevitable as long as monopoly-capitalism rules parts of the world.[83] This seems enough to create the general notion that China resolves not to coexist with the West.[84]

However, the problem is not a clear-cut one. The Chinese adherence to the precept of the inevitability of war, taken as it is, tends to make their regime look aggressive indeed. In order not to miss the gist of their view, we consider it mandatory to analyze the various texts and to see just what qualifying concepts there have been made. Undeniably, Peking has regarded war inevitable. But whether this betrays the invasive traits of its policy-makers is another question. A *Hung-ch'i* article unmistakably declared: "No Marxist-Leninist party advocates that the socialist countries resort to war between states to spread revolution."[85] It was written to refute Tito's (and Russia's) charge that China posed a threat to international order and security. All that the Chinese have assumed is that there are two situations of inevitability: one defensive and one offensive. In order to make this point clear we find it appropriate first to discuss, in the remainder of this section, how the Chinese classified wars, leaving the inevitability argument to the section that follows.

China's inevitability doctrine presupposes that offensive wars unleashed by the reactionaries and defensive wars waged by the progressives are unavoidable. She did not agree with Khrushchev's uninevitability theory and his unreserved opposition to war in its entirety. Her theoreticians sought to be specific about the matter and thought that defensive wars are legitimate and not objectionable at all.[86] At the

---

[83] Chung-kuo ch'ing-nien, *Lun ko-ming jen-hsing-kuan* (Revolutionary Weltanschauung) (Peking: Chung-kuo ch'ing-nien ch'u pan she, 1952), pp. 2–12; Chou Mou-yang, *Lun wo-kuo jen-min nei-pu mao-tun ti ko-kuan ken-yüan* (The objective origins of the internal contradictions of our people) (Shanghai: People's publishers, 1957), pp. 40–60; *Cha hung-ch'i pa pai-ch'i pa tzu-ch'an chieh-chi tsui-hou ti chen-t'i to-ch'ü kuo-lai* (Hoist the red flag, drag down the white flag and storm the final fortress of the capitalists) (Peking: Chung-kuo ch'ing-nien ch'u pan she, 1958), pp. 71–8; *China after Mao*, p. 238.

[84] George F. Kennan wrote: "The Chinese fear anything in the nature of reduction of cold war tension. They view with horror the idea of any agreements at all between the Russians and the western powers.... Were the Chinese attitude to be adopted by the entire communist bloc, a new world war would have to be regarded as practically inevitable. The Russian attitude allows at least a chance of avoiding it," in his article previously cited, *Saturday Evening Post*, 236 (October 5, 1963), 40, 43. It seems that Kennan failed to analyze the cause of the Chinese demeanor, although his conclusion seems correct.

[85] "A basic summing-up...," *Sino-Soviet Dispute*, pp. 162–67. Translation of "Chung-kuo jen-min ko-ming...," *Hung-ch'i*, 20–21 (November 1, 1960), 1–13.

[86] Khrushchev's unqualified opposition to war in his Twentieth Congress speech is manifestly contrary to Leninism. On countless occasions, Lenin taught that one cannot oppose all wars without ceasing to be socialist. He branded as "socialist clergymen" those who unreservedly denounced armed struggle of every kind. The following citations are only a few examples: "O lozunge 'razoruzheniya'" (On the slogan of disarmament), October, 1916,

meeting of the World Federation of Trade Unions in Peking (June, 1960)
Liu Ch'ang-sheng, vice-chairman of that body, first refuted the Russian
position. He stated that the hypothesis that war was not inevitable
needed modification. Although not in so many words, he felt that war
for protection against imperialist aggressors is a necessity; it ought to
be waged for the very existence of the proletariat.[87] Liu suggested four
types of war: (1) imperialist encroachment on the colonies, (2) imperialist pacification of rebels, (3) colonial struggle for independence, (4)
workers' revolts against capitalist rule.[88] In reality, numbers two and
four are internal scuffles between exploitative and exploited classes,
while numbers one and three are colonial in substance. There are only
two types of war involved here; but when one looks at them, as Liu did,
from the stance of the belligerents, he will get four. Liu's classification
was supposed to improve upon, but appears less comprehensive than,
another classification made two months earlier. The author of "Long
Live Leninism" divided wars into four different groups according to
their nature. These are: (1) wars between the imperialists for division
of the world, (2) aggressive wars of the imperialists against the oppressed
nations, (3) revolutionary or counterrevolutionary wars between the
exploitative and working classes, (4) the imperialist wars against the
socialist countries, the latter being forced to defend themselves.[89] Liu

O voine, armii i voennoi nauke (On war, army and military science; 2nd ed.), pp. 312–13;
"Voennaya programma proletarskoi revoliutsii" (Military program of the proletarian revolution), September, 1916, ibid., pp. 302, 303; "O karikature na Marksizm i ob 'imperialisticheskom ekonomizme'" (On the caricature of Marxism and "imperialist economism"),
August–October, 1916, ibid., p. 299, where it is written that "to deny wars entirely is to
make a caricature out of Marxism"; "O broshiure iunius" (On the brochure of Junius), July,
1916, ibid., p. 278; "Sotsializm i voina" (Socialism and war), July–August, 1915, ibid., pp.
255, 269.

    [87] For Lenin's similar statement, see his "Voennaya programma proletarskoi revoliutsii"
(Military program of the proletarian revolution), September, 1916, ibid., p. 308; "O karikature
na marksizm i ob 'imperialisticheskom ekonomizme" (On the caricature of Marxism and
'imperialist economism'), ibid., p. 300.

    [88] Sino-Soviet Dispute, p. 124; "On the question of war and peace," Peking Review, 24
(June 14, 1960), 13–14.

    [89] Sino-Soviet Dispute, p. 98. Lenin made three attempts to classify wars; the first in
August, 1916, the second in October of the same year, and the third in January, 1917. We
shall take the last first. In his "Iz pis'ma I. F. Armand" (From a letter to I. F. Armand),
Lenin divided wars into: (1) wars of oppressed nations against oppressive nations, (2) wars
between two groups of oppressive nations, (3) wars which Lenin described very unsatisfacto-
rily because he lumped together all the wars fought from 1815 to 1905; O voine, armii i voennoi
nauke (On war, army and military science; 2nd ed.), p. 323. In October, 1916, he classified
wars into four groups exactly as the article "Long live Leninism" did. However, the article
gave no credit to Lenin for its classification. See "O lozunge 'razoruzheniya'" (On the slogan
of disarmament), ibid., p. 312. In August, 1916, his classification was: (1) national wars,
(2) civil wars, (3) socialist wars, "[Pis'mo] G. E. Zinov'ev" (Letter to G. E. Zinov'ev),
Sochineniya (Collected works; 5th ed.), vol. 49, p. 287; also in O voine, armii i voennoi nauke
(On war, army and military science; 2nd ed.), p. 288.

emphasized that one may not oppose wars unreservedly, but should back up the proletarians in their resistance to imperialism.[90]

Imperialists' Propensity to War

Peking's view on the inevitability of world war is not free from being ambiguous. In his speech to the World Federation of Trade Unions Liu stated he believed that the interbloc war was avoidable.[91] The same thought was shared by Yu Chao-li.[92] It should also be recalled that China signed the Moscow Declaration of December 6, 1960, thus supposedly endorsing the avoidability doctrine contained therein. On many occasions, the theme of coexistence was chanted by Peking, too.[93] Yet, for all that, Peking's attitude has been characterized by suspicion. The dominant note in the various texts of the Chinese treatises is that the socialist countries ought not to be outmaneuvered or lulled into complacency.[94] Peace offers from the other side, Peking cautioned, should be treated with reservation, because the people of the West in general, and of the United States in particular, did not take to heart the course of detente.[95] At Bucharest, where Khrushchev hammered at his no-war theme, the Chinese delegate, P'eng Chen, sought to remind him that imperialism has always schemed against the socialist nations.[96] The Chinese had no difficulty finding support in various documents issued by international meetings of communists, for each of them made statements on the pugnacious nature of the imperialists, on the one hand, and the possibility of preventing world war, on the other. There is room then for the disputants to emphasize one statement or another, with Peking always haunted by the imperialist specter.[97]

In February 1960, K'ang Sheng spoke to the Warsaw Treaty Confer-

---

[90] *Sino-Soviet Dispute*, pp. 95–98.

[91] "On the question of war and peace," *Peking Review*, 24 (June 14, 1960), 13–14.

[92] "On imperialism as a source of war...," *ibid.*, 15 (April 12, 1960), 17–24. Translation of "Lun t'i-kuo chu-i...," *Hung-ch'i*, 7 (April 1, 1960), 1–12.

[93] The so-called *pencha-shila* (five principles of coexistence), Ch'en Yi, "The current international situation and our diplomacy," *Jen-min shou-ts'e* (People's handbook, 1957), p. 117; "Peace manifesto declared at the 40th anniversary of the Chinese Communist Party, November 16–19, 1957, " *Shih-chieh chih-shih nien-chien* (World encyclopedia, 1958), 13.

[94] *Sino-Soviet Dispute*, p. 11.

[95] *Ibid.*, p. 87.

[96] *Pravda*, June 22, 1960; "The Chinese Communist Party greets the Third Congress of the Romanian Workers' Party," *Peking Review*, 26 (June 28, 1960), 4–6; *Sino-Soviet Dispute*, pp. 139–40.

[97] However, some Soviets are still inclined to believe in the bellicose character of imperialists who "are not interested in easing international tension," W. I. Moschnin, "W. I. Lenin über die Erziehung der Sowjetkämpfer" (Lenin on the education of the Soviet troops), originally published in *Propagandist und Agitator*, no. 6, p. 56, now in *W. I. Lenin als Militärwissenschaftler* (Lenin as a military scientist), p. 49.

ence stressing that his people were wholeheartedly behind the Soviet quest for a peaceful solution of the German unification. But the United States, it was inveighed, was hatching a plan to revive both German and Japanese militarism. This, K'ang continued, did not jibe with the good intentions imputed to the American Government by many credulous souls.[98] With respect to the alleged danger from the two ex-fascist countries, *Jen-min jih-pao* wrote that it was the goal of the West to transform them into a hotbed of jingoism.[99] As the daily saw it, the world was viewing the same kind of drama which led to the Second World War. Like K'ang in the Warsaw Treaty Conference, the paper exhibited its misgiving as to the avoidability of wars.[100] Another editorial in the same media at almost the same time tried to disabuse people of the belief that imperialism was changing its streaks. The administration in Washington, the paper reminded its readers, sought to masquerade itself as a friend of peace,[101] but imperialism can never alter its essence.[102] Yu Chao-li asserted that the rapacity of the bourgeoisie is legendary and that "it is absolutely impermissible for us to mistake certain of imperialism's changes for fundamental changes."[103] In the American effort to ease international tensions, the Chinese saw a sleight of hand "aimed at numbing the fighting spirit of the people of the world" and at their subjugation.[104]

To Peking, Khrushchev's avoidability doctrine was based on several assumptions none of which it considered sound. The first was that the United States has forsaken its acquisitive policy with regard to colonial and semi-colonial peoples in Asia, Africa and Latin America. The Chinese felt there was no sign whatever to substantiate this, for the American Government has not slackened its pressure in those continents. Particularly irritating to Peking was the issue of Taiwan, which is regarded as occupied by the armed forces of the United States.[105] From

---

[98] "On the current international situation," *Peking Review*, 6 (February 5, 1960), 6–9; *Sino-Soviet Dispute*, p.p 72–77.

[99] "Forward along the path of the great Lenin," *ibid.*, pp. 112–14; *Peking Review*, 17 (April 26, 1960), 23–32. Translation of "Yüan-cho wei-ta le-nin ti tao-lu ch'ien chin," *Jen-min jih-pao*, April 22, 1960.

[100] *Ibid.*

[101] Chung Hsin-ching, "Two sources of war...," *Peking Review*, 25 (June 21, 1960), 22–27. Translation of "Wei-sheh shih-chieh...," *Hung ch'i*, 11 (June 1, 1960), 8–15.

[102] "Forward along the path...," *Sino-Soviet Dispute*, pp. 112–14; *Peking Review*, 17 (April 26, 1960), 23–32. Translation of "Yüan-cho wei-ta le-nin...," *Jen-min jih-pao*, April 22, 1960.

[103] "On imperialism as a source of war...," *Peking Review*, 15 (April 12, 1960), 17–24. Translation of "Lun t'i-kuo chu-i...," *Hung-ch'i*, 7 (April 1, 1960), 1–12.

[104] *Sino-Soviet Dispute*, p. 73.

[105] William Henry Chamberlain, *Russian Review*, 23 (July, 1964), 220.

China's stance, this situation constitutes the same sort of provocation as if China took Hawaii or aided insurgents there.[106] The second assumption was that the imperialists are no longer what they used to be. In refutation of such an idea, the Chinese grew verbose. To have faith in the changed nature of imperialism, they objected, is inexcusable. There is a Chinese adage that one can lay down his cleaver and thus become a Buddha at once. But to imperialists, Peking argued, the saying does not apply, since they are too depraved to turn into anything better. "Until their doom the imperialist elements will never lay down their butcher knives, nor will they ever become Buddhas," wrote Yu Chao-li.[107] The Chinese have long held that it is easy to level off a mountain, but it is hard to change one's nature.[108] The deep conviction of the certitude of an armed action against the communist nations was manifested by the Chinese Communist Party in its resolution underwriting the Moscow declaration: "Facts have proved that the aggressive nature of imperialism has not changed . . . . The danger is not yet over that imperialism will launch a new and unprecedentedly destructive war."[109] Another assumption of the avoidability doctrine is that the West will be observant of international commitments. The Chinese, however, pointed out that any treaty concluded with capitalists would be broken by them if they deemed it unfavorable to their evil design.[110] Finally, the doctrine also premised itself on the enemy's halting of military preparedness. This is groundless, too, Peking held. "The United States imperialists made an allocation of nearly sixty per cent of the 1960 budget outlay to arms expansion and war preparations,"

---

[106] "Pu kan-tsou mei-kuo ch'iang-tao, pu chieh-fang tai-wan, shih pu kan hsiu" (Struggle forever until the ouster of the United States from Taiwan), *Jen-min jih-pao*, June 29, 1960. Lin Piao wrote: "This occupation of Taiwan by U.S. imperialism is absolutely unjustified. Taiwan province is an inalienable part of Chinese territory. The U.S. imperialists must get out of Taiwan," *China after Mao*, pp. 260–61.

[107] "The Chinese people's great victory in the fight against imperialism," *Peking Review*, 38 (September 22, 1959), 6–11. Translation of "Chung-kuo jen-min fan-tui t'i-kuo chu-i tou-cheng ti wei-ta sheng-li," written in commemoration of the tenth anniversary of the founding of the People's Republic of China, *Hung-ch'i*, 18 (September 16, 1959), 9–16.

[108] Shih Tung-hsiang, "Refuting the fallacy that the nature of imperialism has changed," *Peking Review*, 25 (June 21, 1960), 11–13. Translation of "Po t'i-kuo chu-i pen-hsing i p'ien ti miu-lun," *Hung-ch'i*, 12 (June 16, 1960), 1–4. *Jen-min jih-pao*, and *Chieh-fang chün-pao*, July 27, 1970. *Peking Review*, 31 (July 31, 1970), 18.

[109] "The CCP resolution on the Moscow Conference, adopted on January 18, 1961 by the Ninth Plenary Session of the Eighth Central Committee," *Sino-Soviet Dispute*, p. 222.

[110] Liu Ch'ang-sheng said that the imperialists would tear into pieces any treaty on banning nuclear bombs and that if they did observe the treaty, they could still resort to conventional weapons to begin a world war; *ibid.*, p. 126.

a clear indicator of their bellicosity, wrote the author of "Long Live Leninism."[111]

It is not to be mistaken, Peking asserted, that imperialism is the source of war.[112] One should never dream of the disappearance of war before the authors of war themselves have disappeared. The bourgeoisie would not quit the historical stage voluntarily.[113] The nearer they come to their end, the more frenzied they get. Hence wars are more likely than ever before.[114] As we stated formerly, both the thoughts of avoidability and unavoidability of war coexist in most communist documents studied in this work. Moscow and Peking are alike prevaricating. Kozlov, for example, after dwelling on the preventability of war stated that the reactionary forces of the monopolies have been preparing armed attack and that this is on account of their insatiable animus for expansion.[115] Khrushchev, the father of the avoidability doctrine, asserted: "Some people would say: but capitalism will remain, and therefore adventurers who start a war will remain also. This is correct and should not be forgotten."[116] Marshal Sokolovskii and his associates were persuaded that until the final jubilee of socialism, or in other words, before capitalism vanishes up to the hilt, the shadow of Mars hangs above us.[117] On their side, the Chinese also thought of the avoidability of war due to the growth of world peace forces.[118] On the whole, however, the Russians put their emphasis on the avoidability, while the Chinese always exerted their efforts to dramatize the idea of imperialist hostility which will surely lead to a collision course. Proceed-

---

[111] *Ibid.*, p. 88. *See* also K. Alexandrov, Institut zur Erforschung der UdSSR, *Bulletin*, 7 (May, 1960), 33.

[112] *Sino-Soviet Dispute*, p. 124.

[113] Lenin iterated this concept numerous times; for example: "Voennaya programma proletarskoi revoliutsii" (Military program of the proletarian revolution), September, 1916, *O voine, armii i voennoi nauke* (On war, army and military science; 2nd ed.), p. 306; "O porazhenii svoego pravitel'stva v imperialistskoi voine" (On defeat of one's own country in imperialist war), July, 1915, *ibid.*, p. 251; "Mezhdunarodnyi sotsialisticheskii kongress v Shtutgarte" (International socialist congress in Stuttgart), September, 1907, *ibid.*, pp. 172–73; "Uroki kommuny" (The lessons of the Commune), March, 1908, *ibid.*, p. 179; "Uroki moskovskogo vosstaniya" (The lessons of Moscow revolt), August, 1906, *ibid.*, p. 144; "Revoliutsionaya armiya i revoliutsionoe pravitel'stvo" (Revolutionary army and revolutionary government), July, 1905, *ibid.*, p. 88; "Bor'ba proletariata i kholopstvo burzhuazii" (Struggle of the proletariat and bourgeois bondage), June, 1905, *ibid.*, p. 86.

[114] "Fa yang mo-ssu-k'o hsüan-yen...," (Carry forward the revolutionary spirit of the Moscow declaration and the Moscow statement), *Jen-min jih-pao*, November 15, 1962.

[115] "43-ya godovshchina velikoi...," *Pravda*, November 7, 1960.

[116] "Dal'neishee ukreplenie mirovoi...," *ibid.*, January 28, 1959.

[117] "Rech' t. N. S. Khrushcheva" (Khrushchev's speech [in Krasnodar District]), *ibid.*, October 16, 1958.

[118] Liu's speech at WFTU (June, 1960), *Sino-Soviet Dispute*, p. 124; K'ang's speech at the Warsaw Treaty Conference (June, 1960), *ibid.*, p. 73; "The CCP resolution...," *ibid.*, p. 222.

ing from this conviction, Peking regarded international war as a sure matter.[119] It follows that the Chinese doctrine of inevitability is not as offensive as it appears. Mao and his followers have not called for a revolutionary crusade against the West to spread communist gospel or to prevent an attack.[120] It seems that China has an indelible suspicion of what they choose to name imperialist. Here lies the basis of her intransigence.

View of Khrushchev: To Prevent the War

Despite their charge of aggressive imperialism, the Soviets appeared more hopeful of peace.[121] The burden of their argument was that although the enemy was bent upon fighting, he no longer felt free to do so. To Moscow, the question was, then, not whether a war would occur, but how to arrest it quickly at the beginning. Soviet polemics evolved around the proposition that the imperialists have been manacled because the odds against them were just too much and that the situation made them behave correctly. Since the socialist system has become a crucial factor in world politics and "is striving to set limits to the activity of the imperialists," they "shall not be able at their own whim to unleash wars."[122] Khrushchev told his partisans that the adventurers have been faced by insurmountable handicaps in their plans to plunge humanity into a blood bath. At Bucharest he admitted that imperialists remain insatiable, just as do wolves. However, he added, it cannot be denied that a weakened beast is less of a nuisance.[123] In the same vein, Frantsev wrote that it was only when the greedy enemy was given the opportunity to take action that wars broke out. Nowadays, he argued,

---

[119] There is the observation that aggressors often so behave themselves as if they are peace-lovers and defenders of alleged encroachment. In this regard, it is interesting to note that when Lenin read Clausewizt's statement that "Der Eroberer ist immer friedliebend (wie Bonaparte auch stets behauptet hat)" (The conquerer is always peace-inclined as Bonaparte also claimed all the time), he wrote on the margin of the book he was reading: "Haha! What a smart guy!" Lenin, *Clausewitz's Werk "Vom Kriege": Auszüge und Randglossen* (Clausewitz's book on war: extracts and annotations), p. 23.

[120] "Socialist countries never permit themselves to send, never should and never will send, their troops across their borders unless they are subjected to aggression from a foreign enemy," in "Long live Leninism," *Peking Review*, 17 (April 26, 1960), 16. It is further stated, "The socialist system determines that we do not need war, and absolutely must not, should not and could not encroach one inch the territory of a neighboring country," *ibid.*, p. 14.

[121] Alexandre Metaxas, *Listener*, 44 (September 8, 1960), 371; George F. Kennan, *Saturday Evening Post*, 236 (October 5, 1963), 43.

[122] "Rech' t. N. S. Khrushcheva" (Khrushchev's speech [in Krasnodar District]), *Pravda*, October 16, 1958.

[123] Khrushchev, *On Peaceful Coexistence*, p. 246.

the opportunity was diminishing.[124] The future of peace, henceforth, gets brighter.

Kozlov saw in the public of the imperialist countries the major curb on armed adventures. The people, he stated, could exercise a great influence in keeping their rulers away from a suicidal path.[125] Such internal obstacles, plus the outside ones of the socialist camp, would be adequate to compel the imperialists to reorient their policy. Thus, the battle for peace was won without either side firing a shot. Khrushchev even saw the possibility of the self-restraint of the warmongers.[126] The realization of the dire consequences of nuclear blows and the certainty of being disowned by the people for their policy may awaken the imperialist-statesmen. Even the most delirious would have refrained from aggression, if there had been inhibiting forces.[127]

The Soviet argument put the Chinese in an awkward position. If they retained their inevitability doctrine, they would betray a lack of confidence in the strength of the communist bloc to stop the enemy from launching a war in the first place. Edward Kardelj had already criticized them on this very point.[128] Conversely, an acceptance of the avoidability doctrine would compromise their views on the nature of the imperialists, who, they always asserted, are irrational and cannot be deterred. Occasionally, the Chinese Government has conceded to the Soviet contention. "The powerful socialist camp is becoming the decisive factor in the development of human society" and can play a role in safeguarding world peace.[129] An editorial in *Hung-ch'i* also spoke of the worn-out beasts, a metaphor used by the Chinese for the imperialists.[130] Thus, Peking seemed to come close to the stand of its opponent. But it tended to think that the Russians were too afraid of the West,[131] and that they too highly esteemed the role of nuclear weapons in international relations.[132] Peking's image of the future world also differ-

[124] Iu. Frantsev, "Problemy voiny i mira...," *Pravda*, August 7, 1960; "Novaya programma" (New program), *Izvestiya*, November 2, 1961; also *Pravda* of the same date.
[125] "43-ya godovshchina velikoi...," *ibid.*, November 7, 1960.
[126] "Marksizm-leninizm...," *Izvestiya*, January 8, 1961; "Za novye pobedy...," *Pravda*, January 7, 1961; *Kommunist*, 1 (January, 1961), 30–35.
[127] *Ibid.*
[128] *Socialism and War*, p. 36
[129] "CCP resolution...," *Sino-Soviet Dispute*, p. 221.
[130] "Hsiang kung-ch'an chu-i chin-chuan ti hao-chiao" (The clarion-call of armed march toward communism), *Hung-ch'i*, 4 (February 16, 1959), 1–8.
[131] "Pao-wei ma-k'e-ssu le-nin chu-i ti shun-chieh hsing" (Defending the purity of Marxism-Leninism), *ibid.*, 22 (November 16, 1962), 1–6. This editorial was written in commemoration of the second anniversary of the Moscow Declaration.
[132] Kozlov once told the Italian communists: "Those who are certain of their historical future have no need to play with thermonuclear fire," see Robert Karl MacCabe, *New Leader*, 45 (December 24, 1962), 9.

ed from Moscow's. This aspect of the dispute is intertwined with the question of tactics and strategy toward the democracies. In order to analyze the respective policy lines, it is necessary for us to investigate the diverse forces which the communists felt have definitely put the East ahead of the West and which have developed a real possibility of eliminating arms.

THE DECLINE OF THE WEST

The Problem of Western Intra-bloc War

The issue of the inevitability of world war is closely linked with the alleged conditions within the enemy camp. If the latter has atrophied from internal erosion, its potential for waging war has become less.[133] This is the platitude that solidarity makes for strength, while disunity is conducive to vulnerability. The question as to whether the Western alliance can be free from strife among its members has not been answered with one voice by the Soviets. Originally it was Lenin's contention that the several imperialist powers would surely head for a showdown in order to grab each other's colonies.[134] Following his postulation, Stalin believed that the tension in the West after the Second World War would cause still another disaster similar to its predecessor. The United States, he argued, under the cover of the Marshall Plan subjected its European partners to its economic dominion; and this bred a sense of resentment in them. Sooner or later, he felt, such resentment would end in armed blows.[135] The rivalry in the imperialist camp, stated Marshal Sokolovskii *et al.*, was the old story of striving for spheres of influence. On account of the inner contradictions the imperialists would soon be "torn asunder" and therefore unable to unite against the socialist forces.[136]

---

[133] The Central Committee of the Chinese Communist Party which met from November 28 to December 10, 1958 noted that the "growing decay and division among the imperialists will permit the maintenance of peace," *see* Richard Lowenthal, *Problems of Communism*, 8 (January–February, 1959), 23.

[134] *Marksizm-leninizm o voine i armii* (Marxism-Leninism on war and army; 4th ed.), pp. 108–15; Lenin, *Sochineniya* (Collected works; 5th ed.), vol. 16, p. 72; *KPSS v rezoliutsiyakh i resheniyahh s'ezdov, konferentsii i plenumov TsK* (A Collection of resolutions, and decisions taken by the CPSU congresses, conferences and plenary sessions of the Central Committee) (7th ed.; Moskva Gospolitizdat, 1953), part I, p. 324; an appeal of the Executive Committee of the Communist International in celebration of the 22nd anniversary of the October Revolution, *Kommunisticheskii internatsional*, 8–9 (1939), 3–4. *Programye dokumenty bor'by za mir, demokratiiu i sotsializm* (The programs of the struggle for peace, democracy and socialism) (Moskva: Gospolitizdat, 1964), p. 42.

[135] Stalin, *Economic Problems of Socialism in the Soviet Union*, pp. 1–10. In Russian: *Ekonomicheskie problemy sotsializma v SSSR*, pp. 5–9.

[136] *Voennaya strategiya* (Military strategy; 2nd ed.), p. 225.

The Western nations are described as leading to a confrontation between themselves due to the uneven development of their economies.[137] After the Second World War, America had outstripped all her allies in business and industry, and progressed at a breakneck tempo. When the "domain of the imperialists ... shrunk more and more," they truly jostled one another. The "grabbing" by the Americans of the "markets ... away from the British" and French was patent.[138] Further, West Germany and Japan were making inroads into the financial empire of the United States. These circumstances, the Chinese held, increased the danger of war.[139] Disagreeing with their Chinese colleagues, the Russians gave a more sober explication.[140] They felt that the dissention in the enemy camp would produce a balance of forces in favor of the East.[141] But they did not envision an intra-imperialist war as the Chinese did.[142] Actually, Khrushchev believed in the avoidability of such a war, a point to be dealt with shortly. With regard to the economic situation in the Western camp, Foreign Minister Ch'en Yi drew a different picture. In analyzing China's diplomacy, he suggested that the American economy was shaken by the industrial recovery of Great Britain and France, a recovery which was ironically due to the assistance of the United States. The rise of the junior and the fall of the senior partners, in his judgment, rocked the imperialist boat.[143] Although he presaged no intra-bloc war in the West, he perceived the decline of imperialism.

From the standpoints of the communists, any quarrel among enemy countries would be welcome because it would tend to eviscerate them.[144] Yet, they blasted scathingly the imperialist war. Does this signify that

---

[137] Lenin, "Lozunge soedinennykh shtatov evropy" (The slogan of the United States of Europe), August, 1916, *O voine, armii i voennoi nauke* (On war, army and military science; 2nd ed.), p. 272. Shieh Fang, "T'i-kuo chu-i chen-ying nei-pu ti ta hun-chan" (The pell-mell inside the imperialist camp), *Shih-chieh chih-shih* (World knowledge), 6 (March 25, 1966), 6–11.

[138] *Sino-Soviet Dispute*, p. 85.

[139] *Ibid.*

[140] Stalin's view on the intra-imperialist war was rejected as unsound and unfounded after his death; *see Politicheskii slovar'* (Political dictionary) (2nd ed.; Moskva: Gos. izd-vo polit. lit-ry, 1958), p. 556.

[141] "Marksizm-leninizm...," *Izvestiya*, January 8, 1961; "Za novye pobedy...," *Pravda*, January 7, 1961; *Kommunist*, 1 (January, 1961), 29.

[142] A few Soviets, however, held the Chinese view; *Voennaya strategiya* (Military strategy; 2nd ed.), p. 225.

[143] "Current international situation and our diplomacy," *Jen-min shou-ts'e* (People's handbook, 1957), p. 117.

[144] Lenin, "O lozunge 'razoruzheniya'" (On the slogan of disarmament), October, 1916, *O voine, armii i voennoi nauke* (On war, army and military science; 2nd ed.), p. 315: "When two robbers are fighting, let them fight each other to death," Lenin wrote, "Iz pis'ma I. F. Armand" (Letters to I. F. Armand), January, 1917, *ibid.*, p. 321.

they have any love for the capitalists and would hate to see them trample each other to death? In answering this question, we need to look at several points. First, the expression "imperialist war" has been loosely used to denote war between East and West, but in strict Leninist terms it means only war between colonial powers. Second, there is the historical fact that Lenin himself fulminated against the First World War, which he called "imperialist." His opposition thereto stemmed not from a fondness for any capitalist regime,[145] but from his contempt for the sordid objective of industrial powers to divide up the world.[146] Following Lenin, Mao wrote: "Unjust wars, such as the first world conflict, are waged for imperialist interests on both sides."[147] Third, intra-imperialist wars were not considered by Khrushchev as inevitable. This seems to be the only revision he made of Lenin's theory of war, for Lenin did believe such wars were inevitable.[148] Khrushchev's stand was adopted by the 1960 Moscow statement.[149] What is the basis for the professed belief in the avoidability of such wars? Three reasons are advanced. It is suggested, first, that because of the growth of communist power, the imperialists would have to be quiet among themselves for fear of being destroyed separately.[150] Second, communism has united them by instilling in their minds a sense of hatred of a competitive ideology. Third, the imperialists have after all shared many basic concepts[151] – an assumption which was once brought out by Karl Kautsky. "The new program" of the Twenty-Second Congress stated that the "Party and the Soviet people always oppose war, even

[145] *Idem*, "Pis'mo A. M. Gor'komu" (Letter to A. M. Gorkii), January, 1913, *Sochineniya* (Collected works; 4th ed.), vol. 35, p. 48; also in *ibid.*, 3rd ed., vol. 16, p. 278.
[146] *Ibid.*, 4th ed., vol. 15, p. 187; vol. 21, pp. 1, 3, 7, 11–12.
[147] Mao, "Lun chih chiu chan" (On protracted war), *Mao Tse-tung hsüan-chi* (Selected works), 1952, vol. 2, p. 438.
[148] Lenin's theory of imperialist war, although elaborated in the book *Imperialism*, which appeared in 1917, was formulated long before that in several of his earlier works including the following tracts: "Mirnaya demonstratsiya angliiskikh i nemetskikh rabochikh" (Peaceful demonstration of English and German workers), September–October, 1908, *O voine, armii i voennoi nauke* (On war, army and military science; 2nd ed.), p. 187; "Konnets voiny Italii s Turtsiei" (End of the Italo-Turkish war), *Sochineniya* (Collected works; 5th ed.), vol. 22, p. 118, also in *O voine, armii i voennoi nauke* (On war, army and military science; 2nd ed.), p. 202; "Voinstvuiushchii militarizm i antiimperialistskaya taktika sotsial-demokratii" (Militarism and anti-imperialist tactics of the Social Democracy), July, 1908, *ibid.*, p. 181; "Mezhdunarodnyi sotsialisticheskii kongress v Shtutgarte" (International socialist congress in Stuttgart), August–September, 1907, *ibid.*, p. 172; "Revoliutsionnaya armiya i revoliutsionnoe pravitel'stvo" (Revolutionary army and revolutionary government), June, 1905, *ibid.*, p. 92.
[149] "Zayavlenie soveshchaniya...," *Pravda*, December 6, 1960.
[150] *Ibid.*
[151] "Marksizm-leniniam...," *Izvestiya*, January 8, 1961; "Za novye pobedy...," *Pravda*, January 7, 1961; *Kommunist*, 1 (January, 1961), 14.

war between the capitalist regimes."[152] A united and strengthened socialist camp has as a result the cessation of quarrels between the otherwise discordant friends. Therefore, along with inter-bloc war, intra-imperialist war could also be warded off.

A Decadent Social Body

The decline of the West is also allegedly seen with increasing clarity.[153] Its viability as a living organism has been much in doubt, and it cannot be made into a fighting unit at all.[154] It is said that the ruling circles of the various regimes have split in their policy orientations and are unable to see eye to eye on diplomacy.[155] This would rob them of leadership. The communists claimed to have discerned a marked symptom of capitalist decay in the rise of communist parties. Standing for the broad masses, communists have operated effectively in organizing workmen's parties almost everywhere on the globe. Kozlov asserted that eighty-seven Marxist-Leninist parties have come into existence with a total membership of thirty-six million communists.[156] They constituted the "front lines" of peace and were ready "to isolate the reactionary monopoly circles."[157] Khrushchev, not as precise as Kozlov, put the number of countries having communist parties as "more than fifty," and extolled their noble espousal for peace.[158] Discontent with the capitalist system was described as mounting, and "inveterate class animosity" as ushering in an era of unrest.[159] "The working class is putting up a stout resistance to the policy of imperialism and the monopolies," reads the 1957 Moscow statement.[160]

[152] "Novaya programma" (New program), *Pravda*, November 2, 1961; *Izvestiya* of the same date; also in *Voennaya strategiya* (Military strategy; 2nd ed.), p. 228.

[153] A good comment on the allegation can be found in Clarence A. Manning, "Khrushchev's new communist program," *Ukrainian Quarterly*, 17 (Autumn, 1961); Rudolf Schlesinger, "The CPSU program: the concept of communism," *Soviet Studies*, 13 (January, 1962), 307.

[154] "One must not exaggerate the possibility of international unity of imperialism. This does not mean that he may ignore it," said Khrushchev, *Nasushchnye voprosy razvitiya mirovoi sotsialisticheskoi sistem* (The pressing problems of the development of world socialist system) (Moskva: Gos. izd-vo polit. lit-ry, 1962), pp. 15–16; also *Voennaya strategiya* (Military strategy; 2nd ed.), p. 131. Shieh Fang, "T'i-kuo chu-i kuo-chia chih chien mao-tun chin i-pu chien jui-hua" (Further aggravation of the inter-imperialist conflicts), *Shih-chieh chih-shih* (World knowledge), 5 (May 10, 1965), 9–12.

[155] Kuusinen, "Pretvorenie v zhizn'...," *Pravda*, April 23, 1960.

[156] "43-ya godovshchina velikoi...," *ibid.*, November 7, 1960.

[157] *Ibid.*

[158] "Marksizm-leninizm...," *Izvestiya*, January 8, 1961; "Za novye pobedy...," *Pravda*, January 7, 1961; *Kommunist*, 1 (January, 1961), 10.

[159] "Novaya programma" (New Program), *Pravda*, November 2, 1961; *Izvestiya* of the same date. Shih Chieh, "Wei-chi ssu-fu ti mei-kuo ching-chi" (The crisis-laden American economy), *Shih-chieh chih-shih* (World knowledge), 7 (April 10, 1966), 8–11.

[160] "Deklaratsiya soveshchaniya predstavitelei...," *Pravda*, November 22, 1957.

The hypothesis that the Soviet Union has its friends in the enemy countries is not new. Once Stalin pointed out that the Red Army had its outposts, manned by the downtrodden, on the other side of the battle front. They were called the "reserves" of the Bolsheviks.[161] Like Stalin, Khrushchev stated that those like-minded workers finding themselves in the enemy camp were getting more numerous and very powerful in opposing the call to arms for aggression.[162] Not knowing it, the imperialist governments are said to be "graduating" out partisans for the world socialist system. Because of more rapid concentration of wealth as a result of the new techniques, the monopoly-capitalists are making fabulous profits at the expense of the common man. There comes to pass in the several imperialist states an ever greater disparity of income; "automation and rationalization under capitalism bring the working people further calamities."[163] It is asserted that the uneven development of capitalism between countries has happened also inside each of them. Some blighted areas are seen as populated by poverty-stricken masses and petty bourgeoisie, all victims of the "domination of the monopolies."[164] Rampant in the West are various forms of struggle between "labor and capital," "democracy and reaction," "freedom and colonialism."[165] The home front of the West, it is believed, has been on the brink of total collapse, and the capitalist economy is swiftly sagging. Otto Kuusinen saw a vast "zone of peace" which is "more closely united and better organized" than ever before.[166] In a word, the days of the West are numbered.[167]

With the break-off of the colonies, the capitalist hinterland and sources of raw material are gone. Shorn of those lands to be exploited to sustain the metropolis, the "capitalist world cannot maintain its high-consumption levels and will sink into an abyss of depression and civil strife."[168] Presently, the imperialists can exist not because of any magic

[161] Stalin, *Sochineniya* (Collected works), vol. 5, p. 108. He termed colonial peoples of the East the "great reserves of our revolution," *ibid.*, vol. 3, p. 26. Ryazanov (an old Bolshevik liquidated by Stalin in 1937) said: "Of course, we have a great strategical advantage, for we have reserves in the enemy's rear," in *Voina i voennoe iskusstvo v svete istoricheskogo materia-lizma* (War and military art in the light of historical materialism), p. 22.
[162] "Marksizm-leninizm...," *Izvestiya*, January 8, 1961; "Za novye pobedy...," *Pravda*, January 7, 1961; *Kommunist*, 1 (January, 1961), 23.
[163] "Zayavlenie soveshchaniya predstavitelei...," *Pravda*, December 6, 1960.
[164] *Ibid.*
[165] *Ibid.*
[166] "Pretvorenie v zhizn'...," *ibid.*, April 23, 1960.
[167] M. Mikhailov, and N. Polyanov, "Printsipy, kotorye dolzhny torzhestvovat'" (The principles which must succeed), *Izvestiya*, August 14, 1960.
[168] "Deklaratsiya soveshchaniya predstavitelei...," *Pravda*, November 22, 1957; Kuusinen, "Pretvorenie v zhizn'...," *ibid.*, April 23, 1960; Marvin L. Kalb, *Dragon in the Kremlin* (New York: Dutton, 1961), p. 241.

economy but because of the arms race.[169] Thus, in spite of the discrepancy "between the productive forces and production relations," the system has not yet broken down. Weakened by the poor economy, the capitalist nations are said to be unable to wage war. Marshal Sokolovskii and his colleagues analyzed this problem and came out with several inferences. First, morale is low in imperialist armies, because "aggression, pillage and slavery of other peoples" is hardly laudable.[170] The soldiers can have no enthusiasm for a policy of war, Lenin said.[171] Second, in a predaceous war, it is impossible to maintain unity among the people, it is claimed. Even during the last war some industries in the United States refused to convert to arms production. The laboring class was also uncooperative. For example, in 1941, there were 4,288 strikes affecting 2,400,000 workmen; in 1943, 3,425 strikes affecting 3,500,000 workmen; in 1944, 4,956 affecting 2,100,000 respectively.[172] Such phenomena cannot be expected to occur in a socialist country. A "planned economy" can produce enormous war potentials, and it is easy to allocate manpower and readjust people's livelihood.[173] Third, "modern war is between coalitions of states. Each coalition must have an agreed-upon strategy which is hard to achieve in the imperialist camp."[174] The authors believed that all military theory "is conditioned by a country's economic possibilities, geographical contours, national characteristics, tradition, etc. Strategy has a definite national imprint." The plans of the North Atlantic Treaty Organization, the authors went on, "represent only mechanical aggregates of the views of many states."[175] In short, the communists argued that the imperialists are getting less and less competent in prosecuting modern war. Their political community is divided and their economy too shaky to weather any great storms.[176] Under these conditions, war is virtually avoided. Before taking the field, the enemy has been deprived of all opportunities to win the battle. Here is another reason for Khrushchev's avoidability doctrine; it is unnecessary to fire a shot to defeat the enemy, an enemy who simply cannot move in the first place.

---

[169] "Deklaratsiya soveshchaniya predstavitelei....," *Pravda*, November 22, 1957.

[170] *Voennaya strategiya* (Military strategy; 2nd ed.), pp. 228, 268, 287.

[171] Lenin, *Sochineniya* (Collected works), vol. 25, p. 337 as quoted in *ibid.*, p. 268. Lin Piao analyzed the vulnerability of the United States on account of her overdiffusion of her forces on the globe and of her internal dissension regarding military policy, *see China after Mao*, pp. 248–49.

[172] *Voennaya Strategiya* (Military Strategy; 2nd ed.), p. 222.

[173] *Ibid.*, p. 287.

[174] *Ibid.*, p. 34.

[175] *Ibid.*

[176] "The Sino-Soviet conflict," *Royal Central Asian Journal*, 50 (January, 1963), 61.

Where lies the Real Strength?[177]

As analyzed above, the Chinese leaders thought war inevitable and were confident of their victory. While Soviets felt that the socialist camp was so strong that the enemy did not even venture an attack, Mao and company were persuaded that the same camp was so powerful that should the enemy strike he would be vanquished. In order to justify their supreme self-assurance, the Chinese had a peculiar way of estimating the strength of both sides. Having in view that China then lagged behind in weapons development, but was blessed with manpower, the leaders in Peking advanced a theory that man is more important than weapons.[178] It must be noted that this concept is not in accord with Mao's precept that power emanates from the barrel of a rifle.[179] Neither is it in consonance with Peking's crash-program of nuclear development which had produced a hydrogen variety. The fact is, however, that in Mao's writings numerous statements can be culled to the effect that rifles do not determine everything.[180] In his "On protracted war" (May, 1938), he asserted that to regard weapons as the only desideratum for victories means falling into the error of "military mechanicalism," and that "such a viewpoint is subjective, defective and not persuasive."[181] The following statements are revealing: "One must strike a balance between men and weapons"; "Weapons are important, but not decisive"; "It is men who are crucial."[182] The whole idea was driven home by the author of "Long Live Leninism." There it was stated that "Comrade Mao dismissed the theory of 'weapons mean-everything' as nonsense, because it was against Marxism-Lenin-

[177] This concept was brought out by Lenin, who wrote in German: "Schein ist noch nicht Wirklichkeit" (The apparent is not yet reality), *Clausewitz's Werk "Vom Kriege": Auszüge und Randglossen* (Clausewitz's book on war: extracts and annotations), p. 16.

[178] *China after Mao*, pp. 225, 230, 250, 254.

[179] Mao's statement is fully endorsed by Lin Piao, *ibid.*, p. 238.

[180] "T'ung-i wen-hua cheng-ts'e" (Unified cultural policy), October 30, 1944, *Mao Tse-tung hsüan-chi* (Selected works), 1953, vol. 3, p. 1009; "Pi-hsü hsüeh tso ching-chi kung-tso" (One must learn how to do economic work), January 10, 1945, *ibid.*, p. 1017; "Yu-chi ch'ü ti sheng-ch'an kung-tso" (Productive work in the guerilla areas), January 31, 1945, *ibid.*, p. 1024; "Sheer military strength is not enough," wrote Mao, in "Chiu-cheng tang ti ts'o-wu" (To correct the Party's errors), December 29, *ibid.*, 1951, vol. 1, p. 91.

[181] *Ibid.*, 1952, vol. 2, p. 432. It is to be noted that the Soviets, too, are speaking of the supreme importance of men in comparison with weapons, *see* W. I. Moschnin, "W. I. Lenin über die Erziehung der Sowjetkämpfer" (Lenin on the education of the Soviet troops), *W. I. Lenin als Militärwissenschaftler* (Lenin as a military scientist), p. 42; M. Karamyschew, "Lenins Ratschläge für die Sowjetsoldaten" (Lenin's advice to the Soviet soldiers), *ibid.*, p. 36; N. Schatagin, "W. I. Lenin über den Aufbau und die Festigung der Sowjetischen bewaffneten Kräfte" (Lenin on the building and strengthening of the Soviet armed forces), *ibid.*, p. 32.

[182] "Lun chih chiu chan" (On protracted war), *Mao Tse-tung hüsan-chi* (Selected works), 1952, vol. 2. p. 432.

ism."[183] Communist ideology has "always maintained that in history it is not technique but persons, the mass of people, that determine the fate of mankind."[184]

To defend the theory of men-over-weapons, the Chinese have gone into some detail. During the Sino-Japanese war, Mao remarked, many believed that China would be subjugated because of her outmoded equipment; but "Mr. Fact" pronounced Cathay the victor in spite of it.[185] It was also argued that in the Korean conflict, China carried the day for all the superiority of the allied firepower.[186] The basis of China's triumph is that her principle is just, while that of her foe is not. "She is admittedly a weak country with a semi-feudal and semi-colonial social structure. Yet she finds herself in a progressive epoch. Here lies the source of her strength," wrote Mao in 1938.[187] In an essay entitled "Some strategical problems of the Chinese revolutionary war" (November, 1936), he stated that "throughout our history there are two kinds of war: just and unjust."[188] A just war is revolutionary, forward and liberatory, while an unjust war is imperialist, reactionary and pillaging.[189] That the former wins and the latter loses is a rule of historical law. When one prosecutes a just war, he will get support from many quarters that conduces to his cause.[190] During the Italian conquest of Ethiopia, Mao predicted victory for the latter, for she was just.[191] In 1939, he wrote that the war then going on in Europe "is unjust from the standpoint of both sides, since the Anglo-French have no better reason than the Germans."[192] They would all be defeated. In sum, mass people and right cause are the most powerful arms and "difference in quality (victory) derives from difference in quantity (number of men)."[193] History has dictated the enthronement of the

[183] *Sino-Soviet Dispute*, p. 92. N. Kushmin, "Fragen der Militärwissenschaft in den Werken W. I. Lenins" (The problems of military science in Lenin's writings), *W. I. Lenin als Militärwissenschaftler* (Lenin as a military scientist), pp. 20–21.

[184] *Sino-Soviet Dispute*, p. 92. See also *China after Mao*, pp. 253–254.

[185] *Ibid.*

[186] *Ibid.*

[187] "Lun chih chiu chan" (On protracted war), May, 1938, *Mao Tse-tung hsüan-chi* (Selected works), 1952, vol. 2, p. 414. *China after Mao*, p. 204.

[188] *Ibid.*, 1951, vol. 1, p. 171. The title of this essay in Chinese reads: "Chung-kuo ko-ming chan-cheng ti chi-ko ts'e-lüeh wen-t'i."

[189] *Ibid.*; also "Su-lien li-i ho jen-lei li-i i-chih" (The interests of the Soviet Union are the interests of all mankind), September 26, 1939, *ibid.*, 1952, vol. 2, p. 560. *Voennaya strategiya* (Military strategy; 2nd ed.), p. 228.

[190] *Ibid.*, p. 286. *China after Mao*, pp. 197, 235.

[191] Mao, "Lun chih chiu chan" (On protracted war), May, 1938, *Mao Tse-tsung hsüan-chi* (Selected works), 1952, vol. 2, p. 415.

[192] "Su-lien li-i ho jen-lei li-i i-chih" (The interests of the Soviet Union are the interests of all mankind), September 26, 1939, *ibid.*, 1952, vol. 2, p. 560.

[193] *Idem*, "shih-chien lun" (On practicum), *ibid.*, 1951, vol. 1, p. 284.

proletarians; in the long run, they are invincible, irrespective of temporary odds against them.[194]

Another significant facet in Mao's confidence in victory is his "paper-tiger" theory. The phrase means that the "apparent is not real." The Chinese believed that there can be a disagreement between what men subjectively perceive and what reality objectively signifies.[195] Whenever our judgment on a given matter happens to be out of focus with the true essence, we are misled and tend to run into trouble. In military problems, grave disasters often result from erroneous appraisals. It happens that a seemingly strong enemy often turns out to be weak. "In history, many doomed reactionaries would fight a last-ditch battle with revolutionary forces. The latter have often taken the enemy's bluffing for his invincibility," wrote Mao.[196] The remark referred to the 1916 Verdun campaign when "Great Britain, America [sic] and France did not know that they were on the threshold of victory."[197] In 1943, Mao taught his comrades never to be deceived by the troop build-up of the Kuomintang which numbered then three million men. He said that they were really "a broken reed."[198] From 1943 to 1946, the cohorts of Mao and Chiang engaged in a series of dog fights in which the former came out on top. In an interview (1946) with Anna Louise Strong, Mao used the phrase "paper tiger" for Chiang and all reactionary forces.[199] Iterating Mao's concept, a *Hung-ch'i* article declared: "What the Right opportunists saw was only the superficial strength of the Chiang reactionaries, not their true weakness."[200] Later the phrase has applied exclusively to the United States, which is really weak, Peking said, and must not be feared.[201] However, Mao believed

[194] Lenin taught that "even a hopeless struggle is good for the proletarians because they gain experience therefrom," in "Iz 'predisloviya k russkomy perevodu pisem K. Marksa k L. Kugel'manu'" (Preface to the Russian translation of Marx's letters to L. Kugelman), February, 1907, *O voine, armii i voennoi nauke* (On war, army and military science; 2nd ed.), p. 162.

[195] "Hsing-hsing chi huo k'o-i liao yüan" (A spark may start a conflagration), January 5, 1930, *Mao Tse-tung hsüan-chi* (Selected works), 1951, vol. 1, p. 105; *China after Mao*, p. 240.

[196] "Ti erh-tz'u shih-chieh ta-chan ti chuan-li tien" (The turning point of the Second World War), October 12, 1943, *ibid.*, 1953, vol. 3, p. 885.

[197] *Ibid.*

[198] "P'ing kuomintang shih-i chung chuan-hui" (A critique on the Eleventh Plenary Session of the Kuomintang), October 5, 1943, *ibid.*, p. 920.

[199] *Idem*, "Talk with the American correspondent Anna Louise Strong," August, 1946, *Selected Works* (New York ed.), vol. 5, p. 100.

[200] "A basic summing up...," *Sino-Soviet Dispute*, p. 165. Translation of "Chung-kuo jen-min ko-ming...," *Hung-ch'i*, 20–21 (November 1, 1960), 12.

[201] Allen S. Whiting wrote that Peking has never underestimated America's "ability to attack and to destroy. If anything, it has long exaggerated the readiness of the United States to engage in all-out war with the People's Republic," in *Journal of Politics*, 20 (February 1958) 160.

in no adventurism either, for as he told Miss Strong: "Strategically we should slight all enemies, but tactically we should take full account of them."[202]

VIEWS ON EAST-WEST RELATIONS

Has the World Been Made Safe for the People's Democracy?

The Chinese doctrine of the inevitability of a world war is to be appreciated in defensive terms and manifests a feeling of insecurity. This state of mind is to be expected in view of Peking's being repudiated by the Soviet Union and its allies and by the Western powers.[203] The history of Cathay since the mid-19th century has been a record of humiliation at the hands of foreigners.[204] With the advent of the communist regime, the old fear of national persecution has been played up through the use of mass propaganda. The view of the Chinese Communists has been that it is not China that would not coexist with the West; it is the West that would not coexist with China.[205] The same thought was embraced by the Russians during the time of the foreign intervention of 1918–21 when Lenin grimly foretold the life-and-death struggle. If one follows Mao's theorem that the apparent is not real, the hostile encirclement may be imagined, while in actuality, Russia and China are quite secure. Although insisting on the imminent danger of war, Mao felt that world war, unless the allied aggressors unleash it, would not occur.[206] His truly belligerent traits are shown in his view on civil

[202] Mao, "Hsing-hsing chih huo k'o-i liao yüan" (A spark may start a conflagration), January 5, 1930, *Mao Tse-tung hsüan-chi* (Selected works), 1951, vol. 1, p. 105. For Lin Piao's statement to the same effect, *see China after Mao*, p. 240.

[203] Richard Harris, *Political Quarterly*, 35 (July–September, 1964), 330.

[204] *Ibid.*, John Gittings; *International Affairs* (London), 40 (January, 1964), 60–61; Merner Levi, "China and the two great powers," *Current History*, 39 (December, 1960), 321; Rodger Swearingen, *ibid.*, 43 (October, 1962), 229–30; Obata Misao, *Japan Quarterly*, 8 (January–March, 1961), 31.

[205] A. M. Halpern, "Communist China and peaceful coexistence," *China Quarterly*, 3 (July–September, 1960), 26.

[206] American military restraint intimated to Mao Tse-tung that the United States was not disposed to plunge the world into a hecatomb of nuclear war. The American people, thus, refrained from a general war on account of its dreadful consequences, *see* Mao Tun, "The way to general disarmament and world peace," *Peking Review*, 29 (July 10, 1962), 11. America has not resorted to nuclear war when faced with the communist revolution in Vietnam and Laos, the 1956 counterrevolution in Hungary, or the conventional war in Korea; *see* Chinese People's Institute of Foreign Affairs, *Two Tactics, One Aim: an Exposing of the Peace Tricks of U.S. Imperialism* (Peking: The Institute, 1960), p. 38; "Peking rally backs Tokyo Conference," *Peking Review*, 5 (August 31, 1962), 9. The fact that the United States "through words and deeds has assured of its commitment not to attack China" further strengthens Peking's conviction of non-escalation; *see* Y. L. Wu, "Can Communist China afford war?" *Orbis*, 6 (October, 1962), 455. American assurance must have been believed by the Chinese communists in spite of their charge that the imperialists are treacherous, for Lenin himself acknowledged

war within each capitalist state, a topic to be discussed in the next chapter.

As pointed out previously, the Russians, defending the avoidability theme, are unsure if war can be excluded after all, for they said they are not in a position to vouch for the imperialists.[207] Thus, the differences between Peking and Moscow are not so pronounced. Neither wants world war, which they asserted would be started by the enemy at any rate. However, China's emphasis on the hostility of the West, and Russia's on the deterrent capacity of the East have led to divergent views on policy. In Mao's thinking, the West seeks to exact concessions from the communist side and to gain advantages in planning a war against it. Khrushchev's detente should be discontinued because it benefits the West, which Peking feels is racing against time. If the East persists in conducting a low-risk policy, war will definitely draw near, for it is by showing the white feather that an aggressor finds it tempting to attack. The argument is not unusual in the world today. The West as well as the Chinese are all deducing from the events leading to Hitler's aggression the lesson: retreat means war. The Russians, however, take the view that an inflexible stand toward the imperialists would generate hard feelings. In a nuclear age, war may easily result from misunderstanding compounded with irritation. It has been reasoned by them that after all, to risk a general collision with the west is unnecessary because socialism has come here to stay.[208] The balance of forces secures the longevity of the socialist system, a system which not only cannot be effaced from the earth, but will become a universal way of life. So long as this noble objective has been within striking distance, the Russians would question the wisdom of accelerating its final arrival. In a contest on the battlefield, the East might even not do well. In various ways, the Soviets have counseled against too much confidence in the bloc's military strength, a confidence they themselves cultivated in the first place.

Some Soviets have acknowledged that "a socialist triumph is not automatic," and that "it entails a preparation as thorough as possible."[209] The suggestion implies that history does not unfailingly side with the communists and that the capitalists, if well readied, can be

the "unbeclouded American frankness" *see* Lenin, "Voina i revoliutsiya" (War and revolution), May, 1917, *O voine, armii i voennoi nauke* (On war, army and military science; 2nd ed.), p. 368.

[207] "Rech' t. N. S. Khrushcheva" (Khrushchev's speech [in Krasnodar District]), *Pravda*, October 16, 1958.

[208] "Otchetnyi doklad Tsentral'nogo Komiteta...," *Pravda*, February 15, 1956; Kozlov, "43-ya godovshchina velikoi...," *ibid.*, November 7, 1960.

[209] *Voennaya strategiya* (Military strategy; 2nd ed.), p. 258.

formidable enough to knock off the communists from the historical stage which they are allegedly occupying.[210] After arguing for the "socialist world system," Khrushchev, in his speech before the party conference, conceded that "this does not mean that imperialism is an insignificant factor which can be ignored. Not at all. Imperialism is still robust. It has a powerful military machine."[211] "Godly blessing of history" is not invoked. Whether Karl Kautsky's remark holds true that "war is not a strong point in socialism,"[212] the plain fact in the present context is that the Soviet leaders do not seem to hold war necessary, or desirable.[213] Besides, Peking has much more frequently urged readiness for a break with the West than Moscow has.[214] Western proposals to discuss world problems are deemed to be either a trap or a lullaby. The statement that as long as imperialism exists, war is inevitable is another way of saying that socialism is never at ease with imperialism as its neighbor. A complete security of socialism requires the complete perdition of monopoly-capitalism.[215] In Chinese eyes, the world is not yet being made safe for people's democracy. The system

[210] In November, 1957, Mao, while attending the Moscow Conference, stated that "in the end the socialist system will replace the capitalist system. This is an objective law independent of human will," as quoted in Werner Levi, *Current History*, 39 (December, 1960), 322.

[211] "Marksizm-leninizm...," *Izvestiya*, January 8, 1961; "Za novye pobedy...," *Pravda*, January 7, 1961; *Kommunist*, 1 (January, 1961), 33. One Western student rightly observed that "Khrushchev seems to recognize that the balance of power lies with the West, in spite of Mao's insistence on the strategical superiority of the Soviet camp," R. Hilsman, State Department, *Bulletin*, 47 (November 26, 1962), 808; *see* also James O'Gara, "Battle of the giants," *Commonweal*, 77 (March 22, 1963), 654.

[212] As quoted in Erich Wollenberg, *The Red Army: A Study of the Growth of Soviet Imperialism* (London: Secker and Warburg, 1940), pp. 15, 53.

[213] A noted Chinese economist and President of Peking University, Ma Yin-ch'u, took the Soviet stand and was promptly dismissed from his post. He wrote that China was to be careful of her international conduct, because future nuclear war depends not so much on quantity as on quality of manpower. The numerical superiority of the Chinese population is not her asset in war; *see* "Die Absetzung des Rektors der Universität Peking, Ma Jing-tschus Kritik am 'Grossen Sprung'" (Dismissal of Ma Yin-ch'u, President of Peking University, for his criticism of the 'Great leap forward'), *Neue Zürcher Zeitung*, April 20, 1960, p. 12.

[214] "In fact, if you look back on the Chinese communist position in every crisis, you will find Peiping has told Moscow to 'go for broke,' – in 1958 it was Lebanon, in 1959 Berlin, in 1961 Berlin again, and now in 1962 Cuba," wrote R. Hilsman, State Department, *Bulletin*, 47 (November 26, 1962), 808.

[215] Lenin said, "Revolution has to be universal if it is to be a complete success," in "O proletarskoi militsii" (On proletarian militia), May, 1917, *O voine, armii i voennoi nauke* (On war, army and military science; 1st ed.), col. 2, p. 45. Maurice Duverger wrote: "...le communisme s'affirme lui-même une doctrine internationale, dont le triomphe total et définitif n'est pas possible dans un seul pays, mais seulement à l'échelle mondiale" (Communism is an international doctrine whose total and definitive success results from its universal application, not just its application in a few countries), *Les Partis Politiques*, (4th ed.; Paris: Librarie Armand Colin, 1961), p. 306. George Modelski said that "communism will not have been constructed unless it has become universal," *see* his *The Communist Internationalist System* (Research Monograph, no. 9; Princeton: N. J.: Princeton University press for Center of International Studies, 1960), pp. 54–5.

may unfortunately die before it reaches its maturity or, to abandon the figure of speech, before it becomes the only ideology of humanity.

Can Capitalism Be Contained?

Whether the socialist system can become dominant hinges upon the possibility of warding off the danger from capitalism. Certainly, an ideal world is one in which monopoly capitalism has gone with the wind. When the proletariat holds sway in every corner of the globe, the communists can then sleep well.[216] Although the Chinese do not intend to declare a jihad on others, their disdainful attitude toward what they call imperialism makes it hard to believe that they earnestly desire peace on earth. Aside from the fact that there have been a number of treaties signed by China with several of her neighbors in which the principles of mutual respect and friendship were pledged, Peking has not desisted from aiding subversives in the states of South Asia and Africa. This, viewed against Mao's vials of hate for the West, does not help to conjure up a good image of Peking. It is perhaps because of the conspiratorial deeds and denunciatory words of China that the Russian charge of warmongering becomes increasingly plausible. But Peking is obsessed by a fancied imperialist attack; the Soviets think the Chinese fear is groundless and find it necessary to dispel it through an array of arguments.

Moscow contended that the dichotomized world is a temporary phenomenon with one camp definitely atrophying. In reference to the new epoch, Khrushchev made a passing remark on recent history as follows. The greatest event is, as one would expect, the Bolshevik revolt of November 7, 1917, the importance of which lies in its breakthrough of the solid capitalist chain.[217] Previously there had existed in the minds of the Marxists only a vague notion of what a socialist regime would look like, but not whether it could endure after it came into being. The death knell of capitalism rang its first peals on that November day. From then until the Great Patriotic war, the world witnessed only the Soviets and the outer Mongolians embracing socialism.[218] The situation changed quickly in the aftermath of the downfall of fascism. The upshot was a socialist system. The old concept of "knocking off of

[216] Lenin once wrote that "When the communist flag flies atop the government buildings of the Paris Commune, world capitalists cannot sleep well," in "Mamyati communy" (Memory of the Commune), April, 1911, *O voine, armii i voennoi nauke* (On war, army and military science; 2nd ed.), p. 196.

[217] "Marksizm-leninizm...," *Izvestiya*, January 8, 1961; "Za novye pobedy...," *Pravda*, January 7, 1961; *Kommunist*, 1 (January, 1961), 26.

[218] "Otchetnyi doklad Tsentral'nogo Komiteta...," *Pravda*, February 15, 1956.

one or more links in the imperialist chain" has to be modified in order to fit with the new circumstances.[219] The true picture suggests that the old chain has been shattered into pieces and, in its place, a new socialist chain is being forged, said Khrushchev.[220] "The dictatorship of the working class has outgrown the confines of one country and assumed a world stature."[221] Presently it is the socialists who encircle the capitalists. The latter have been contained now. If one still fears them, he really mistrusts the power of the socialist system. When capitalist regimes on earth are reduced to no more than a button in a coat, they will be on the way out.[222] Even though the reasoning sounded logical, the Russian leader did not say just when that situation would materialize. This vista is not unlike what Lenin depicted in his work "State and revolution."

The Russians are not sure of the highly proclaimed superiority of the bloc. As a matter of fact, the Chinese are more confident than the Russians. In Peking's analysis, the "present situation is extremely favorable to us," and the time is ripe for the communist to "march victoriously toward our great goal" of world socialism.[223] The Soviet Government was accused of overestimating the enemy; that is why, Peking explains, it acquits itself so timidly.[224] The Chinese would like to advise the Soviets that since the bloc grows more powerful than the West, it had better exploit its advantage and drive a hard bargain with the democracies. In other words, when you are stronger, you must press forward. The Soviets were rebuked as tactless by the Albanian delegate in the World Peace Conference, which met in December, 1961, in Stockholm. His speech was carried in the bulletin of the New China News Agency,[225] thus signifying Mao's endorsement. On November 18, 1957, the Chinese leader made the now famous remark of the "east wind" prevailing over the "west wind."[226] The concept, aside from showing his confidence in the bloc's power, meant that the balance of

[219] "Marksizm-leninizm...," *Izvestiya*, January 8, 1961; "Za novye pobedy...," *Pravda*, January 7, 1961; *Kommunist*, 1 (January, 1961), 34.
[220] His speech to a mass meeting in Sophia (Bulgaria), May 19, 1962, *Predotvratit' voinu, otstoyat' mir!* (Prevent war and defend peace!), p. 108.
[221] "Marksizm-leninizm...," *Izvestiya*, January 8, 1961; "Za novye pobedy...," *Pravda*, January 7, 1961; *Kommunist*, 1 (January, 1961), 21–25.
[222] Khrushchev, *On Peaceful Coexistence*, p. 246.
[223] K'ang Sheng's speech at the Warsaw Treaty Conference, *Sino-Soviet Dispute*, p. 77.
[224] "Give full play to the revolutionary spirit of the 1957 Moscow declaration," *Peking Review*, 48 (November 29, 1960), 6–8. Translation of "Fa yang i chiu wu-ch'i mo-ssu-k'o hsüan-yen ti ko-ming ching-shen," *jen-min jih-pao*, November 21, 1960.
[225] In English to Asian readers, December 18, 1961.
[226] Mao, *Imperialism and All Reactionaries Are Paper Tigers* (Peking: Foreign languages press, 1958), p. 28.

power had changed. The example of wind denotes that the equilibrium always tips one way or another. Wind is seasonal, and the west wind may later prevail over the east wind. In the essay "On protracted war" (May, 1938), Mao said: "The relative strength of two opponents is not absolute. Everything in war keeps changing."[227] "The correct strategy is to make use of one's forte."[228] Finally, the Chinese dislike the policy of containment of capitalism because a seemingly harmless power might grow until it becomes uncontrollable, just as the little "Red pockets" in China were the origin of the present Peking regime.[229] With a strange fellow at one's side, one is not secure.

Can Communism Be Exemplary?

Connected with the strategic thinking of both disputants is the issue of whether it is possible to conquer the world not by arms but by bettering the people's livelihood. It has been assumed that since the socialist system is being accepted by millions upon millions of people,[230] it must have merits other than military muscle. Khrushchev in an interview with Gardner Couls of *The Des Moines Register* (April 20, 1962), stated that under socialism both the private and public life of citizens develops at a greater speed than under capitalism, and that this explains why the latter is doomed.[231] Ages ago, during its ascent, capitalism replaced feudalism because it proved superior.[232] The Russian leader did not consider the capitalist victory over feudalism as a result of war.[233] When the socialist way of life demonstrates its true value, one cannot keep it from being adopted. On the contrary, should a system lose its appeal, it is foolish to keep it for oneself, let alone impose

[227] *Mao Tse-tung hsüan-chi* (Selected works), 1952, vol. 2, p. 423.
[228] *Ibid.*, p. 424.
[229] "Wei shen-mo hung-se ch'ü-yü neng ts'un-tsai?" (Why the little red pockets can exist?"), October 25, 1928, *ibid.*, 1951, vol. 1, pp. 51–52.
[230] Khrushchev's address to the constituency of Kalinin District (Moscow) in the campaign for re-election to the Supreme Soviet, March 16, 1962, *Predotvratit' voinu, otstoyat' mir!* (Prevent war and defend peace!), pp. 12–13.
[231] *Ibid.*, pp. 48–50.
[232] "The work of the Soviet delegation at the Fifteenth General Assembly of the United Nations," from the speech given at a mass meeting in Moscow, October 20, 1960, *On Peaceful Coexistence*, p. 328. "Socialism is strong because it is a vital necessity and because it meets the most cherished interests of the people... Socialist ideas do not have to be spread among the people by force," said Khrushchev.
[233] *Ibid.* It was stated that international war and what it inevitably involves such as arms race would slow down the economic development in the Soviet Union; "Novaya programma" (New Program), *Pravda*, November 2, 1961; *Izvestiya* of the same date. However, Lenin once taught that Marxism dictates that socialist movement be given a push by revolutionary war, "Mezhdunarodnyi sotsialisticheskii kongress v Shtutgarte (International socialist congress in Stuttgart), August–September, 1907, *O voine, armii i voennoi nauke* (On war, army and military science; 2nd ed.), p. 172.

it upon others.[234] Socialism became a system after the end of the last war not because of coercion but because of its meritorious appeal. Embarking upon socialist construction, various countries have already found the old way of life unsuitable to men's needs. Capitalist exploitation antagonizes people and digs its own grave. Wars have nothing to do with the flourishing of the socialist system.

In the future, when socialism further develops, it will do so without wars.[235] Exemplariness is its aim and desert.[236] On the other hand, the waning of capitalism is also not a result of defeats on the battleground, but the growth of the destructive seeds within the body politic. They will collapse sooner or later without a push from outside. The disintegration cannot be arrested by either armament or "prayers."[237] The Soviets have minimized the military, for "wars between the socialist and capitalist countries" cannot be counted as an "objective necessity."[238] The Russian argument can hardly be denied by any communist who claims to be a votary of Marxism-Leninism. However, as to the imminent fall of capitalism, not all communists are in agreement.[239] The late Eugene Varga, a Russian economist of Hungarian descent, wrote that the capitalist system has its vitality and has survived many a crisis.[240] No matter how acrid the Chinese are in raving against capitalism, which they scoff at as "man-eating," they still feel that it "will not crumble of itself."[241] Hence it is urged that an outside force is called for to hasten its last gasp.[242] In actively supporting the

[234] Khrushchev, *On Peaceful Coexistence*, p. 328.

[235] Neal Stanford, "Moscow-Peiping feud grows," *Foreign Policy Bulletin*, 40 (October 1, 1960), 11.

[236] "What can better win the sympathy for socialism than the example set by the Soviet Union and other socialist states?" asked Khrushchev, *On Peaceful Coexistence*, p. 328.

[237] Khrushchev's address to the constituency of Kalinin District (Moscow) in the campaign for re-election to the Supreme Soviet, March 16, 1962, *Predotvratit' voinu, otstoyat' mir!* (Prevent war and defend peace!), p. 12.

[238] "The work of the Soviet delegation at the Fifteenth General Assembly of the United Nations," from the speech given at a mass meeting in Moscow, October 20, 1960, *On Peaceful Coexistence*, p. 328.

[239] K. S. Karol, *New Statesman*, 65 (March 22, 1963), 414. He reported that Fidel Castro of Cuba never gives credence to the possibility of capitalist breakdown due to internal decomposition.

[240] *Osnovye voprosy ekonomiki i politiki imperializma posle vtoroi mirovoi voiny* (The fundamental problems of imperialist economy and politics after the Second World War) (Moskva: Gos. izd-vo polit. lit-ry, 1953), chap. 1.

[241] *Sino-Soviet Dispute*, pp. 94–95.

[242] On this point, Lenin was most articulate and verbose. The following citations are only a few examples: "O lozunge 'razoruzheniya'" (On the slogan of disarmament), October, 1916, *O voine, armii i voennoi nauke* (On war, army and military science; 2nd ed.), pp. 311–13; "Voennaya programma proletarskoi revoliutsii" (Military program of the proletarian revolution), September, 1916, *ibid.*, pp. 305–7; "O broshiure iuiysa" (On the brochure of Junius), July, 1916, *ibid.*, pp. 285–86; "Sotsializm i voina" (Socialism and war), July–August, 1915, *ibid.*, p. 269; "O porazhenii svoego pravitel'stva v imperialisticheskoi voine" (On defeat of

removal of capitalism by violence, the Chinese leaders do not in the meantime admit their lack of confidence in their own mode of life.

The advocacy of violence lends credit to the charge that Peking is in favor of a world war. It cannot be gainsaid that in suggesting the use of revolution to overthrow governments which exist, Peking has little trust in the supposed magnetic power of communism, for, otherwise, force would be unnecessary. It should not be admitted, of course, that Peking intends to send its troops into other countries in order to get rid of the ruling classes there. The proletarians, Mao argued, should make use of civil war to take political power. Yet, an incitement of domestic rebels is so close to direct intervention that to label Mao "warmongering" does not seem inapt. Peking, in short, has little faith in the exemplariness of socialism. That explains why it puts so much of a premium on rifles. On account of this lack of confidence, too, Peking does not hesitate to instigate civil dissent in non-communist countries, with the result that it is waging an international war by abetting civil strife.

There is another reason for exemplary communism, insofar as the Soviets are concerned. It is Khrushchev's persuasion that a new life cannot be instituted by a decree. When conditions do not exist, to try communism would bring miseries, not happiness.[243] His remark to Gardner Couls of the Iowan newspaper that "starvation communism" goes against the grain of Marxism-Leninism was directed at the Chinese. He described the latter as having one pair of trousers for every ten individuals; it ended with nobody having enough to cover himself.[244] It is simply foolhardy to quicken the pace toward workers' paradise

one's own government in the imperialist war), July, 1915, *ibid.*, pp. 251–53; "Proekt revoliutsii levykh sotsial-demokratov k pervoi mezhdunarodnoi sotsialisticheskoi konferentsii" (The project of left Social-Democrats to be submitted to the first international socialist conference), *ibid.*, pp. 247–49; "Referat na temu 'proletariat i voina'" (Concerning the topic "proletariat and war"), October, 1914, *ibid.*, pp. 225, 229; "Voina i rossiiskaya sotsial-demokratiya" (War and Russian Social Democracy), October, 1914, *ibid.*, p. 222; "Mezhdunarodnyi sotsialisticheskoi kongress v Shtutgart), internationaal socialist congres in Stuttgart, August–September, 1907, *ibid.*, pp. 172–73; "Bor'ba proletariata i kholopstvo burzhuazii" (Struggle of the proletariat and bourgeois bondage), June, 1905, *ibid.*, p. 86; "Partizanskaya voina" (Partisan war), September, 1906, *ibid.*, pp. 154–56; "Uroki moskovskogo vosstaniya" (The lessons of Moscow revolt), August, 1906, *ibid.*, p. 144; "Evropeiskii kapital i samodarzhavie" (European capital and autocracy), April, 1905, *ibid.*, pp. 71–72; "Voisko i revoliutsiya" (Troops and revolution), November, 1905, *ibid.*, p. 135; "Dve taktiki sotsial-demokratii v demokraticheskoi revoliutsii" (Two tactics of Social-Democracy in democratical revolution), June–July, 1905, *ibid.*, p. 107; "Revoliutsionnaya armiya i revoliutsionnoe pravitel'stvo" (Revolutionary army and revolutionary government), July, 1905, *ibid.*, pp. 90, 92; "Novye zadachi i novye sily" (New tasks and new forces), March, 1905, *ibid.*, p. 65.
[243] *Predotvratit' voinu, otstoyat' mir!* (Prevent war and defend peace!), p. 56.
[244] *Ibid.*

by combining several steps in one stride.[245] Moreover it is disastrous to enforce upon others a system alien to them, for time is required to advance into a classless world, and all the circumstances have to be auspicious.

---

[245] *Ibid.*, p. 55.

CHAPTER IV

CIVIL WAR

THE PEACEFUL TRANSITION TO SOCIALISM

A response to Oppression

With regard to world war there was the marked difference that Moscow considered it avoidable, while Peking did not. Hoewver, they were in substantial agreement in believing civil wars would occur.[1] But it is not until after Peking made a distinction among several types of war that Moscow gradually modified its original view that war in general is not inevitable. According to the Chinese, there are three kinds of war: world, civil, and national liberation.[2] All three are inescapable: the first, because the imperialists will initiate it; the second and third, because they have already initiated them. In this chapter, civil war will be taken up, with wars of national liberation left to the following chapter.

What is civil war?[3] Both Mao and Khrushchev have spoken about it, but not defined it. In one of his early works, Mao wrote that a struggle waged by the poor peasantry to get rid of landlordism is an engagement between the forces of revolution and counterrevolution and that that is civil war.[4] The *fons et origo* is the incompatibility of productive

---

[1] George F. Kennan, *Saturday Evening Post*, 236 (October 5, 1963), 38.

[2] Mao made the differentiation in the essay "Lun lien-ho cheng-fu" (On coalition government), April 24, 1945, *Mao Tse-tung hsüan-chi* (Selected works), 1953, vol. 3, p. 1031; also in "Yü kung i-shan" (A foolish man wants to move the mountain), June 11, 1945, *ibid.*, p. 1103. Mao cited Stalin's classification of contradictions culminating in wars: (1) between proletariat and bourgeoisie, (2) between imperialist countries, and (3) between colonial (or semi-colonial) states and imperialists.

[3] Lenin defined it as an inter-class armed conflict, *Sochineniya* (Collected works), 4th ed. vol. 5, p. 54; vol. 8, p. 87; vol. 9, p. 51. A Soviet source defines "civil war as one waged by the workers against the internal class enemy and foreign interest for their own defense," in "Grazhdanskaya voina v SSSR" (Civil war in the Soviet Union), *Politicheskii slovar'* (Political dictionary) (2nd ed.; Moskva: Gos. izd-vo polit. lit-ry, 1958), p. 137.

[4] "Hunan nung-min yün-tung pao-kao" (A report on the peasant movement in Hunan Province), March, 1927, *Mao Tse-tung hsüan-chi* (Selected works), 1951, vol. 1, pp. 15–18.

methods and proprietorship. Khrushchev termed civil war "a popular uprising" whereby a "tyrannical regime" with imperialist support is replaced with a people's democracy.[5] Both leaders felt that the proletariat is righting the wrong suffered at the hands of the exploiters. It is supposed that the bourgeois regime has already fought the toilers by the mere fact that it sustains the status quo and keeps them in bondage.[6] Treated as beasts of burden, the workers have every reason to revolt. One must not "talk indiscriminatingly about whether or not war should be supported or whether or not it should be opposed without making a specific analysis of its nature," declared Liu Ch'angsheng.[7] To justify the legitimacy of what he called "popular uprisings," Khrushchev stated that under the feet of capitalism the workmen's "cup of patience overflows" and that it seemed only natural that they should have recourse to revolutionary war.[8] Because the latter is said to be the affair of a given people it follows that neither China nor Russia is to be held responsible for such uprisings.[9]

Civil War – Internal Affairs

The concept of civil war for both Mao and Khrushchev has its Leninist derivative. Lenin visualized a revolutionary situation prevailing in capitalist countries. Whenever a society, he wrote, develops to such a stage that the "lower stratum thereof can no longer keep on living and the political apparatus has rotted through and through, an armed crisis will develop."[10] This symbolizes the birth pang of a new life. In January, 1961, a textbook for Russian universities, *Fundamentals of Marxism-Leninism*, was published. It devoted a whole chapter to

[5] "Marksizm-leninizm...," *Izvestiya*, January 8, 1961; "Za novye pobedy...," *Pravda*, January 7, 1961; *Kommunist*, 1 (January, 1961), 8.
[6] Lenin, "O lozunge 'razoruzheniya'" (On the slogan of disarmament), October, 1916, *O voine, armii i voennoi nauke* (On war, army and military science; 2nd ed.), p. 313.
[7] His address to the World Federation of Trade Unions, June 8, 1960, *Sino-Soviet Dispute*, p. 124. In reality, Liu repeated what Lenin had said in "Iz 'Otkrytogo pis'ma Borisu Suvarinu'" (From an open letter to Boris Souvarine), December,1916,*O voine, armii i voennoi nauke* (On war, army and military science; 2nd ed.), p. 321.
[8] "Marksizm-leninizm...," *Izvestiya*, January 8, 1961; "Za novye pobedy...," *Pravda*, January 7, 1961; *Kommunist*, 1 (January, 1961), 24.
[9] Khrushchev's speech to the Supreme Soviet, December 12, 1962, *Predotvratit' voinu, otstoyat' mir!* (Prevent war and defend peace!), p. 375. "Revolution cannot be tailored," wrote Lenin, "O broshiure Iuniysa" (On the brochure of Junius), July, 1916, *O voine, armii i voennoi nauke* (On war, army and military science; 2nd ed.), p. 285.
[10] "There are three revolutionary situations from which civil war may break out: (1) the ruling class can no longer rule, (2) aggravation of popular misery, (3) mass action," in "Khrakh II internatsionala" (Collapse of the Second International), May–June, 1915, *ibid.*, p. 235. Further information can be found in his *Sochineniya* (Collected works; 4th ed.), vol. 6, pp. 249–60; vol. 9, p. 382; vol. 15, p. 270; vol. 19, pp. 194–96.

defining revolutionary situations, the point being stressed was that personal volition, even that of an elite, can no more make a revolt than a swallow can make a summer.[11] There must be "objective conditions" such as economic deterioration and political consciousness of the workmen.[12] Civil disobedience is the spontaneous reaction of the people to the stimuli of political realities of life. Any revolution truly originates from the "peoples' heart."[13] Whether there will be an insurrection is decided by the oppressed class itself, wrote Frantsev.[14]

In spite of the assertion of the spontaneity of revolution, the authors of *Fundamentals of Marxism-Leninism* did not counsel against leading it or giving it aid. The problem they raised is how can the vanguard discern with reasonable surety the crisis situation and give it a nudge. Certainly it takes an acumen such as Lenin's to pinpoint the moment when the conditions are timely. "In November, 1917, many Bolsheviks were convinced that the circumstances were not yet ripe for the attempted seizure of power in Russia," the textbook stated. It was Lenin who could see through the fog and infer that it was opportune to act.[15] The authors chided those who strove to bring civil war by blind marches. China was made the direct object for criticism, for, as the book put it, she sought prematurely to encourage such "revolutionary forces in Iraq in the summer of 1958."[16] However, the book did analyze the question of how to synchronize a war cry with a critical juncture in a given country. The issue concerned is adventurism versus revisionism; the former racing ahead "to speed up the pace of socialist revolution," the latter "limping behind events."[17] The Soviets assumed the air of a

[11] The imprint is: Moscow: Foreign languages publishing house, 1961, pp. 610–14 (Russian title: *Osnovy marksizma-leninizma*, Moskva: Gos. izd-vo polit. lit-ry, 1961); also Engels, *Izbrannye voennye proizvedeniya* (Selected military works) (Moskva: Gospolitizdat, 1937), vol. 1, p. 6; E. A. Prokof'ev, *Voennye vzglyady dekabristov* (The military ideology of the Decembrists) (Moskva: Voen. izd-vo, 1953), p. 123. On this point the textbook is only paraphrasing Lenin's statement that "even the capitalists go to war involuntarily because they are pressured to do so by their exploitative social environment," in his "Zadachi proletariata v nashei revoliutsii" (Tasks of the proletariat in our revolution), April, 1917, *O voine, armii i voennoi nauke* (On war, army and military science; 2nd ed.), p. 338.
[12] Lenin, "Krakh II internatsionala" (Collapse of the Second International), May–June, 1915, *ibid.*, p. 235. The Soviets cautioned that "to advance a slogan of armed uprising when there is no revolutionary situation in the country would doom the working class to defeat," in "Otkrytoe pis'mo Tsentral'nogo Komiteta...," *Pravda*, July 14, 1963.
[13] The concept was expressed by Chu Teh in his address to the People's Liberation Army anniversary meeting, *Chieh-fang chün-pao* (Liberation army paper), April 1, 1958.
[14] "Problemy voiny i mira...," *Pravda*, August 7, 1960.
[15] *Fundamentals of Marxism-Leninism*, p. 607.
[16] Donald S. Zagoria, *The Sino-Soviet Conflict, 1956–1961*, p. 230.
[17] Iu. Krasin, "Razvitie leninym marksistskoi teorii sotsialisticheskoi revoliutsii" (The development by Lenin of Marxist theory of socialist revolution), in *V. I. Lenin – Velikii teoretik* (Lenin, a great theorist), p. 157.

detached critic and slashed at Peking as Blanquist.[18] The idea they attempted to convey was that the Chinese government was unduly hasty with its militant internationalism.[19] The Chinese were reminded that "it is impossible to introduce revolution from outside because revolution evolves out of both internal and external contradictions of capitalism."[20] The most that a socialist country can do is to call upon the people in the country "to unite and to mobilize all the forces" to vanquish the exploiters.[21]

Although the proletarian revolution is properly world-wide by nature,[22] it partakes of national characteristics, for no two countries are alike in their heritages and material settings. A true Marxist-Leninist ought to allow for the internal differences of every political community when he seeks to survey concretely the revolutionary status of a people. Each and every state bears its own special marks which often elude the insight of a bona fide observer. In an attempt to emphasize the unique qualities of every civil war, the Soviets referred to Lenin's upbraiding of some "left phrase-mongers" who were inclined to start revolution almost everywhere.[23] Such a policy is of no avail, since people would not respond, unless otherwise ready.[24] E. Zhukov pointed out that it took a reckless Marxist to try to impose "upon other countries ... systems and institutions which are not the outgrowth of internal development."[25] It is injudicious for the socialist camp to drag an unwilling nation along toward the revolutionary goal. Before the splendid idea of Marxism-Leninism conquers the minds of the millions all over the world, it will be useless to try to communize

---

[18] *Ibid.*; also *Fundamentals of Marxism-Leninism*, p. 607.

[19] James O'Gara, *Commonweal*, 77 (March 22, 1963), 654.

[20] *Voennaya strategiya* (Military strategy; 2nd ed.), p. 227.

[21] *Ibid.*

[22] Lenin explained that the revolution is universal because the capitalist oppression and counterrevolution is universal, in his "Iz pis'ma I. F. Armand" (From a letter to I. F. Armand), November, 1916, *O voine, armii i voennoi nauke* (On war, army and military science; 2nd ed.), p. 316.

[23] Iu. Frantsev, "Problemy voiny i mira...," *Pravda*, August 7, 1960; Kuusinen, "Pretvorenie v zhizn' ...,"*ibid.*, April 23, 1960.

[24] The Soviets tend to think realistically that class contradiction and civil war in the imperialist countries are less likely than ever before because of the betterment of livelihood of all people; *see* K. Alexandrov, Institut zur Erforschung der UdSSR, *Bulletin*, 7 (May 1960), 24. E. Ya. Batalov i Iu. F. Polyakov, "Burzhuaznye kontseptsii dekolonizatsii i raspad kolonial'-noi sistemy imperializma" (The bourgeois concepts of decolonization and the collapse of colonial system of imperialism), in *Mirovaya sotsialisticheskaya sistema i antikommunizm* (The world socialist system and anticommunism) (Moskva: Izd-vo "Nauka," 1968), p. 250, note 21, and p. 280.

[25] "Znamenatel'nyi faktor nashego vremeni" (Outstanding factor of our time), *Pravda*, August 26, 1960.

them suddenly and prematurely.[26] Khrushchev saw the danger, nay the futility, in transplanting an ideology, should the soil be inhospitable.[27] In Novosibirsk (October 10, 1959), he seemed considerate toward the capitalists who "will fight," he stated, "rather than be coerced to abandon their way of life."[28] It should be recalled that the averment was made after he returned from his American tour. A communist party in a non-communist country has the right to decide whether civil war is needed to seize power.[29] Other communist parties may not interfere with the matter. In a word, civil war is homespun and impossible to ship from abroad.[30]

In their depreciation of exporting revolution, the Soviets have sought to purge themselves of the subversive image among the people in the West.[31] By describing Peking as prone to enkindle civil war in order to disseminate communism the Soviet leaders wished to make their detente policy that much more credible. The position taken by Mao regarding civil war is not unlike that taken by Khrushchev with, however, some nuances of difference. It should be noted that on a few occasions, the Soviet media had also counseled aid and comfort to rebels.[32] Therefore, the Sino-Soviet discrepancy is really not a matter of black and white. On their part, the Chinese refuted the smear that they sought world conflict to trigger off civil wars; they branded it as Titoist slander.[33] Like the Soviets, they reasoned that "history tells us that people's revolution in all countries stems from the needs of the people and is the result of the development of the class struggle."[34] In effect, Peking concurred with Khrushchev, who said in 1956 that

[26] Khrushchev's speech at the reception given to the President of the Republic of Mali, March 29, 1962, *Predotvratit' voinu, otstoyat' mir!* (Prevent war and defend peace!), p. 128; also *idem*, "Otchetnyi doklad Tsentral'nogo Komiteta...," *Pravda*, February 15, 1956.

[27] "Who, pray, would heed the struggle for the dictatorship of the proletariat in those countries where there is no proletariat and no proletarian party, and what kind of dictatorship of the proletariat can there be without a proletariat?" asked the Soviets, in "Za torzhestvo tvorcheskogo marksizma-leninizma, protiv revizii kurza mirovogo kommunisticheskogo dvizheniya" (For victorious and creative Marxism-Leninism in opposition to revisionism of world communist movement), *Kommunist*, 11 (July, 1963), 25.

[28] "Rech' t. N. S. Khrushcheva na mitinge trudyashchkhsya goroda Novosibirska" (Khrushchev's speech to a mass meeting in Novosibirsk,) *Pravda*, October 11, 1959.

[29] "Zayavlenie soveshchaniya predstavitelei...," *ibid.*, December 6, 1960.

[30] Erich Wollenberg, *op. cit.*, p. 146.

[31] Khrushchev's speech to the Supreme Soviet, December 12, 1962, *Predotvratit' voinu, otstoyat' mir!* (Prevent war and defend peace!), p. 375.

[32] *Ibid.*, pp. 375–76.

[33] "A basic summing-up of experience...," *Sino-Soviet Dispute*, p. 167. Translation of "Chung-kuo jen-min ko-ming...," *Hung-ch'i*, 20–21 (November 1, 1960), 1–13.

[34] *Ibid.; see* also *China after Mao*, pp. 232–33, there Lin Piao writes "Revolution or people's war in any country is the business of masses in that country and should be carried out by their own efforts; there is no other way."

"Romain Rolland was right when he stated that 'freedom is not brought in from abroad in baggage trains like Bourbon whiskey.'"[35] Furthermore, like the Soviets, the Chinese objected to too rashly or too slowly engineering a civil war. Mao wrote: "Adventurism tends to maximize the subjective revolutionary ethos, and minimize the counterrevolutionary ethos, while objectivism tends to do otherwise."[36] His paper-tiger theory assumes that one is often misguided by the ostentation of a regime and thinks wrongly that civil war is not ripe, while in reality it might have been overdue.[37] From this precept the Chinese theorists drew several conclusions as follows.

First, Peking put its emphasis on the impossibility to "hold back a revolution in any country if there is a desire for that revolution on the part of the people and when the revolutionary crisis there has matured."[38] This argument was set forth to counter the Soviet stand of not accelerating the revolutionary situation.[39] "No matter how hard the reactionaries may try to prevent the advance of the wheel of history, revolutions will take place," Peking asserted.[40] Second, while Moscow objected to the export of revolution, Peking pointed out that counterrevolution has been exported by the imperialists, and that the West would use force to quell workers' outbreaks in other countries.[41] On this issue the Chinese got their point adopted by the 1960 Moscow Conference.[42] Third, Peking did not exclude the possibility of changing the "state of another country,"[43] to use Stalin's phrase, if the socialist

[35] "Otchetnyi doklad Tsentral'nogo Komiteta...," *Pravda*, February 15, 1956.
[36] Mao, "Hsing-hsing chih-huo k'o-i liao yüan" (A spark may start a conflagration), January 5, 1930, *Mao Tse-tung hsüan-chi* (Selected works), 1951, vol. 1, p. 105.
[37] *Ibid.*; Khrushchev retorted that the paper-tiger was provided with nuclear teeth; *see* P. Royle, *Political Quarterly*, 34 (July–September, 1963), 292.
[38] *Sino-Soviet Dispute*, p. 101. "Ninety percent of the people of the capitalist world demanded revolution... and demanded the joint support of the socialist camp, particularly of the Soviet Union and China," wrote *Hung-ch'i*, 1 (January 1, 1961), 5.
[39] After the 1957 Moscow Declaration, China submitted a separate memorandum dissociating herself from the thesis of peaceful transition to socialism; *see* "The origin and development of the difference between the leadership of the CPSU and ourselves," *Peking Review*, 37 (September 13, 1963), 6–20.
[40] *Sino-Soviet Dispute*, p. 101. *See* also A. F. Kulov, "Razvitie leninym filosofii marksizma" (Development by Lenin of the philosophy of marxism), in *V. I. Lenin-velikii teoretik* (V. I. Lenin, a great theorist), p. 14.
[41] *Sino-Soviet Dispute*, p. 86; Khrushchev also availed himself of the idea of counterrevolution by the Western nations, *Predotvratit' voinu, otstoyat' mir!* (Prevent war and defend peace!), p. 376.
[42] "Zayavlenie soveshchaniya predstavitelei...," *Pravda*, December 6, 1960.
[43] On March 3, 1936, Stalin denied to M. Howard that "men of the Soviet Union would ever want to change the state of another country by any means, let alone by force," as quoted in Erich Wollenberg, *op. cit.*, p. 146. Lenin's similar assertion is in "Sed'maya (aprel'skaya) vserossiiskaya konferentsiya RSDRP (B)" (The Seventh (April) All-Russian Conference of the RSDRP (B)), April, 1917, *O voine, armii i voennoi nauke* (On war, army and military science; 2nd ed.), p. 356.

regime sends its troops across its borders to pursue the enemy forces.[44] Should such an eventuality occur, it was contended, the native people would not fail to be attracted by the socialist system and to discard their obsolete mode of life. Fourth and last, the Chinese felt that the fate of proletarians everywhere must be the concern of all socialists,[45] and that to be apathetic to them amounts to disloyalty to Marxism-Leninism.[46] Civil war, Peking believed, should not be left alone when it is threatened by counterrevolution. Yet, like the Chinese, the Soviets have also pledged aid to rebels. Khrushchev said that he would offer wholehearted support to the Cuban type of civil war.[47] Peaceful co-existence, Sokolovskii, *et al.* wrote, did not mean being neutral to the proletarian struggle in the capitalist countries.[48] More outspoken is the 1960 declaration which stated that the communists "consider it their international commitment to incite the peoples of all nations to overthrow their imperialist regimes."[49] This is nothing but straight abetment of civil war.

The Parliamentary Avenue to Socialism

In his address to the Twentieth Congress Khrushchev counted as one of the cardinal features of his "new epoch" the bloodless passage to socialism. Parliament, he declared, could be availed of to reach the goal of Marxism-Leninism. The theme is the corollary of his avoidability doctrine, for if social reform be realized democratically and lawfully, wars within a nation as well as between nations are useless. There is no doubt that he had made a bold departure from the precept of Lenin, who defamed parliamentarianism as a bourgeois tool,[50] which should, in certain circumstances, be uprooted before its replacement can be

---

[44] *Sino-Soviet Dispute*, p. 100.

[45] "Pu yao wang-chi shih-chieh shong huan-yu san-fen-chih-erh ti pei ya-pe jen-min" (Don't forget the oppressed two-thirds of the world's people), *Shih-chieh chih-shih* (World knowledge), 5 (May 10, 1966), reverse side of the title page.

[46] *China after Mao*, p. 235.

[47] "Marksizm-leninizm...," *Izvestiya*, January 8, 1961; "Za novye pobedy...," *Pravda*, January 7, 1961; *Kommunist*, 1 (January, 1961), 4–6.

[48] *Voennaya strategiya* (Military strategy; 2nd ed.), p. 226.

[49] "Zayavlenie soveschchaniya predstavitelei...," *Pravda*, December 6, 1960.

[50] "Partizanskaya voina" (Partisan war), September, 1916, *O voine, armii i voennoi nauke* (On war, army and military science; 2nd ed.), p. 156. "Peaceful means are helpful, but bloody battles are most vital," Lenin taught, "Uroki Kommuny" (The lessons of the Commune), March, 1908, *ibid.*, p. 179; "Uroki moskovskogo vosstaniya" (The lessons of Moscow revolt), August, 1906, *ibid.*, p. 144; there he said that it is a plain humbug to tell people that bloody battles are not needed to take political power). Edward Crankshaw observed correctly that "when all is said, the Chinese are, in fact, showing themselves better communists than the Russians. Khrushchev knows this." Lenin was unmistakably for violence toward, not compromising with, the capitalists; *see New York Times Magazine*, May 26, 1963, p. 90.

brought up.[51] Except in the essay "Left-wing communism, an infantile disorder" where he sanctioned cooperation with other parties,[52] Lenin never thought much of democratic procedure.[53] The transition from capitalism to communism is not a gentle one, he realized.[54] To make the leap, what is more important for the proletariat than guns, he was wondering.[55] "The great questions of class struggle are decided only by force, and we must get busy, gathering, organizing and using the means of force in a dynamic way."[56] Although Khrushchev did not bluntly suggest that Lenin's violent approach to socialism was no longer sound, his advice to the workmen in non-socialist countries was to avail themselves of all legal means to achieve the revolutionary goal; this statement amounted to a repudiation of Lenin on this point.

Yet Khrushchev's view underwent a noticeable change from the unqualified advocacy of parliamentarianism in 1956 to a qualified one in 1961. On February 15, 1956, he held out to the Party Congress the prospect of tranquility in every part of the world as a result of the balance of forces, on the one hand, and the inadvisability of nuclear war, on the other.[57] There would be interstate as well as intra-state peace, according to him. The proletariat does not have to shed blood in order to attain dictatorship in every country. Such a stand was, however, emphatically revised in his early 1961 speech to the meeting of the party apparatus.[58] He began by iterating the familiar lines like "correlation of forces," and "increasingly propitious conditions for the socialist future."[59] In countries which have a parliamentary system of some kind, the proletariat would use it to seize the reins of government. But, he talked forcibly, in case such a system were not available, the sword

[51] Lenin, "Gosudarstvo i revoliutsiya" (State and revolution), August–September, 1917, Sochineniya (Collected works; 4th ed.), vol. 25, pp. 461–63.

[52] Ibid., vol. 27, pp. 70, 124–25, 175, 204.

[53] "Parliamentarianism and trade-unionism could be used only temporarily," said Lenin, "Partizanskaya voina" (Partisan war), September, 1906, O voine, armii i voennoi nauke (On war, army and military science; 2nd ed.), p. 150.

[54] "The Social-Democrats are to transform radically the social conditions of all people," Lenin taught his comrades, "Shto nachat'?" (What to begin), 1901–2, ibid., p. 40. "The workers who deny the use of rifles to destroy their enemy regimes deserve to be treated as slaves," declared Lenin, "O lozunge 'razoruzheniya'" (On the slogan of disarmament), October, 1916, ibid., p. 312.

[55] Ibid., p. 313; there he said: "The proletariat would not lay down its arms until the vanishment of the capitalists,." Also ibid. 1st ed., vol. 1, pp. 127, 131.

[56] Idem, Sochineniya (Collected works; 4th ed.), vol. 9, p. 16.

[57] "Otchetnyi doklad Tsentra'nogo Komiteta...," Pravda, February 15, 1906.

[58] Even in the 1956 speech his position is a nebulous one, for he did not exclude the force of arms as a means to power. But the point was not belabored.

[59] "Marksizm-leninizm...," Izvestiya, January 8, 1961; "Za novye pobedy...," Pravda, January 7, 1961; Kommunist, 1 (January, 1961), 5.

offered the only alternative.[60] Even if a parliament existed, the struggle
for power as suggested by him is far from peaceful.[61] What is involved,
he told his partisans, "will not be a matter of electoral speeches or plain
skirmish around the polls"; instead, the problem is to employ the
"parliamentary form and not the bourgeois parliament as such" in
order to place it at the service of the people. Finally, displaying his
Bolshevik mettle, he equated the winning of a "majority of the parliament" to "smashing the military-bureaucratic machine . . . and setting
up a new proletarian people's state."[62] This is precisely what has been
taught by Lenin,[63] Marx,[64] and Engels.[65]

A few months before Khrushchev's speech just cited, Belyakov and
Burlatskii co-authored an article propounding the same idea. Apart
from the violent taking over of power which was said inescapable,
the two also suggested peaceful means because of the necessity of
diversified forms of struggle.[66] It is interesting to note what they
meant by the word "peaceful." They contended that the conditions
for the exclusion of "civil war" or "armed uprising" are such that the
ruling class be deprived of army, police and bureaucracy so that they
could not wage counterrevolution.[67] When the government is isolated

[60] *Ibid.* The same was stressed in chapter V of "Novaya programma" (New program),
Pravda, and *Izvestiya,* November 2, 1961.
[61] Lenin ridiculed the Duma as not being non-violent parliamentarianism, *see* "Armiya i
narod" (Army and people), in his *Sochineniya* (Collected works; 5th ed.), vol. 13, p. 282.
[62] "Marksizm-leninizm...," *Izvestiya,* January 8, 1961; "Za novye pobedy...," *Pravda,*
January 7, 1961; *Kommunist,* 1 (January, 1961), 15.
[63] "Gosudarstvo i revoliutsiya" (State and revolution), August–September, 1917, *Sochinenyia* (Collected works; 4th ed.), vol. 25, pp. 461–63; also in *O voine, armii i voennoi nauke*
(On war, army and military science; 2nd ed.), pp. 384–98. "Partizanskaya voina" (Partisan
war), September, 1906, *ibid.,* pp. 154 (here it is said that Marxists must always stand for
civil war), 156. "Voisko i revoliutsiya" (Troops and revolution), November, 1905, *ibid.,* p. 135;
"Dve taktike sotsial-demokratii v demokraticheskoi revoliutsii" (Two tactics of the Social-
Democracy in democratic revolution), June–July, 1905, *ibid.,* p. 107; "Revoliutsionnaya
armiya i revoliutsionnoe pravitel'stvo" (Revolutionary army and revolutionary government),
July, 1905, *ibid.,* p. 92; "Novye zadachi i novye sily" (New tasks and new forces), March,
1905, *ibid.,* p. 65; "Proekt rezoliutsii levykh sotsial-demokratov k pervoi mezhdunarodnoi
sotsialistichekoi konferentsii" (Project of the resolutions to be submitted by the Social-
Democrats to the first international socialist conference), July, 1915, *ibid.,* p. 248 (here it is
clearly asserted that civil peace is betrayal of Marxism); "Referat po temu 'Proletariat i
voine'" (On the topic of proletariat and war), October, 1914, *ibid.,* p. 229.
[64] *Der Bürgerkrieg in Frankreich* (Civil war in France) (Moskau: Verlagsgenossenschaft
ausländischer Arbeiter in der UdSSR, 1937), pp. 1–12. Also *Manifesto kommunisticheskoi partii*
(Moskva: Gos. izd-vo polit. lit-ry, 1952), pp. 25–50.
[65] *Der Ursprung der Familie, des Privateigentums und des Staates* (The origin of family,
private property and state), p. 138.
[66] Diversity of the forms of struggle was suggested by Lenin, "Partizanskaya voina"
(Partisan war), September, 1906, in *O voine, armii i voennoi nake* (On war, army and military
science; 2nd ed.), p. 149.
[67] Belyakov and Burlatskii, "Leninskaya teoriya...," (Lenin's theory of siocalist revolution in present conditions), *Kommunist,* 13 (September, 1960), 20. Lenin's teaching on this
matter can be found in "Pis'mo iz daleka" (Letter from afar), March, 1917, *O voine, armii i*

and the disarmament program leaves it with no sinews of war, the passage to socialism can be tranquil. The writers warned that if these conditions are absent, the people have recourse to nothing but arms. "Lenin constantly stressed that the proletariat ought to master the techniques of all sorts, non-peaceable as well as peaceable," advised the authors.[68] It is only clear that Khrushchev's original stand on parliamentarianism gave way to advocating either open civil war or coup d'état.[69] In contrast to him, Mao never believed in parliamentarianism,[70] at least in his own country. In one of his early essays he suggested that "without armed struggle there cannot be a place for the proletariat, nor can there be a place for our Communist Party."[71] In answering the question whether bourgeois legislatures could be harnessed for revolutionary purposes, he quoted Stalin: "In China, the unique point is to wage revolutionary war against counterrevolutionary war. Here lies the superiority of the Chinese revolution."[72] The problem, he said, was that China had no parliament in the first place, and "our Communist Party is not going to engage in legal battles."[73]

Again and again, Mao pointed to the significance of civil war and saluted the rifles that made possible the establishment of his regime.[74] As to whether he thought it feasible to remake the parliament into a congress of workers' deputies in the capitalist nations, Mao did not go beyond saying that there the struggle may take "multifarious ave-

voennoi nauke (On war, army and military science; 2nd ed.), p. 329; "O zadachakh proletariata v dannoi revoliutsii" (On the tasks of the proletariat in the revolution), April, 1917, *ibid.*, p. 337.

[68] Belyakov and Burlatskii, "Leninskaya teoriya...," *Kommunist*, 13 (September, 1960), 15–16.

[69] Brian Crozier, *International Affairs* (London), 40 (July, 1964), 449.

[70] Mao's innate hatred of parliamentarianism is solidly based on the teaching of both Marx and Lenin. Marx said that "parliamentarians are to oppress the people," in "Grazhdanskaya voina vo Frantsii" (Civil war in France), as quoted in Lenin, *O voine, armii i voennoi nauke* (On war, army and military science; 2nd ed.), p. 346. Lenin remarked that "parliament is a whorehouse," in "Partizanskaya voina" (Partisan war), September, 1906, *ibid.*, p. 156.

[71] Mao, "Kung-ch'an tang-jen fa-kan-tsu" (A few words to introduce the journal *Communist*), October 4, 1939, *Mao Tse-tung hsüan-chi* (Selected works), 1952, vol. 2, p. 560.

[72] "Chan-cheng yü chan-lüeh wen-t'i" (The problems of war and strategy), *ibid.*, p. 507.

[73] *Ibid.*, p. 506.

[74] "Hsing-hsing chih-huo k'o-i liao-yüan" (A spark may start a conflagration), January 5, 1930, *ibid.*, 1951, vol. 1, p. 103; "Lun lien-ho cheng-fu" (On coalition government), April 24, 1945, *ibid.*, 1953, vol. 3, p. 1031. Mao has firmly built upon Leninism. Lenin's preaching of civil war to overthrow a bourgeois regime is vibrant and verbose, "Iz 'Otkrytogo pis'ma Borisu Suvarinu'" (From an open letter to Boris Souvarine), December, 1916, *O voine, armii i voennoi nauke* (On war, army and military science), p. 320; "O lozunge 'razoruzheniya'" (On the slogan of disarmament), October, 1916, *ibid.*, pp. 312, 313; "Voennaya programma proletarskoi revoliutsii" (Military program of the proletarian revolution), September, 1916, *ibid.*, pp. 301–8; "Sotsializm i voina" (Socialism and war), July–August, 1915, *ibid.*, p. 269.

nues.''[75] Judged by Mao's near-obsession with the role of the military, political transformation, for him, cannot be free from violence in effect.[76] Indeed, Mao gives no more credit to parliament than the Russians. To him, it "is nothing but an adornment for bourgeois dictatorship even if the working-class party commands a majority in parliament or becomes the biggest party in it."[77] Further, the ruling circles could advance any pretext to dissolve the legislature or turn it into an innocuous body or simply penalize the representatives of the workmen. It is just unbelievable that the bourgeois Solons could take steps to implement socialism.[78] This remark of Mao's answers directly Khrushchev's assertion that the "winning of a firm parliamentary majority based on the mass revolutionary movement of the proletariat and of the working people could bring about conditions to ... make social changes."[79] Peking's concept is typically Leninist. When suggesting the Soviet as an apparatus of governance fusing both legislative and political sovereignties, Lenin declared that yesterday's legislature could not be remodeled to serve today's proletariat.[80] From the viewpoint of revolutionaries, all systems which have been tarred with the capitalist brush would have to be jettisoned; and any organism of Western democracy has no room in a workers' body politic.

Khrushchev and company in propounding parliamentarianism held that it is at once the natural and desirable way to socialism. According to them, capitalism draws to its end. The 1957 Moscow declaration lavished much space to diagnosing the economic health of the West. A dismal picture was painted of the people's livelihood, which was depicted as beyond remedy; the whole structure ought to be relinquished.[81] The 1960 Moscow statement bemoaned the rampant unemployment, increasing poverty of the broad masses, and "monopoly profits and superprofits" of a small group of individuals, all leading to class enmity.[82] Granted all these, it would have been superfluous for civil wars to finish up the regime, because the ripe plum is ready to drop into the lap of the proletariat. Peking, however, believed that a push is yet needed. It little trusted the slow process of the decay of capital-

[75] Mao, "Chan-cheng yü chan-lüeh wen-t'i" (The problems of war and strategy), *Mao Tse-tung hsüan-chi* (Selected works), 1952, vol. 2, p. 507.
[76] James O'Gara, *Commonweal*, 77 (March 22, 1962), 654.
[77] *Sino-Soviet Dispute*, p. 107.
[78] *Ibid.*
[79] "Otchenyi doklad Tsentral'nogo Komiteta...," *Pravda*, February 15, 1956.
[80] Lenin, "Aprel'skie tezisy" (April thesis), 1917, *Sochineniya* (Collected works: 4th ed.), vol. 24, pp. 1–4.
[81] "Deklaratsiya soveshchaniya predstavitelei...," *Pravda*, November 22, 1957.
[82] "Zayavlenie soveshchaniya predstavitelei...," *ibid.*, December 6, 1960.

ism. Another reason for the peaceful transition which the Soviets set forth was explained in the textbook *Fundamentals of Marxism-Leninism*.[83] After underwriting Khrushchev's view as set forth in his Twentieth Congress speech, the publication stated that parliamentary methods to attain socialism had a great advantage in that they entailed no destruction and could effect an overhaul of the state structure.[84] Civil war, it was reasoned, would inflict too much harm on both the productive forces and the fruits of labor accumulated by the workers over a long period of time.[85] However, the book admitted that although no Marxist can deny the desirability of a pacific transformation, the real question is whether the "objective premises for it exist."[86] It is assumed that should they be not forthcoming, civil war is in order.

THE ROLE OF CIVIL WAR

Historical Necessity

Although from time to time the Soviets held a brief for civil war, they did not find it particularly expedient to laud it. True, the possibility of the toilers' insurgence in a capitalist nation was not overlooked by Khrushchev and company. But they have nothing of Peking's engrossment in the non-peaceful approach to power. The Chinese communist leaders adhered tenaciously to the legacy of Marx and Lenin, as they saw it, in their refusal to accept the formula of the parliamentary avenue to socialism.[87] The central idea on which Peking builds has been that it is only through armed insurrection that an existing regime can be totally blown up.[88] For the starting point of their contention, the Chinese took the Paris Commune of 1871.[89] It was written that that heroic event signifies a landmark on the road to a labor paradise. It is the "first dress rehearsal ... in the proletariat's attempt to overthrow

---

[83] *Fundamentals of Marxism-Leninism*. p. 614.

[84] *Ibid.*, pp. 610–14.

[85] The authors of the textbook seemed to base their argument on Lenin's occasional references to the adverse effects of war; *see* Lenin, *Sochineniya* (Collected works; 5th ed.), vol. 36, p. 396; N. P. Mamai, "Predislovie" (introduction), in Lenin, *O voine, armii i voennoi nauke* (On war, army and military science; 2nd ed.), p. 8.

[86] *Fundamentals of Marxism-Leninism*, pp. 610–14.

[87] Lenin, "Partizanskaya voina" (Partisan war), September, 1906, *O voine, armii i voennoi nauke* (On war, army and military science; 2nd ed.), p. 154.

[88] *Idem*, "Voennaya programma proletarskoi revoliutsii" (Military program of the proletarian revolution), September, 1916, *ibid.*, pp. 302–8; "Mezhdunarodnyi sotsialisticheskii kongress v Shtutgarte" (International socialist congress in Stuttgart), August–September, 1907, *ibid.*, p. 172; "Sotsializm i voina" (Socialism and war), July–August, 1915, *ibid.*, p. 269.

[89] Lenin took the Paris Commune as the classical example for the proletariat to come to power; *see* "Voennaya programma proletarskoi revoliutsii" (Military program of the proletarian revolution), September, 1916, *ibid.*, p. 305.

the capitalist system."[90] Deducing from Marx's observation made on the eve of the crushing of the Commune that the same communist effort would be repeated until the final victory,[91] the Chinese believed that it was the invariable pattern of power transfer from one class to another. When the social body has suffered from incurable diseases, there would grow in it a genesis of new life by the law of dialectics. However, the moribund organism may linger on indefinitely. Hence it is imperative to deliver the dying Leviathan a coup de grâce, for Marx said that war has the ultimate word in any complete revamping of social structure.[92]

The use of war in excising the dysfunctional tissue from a living organism causes it to be called the "milestone of world history."[93] Peking was convinced of the unavoidability of ousting the bourgeoisie by arms and not by peace. "The capitalist-imperialist system absolutely will not crumble of itself. It will be overthrown by the proletarian revolution within the imperialist country concerned."[94] There has never been an instance, it was asserted, where a senile class yields its place to a new class as the ruler. If the workers and peasants have to wait their turn for the voluntary handover of the reins of government by the exploiters, they may as well quit. The truth, Peking argued, is that even if the toiling people should prefer peace to force, their opponent would not appreciate it.[95] As Lenin said, the "bourgeois gentlemen" will do all they can to thwart the orderly advance toward a socialist state; any great revolution, like the French one in 1789, always winds up in war which is "unleashed by the counterrevolutionary bourgeoisie."[96] Next to the French, the Russian and Chinese peoples were adduced as setting shining examples, showing how force has been successfully utilized as a tool of political surgery.[97]

The difference, Peking felt, between Marxism and pseudo-Marxism is that the former upholds the "perpetual and indestructible truth" of proletarian revolt, while the latter deceives by prattling of civil peace.[98]

---

[90] *Sino-Soviet Dispute*, p. 82.

[91] Lenin, *Sochineniya* (Collected works; 4th ed.), vol. 5, p. 344; vol. 8, pp. 361–62; vol. 9, p. 42; vol. 19, p. 506; vol. 21, p. 357.

[92] Ryazanov, "Voennoe delo i marksizm" (Military affairs and Marxism), *Voina i voennoe iskusstvo v svete istoricheskogo materializma* (War and military art in the light of historical materialism), p. 14.

[93] Rotstein, "Voina kak sotsial'noe yavlenie" (War as a social phenomenon), *Bol'shaya sovetskaya entsiklopediya* (The great Soviet encyclopedia; 1st ed.), vol. 12, col. 571.

[94] *Sino-Soviet Dispute*, p. 94.

[95] *Ibid.*, p. 102.

[96] Lenin, *Sochineniya* (Collected works; 4th ed.), vol. 29, p. 334.

[97] *Sino-Soviet Dispute*, p. 83.

[98] *Ibid.*, pp. 83, 102. For Lenin's denunciation of civil peace, *see* his " O lozunge 'razoruzheniya'" (On the slogan of disarmament), October, 1916, *O voine, armii i voennoi nauke* (O

Rebuking Khrushchev's no-war policy, Yu Chao-li stated: "Civil wars are also wars. Whoever recognizes the struggle of classes cannot fail to recognize civil wars." The Russians were lamented as "sinking into extreme opportunism and renouncing socialist revolution" by fetishizing piecemeal and peaceful reforms.[99] Short of armed rebellion, there would have been no socialist Russia and China. On the eve of the November Revolution, *Hung-ch'i* wrote, Lenin was confronted with the decision whether to take action, and after analyzing the various factors, ordered the Bolsheviks to go ahead with the planned strike.[100] Lenin's idea, the journal went on, was embodied in the essay "State and revolution"; short of riddance of the old state organ, it was impossible to erect a new one. The more thorough the spade work in razing the condemned structure, the more magnificent the edifice freshly constructed.[101] Simply by attaching so many wings here and there onto a shaky house, one cannot expect it to be habitable and lasting. Because parliament indicates not just the law-making machinery, but the whole web of the community life, it is "bound by thousands of threads to the bourgeoisie and permeated through and through with routine and inertia."[102] Liu Shao-ch'i and Teng Hsiao-p'ing (both

war, army and military science; 2nd ed.), pp. 312, 313; "O porazhenii svoego pravitel'stva v imperialistkoi voine" (On the defeat of one's own government in the imperialist war), July, 1915, *ibid.*, p. 253; "Proekt rezoliutsii levykh sotsial-demokratov k pervoi mezhdunarodnoi sotsialisticheskoi konferentsii" (Project of the resolution submitted to the first international socialist conference by the left Social-Democrats), July, 1916, *ibid.*, p. 248; "Sozhalenie i styd" (Sorrow and shame), May, 1911, *ibid.*, p. 198; "Partizanskaya voina" (Partisan war), September, 1906, *ibid.*, p. 154; "Uroki moskovskogo vosstaniya" (The lessons of Moscow revolt), August, 1906, *ibid.*, p. 144; "Evropeiskii kapital i samoderzhavie" (European capital and autocracy), April, 1905; *ibid.*, p. 72; here it was written that civil peace is worse than civil war.

[99] "On imperialism as a source of war...," *Peking Review*, 15 (April 12, 1960), 20. Translation of "Lun t'i-kuo chu-i...," *Hung-ch'i*, 7 (April 1, 1960), 1–12. The statement that "civil wars are wars" was used to refute Khrushchev's indiscriminate denunciation of all wars in his Twentieth Congress speech. Yu said that even if the socialist countries were opposing international war, civil war may not be objected to. The concept of civil wars being wars was expressed by Lenin at least twice in his criticism on the revisionists: "Otvet P. Kievskomu" (Answer to P. Kievskii), August–September, 1916, *O voine, armii i voennoi nauke* (On war, army and military science; 2nd ed.), p. 293; "Voennaya programma proletarskoi revoliutsii" (Military program of the proletarian revolution), September, 1916, *ibid.*, p. 302.

[100] "The path of the great October revolution is the common path of the liberation of mankind," *Peking Review*, 45 (November 8, 1960), 5–7. Translation of "Wei-ta shih-yüeh ko-ming ...," *Hung-ch'i*, 20–21 (November 1, 1960), 14–17.

[101] "Revolution is to destroy the old superstructure and to build up a new one," wrote Lenin, "Novye zadachi i novye sily" (New tasks and new forces), March, 1905, *O voine, armii i voennoi nauke* (On war, army and military science; 2nd ed.), p. 65. *See* also "Dve taktiki sotsial-demokratii v demokraticheskoi revoliutsii" (Two tactics of the Social-Democrats in democratic revolution), June–July, 1905, *ibid.*, p. 107.

[102] "The path of the great October revolution...," *Peking Review*, 45 (November 8, 1960), 5–7. Translation of "Wei-ta shih-yüeh ko-ming...," *Hung-ch'i*, 20–21 (November 1, 1960), 14–17. For Lenin's statement, *see* his "Zadachi proletarita v nashei revoliutsii" (Tasks of the

expelled from the CCP in 1968) fought valiantly in the 1960 Moscow Conference for the primacy of revolutionary war in the seizure of power. Half way through the meeting, *Jen-min jih-pao* carried an article against parliamentarianism which, however, was favored by the majority in the conference. The paper commented satirically that the exploiters and the exploited can no more coexist than a "rider and his horse."[103] Without bucking him off, the horse cannot be free.[104]

Destruction of the Principal Agents of the State

In the preceding pages, we have presented the position the Chinese took on the necessity of civil war. What specifically did they have in mind when they spoke of the forceful eradication of an obsolete regime? According to the materialist accounting of history, the superstructure of a community reflects man's activity in making and sharing goods. A revolution is to bring the cultural and political life in correspondence with the economic system.[105] A change in the way men earn their living would entail other changes in social relations as a whole. However, in reality, the communists seem to reverse the process. It is the new superstructure brought by revolution that is instrumental in transforming the material pattern of the people.[106] That is to say, the alteration of the methods of production and distribution is a result of the coming into being of the superstructure.[107] Against this anomaly we seek to examine the revolutionary tactics of the communists. If dialectical materialism

proletarians in our revolution), April, 1917, *O voine, armii i voennoi nauke* (On war, army and military science; 2nd ed.), p. 338.

[103] *Jen-min jih-pao*, November 21, 1960; *NCNA*, November 21, 1960.

[104] Lenin suggested that the interests of the workers and their capitalist slave-drivers just cannot be harmonized and, hence, they may not live together peaceably; "Sozhaleinie i styd" (Sorrow and shame), May, 1911, *O voine, armii i voennoi nauke* (On war, army and military science; 2nd ed.), p. 198; also in *Sochineniya* (Collected works; 5th ed.), vol. 20, p. 245. "There is fundamentally no possibility for people of different classes to share common sentiment. The revisionists think they can," wrote *Chung-kuo ch'ing-nien* (Chinese youth), 11 (June 1, 1960), 5. For Engels' concept on this point, *see* his *Der Ursprung der Familie, des Privateigentums und des Staates* (The origin of family, private property and state), pp. 177–78.

[105] R. N. Carew-Hunt, *Theory and Practice of Communism* (London: Bles, 1950), pp. 1–50.

[106] "Dve taktiki sotsial-demokratii v demokraticheskoi revoliutsii" (Two tactics of the Social-Democrats in democratic revolution), June-July, 1905, Lenin, *O voine, armii i voennoi nauke* (On war, army and military science; 2nd ed.), p. 107; "Novye zadachi i novye sily" (New tasks and new forces), *ibid.*, p. 65.

[107] "The very triumph of Bolshevism in the last forty years constitutes a refutation of Marx's theory of historical determinism in which he expressed it. The mode of political decision determines the mode of economic production, not vice versa," wrote correctly Sidney Hook in a previously cited article, *Encounter*, 19 (September, 1962), 65. Hook's observation was shared by some Soviet students who, however, denied a violation of orthodox Marxism; *see* M. M. Rozental' and G. M. Shtraks (eds.), *Kategorii materialisticheskoi dialektiki* (Categories of materialist dialectics) (Moskva: Gos. izd-vo polit. lit-ry, 1956), pp. 128–31. "Politics does influence economy," it was written.

works the way we are told, the termination of an existing government by arms should not be wanted.[108] This theoretical dilemma has not been squared away by the communists.[109] At any rate, the civil-warmongers are realistic and have been concerned not so much with the gulf between the productive mode and proprietorship as with the very agents of the state which are to counter their revolutionary activities.[110] It is rightfully assumed that if those agents are put out of the way, the old regime is done for and a room is found for the new power complex.

The communists believe that the principal target of the revolutionary is the state machinery which keeps peace and security for the bourgeoisie, but threats and repression for the toilers. In the essay "Revolutionary army and revolutionary government," Lenin taught that the Bolsheviks ought to focus their efforts on how to deal lethal blows to the government troops, because he said, if that job is done, a revolt then scores its success.[111] Building upon Lenin's precept, Mao and company insisted that the proletariat should break the military resistance of the enemy class first and foremost, since "according to the Marxist theory of state, the army is the main prop of the political power ... Whoever wants to seize state power and to keep it must have a strong army."[112] Peaceful means are no match for non-peaceful ones. Any conquest of authority begins with the annihilation of hostile opponents. "The standing army," wrote Lenin, "is used not so much against the external enemy as against the internal enemy."[113] The Chinese regard this legacy "valid for all countries."[114] The military units of any imperialist nation are said to keep the workpeople from revolt.[115] Hence it is only right that the workpeople have to treat them

---

[108] "La critique du capitalisme, dévelopée dans *Le Capital*, laisse supposer que, par le seul jeu des lois du système, celui-ci s'effondrera. En fait, cette conception se concilie difficilement avec celle de la révolution catastrophique" (The critique of capitalism elaborated in *Das Kapital* tells us that the system will inevitably collapse, simply as the result of the interplay of its own laws. Actually, however, this conception is not easily reconciled with the idea of a catastrophic revolution), wrote Henri Chambre, *De Karl Marx à Mao Tse-tung* (Paris: Spes, 1958), p. 19.

[109] A. N. V. Tropkin, *op. cit.*, p. 180.

[110] Georg von Rauch, *A History of Soviet Russia* (rev. ed.; New York: Praeger, 1959), pp. 45–60.

[111] Lenin, *Sochineniya* (Collected works; 4th ed.), vol. 8, pp. 524–25.

[112] "A basic summing-up of experience...," *Sino-Soviet Dispute*, p. 164; translation of "Chung-kuo jen-min ko-ming...," *Hung-ch'i*, 20–21 (November 1, 1960), 1–13.

[113] Lenin, "Armiya i revoliutsiya" (Army and revolution), November, 1905, *Sochineniya* (Collected works; 4th ed.), vol. 10, p. 38; also in *O voine, armii i voennoi nauke* (On war, army and military science; 2nd ed.), p. 135. This essay sometimes takes up the title "Voisko i revoliutsiya" (Troops and revolution).

[114] *Sino-Soviet Dispute*, p. 104.

[115] Lenin, "O lozunge 'razoruzheniya'" (On the slogan of disarmament), October, 1916, *O voine, armii i voennoi nauke* (On war, army and military science; 2nd ed.), p. 313.

as the gravest menace. In the 1870's Marx observed that both Great Britain and the United States could follow the pacific road to socialism because neither had a formidable standing army or bureaucracy. But presently, the Chinese argued, the situation has changed; the two nations have come to possess the punitive means of the most efficient kind in the world which "subordinate everything to themselves and trample everything underfoot."[116] It is assumed that to wage civil war in order to smash the armed might of these two regimes is now necessary, although it was not so in Marx's time.

Since the stumbling block of the proletarian liberation in the imperialist countries is the military, the parties of the working class are compelled to organize and defend themselves.[117] The bourgeois class is charged with preventing the exploited from democratic practice, in spite of the fact that the exploited have tried that way.[118] As pointed out by the 1957 Moscow declaration, now that the "ruling classes never relinquish their power voluntarily," it is imperative to storm the bulwark, viz., the war machine.[119] Revolution, *Hung-ch'i* wrote, is nothing but the application of force to liquidate the army.[120] Along with the army, the state organ and police formation are also slated as the targets of attack; all three are mordantly execrated by Lenin in the essay "Tasks of the proletariat in our revolution."[121] He preferred a universal militia to replace the army, and simple officialdom to take the place of the state bureaucracy. There should be no police at all. It was his belief that if this was done, capitalism would be swept away completely.[122] However, the Chinese literature spoke of "smashing the bourgeois state machinery,"[123] or "smashing the military and bureaucratic machines";

---

[116] *Sino-Soviet Dispute*, p. 104. Lenin, "Gosudarstvo i revoliutsiya" (State and revolution), *Sochineniya* (Collected works; 4th ed.), vol. 25, pp. 353–63.

[117] *Sino-Soviet Dispute*, p. 104.

[118] *Ibid.*

[119] "Deklaratsiya soveshchaniya predstavitelei...," *Pravda*, November 22, 1960.

[120] "A basic summing-up of experience...," *Sino-Soviet Dispute*, p. 166. Translation of "Chung-kuo jen-min ko-ming...," *Hung-ch'i*, 20–21 (November 1, 1960), 1–13.

[121] "Zadachi proletariata v nashei revoliutsii," in *O voine, armii i voennoi nauke* (On war, army and military science; 2nd ed.), pp. 338–42; also in *Sochineniya* (Collected works; 5th ed.), vol. 31, pp. 161–65, and *O voine, armii i voennoi nauke* (On war, army and military science; 1st ed.), vol. 2, pp. 31–42. *See* also "Rech' k soldatam na mitinge v izmailovskom polku" (Speech to the troops of the Izmailovskii regiment), April, 1917, *ibid.*, 2nd ed., pp. 343–44; "O proletarskoi militsii" (On proletarian militia), May, 1917, *ibid.*, pp. 345–47.

[122] "O zadachakh proletariata v dannoi revoliutsii" (On the tasks of the proletarians in the revolution), April, 1917, *ibid.*, p. 337; "Pis'ma iz daleka" (Letters from afar), March, 1917, *ibid.*, pp. 329–30.

[123] "The path of the great October revolution...," *Peking Review*, 45 (November 8, 1960), 5–7. Translation of "Wei-ta shih-yüeh-ko-ming...," *Hung-ch'i*, 20–21 (November 1, 1960), 14–17.

it mentioned no police.[124] One explanation may be that the concept of government includes both bureaucracy and police. Or, the Chinese think little of civilian arms like police as a hindrance of revolution. Their own operation in the rise to power suffered from no police harassment. In general, the Russians do not talk about such civil war techniques as demolition of the state apparatus; because, if they do, they would detract from their emphasis on parliamentarianism. For all that, Khrushchev still enunciated that it is in the capitalist states, where a "dread military and police machine" exists, that civil war proves inevitable.[125]

Violence and Counter-violence

Although war is a form of violence, the two are different categories: the former is a social phenomenon, the latter a psychological attribute. In the communist literature there appears a limited but elucidating treatment of violence. The central idea is that from the moral point of view, war is not to be condemned, because a wholesome end may justify otherwise abominable means. Before proceeding further, we shall define three allied terms. According to the *Soviet Encyclopedia*, violence pertains to a "criminal action against persons, including assault, battery or other activities accompanied by an application of physical force."[126] "Terror" is described as a "policy of frightening a class or political enemy by way of coercive measures."[127] "Terroristic action" means an attempt upon life, or other forms of violence with politicians or other state figures as its objects; it is committed out of public motives."[128] The first is a term in penal law, while the latter two are more political than juridic. But violence also has its definite revolutionary import.[129] Once Lenin was asked if his partisans (Social Democrats) should dispense with violence in carrying out their mission, he replied curtly: "Of course, they cannot";[130] "to promise to do away with terror would

---

[124] *Sino-Soviet Dispute*, p. 82.

[125] "Otchetnyi doklad Tsentral'nogo Komiteta...," *Pravda*, February 15, 1956.

[126] *Bol'shaya sovetskaya entsikopediya* (The great Soviet encyclopedia; 2nd ed.), vol. 29, p. 193.

[127] *Ibid.*, vol. 42, p. 366.

[128] *Ibid.*

[129] "When violence is committed by the toiling and exploited masses, it is the kind of violence we approve," taught Lenin; "Doklad o deyatel'nosti soveta narodnykh kommisarov" (Report on the activities of the Council of People's Commissars), January 24, 1918, *Sochineniya* (Collected works; 3rd ed.), vol. 22, p. 208. Stalin said: "The GPU is necessary for the revolution and will continue to exist to the terror of the enemies of the proletariat," in "Beseda s inostrannymi rabochimi deligatsiyami" (Interview with foreign workers' delegation), his *Sochineniya* (Collected works), vol. 10, p. 234.

[130] Lenin, *Sochineniya* (Collected works; 4th ed.), vol. 22, p. 314.

be to fool either ourselves or others."[131] "As a matter of principle, we never refrain from resorting to terror," Lenin declared at the very inception of his revolutionary life.[132]

In 1957, a communist journal published a theretofore classified speech by Lenin (to a Cheka meeting) in which he stated: "History has proved that it is impossible to gain a victory without violence."[133] The latter is legitimate in two situations: one is to win the battle in civil war, the other to win the battle in world war.[134] Lenin deprecated individual terror perpetrated out of the political context.[135] The use of violence has its justification in crippling the resistance of the enemy and forcing him to capitulate. Trotskii urged the proletarians to appeal to terror against counterrevolutionaries in order to demoralize them.[136]

In the Sino-Soviet dispute, the problem of violence was brought up by China to vindicate her view on civil war.[137] In general, her theory on this subject does not go beyond where Lenin and Trotskii had left off. In all there are four cardinal points in China's contention. In the first place, Peking cited Lenin's well-known dictum on revolutionary and counterrevolutionary outrages.[138] The initial assertion is that violence is first used against the proletariat and this impels the latter to take measures for self-preservation. In the second place, the Chinese leaders averred that the system of capitalism itself is an embodiment of violence. Its oppression of the toilers is said to be maleficent and inexcusable. This standing agony inflicted by the exploitative state comes to an end only when "it is overthrown and replaced by the people's

---

[131] *Idem*, "Pis'mo D. I. Kurskomu po voprosu o terror" (Letter to D. I. Kurskii on the question of terror), *ibid.*, 3rd. ed, vol. 27, p. 269.

[132] *Idem*, "Chego nachat'?" (Begin with whom?) May, 1901, *O voine, armii i voennoi nauke* (On war, army and military science; 2nd ed.), p. 32.

[133] *Idem*, "Rech' na chetvertoi konferentsii gubernskykh chrezvyzhainykh komissii, fr. 6, 1920" (Speech to the fourth conference of the provincial extraordinary commissions, February 6, 1920), *Kommunist*, 5 (April, 1957), 19–23. Also in his *O voine, armii i voennoi nauke* (On war, army and military science; 2nd ed.), p. 664.

[134] Lenin, *Sochineniya* (Collected works; 4th ed.), vol. 21, p. 276.

[135] *Ibid.*, vol. 35, p. 191.

[136] Trotskii wrote: "Terror as the demonstration of the will and strength of the working class is historically justified precisely because the proletariat was able thereby to destroy the political conscience of the intelligentsia, pacify the professional men of various categories and gradually subordinate them to its own aims within the field of their specialities," in his article "Voennye spetsialisty i Krasnaya Armiya" (Military specialists and the Red Army), *Izvestiya*, January 10, 1919.

[137] John S. Reshetar, *Western Political Quarterly*, 14 (September, 1961, supplement), 74.

[138] *Sino-Soviet Dispute*, p. 94. "We support proletarian violence," wrote Lenin, "O lozunge 'razoruzheniya'" (On the slogan of disarmament), October, 1916, *O voine, armii i voennoi nauke* (On war, army and military science; 2nd ed.), p. 312. Elsewhere he stated: "Only Christian anarchists and Tolstoyists opposed revolutionary violence," in "Proletarskaya revoliutsiya i renegat Kautskii" (Proletarian revolution and renegade Kautsky), November, 1918, *ibid.*, p. 546.

state, the state of the dictatorship of the proletariat of that country."[139] Such a straight equation of capitalism with violence does not appear in Lenin's writings, although a strong allusion to that effect is not lacking.[140]

In the third place, it is argued that the concept of proletarian ascendancy has "revolutionary violence" as its "root."[141] This view is advanced to counter the non-violence idea as implied in parliamentarianism. The perpetuation of the status quo in the capitalist world is to freeze exploitation. It is only by removing forcibly the shackles of such oppression that the workpeople can be emancipated. In the fourth place, an issue was made by Peking with regard to violence to capture the state power and violence to build up a state afterwards. *Hung-ch'i* contended that the two must not be confused because while state-building ought to be peaceful, the avenue to the seat of power cannot but be violent.[142] Peking impugned the Kremlin leaders for their over-stressing the democratic way of coming to power. Citing Lenin, it reminded Moscow time and again that the "reactionary classes themselves are usually the first to have recourse to violence; they are the first to place the bayonet on the agenda."[143] Moreover, it warned, the new devices like "atomic bombs and rocket weapons symbolize new means in store for the downtrodden."[144] In meeting the threat, the workers are bound to avail themselves of more vigorous measures, too. Parliamentarianism is to persuade them to suffer and not to rataliate, it was charged. Civil violence,[145] in a word, is the hallmark of all great

[139] *Sino-Soviet Dispute*, p. 94.

[140] Lenin wrote: "For politically imperialism is in general striving toward violence," *Selected Works* (New York: International publishers, 1945), vol. 5, p. 83. *See* also his "O lozunge 'razoruzheniya'" (On the slogan of disarmament), October, 1916, *O voine, armii i voennoi nauke* (On war, army and military science; 2nd ed.), p. 313; here it is written that capitalist society is a terroristic society: "Voennaya programma proletarskoi revoliutsii" (Military program of the proletarian revolution), September, 1916, *ibid.*, p. 305. Lenin also taught that one must avail oneself of the bourgeois democracy's freedom offered the citizens to destroy that democracy," *see* "Otvet P. Kievskomu" (A reply to P. Kievskii), August–September, 1916, *ibid.*, pp. 292, 293; "Proletarskoi militsii" (Proletarian militia), May, 1917, *ibid.*, p. 746.

[141] Yu Chao-li, "On imperialism as the source of war...," *Peking Review*, 15 (April 12, 1960), 17–24. Translation of "Lun t'i-kuo chu-i...," *Hung-ch'i*, 7 (April, 1 1960), 1–12.

[142] Commentary on the issuance of the fourth volume of *Mao-Tse-tung hsüan-chi* (Selected works) in *Hung-ch'i*, 21 (November 2, 1960), 5; also in "Chung-a lien kuo jen-min ti chan cheng yu-i wan sui" (Long live the Sino-Albanian military friendship), *Jen-min jih-pao*, October 6, 1960.

[143] Lenin, "Dve taktiki sotsial-demokratii v demokraticheskoi revoliutsii" (Two tactics of the Social-Democrats in the democratic revolution), June–July, 1905, *O voine, armii i voennoi nauke* (On war, army and military science; 2nd ed.), pp. 102–8.

[144] *Sino-Soviet Dispute*, p. 94.

[145] The very concept of the Soviet was initially one of organizing the revolutionary violence of the proletariat, *see* Lenin, "Pis'ma iz daleka" (Letters from afar), March, 1917, *O voine,*

revolutions; it is the common denominator of the Chinese and Russian kinds, as Lin Piao said.[146] We may sum up by saying that the Chinese have regarded violence as inevitable for the conquest of political power, while the Russians, on their part, are double-tongued in the matter. This is understandable since Khrushchev did not want to be discredited in his diplomacy of detente.

Diversifying the Forms of Struggle

Despite differences of stress the Soviet and Chinese outlooks on the problem of civil war have shown marked analogy. On the one hand, in his address to the Twentieth Congress, Khrushchev did not refute the necessity of forceful solutions of class antagonism. This is how he put it: "The use or non-use of violence in the transition to socialism depends on the resistance of the exploiters, on whether the exploiting class itself resorts to violence, rather than on the proletariat."[147] On the other hand, Peking thought that it was "in the best interests of the people if the transition to socialism is by peaceful means. "It would be wrong not to make use of such a possibility when it occurs."[148] The supreme objective of world communism, in Lenin's words, requires that the "methods of struggle with an enemy be adjusted in tune with the altered circumstances."[149] Hinging on local variations, the revolutionists ought to search for the handiest ways. As suggested by the Conference of the Ruling Communist Parties (December, 1960), "Marxism-Leninism calls for a creative application of the general principles of the socialist revolution" according to the "concrete conditions of each country."[150] At the same time it cautioned that one should eschew "blind imitation of the policies and tactics" as practiced by others.[151] In one of his early works, Mao wrote that the "manner of battle short of a shooting

armii i voennoi nauke (On war, army and military science; 2nd ed.), p. 328. *Voprosy sovetskogo gosudarstva i prava* (Problems of Soviet state and law) (Moskva: Izd-vo Leningradskogo Universiteta, 1955), p. 18.

[146] *China after Mao*, p. 236. Lenin said that not a single revolution has been carried out short of civil war and that no Marxist ever believed in a warless revolution; *Sochineniya* (Collected works; 4th ed.), vol. 9, pp. 12, 31–32. Lenin's violence theme is elaborated in the article "Long live Leninism," *Sino-Soviet Dispute*, pp. 94–8.

[147] "Otchetnyi doklad Tsentral'nogo Komiteta ...," *Pravda*, February 15, 1956.

[148] *Sino-Soviet Dispute*, p. 103.

[149] Lenin, "Partizanskaya voina (Partisan war), September, 1906, *O voine, armii i voennoi nauke* (On war, army and military science; 2nd ed.), pp. 149–50; "Uroki moskovskogo vosstaniya" (The lessons of Moscow revolt), August, 1906, *ibid.*, p. 144; "Uroki kommuny" (The lessons of the Commune), March, 1908, *ibid.*, p. 179; "Voennaya programma proletarskoi revoliutsii" (Military program of the proletarian revolution), September, 1916, *ibid.*, p. 307. *See* also N. P. Mamai, "Predislovie" (Introduction), *ibid.*, p. 8.

[150] "Deklaratsiya soveshchaniya predstavitelei...," *Pravda*, November 22, 1957.
[151] *Ibid.*

war is also in order."[152] Perhaps no revolutionist may stick to one specific method alone. Tactical retreat as a *modus operandi* is deemed by Lenin vital to the goal of socialism.[153] Yet different appraisals of a given situation often lead the communists to accentuate either violence or non-violence; and as often they accuse each other of deviating from Marxism-Leninism.

The dialogue between Moscow and Peking intimate that they are in accord regarding the objective of socialist triumph but are unable to agree on the ways and means to achieve it. With Moscow the center of gravity is on gradualism, while Peking persistently clamors for mass violence to topple capitalist regimes.[154] The Soviet theme was spelled out in some detail by the Moscow conference (January, 1961) and the Rome conference of communist parties of Western Europe (March, 1960). In the Italian capital, the conference suggested a "minimum program" which embraces the following planks: nationalization of monopoly-industries, decentralization of the economy, greater workers' initiative and role in planning, popular control of investment, and agrarian reforms.[155] The proposed measures, according to the Soviet writers, were derided by the "Chinese dogmatists."[156] The Moscow gathering calls for "nationalization of the key branches of the economy and democratization of their management, the use of the entire material resources to satisfy the needs of the populace."[157] That there is the danger of isolating the communist parties from the masses through dogmatic and bookish application of Marxist-Leninist theory was voiced by the 1957 Moscow declaration.[158] It was felt by Butenko and Plechin, both academicians, that the favorable "east wind" on the international horizon would have its effect within the imperialist nations, because the bourgeoisie dared not face the music and elected to retire from the helm of state.[159] In the new epoch circumstances will be such as to enable the proletariat to walk quietly onto the seat of power to which they are said entitled by the rule of dialectical law.

[152] Mao, "Chung-kuo ko-ming yü chung-kuo kung-ch'an tang" (Chinese revolution and the Chinese Communist Party), *Mao Tse-tung hsüan-chi* (Selected works), 1952, vol. 2, p. 606.
[153] Lenin, "O levom rebyachestva" (Left communism, an infantile disorder), *Sochineniya* (Collected works; 4th ed.), vol. 27, pp. 291–99.
[154] James O'Gara, *Commonweal*, 77 (March 22, 1963), 654.
[155] Belyakov and Burlatskii, "Leninskaya teoriya ...," (Lenin's theory of socialist revolution in present conditions), *Kommunist*, 13 (September, 1960), 20.
[156] *Ibid.*
[157] "Zayavlenie soveshchaniya predstavitelei...," *Pravda*, December 6, 1960.
[158] "Deklaratsiya soveshchaniya predstavitelei...," *ibid.*, November 22, 1957.
[159] A. Butenko and V. Plechin, "Sovremennyi epokh i tvorcheskoe razvitie marksizma-leninizma" (Contemporary epoch and creative development of Marxism-Leninism), *Kommunist*, 12 (August, 1960), 15.

The burden of the Chinese polemics is definitely on armed rebellion. The Maoists dismissed peaceful tactics as a rare exception.[160] It is only once in a blue moon, they suggested in effect, that a revolution could erupt without carnage.[161] To employ only bloodless methods would doom proletarian internationalism. Peking could not fail to observe that its opponent on occasions held a brief for the forcible riddance of the *ancien regime*. But the infrequence with which the Soviets referred to it was taken by Peking as refusal thereof. "The peaceful development of the revolution should never be regarded as the only possibility and it is therefore necessary to prepare at the same time for the other possibility," declared Peking.[162] This statement clearly distorted the position of Moscow, for neither Khrushchev nor any of the rendezvous of communist parties abjured the removal of bourgeois ruler by arms. The Chinese distortion, in turn, evoked counter-distortion. Owing to the standing advocacy by Peking of revolutionary war, the Soviets chose to overlook its few references to peaceful struggle. Matkovskii wrote that "Lenin demonstrated the unsoundness and harm of the slogan of the leftist who rejected the idea of communist compromise with other parties and groups."[163] Adducing words from Lenin, other Soviet writers berated the Chinese in this way: "Lenin wrote that for a genuine revolutionary the greatest danger, nay the only danger, is to overrate revolutionary ardors."[164] There are acknowledged ambits beyond which the true Marxist-Leninists just cannot go. They should not "break their necks," or "write the word 'revolution' in block letters," or "exalt revolution as something almost divine," or "lose their heads."[165] This kind of charge, though not fair to the Chinese, does point to the drift of their argument.[166]

---

[160] Lenin said that parliamentarianism was once in a while needed in the struggle for power of the socialists, "Partizanskaya voina" (Partisan war), September, 1906, *O voine, armii i voennoi nauke* (On war, army and military science; 2nd ed.), p. 150. Also in *Sochineniya* (Collected works; 5th ed.), vol. 14, pp. 1–2.

[161] *Sino-Soviet Dispute*, p. 103. "Every great revolution cannot do without civil war," said Lenin, in "Voennaya programma proletarskoi revoliutsii" (Military program of the proletarian revolution), September, 1916, *O voine, armii i voennoi nauke* (On war, army and military science; 2nd ed.), p. 302. "Is there a war-free revolution?" he asked; *ibid.*, p. 305.

[162] *Sino-Soviet Dispute*, p. 103.

[163] N. Matkovskii, "ideinoe oruzhie kommunizma" (The ideological weapon of communism), *Pravda*, June 12, 1960.

[164] Belyakov and Burlatskii, "Leninskaya teoriya ...," (Lenin's theory of socialist revolution in present conditions), *Kommunist*, 13 (September, 1960), 20–24.

[165] *Ibid.*

[166] Tsou Tang, *Orbis*, 8 (Spring, 1964), 44.

CIVIL WAR IN COMMUNIST WORLD STRATEGY

Civil War and Capitalist Stability

The controversy on civil war of the two disputants reveals principally their tactical differences. Inspired by world communism, both are in agreement on the call for diversified modes of struggle. But they have not concurred as to whether one method is superior to another for the present epoch. The manner in which each interprets the world situation is right in its own way. Building on the assumption that the East is now outstripping the West in terms of military power and industrial capacity, Khrushchev and Mao proceeded to draw their respective conclusions. The former was persuaded that since the bloc has become better situated, it would be either imprudent or pointless to rush ahead with plans for world communism. Refuting him, Mao felt that the propitious moment for one to take bold action is when he rides on the crest of the wave. It is hard to tell which of the two judgments is superior, and harder yet is it to dismiss either view as senseless. The accusation unfolded in the Sino-Soviet dialogue shows that each seeks to falsify the other's stand. The low-risk policy preferred by Moscow has been deemed overcautious by the Chinese. Mao taught that "one must know how to wrest the initiative from the enemy, and more important, how to make the best use of the initiative after he gets it."[167] At the same time, any margin in the balance of forces "is not absolutely constant."[168] A strategist should lose no time in turning that margin into his own victory at the earliest moment. To hesitate is to forfeit one's chances. Now that the Soviet bloc has gotten an edge over its adversary, it cannot afford to sit down and idly talk peace.

But Mao did not press for an inter-bloc showdown. Peking stated clearly: "We do not need war, absolutely would not start a war, and absolutely must not, should not, and could not encroach one inch on the territory of a neighboring country."[169] We ought to note, however, that the war Peking here categorically disavowed is war between China and other countries. With respect to war inside the capitalist states, Peking has different thoughts. This is rather to be expected, for how could China care for the internal calm of a bourgeois regime. It only

---

[167] "Lun chih chiu chan" (On protracted war), *Mao Tse-tung hsüan-chi* (Selected works), 1952, vol. 2, p. 459.

[168] *Ibid.*, p. 457.

[169] "Long live Leninism," *Peking Review*, 17 (April 26, 1960), 14; also in *Sino-Soviet Dispute*, p. 97. *See* also "The different lines on the question of war and peace: comment on the open letter of the Central Committee of the CPSU, by the Editorial Departments of *Renmin Ribao* and *Hongqi*," *Peking Review*, 47 (November 22, 1963), 12.

suits her well if the toilers of each state should arise and massacre their rulers.[170] Perhaps the most desirable way to "bury" the imperialists is to appeal to the workers to do that in their own country.[171] This view has been shared by both Chinese and Russian communists, for they called for the "broadest united front" to thwart the alleged aggressive designs of the capitalist governments.[172] The mighty power of the revolutionary masses of people, it is averred, has indeed forestalled world war, which could otherwise have broken out.[173] On account of the block put up by the workers, the imperialists are said to be forced to wage a "cold war," "without risking going over to open direct action."[174] Lu Ting-yi, the now deposed propaganda chief of the Peking regime, wrote that world conflict could be warded off "only by linking up the struggles of the proletariat in the capitalist countries."[175] Revolutionary struggles, so-called, include (in Raymond Garthoff's words) "subversion, sabotage, colonial rebellion, and satellite aggression. These are not dependent on a formal war or total involvement nor on the risks inherent in total war."[176] The chances of world war are in inverse ratio to civil war: the more likely the civil war, the less likely the world war. Or, the less probable the civil war, the more probable the world war.

Civil Peace Dampening the Revolutionary Spirit

Civil war inside the capitalist country is highly welcomed by Peking because it is to the advantage of the proletariat of the world to enervate the imperialist camp. In order to make civil war possible, it is necessary to cultivate the fighting morale among the masses.[177] *Jen-min jih-pao* stated that "revolutionary spirit is the core of Marxism-Leninism."[178] The slogan of no civil war, it is written, should not be taken to mean

---

[170] "A basic summing-up of the experience...," *Sino-Soviet Dispute*, pp. 162–67; translation of "Chung-kuo jen-min ko-ming...," *Hung-chi' i*, 20–21 (November 1, 1960), 1–13.

[171] Lenin was very articulate on this point, *see* his "I vse rossiiskii s'ezd sovetov rabochikh i soldatskikh deputatov" (The first session of the Soviets of Workers' and Soldiers' Deputies), June, 1917, *O voine, armii i voennoi nauke* (On war, army and military science; 2nd ed.), p. 382.

[172] "The path of the great October revolution...," *Peking Review*, 45 (November 8, 1960), 5–7; translation of "Wei-ta shih-yüeh ko-ming...," *Hung-ch'i*, 20–21 (November 1, 1960), 14–17.

[173] "Give full play to the revolutionary spirit of the 1957 Moscow declaration," *Sino-Soviet Dispute*, p. 172. Translation of "Fa yang i-chiu wu-ch'i mo-ssu-k'o...," *Jen-min jih-pao*, November 21, 1960.

[174] Iu. Frantsev, "Problemy voiny i mira...," *Pravda*, August 7, 1960.

[175] "United under Lenin's banner," in *Long Live Leninism* (Peking: Foreign languages press, 1961), p. 103.

[176] *Soviet Military Doctrine* (Glencoe, Ill.: Free Press, 1953), pp. 11–12.

[177] Victor Zorza, *Guardian*, January 7, 1963, p. 7.

[178] "Give full play to the revolutionary spirit of the 1957 Moscow declaration," *Sino-Soviet Dispute*, p. 172. Translation of "Fa yang i-chiu wu-ch'i mo-ssu k'o...," *Jen-min jih-pao*, November 21, 1960.

civil peace, for a compromise between the opposing interests goes against the very essence of class antagonism. Having Tito as its object, Peking impugned him along with those of his ilk for the apologia of domestic rapprochement which could only conduce to "tranquility" within the bourgeois body politic and could only dilute the proletarian faith in revolution.[179] The question was asked how the oppressed people in the imperialist countries could relax.[180] Not until the doomsday of the capitalists may peace and harmony reign there.[181] It will be recalled that the 1960 Moscow conference wrought out a formula to propitiate the "sectarians and dogmatists" (the Chinese), on the one hand, and "revisionists" (the Russians), on the other.[182] Having disagreed with impetuous proletarian internationalism, the document recommends that the dour spirit of revolution ought not to be depressed either.[183] The conference decried the moral demobilization of the people as abominable. Peking taunted Moscow with sacrificing the lofty goal of the revolution in return for myopic gains. It felt that the plea for parliamentarianism tended to pin the hope of the workers on the most frivolous handouts of the exploitative class. Gradually they would flock to the trade unions and thus deflect themselves from their path of revolt.[184] In truth, said Peking, the class armistice as propounded by the opportunists helps secure bourgeois peace; it serves to "lower the revolutionary standards of the peoples."[185]

The most vital task of the revolutionary Marxist-Leninist is to steel the will of the toiling masses and to point to them the irreconcilability of their interests with the interests of the capitalists.[186] Inter-class barriers can never be removed,[187] and any attempt to better industrial

---

[179] *Ibid.*, p. 87.

[180] *Ibid.*

[181] "The property-owning classes in the non-communist countries cannot be made to vanish by the wave of a magic hand," thought Mao; *see* K. S. Karol, *New Statesman*, 65 (March 22, 1963), 414.

[182] "The December 1960 81-party declaration was generally regarded as a compromise between the divergent theoretical positions which had arisen among the communist parties," wrote Leonard Schapiro, *India Quarterly*, 18 (January–March, 1962), 3. *See* also Norman MacKenzie, "Chinese crackers," *New Statesman*, 65 (February 1, 1963), 144.

[183] "Zayavlenie soveshchaniya predstavitelei...," *Pravda*, December 6, 1960.

[184] *Sino-Soviet Dispute*, p. 106.

[185] *Ibid.*, p. 110. *See* also the article "Two different lines on the question of war and peace: comment on the open letter of the Central Committee of the CPSU, by the Editorial Departments of *Renmin Ribao* and *Hongqi*," *Peking Review*, 47 (November 22, 1963), 15.

[186] On June 4, 1960, General Hsiao Hua, Deputy Chief of Political Affairs of the Chinese People's Liberation Army, stated that to be afraid of war and to oppose even just war would lessen our people's will to fight and increase the insolence of our adversaries; *see* Alexandre Metaxas, "China versus Russia," *Nation*, 191 (July 2, 1960), 12.

[187] Lenin, "Sozhalenie i styd" (Sorrow and shame), May, 1911, *O voine, armii i voennoi nauke*

relations is treacherous and cannot succeed. "We support the revolutionary wars of the oppressed people for their own liberation," declared Peking.[188] The revisionists, it was charged, strove to patch up class differences and thus enabled the bourgeoisie to continue their blood sucking.[189] This is to sell out the downtrodden. It will be noted that the Russians considered the new scientific developments along with the rise of the East as an index of the modern epoch. This view is subject to the Chinese derision for its undue weight placed on techniques rather than on man who, after all, contrives the techniques in the first place.[190] In his address marking Lenin's ninetieth birthday anniversary, Lu Ting-yi stated sardonically that the tenet of the so-called new epoch was to disclaim the "need for further revolutionary struggle in the transition to the higher stage of communism."[191] He regarded dedication to internationalism as the most redoubtable item in the workers' arsenals. In his view, the Soviets stressed material things to the neglect of the invincible and invisible power of the people who are the writers of history. This led them astray into the idealist camp. The disarmament program of the Soviet Government also came in for attack by Peking as (1) putting too heavy an accent on military hardware and (2) minimizing the potentials of the broad masses.[192] To spiritual demobilization there is added physical demobilization.[193] All this redounds to the advantage of the imperialists, the Chinese deplored.[194]

(On war, army and military science; 2nd ed.), p. 148; also in his *Sochineniya* (Collected works; 5th ed.), vol. 20, p. 246.

[188] *Sino-Soviet Dispute*, p. 110.

[189] Peking believed that Khrushchev's general line was leading the communist movement into a position where, ultimately, some form of capitalism would occur; *see* Norman Mac-Kenzie, *New Statesman*, 65 (February 1, 1963), 144.

[190] "Le marxisme affirme que les artisans de cette transformation du monde sont les hommes eux-mêmes par leur activité intellectuelle et practique" (Marxism holds that it is men who transform the world by their intellectual and practical activities), Henri Chambre, *op. cit.*, p. 9. *See* also Lenin, "Iz predisloviya k russkomu perevodu pisem K. Marksa k L. Kugel'manu" (Preface to the Russian translation of Marx's letters to L. Kugelman), February, 1907, *O voine, armii i voennoi nauke* (On war, army and military science; 2nd ed.), p. 162; "Rech' na shrokoi raboche-krasnoarmeiskoi konferentsii v Rogozhsko-Simonoskom raione, 13 maya 1920 g." (Speech to the joint conference of workers and red-army troops of the Rogozhsko Simonoskii district, May 13, 1920), *ibid.*, p. 688.

[191] *NACA*, April 22, 1960.

[192] Khrushchev, however, stated that disarmament would economically benefit the nations of the world, east or west; *Predotvratit' voinu, otstoyat' mir!* (Prevent war and defend peace!), p. 269. The remark was made in his address to the World Disarmament Conference, July 10, 1962.

[193] "To hold out the atomic scare is to disarm the anti-imperialist zeal" of the workers, thought the Chinese; *see* Leonard Schapiro, *India Quarterly*, 18 (January–March, 1962), 6.

[194] "Between national liberation and the struggle for peace and disarmament there exists a close relationship, because strengthening the former makes the latter so much easier," Khrushchev said; *Predotvratit' voinu, otstoyat' mir!* (Prevent war and defend peace!), p. 270.

Peking claimed that it alone has clung to true Leninism and chided the Soviets as ignorant of the ontology of communist philosophy.[195] Lenin's teaching that "without revolutionary theory there can be no revolutionary movement"[196] is adduced to prove the significance of the personal element, for no movement can prosper unless there is a popular base to support it. The matter which really counts in history is the people's enthusiasm; without it, little can be accomplished, let alone such a majestic task as revolution. Peking questioned the Soviets rhetorically just what brought about the November Revolution? In the first place, Peking answered itself, Lenin provided a sound revolutionary ideology; in the second place, the hearts of the Russians were kindled by the Bolshevik propaganda.[197] The Chinese contended the government of the Romanoffs would still exist, had Lenin and company denounced force.[198] "We are not pacifists, we have always declared that it is stupid to the extreme for the proletariat to promise to forego revolutionary war," Lenin wrote.[199] However, one must note that Khrushchev never disparaged the proletariat, for he advised socialist governments to "awaken the conscience of the people, enhance their vigilance, organize and strengthen their struggle against the aggressive policies of imperialists."[200] Yet, he did not seem to have the "Chinese Government's missionary zeal,"[201] for his advocacy of civil strife is not nearly as militant as Mao's.

Civil Peace Increases the Chances of World War

Peking considered that to negate war in general, besides disheartening the people, would be a bad strategy. It felt that the best way to keep the West from starting an armed invasion would be to incapacitate it. The edge of superiority of the East over the West can be even more enlarged through subverting the enemy. "The development of the revolutionary forces of the people ... and their successes in revolution

He further explained that disarmament meant the preclusion of modern weapons which the downtrodden people do not have anyway; thus only the imperialists are disarmed.

[195] James O'Gara, *Commonweal*, 77 (March 22, 1963), 654.

[196] Lenin, "Shto delat'?" (What is to be done?) 1901–1902, *Sochineniya* (Collected works; 4th ed.), vol. 5, pp. 319–24.

[197] *Sino-Soviet Dispute*, p. 107.

[198] It is interesting to note that once Stalin advised the Chinese communists to reconcile their differences with the Kuomintang. The advice was declined promptly. *See* Vladimir Dedjer, *Tito* (New York: Simon and Schuster, 1953), p. 322.

[199] Lenin, *Sochineniya* (Collected works; 4th ed.), vol. 23, pp. 360–61; also in *Kommunist*, 5 (April, 1957), 21.

[200] "Rech' t. N. S. Khrushcheva na III s'ezde...," (Khrushchev's speech to the Third Congress of the Romanian Workers' Party), *Pravda*, June 22, 1960; *Izvestiya*, June 23, 1960.

[201] Donald S. Zagoria, *The Sino-Soviet Conflict, 1956–1961*, p. 104.

are fundamental factors in preventing imperialism from launching a world war," wrote *Hung–ch'i*.[202] Those who can best tie the hands of the aggressors are the very people of the capitalist nations. Should the people there be submissive, the imperialists would feel free to embark on foreign adventures. The possibility of world war, therefore, is greatest when the enemy government has the maximum confidence in taking the country to war without any worry about unrest at home. To put it differently, stability inside the Western states tends to embolden rulers to disturb international peace. A good strategy is to seek to paralyze the enemy's ranks. The proletariat of each land, Peking felt, should turn on its own exploiters as was done in Russia after the first, and in China after the second, world conflict.[203] The argument is made more plausible by the paper-tiger theory, which postulated that the selfsame beast is as vulnerable internally as it is externally. By the theory Mao taught that one should not overestimate the potential of an adversary, for it is more apparent than real.[204] Perhaps that explains why the Chinese leader wished to "test the stability of the Western camp," an action which Khrushchev supposedly dissuaded him from taking.[205]

The last mentioned advice was tendered when Khrushchev visited Peking immediately after returning from his journey to Washington. He analyzed the world scene differently from Mao for he saw no imminent collapse in the countries he traveled to. Although he pointed out that the "American workers will eventually overthrow their government and hoist the banner of revolution,"[206] he did not refer to it as an event in sight. Moreover, civil war is of doubtful value, it has become too dangerous during the present epoch, for world war would easily evolve from it. True, as a "son of the October Revolution," Khrushchev cannot afford to be a professed man of peace. At a meeting of the party workers, he said that the Cuban type of insurgents must be buttressed through might and main, because they were burying the

---

[202] "A basic summing-up of the experience...," *Sino-Soviet Dispute*, p. 167. Translation of "Chung-kuo jen-min ko-ming...," *Hung-ch'i*, 20–21 (November 1, 1960), 1–13.
[203] *Ibid.*
[204] Mao, "Hsing-hsing chih-huo k'o-i liao-yüan" (A spark may start a conflagration), *Mao Tse-tung hsüan-chi* (Selected works), 1951, vol. 1, p. 105. Yu Chao-li, "The forces of the new are bound to defeat the forces of decay," *Peking Review*, 25 (August 19, 1958), 9. Translation of "Hsin-sheng li-liang i ting chan-sheng fu-hsiu li-liang," *Hung-ch'i*, 6 (August 16, 1958), 1–6.
[205] *Pravda*, October 1, 1959.
[206] Khrushchev's speech at Obnova (Bulgaria), May 18, 1962, *Predotvratit' voinu, otstoyat' mir!* (Prevent war and defend peace!), p. 88.

capitalists.[207] But, in doing this, he hastened to caution, care should be taken not to internationalize the conflict. It was intimated that the pledged assistance was rendered solely to deter the imperialists from intervention.[208] The course taken by the counter-intervention was defensive in essence. Here it is pertinent for us to observe that in the First World War Lenin counseled the socialists to turn the international war into civil war in each country.[209] Now Khrushchev did not think that the reverse course should be taken; besides, civil war itself is no longer needed for the proletarian seizure of power.[210] The Russians also thought that even if the imperialists intervened, one ought not plunge rashly into counter-measures, thus to precipitate a crisis. It is necessary to be wary and to be excited by no "slight aggravation of the international situation."[211] In a word, the likelihood of escalation of armed struggle was taken to heart by the Soviets.

On their side, the Chinese did not appreciate the likelihood of civil war ending up in a general conflict. According to their analysis, the calculated risk of an inter-bloc showdown may have to be taken. Behind the nuclear shield of the Soviet Union,[212] disturbances can be abetted, with relative impunity, inside the non-communist countries.[213] As Yu Chao-li saw it, the imperialists were full of Achilles' heels, and sat on a volcano.[214] Hence Moscow was reminded of the cardboard house of the West and urged to shelve the idea of the new epoch with its international comity.[215] After the Bucharest meeting, the Chinese urged an all-out offensive against the West including aid to civil wars, and dismissed the curtailment of arms as frustrating the proletarians

[207] "Marksizm-leninizm...," *Izvestiya*, January 8, 1961; "Za novye pobedy...," *Pravda*, January 7, 1961; *Kommunist*, 1 (January, 1961), 4–6.

[208] *Ibid.*

[209] Lenin, "Iz 'otkrytogo pis'ma Borisu Suvarinu'" (From an open letter to Boris Souvarine), December, 1916, *O voine, armii i voennoi nauke* (On war, army and military science; 2nd ed.), p. 322; N. P. Mamai, "Predislovie" (Introduction), *Ibid.*, p. 8.

[210] Otchetnyi doklad Tsentral'nogo Komiteta...," *Pravda*, February 15, 1956.

[211] D. Shevlyagin, "Oruzhiya srazheniya kommunisticheskikh partiyakh" (Fighting weapon of communist parties), *Sovetskaya Rossiya* (Soviet Russia), 5 (June 10, 1960), 5.

[212] Yu Chao-li, "The forces of the new are bound to defeat the forces of the decay," *Peking Review*, 25 (August 19, 1958), 9. Translation of "Hsin-sheng li-liang...," *Hung-ch'i*, 6 (August 16, 1958), 1–6.

[213] One author wrote: "Communist China can afford to be hostile and intransigent because this country, America, through words and deeds, has given the communist leaders cause to believe that the United States would not start a war against China"; *see* Y. L. Wu, *Orbis*, 6 (October, 1962,) 455–45. He also suggested that "since Chinese domestic policies and problems must be blamed on external forces, and since the maintenance of an arrogant and defiant attitude is believed to enlarge international prestige, a provocative posture toward the United States actually brings rewards," *ibid.*, p. 455.

[214] Yu Chao-li, "The forces of the new...," *Peking Review*, 25 (August 19, 1958), 9. Translation of "Hsing-sheng li liang...," *Hung-ch'i*, 6 (August 16, 1958), 1–6.

[215] *Sino-Soviet Dispute*, p. 90.

because it would defer their final triumph.[216] Li Fu-ch'un, Vice-Premier of China, in his speech on Vietnam Day in the Chinese capital suggested that it was the highest duty to extend fraternal succor to those fighting imperialism and that such a course proved the most effective way to win the East-West contest.[217] In defending their stand, the Chinese drew upon the 1960 Moscow declaration which denounced the hands-off policy on civil war as well as unwarranted audacity in intervention. The document demanded the "most determined international support, by both mass movement and the power of the socialist world system, to the revolutionary movements anywhere."[218] Likewise, Liu Ch'ang-sheng spoke to the World Federation of Trade Unions that to ward off world war "we should mainly rely on the struggle waged by the peoples of various countries."[219] In this way, he went on, the socialist forces would be augmented. The same line was previously followed by Liu Shao-ch'i who reported to the Eighth Congress of the Chinese Communist Party that any success scored by the proletariat inside the capitalist camp would "swell the strength of peace."[220]

Peking did not perceive any logical discrepancy between world tranquility, on the one hand, and civil war, on the other.[221] When one supports the first, it is not necessary that he stop supporting the second.[222] The more civil wars in the West, the less inter-bloc wars. In the aftermath of the collapse of the capitalist regimes from within there would come into being a growing number of socialist countries, and the imperialist domain would shrink still further. In his essay "On coalition government," Mao thought that peace in the several regions of the world depended on the balance of forces there. Japan's breaking away from the capitalist chain and becoming socialist would lessen the contingency of war in the Pacific area.[223] Similarly, if India were to be detached from the same chain, the imperialist frontiers would be pushed

---

[216] *Jen-min jih-pao*, June 29, 1960, editorial comment on the Bucharest Communique; Liao Ch'eng-chih's speech to the World Peace Conference (Stockholm), *ibid.*, June 10, 1960; Ch'en Yi's speech in Peking, *NCNA*, July 15, 1960.

[217] *NCNA*, September 6, 1960.

[218] "Zayavlenie soveshchaniya predstavitelei...," *Pravda*, December 6, 1960.

[219] *Sino-Soviet Dispute*, p. 126.

[220] *Jen-min shou-ts'e* (People's handbook, 1957), p. 23. On the communist tricky semantics of peace and war, *see* Peter Tang, *Orbis*, 5 (Spring, 1961), 15–16; Edgar Snow, *Look*, 25 (January, 1961), 86–104.

[221] "Splochenie pod znamenem marksizma-leninizma" (Unite under the banner of Marxism-Leninism), *Pravda*, November 23, 1960.

[222] It was said by the Chinese that "opposition to colonialism and striving for national independence should not be subservient to a policy of peaceful coexistence," *see* John Gittings, *International Affairs* (London), 40 (January, 1964), 65.

[223] *Mao Tse-tung hsüan-chi* (Selected works), 1953, vol. 3, p. 1086.

farther back yet and "world peace would ensue."[224] Should this process continue, as Mao believes it will, global war would not occur and communism would triumph. To this argument we must relate another strategical thinking of Mao's. In 1946, when he was asked by Anna Louise Strong if he felt the United States would attack the Soviets soon, he replied, the American action could take place only if Uncle Sam conquered the "vast intermediate zone." [225]His remarks on Japan and India just cited indicated his strategy of making inroads in the sphere of the West and pre-empting the area.[226] As *Hung-ch'i* said, the "socialist revolution cannot triumph at a single stroke in all the countries simultaneously"; it depends on peoples' "efforts and their preparation for revolution."[227] The problem, however, involves indirect aid to stir up internal troubles and assist the rebels. The Chinese concept of world revolution is a series of national revolutions executed by the proletarians concerned, with material and moral props from the communist bloc. It does not seem that China intends to release her armed blue-ants to overrun capitalist lands in an attempt to communize them.[228]

---

[224] *Ibid.*, p. 1087.

[225] *Idem, Selected Works*, vo. 5, p. 99.

[226] Charles Malamuth, "Mao's theory of intermediate zones," *Communist Affairs*, 4 (July–August, 1964), 5.

[227] "A basic summing-up of experience...," *Sino-Soviet Dispute*, p. 167. Translation of "Chung-kuo jen-min ko-ming...," *Hung-ch'i*, 20–21 (November 1, 1960), 1–13.

[228] One author wrote that the Chinese intend to export proletarian revolution; *see* Axel Heyst, *Contemporary Review*, 204 (August, 1963), 76. It appears to the present writer that such a concept of exporting revolution can only imply military and technical assistance to communist rebels in other countries. Except for Korea the People's Liberation Army of China has not marched across international boundaries to overthrow non-communist regimes.

CHAPTER V

WARS OF NATIONAL LIBERATION AND LOCAL WARS

WORLD PEACE AND WARS OF NATIONAL LIBERATION

The Significance of National Liberation

The Chinese *min-tsu chieh-fang* and the Russian *Natsional'noe osvo-bozhdenie*, although translated as "national liberation," have their peculiar connotations. Should we make bold to use clumsy English, we may render the former something like the "release and unwinding of the people and race," and the latter as the "deliverance and unstringing of a nation."[1] To a man on the street in Moscow or Peking, the word "liberation" signifies the fight of an enslaved people for their manu-mission. He supposes, first, some forces which take away freedom and, second, the struggle required to win it back. However, not all liberations sought for by masses are national in substance, because a mere resistance to a despotic rule which has no foreign backing is properly an intra-national affair of two opposing forces. Here is involved nothing national in the sense of one nation vis-à-vis another.

The earliest employment of the term "national liberation," insofar as this writer can ascertain, was made by Lenin in the middle of 1915. His essay "Sotsializm i voina" (Socialism and war) refers to it as a

---

[1] "In the period of imperialism, there developed national liberation movements of the colonial and dependent nations. National sentiment of the people was directed at fighting feudalism and colonial oppression. This is progressive." *See* "Natsionalizm" (Nationalism), *Politicheskii slovar'* (Political dictionary; 2nd ed.), p. 378. "When imperialism obtained, national colonialism grew out of the disconnected struggles against national oppressions into a general and international movement of emancipation from imperialism of the subdued people in the colonial and dependent nations. The interests of proletarian movements in the capitalist countries and national liberation movements in the colonies need to be combined into a common front of war with imperialism." *See* "Natsional'no-kolonial'nyi vopros" (National-colonial problem), *ibid.*, 1st ed., p. 370. Lenin also used the term "national war" to denote the pre-capitalist war between national states fought for the sake of dynastic interests alone. *See* Lenin, "Iz 'otkrytogo pis'ma Borisu Suvarinu'" (From an open letter to Boris Souvarine), December, 1916, *O voine, armii i voennoi nauke* (On war, army and military science; 2nd ed.), pp. 320–21.

military secession of the colonies from their mother country.[2] Wars
undertaken for this purpose, he wrote, were always defensive and, on
this ground, must be regarded as lawful. It mattered little, in his judgment, whether the dependent nations should fire the initial shot and
drive the imperialists at bay.[3] Such possible wars as those Morocco or
Algeria or Tunisia might declare on France, Ireland or India on England,
Iran or China or the Ukraine on Imperial Russia were national liberation wars, and hence just;[4] and the people who are made the objects
of bondage have every right to appeal to the flaming sword.[5]

Wars of national liberation, Lenin asserted, are an accompaniment
of imperialism.[6] In a letter to G. E. Zinoviev he observed that "it is
nonsense to imagine that under imperialism such wars can be counted
out."[7] The logical answer of the colonies to the question of self-
determination is to take the field and to eject the foreign settlers.[8]
He diagnosed that the twentieth century would be a century of national
wars,[9] and that with the liquidation of the thraldom of one people by
another a foundation would be laid for the universal communist
republic.[10] Clearly distinct from socialist revolution aimed at home-
grown exploiters is national revolution aimed at foreign-bred exploiters.[11]

Lenin's teachings just cited are followed by his disciples. In a monograph entitled "Evropeiskie tsivilizatory i Marokko" (European civil-
izers and Morocco), M. V. Frunze, Commissar of War in 1925–26,

[2] The essay was done in July-August, 1915, showing the stand of the Russian Social-
Democratic Labor Party toward the European War. This readily available essay can be found
in Lenin, *Sochineniya* (Collected works; 4th ed.), vol. 21, pp. 271–93; or *O voine, armii i
voennoi nauke* (On war, army and military science; 2nd ed.), pp. 256–69; 1st ed., vol. 1, pp.
417–36. The work was co-authored by Lenin and Zinoviev, being written in both German and
French, but now attributed to Lenin alone (in spite of Lenin's own statement of the co-author-
ship). *See* Lenin, "O karikature na marksizm i ob 'imperialisticheskom ekonomizme'" (On
the caricature of Marxism and the "imperialist economism"), August–October, 1916, *ibid.*,
2nd ed., p. 297.
[3] "Iz 'otkrytogo pis'ma Borisu Suvarinu'" (From an open letter to Boris Souvarine),
December, 1916, *ibid.*, p. 321; *see* also "Voina i revoliutsiya" (War and revolution), May, 1917,
ibid., p. 364.
[4] "Iz 'otkrytogo pis'ma Borisu Suvarinu'" (From an open letter to Boris Souvarine),
December, 1916, *ibid.*, pp. 320–21.
[5] *Ibid.*; also "Sotsializm i voina" (Socialism and war) July–August, 1915, *ibid.*, p. 256.
[6] "O broshiure Iunius" (On the brochure of Junius), July, 1916, *ibid.*, p. 261. Lenin emphatically regarded capitalism the basic cause of war, "Evropeiskii kapital" (European capital),
an essay originally appearing in *Vpered* (Forward), 13 (April 15, 1905), now in *ibid*, p. 71.
[7] "[Pis'mo k] G. E. Zinoviev" (A letter to G. E. Zinoviev), August, 1916, *ibid.*, p. 287.
[8] "O karikature na marksizm i ob 'imperialisticheskom ekonomizme'" (On the caricature
of Marxism and "imperialist economism"), August–October, 1916, *ibid.*, pp. 295–300.
[9] "Voennaya programma proletarskoi revoliutsii" (Military program of the proletarian
revolution), originally written in German, September, 1916, *ibid.*, p. 302.
[10] *Idem, Sochineniya* (Collected works; 4th ed.), vol. 30, p. 54.
[11] *Ibid.*, 5th ed., vol. 39, p. 327.

envisaged on the world horizon a broad front of national struggle of which Morocco, in her battle against the Spaniards, formed the shock force. "If she can hold on," the Commissar felt, "the entire colonial structure will end in smoke."[12] Through their success, the Moroccans would write a new chapter in man's history.[13] The devastating impact of national liberation on the imperialist regime is appraised so highly by the communists that they regard it the second most significant feature in the new epoch, ranking next only to the erection of the global system of socialism.[14] "The liberation effort of the people in slavery," alleged N. Y. Sushko and his associates, "symbolizes a dynamo of world revolution."[15]

National liberation has been considered instrumental in eradicating the "intrusive monopoly" and, along with proletarian revolution, "paving the way to peoples' democracy."[16] Owing to the fact that the compradors always work hand in glove with their foreign principals, the movement is against both the imperialists from abroad and the native parasites.[17] Hence the inseparable ligament of wars of national liberation and civil wars.[18] The theoretical basis therefor is laid down by Marx and Engels in the "Communist manifesto" which postulates that to the extent that one class ceases to oppress another class, one nation ceases to oppress another nation.[19] Like the killing of two birds with one stone, so to speak, the communists tend to consider the two kinds of war having practically the same objective.[20]

[12] The monograph appears in his *Izbrannye proizvedeniya* (Selected works, 1957), vol. 2, pp. 392–472; the citation is on p. 436. The work was painstakingly written shortly before he was ordered to undergo a fatal operation (in a Moscow hospital) by the Politburo.

[13] *Ibid.*, p. 442.

[14] *Programmye dokumenty bor'by za mir, demokratiiu i sotsializm* (The program of the documents of the struggle for peace, democracy and socialism) (Moskva: Gospolitizdat, 1964), p. 64.

[15] *Marksizm-leninizm o voine i armii* (Marxism-Leninism on war and army) (under the general editorship of N. Y. Sushko; 4th ed., Moskva: Voen. izd-vo, 1965), pp. 101–2.

[16] *Ibid.*, p. 103.

[17] "The liberation of the oppressed peoples in the dependent nations from the yoke of imperialism, and the establishment of actual equality between peoples constitute the essence of modern nationalism. This problem is related to the general problem of revolutionary struggle of the working class for proletarian dictatorship and has as its object the creation of friendship for the toilers," wrote I. Tsameryan, *see* "Natsional'yi vopros" (The national question), *Bol'shaya sovetskaya entsiklopediya* (The great Soviet encyclopedia; 2nd ed.), vol. 29, p. 296.

[18] "In fighting the enemies at home, we are fighting the counter-revolutionary element of all countries," Stalin wrote. See his "Beseda s inostrannymi rabochimi delegatsiyami" (Interview with foreign workers' delegation), *Sochineniya* (Collected works), vol. 10, p. 234.

[19] Marx and Engels, *Izbrannye proizvedeniya* (Selected works) (Moskva: Gospolitizdat, 1952), vol. 1, pp. 16–56 at 26.

[20] N. P. Mamai, "Predislovie (Introduction), in Lenin, *O voine, armii i voennoi nauke* (On war, army and military science; 2nd ed.), pp. 18–19. He argues that the aim of the "civil war in Russia was to liquidate international imperialism and counterrevolution inside the country."

How have Mao and Khrushchev viewed the question? On September 1, 1939, the Chinese statesman for the first time used the term *min-tsu chieh-fang* (national liberation) referring to the rebeldom he set up in various parts of China.[21] Strictly speaking, his was civil war, a war against the Kuomintang (KMT). However, the ideology has it that the KMT Government was nothing else but a tool of the imperialists.[22] Therefore, the term "national liberation" has been handily but incorrectly applied to civil war. The main import of the Chinese victory in 1949, thought L. Leont'ev, was the storming of the colonial citadel in that part of Asia.[23] To the Chinese, the banishment of the KMT was an epiphenomenon of the dismantling of imperialist sway. The conventional term of "civil war" is thought not designative enough for a Red revolution because it suggests merely one of the many political changeovers in the long history of China.

Nevertheless, the two concepts of "civil war" and "war of national liberation" are not identical, for each has a separate object. For propaganda purposes, it was perhaps more effective to point to some individual compatriots as the concrete target than to bandy vaguely about the notion of imperialism with which most people were unfamiliar. It was on these grounds that the Chinese communists in their drive to power centered their agitation on a few personages of the KMT regime. Only after the complete military success of the revolution has the new authority re-emphasized the slogan of national liberation.[24] In 1939, Mao differentiated "national liberation" from "people's liberation." The latter was civil war in the proper sense, while the former was illustrated by the "Soviet entry into Poland to emancipate the Ukrainians and Belorussians."[25] This observation of Mao's intimates that national liberation has as its kernel the conflict of diverse states, whereas civil war involves class rivalry within a national community. So much for Mao. On this part, Khrushchev did not make a distinction

[21] Mao, "Ho hsin-hua-she chi-che ti t'an-hua" (An interview with the reporters of the New China News Agency on current world politics), *Mao Tse-tung hsüan-chi* (Selected works), 1952, vol. 2, p. 548.

[22] *China after Mao*, p. 200. Lenin once referred to his "revolutionary workers and soldiers" as the "world liberation army"; see his "Rech' k soldatam na mitinge v izmailovskom polku" (Speech to the soldiers of the Izmailovskii regiment), April 23, 1917, *O voine, armii i voennoi nauke* (On war, army and military science; 2nd ed.), p. 343.

[23] L. Leont'ev, *op. cit.*, p. 49.

[24] According to Mao, the "vanguard of the Chinese national liberation was organized in Peiping under communist leadership on December 9, 1935." *See* his "Lun lien-ho cheng-fu" (On coalition government), April 24, 1945, *Mao Tse-tung hsüan-chi* (Selected works), 1953, vol. 3, p. 1037.

[25] Mao, "Su-lien li-i ho jen-lei li-i i-chih" (The interests of the Soviet Union are the interests of all mankind), September 26, 1939, *ibid.*, 1952, vol. 2, p. 560.

between the two types of war. He contended that such wars as has been waged by the Cuban rebels against the Batista administration were at once civil war and war of national liberation, since the people's enemy was the joint force of the domestic tyrants and American vampires.[26]

The Basis of Imperialist Power

In discussing civil war, we have noted how the communists foretold apodictically the aggravation of class enmity as a result of a hopeless situation within a capitalist nation. The enmity was to be assuaged by the capitalists through embarking on a course of colonial expansion. The argument derived from Lenin's theory of modern monopolism signifying the last leg of the capitalist journey. Since the main points of the theory were introduced early in this work, here we relate them only as they bear on the problem of national liberation. After the capitalists had squeezed the home market dry, they directed their attention to building up financial empires abroad.[27] They could turn out merchandise with little overhead, thanks to the cornucopia of the means of production, and sell it overseas.[28] On the material extracted from afar, the people back in the mother country could exist. Therefore, the nation's business pulse shifted its center of gravity. Formerly, at the time of free competition, the fulcrum of economy was the homeland where the industrial plants and enterprises were founded. It is admitted that there had been colonies even then.[29] But they played only second fiddle in sustaining the national life. Colonial acquisition was not vital to the needs of an idyllic society.[30] But with the advent of monopoly capitalism, the hub of economic activity had to move abroad just to keep the metropolis alive.[31] According to Karl Kautsky,[32] Otto Bauer,[33]

[26] "Marksizm-leninizm...," *Izvestiya*, January 8, 1961; "Za novye pobedy...," *Pravda*, January 7, 1961; *Kommunist*, 1 (January, 1961), 30.
[27] L. Leont'ev, *op. cit.*, p. 40.
[28] Lenin, "Imperializm, kak vysshaya statiya kapitalizma" (Imperialism as the highest development of capitalism), January–June, 1916, *Sochineniya* (Collected works; 4th ed.), vol. 22, pp. 17–80. The same source can be found in *idem, O voine, armii i voennoi nauke* (On war, army and military science; 2nd ed.), pp. 274–76.
[29] *Idem,* "O broshiure Iunius" (On the brochure of Junius), June, 1916, *ibid.*, p. 279; "K peresmotru partiinoi programmy" (Toward review of the party program), October, 1917, *ibid.*, p. 437.
[30] Lenin also mentioned capitalist (instead of imperialist) colonial wars; see "Voennaya programma proletarskoi revoliutsii" (Military program of the proletarian revolution), September, 1916, *ibid.*, p. 303.
[31] Rosa Luxemburg, *loc. cit.*
[32] "Krisentheorien" (The crisis theory), *Die Neue Zeit*, 2 (1901–1902), 133.
[33] Otto Bauer, *loc. cit.*

Jules Guesde,[34] John Hobson,[35] and Rudolf Hilferding,[36] the search for unprocessed goods was a crucial matter for the imperialists who were unable to live on their own resources.

The above analysis has been availed of today by the communists to measure Western strengths or rather weaknesses.[37] It is asserted that the intake of supplies from outside helps to keep life going in the metropolis, a metropolis which is a superstructure with its cornerstone thousands of miles away. The whole weight of the bulky political body is buttressed by pillars of imperialism. In this way, the very being, let alone the commonweal of the imperialists, relies on their financial empire. To let the colonies or economic dependencies secede voluntarily would be suicidal. The 1960 Moscow declaration visualized a "new stage ... in the unfolding of the sweeping crisis of capitalism" as one which arose out of the "national liberation struggle and the rapid disintegration of the colonial edifice."[38] The upsurge of anti-imperialism would spell the end of Western monopoly capitalism.[39] The oppressed and exploited masses on the continents of Asia, Africa and Latin America have awakened and become conscious of their identity. "As a result, the domain of imperialism has become daily smaller."[40] The Chinese asserted that from now on the "imperialist countries will have a very hard time."[41] Class contradictions which face them would multiply and get out of hand. Liu Shao-ch'i gloated over the alleged erosive effect of liberation wars on the still dominating nations.[42] He noted such consequences as further stimulating the growth of people's democracies, thwarting the scheme of the aggressors, and divesting

[34] *En Garde: Contre les Contrefacon, les Mirages et la Fausse Monnaie des Reformes Bourgeoises: Polemique* (On guard against the counterfeit coinage of the bourgeois reforms) (Paris: J. Rouff, 1911), pp. 175–76. It is to be noted that Lenin himself attributed his theory of imperialism to this French socialist. *See* Lenin, "Iz 'otkrytogo pis'ma Borisu Suvarinu'" (From an open letter to Boris Souvarine), December, 1916, *O voine, armii i voennoi nauke* (On war, army and military science; 2nd ed.), pp. 320–21.

[35] John Hobson, *loc. cit.*

[36] Rudolf Hilferding, *loc. cit.*

[37] I. Kuz'minov, "Ob ekonomicheskom polozhenii kapitalisticheskogo mira" (On the economic situation of the capitalist world), *Mezhdunarodnaya zhizn'* (International life), 10 (October, 1960), 48–56. *See* also a Chinese source: Chi Lung, "Mei-kuo ti chan-lüeh tsou-yu chiung tu" (The United States strategy is in a blind alley), *Shih-chieh chih-shih* (World knowledge), 23 (December 5, 1957), 1–10.

[38] "Zayavlenie soveshchaniya predstavitelei....," *Pravda*, December 6, 1960.

[39] George F. Kennan, *Saturday Evening Post*, 236 (October 5, 1963), 38, 40. There is a Sino-Soviet agreement, he wrote, on the wholesome effect (from the communist point of view) of colonial uprisings to oust the settlers.

[40] "The path of the great October revolution....," *Sino-Soviet Dispute*, p. 161; translation of "Wei-ta shih-yüeh ko-ming...," *Hung-ch'i*, 20–21 (November 1, 1960), 14–17.

[41] *Ibid.*

[42] His report to the Eighth Plenary Session of the Chinese Communist Party, September 15, 1956, *Jen-min shou-ts'e* (People's handbook, 1957), p. 22.

them of their rear.[43] This plight having obtained in the Western bloc, the East would greatly widen its margin of power.

The communists believe the seeds of self-destruction in capitalism have been sown. The imperialists can no longer maintain solid metropolitan centers or keep under foot their dependencies.[44] They all are now exposing themselves to blows from many quarters: the proletariat, the socialist camp, and the nationals of the colonies.[45] Imperialism is no more the same as existed a generation ago. In the Hungarian capital (June, 1960) Khrushchev told his audience that the capitalists have found themselves literally besieged, with the last front against them being now forged by the liberation revolutionaries.[46] Without colonial possession, they would fade away, since the stamina of the capitalist world wholly springs from there.[47] In strategic as well as economic terms, the outlying territories have stood the mother countries in good stead. Presently, the fountain of imperialism is desiccating as one dependency after another is gone. Otto Kuusinen descried the mounting power of the "world system of socialism," in vivid contrast with the enervation of the capitalist system.[48] However, he was only cautiously sanguine, because he observed that the newly freed people did not go socialist at once, but constituted merely a "zone of peace."[49] L. Leont'ev wrote that the more the imperialist powers tyrannized over the dependent nations, the more the latter were driven to the brink of revolt. In this way, he believed, the colonies were being transformed from a "reserve of the capitalists" to a "reserve of the proletariat."[50]

Because imperialism thrives on the overseas hinterland, the communist ideologues regard the war of national liberation just as momentous as civil war in bringing Western monopoly capitalism to its knees. In 1938, Mao in the essay "On protracted war" implored the world proletariat to gird its loins to storm the "backfield" (colonies) of the im-

---

[43] *Ibid.*

[44] "Imperialism does not have the former hinterland in the form of the colonial system," argued Iu. Frantsev, "Problemy voiny i mira...," *Pravda*, August 7, 1960.

[45] Lenin, "Sotsializm i voina" (Socialism and war), July–August, 1915, *O voina, armii i voennoi nauke* (On war, army and military science; 2nd ed.), p. 257.

[46] "Rech' t. N. S. Khrushcheva na III s'ezde...," (Khrushchev's speech to the Third Congress of the Romanian Workers' Party), *Izvestiya*, June 23, 1960; *Pravda*, June 22, 1960.

[47] Donald S. Zagoria, *Asian Survey*, 1 (April, 1961), 4.

[48] "Pretvorenie v zhizn' idei lenina" (To implement Lenin's ideas), *Pravda*, April 23, 1960.

[49] *Ibid.*; *see* also Brian Crozier, *International Affairs* (London), 40 (July, 1964), 449. "Both the Soviet and the Chinese communist parties are indeed handicapped by the fact that black African societies defy Marxian analysis, and by the scarcity of truly Marxist parties. The dependence of most African countries on Western aid and trade is an even more powerful barrier to communist expansion," wrote Crozier.

[50] L. Leont'ev, *op. cit.*, p. 98.

perialists.[51] When that mission is fulfilled, he waxed confident, colonialism will have disappeared without a vestige, and global revolution gone a long way toward its final success.

Such a delineation is roseate indeed, but the fact abides that none of the powers which have bestowed independence on their possession has gone broke due to the supposed disappearance of sources of exploitation. It looks as if the cornerstone has given way, but the superstructure stands. It is doubtful indeed if the colonies ever constituted the mainstay of the ship of the capitalist state as argued by the communists. If the capitalist powers are truly faced with famine for the loss of the supply bases, they would die a natural death in the not too distant future. But the standard line of Sino-Soviet propaganda did not support their theory. One may wonder, if the imperialists get weaker every day, why they are still described as strong enough to hatch up a new war against the peoples' democracies? The Russians even openly acknowledge the economic as well as the military might of the West. Khrushchev demonstrated with figures the growth of the industrial capacity of the capitalist world even though percentage-wise it is rated at a much slower pace than that of the Soviet Union.[52] Furthermore, both Peking and Moscow still insist upon the necessity of aiding civil wars to hasten the downfall of capitalism.[53] The Chinese have anticipated the difficulties in store for the wars of national liberation by admitting that the "struggle naturally has its twists and turns."[54] Neither do the Russians see the swift victory of national liberation,[55] for it is presaged that only toward the end of the present century will the dependent peoples be entirely emancipated.[56]

The Nature of Wars of National Liberation

A salient characteristic of the national liberation struggle is that it differs from proletarian struggle by the fact that it is neither planned, nor led, by the vanguard of the toilers. The organizers of the movement are heterogeneous with the bourgeois element dominating. This is so

---

[51] *Mao Tse-tung hsüan-chi* (Selected works), 1952, vol. 2, p. 434.

[52] "Otchetnyi doklad Tsentral'nogo Komiteta...," *Pravda*, February 15, 1956.

[53] Milton Kovnar, "The Sino-Soviet dispute: communism at the crossroads," *Current History*, 47 (September, 1964), 130.

[54] *Sino-Soviet Dispute*, p. 85.

[55] "Za torzhestvo tvorcheskogo marksizma-leninizma, protiv revizii kursa mirovogo kommunisticheskogo dvizheniya" (For victorious and creative Marxism-Leninism in opposition to revisionism in the world communist movement), *Kommunist*, 11 (July, 1963), 25.

[56] Kuusinen, "Predvorenie v zhizn' idei lenina" (To implement Lenin's ideas), *Pravda*, April 23, 1960.

because the workers in the underdeveloped countries are few in number and lack proper guidance.[57] These difficulties are considered hard to overcome. From the inception there may be a score of bourgeois intellectuals who are aware of the aggrieved status of their country. Then they proceed to form a skeletal society to disseminate the idea of nationalism; meanwhile some action may also be taken toward secession. Because the movement is multi-class in nature, being made up of factory hands, intelligentsia, shopkeepers, bureaucrats, petty bourgeoisie, and peasants, it constitutes a nation-wide campaign against imperialism and its running dogs.[58] As *Hung-ch'i* wrote, national liberation connotes a broad and torrential current in which each and every anti-foreign force has its role to play.[59] In an essay "The Chinese revolution and the Chinese Communist Party" (December, 1939), Mao suggested that the "kind of revolution ... in China as well as in all colonial and semi-colonial countries" is not the "dictatorship of the bourgeoisie" but the "united front of all revolutionary classes under the leadership of the proletariat."[60] It should be noted, however, that the initial cooperation of a motley group of native people may not invariably find itself under the hegemony of the "proletarians" as Mao well knew from his own experience early in his revolutionary career.[61] Sushko and his fellow authors observed that the elites in a modern national movement often go bourgeois,[62] and suggested, however impractically, that the peasantry should set the tone for the liberation war.[63]

Like civil war, the war of national liberation is described as a response to aggression, this time not from inside, but from outside. The imperialists have already committed outrage toward colonies by their mere control over them. "The independence war is to react against the

---

[57] *Marksizm-leninizm o voine i armii* (Marxism-leninism on war and army; 4th ed.), p. 102. It was written that the legacy of retarded economic development inherited by many countries from their colonial past resulted in lack of proletarian populace. Where the latter can be found, the number is wretchedly small and often poorly articulated." *Aziay i Afrika segodnya* (Asia and Africa of today), 7 (July, 1963), 4.

[58] *Marsizm-leninizm o voine i armii* (Marxism-leninism on war and army; 4th ed.), pp. 102-3.

[59] "The path of the great October Revolution...," *Sino-Soviet Dispute*, p. 161. Translation of "Wei-ta shih-yüeh ko-ming...," *Hung-ch'i*, 20-21 (November 1, 1960), 14-17.

[60] Mao, *Selected works* (New York ed.), vol. 4, pp. 96-97.

[61] Mao hence questioned the wisdom of helping the ruling bourgeoisie in the newly emerging nations on the part of the toiling people. *See* Michael Lindsay, *Annals of the American Academy of Political and Social Science*, 336 (July, 1961), 60; Leonard Schapiro, *India Quarterly*, 18 (January–March, 1962), 6.

[62] *Marksizm-leninizm o voine i armii* (Marxism-leninism on war and army; 4th ed.), p. 103.

[63] *Ibid.*, p. 102. The Soviets, nevertheless, maintain that the "numerous instances of inconsistency and vacillation by the national bourgeoisie do not furnish grounds for the national revolutionary movement." *See* S. Mikhailov, "Cuban revolution and Latin America," *International Affairs* (Moscow), 12 (December, 1963), 47, 48.

incursion and violence of the imperialists whose policy lies at the foot of popular unrest," wrote the Soviets.[64] Armed struggle is therefore the natural counteraction to foreign bondage; it is undertaken to recover what has been denied and not to obtain something the natives did not have inherently. On account of this, the war is righteous both by the law of nations in general, and by the Universal Declaration of Human Rights in particular. It was enunciated that absolutism and iron-handed rule impel one to clutch at arms as a last straw.[65] This spontaneous yearning cannot be stymied. National self-dertemination has become an overpowering stream in the world, which the imperialists seek vainly to stem, the communists regretted.[66] The intractable stand of the exploiters only shocks the conscience of the proletariat everywhere. The Soviets have invariably pretended that they hold the freedom of the downtrodden uppermost in their hearts. "The CPSU deems it its historical obligation to help peoples fighting for independence, thereby doing away with the colonial yoke," declared the Twenty-Second Congress.[67] These pretensions are belied by Soviet behavior on the Eurasian continent such as exemplified by the 1968 Czech invasion, an invasion which manifests communist imperialism beyond any doubt. Still another feature of the war of national liberation is that it assumes various forms comprising peasant revolts, street fighting, mass riots, partisan and pitched battles.[68] The Soviets cited Engels as saying that "people who desire their independence must not have any scruple in the choice of the battle methods."[69] It is reasoned that the irreproachability of the aims would redeem the foulness of almost any means.

World War and Wars of National Liberation

The Sino-Soviet ideologues considered the colonial front as at once their own most hopeful area of operation and the most vulnerable sector of

---

[64] *Marksizm-leninizm o voine i armii* (Marxism-Leninism on war and army; 4th ed.), p. 105; "La révolution est l'oeuvre d'hommes profondément engagés dans la vie sociale et politique, qui ne sont pas prolétariens" (Revolution is the work of men deeply engaged in social and political life, and not all of them are proletarians), wrote Henry Chambre, *op. cit.*, p. 11.

[65] *Mezhdunarodnie pravo v izbrannykh dokumentakh* (International law in selected documents) (Moskva: Izd-vo IMO, 1957), vol. 1, p. 207.

[66] It is highly interesting to note that once Lenin cited with approval the statement of Marx and Engels that "a people oppressing others cannot be free themselves," in Marx and Engels, "Emigrantskaya literatura" (Emigrant literature) which appears in their *Sochineniya* (Collected works), 2nd. ed., vol. 18, p. 509. The latter source is quoted in Lenin, *O voine, armii i voennoi nauke* (On war, army and military science; 2nd ed.), p. 269, and note 138 on p. 759.

[67] *Materialy XXII s'ezda KPSS* (Documentary materials of the Twenty-Second Congress of the CPSU) (Moskva: Gospolitizdat, 1961), p. 357.

[68] *Marksizm-leninizm o voine i armii* (Marxism-Leninism on war and army; 4th ed.), p. 105.

[69] Marx and Engels, *Sochineniya* (Collected works), vol. 9, p. 230, as quoted in *ibid.*

the enemy. The emancipatory voices in all continents have obliged the imperialists to call a general retreat. *Jen-min jih-pao* commented that the global "revolutionary struggle constitutes a mighty force for preventing imperialism from unleashing war."[70] The Chinese thought figuratively that the two wings of a ferocious vulture are being broken by the insurgence of the dependencies and the restive proletariat in the rear.[71] Colonial victories have double results in that they materialize the independence of many peoples as well as debilitate imperialism. To his partisans Liu Shao-ch'i reported that "any successful move in the war of national liberation would add to the strength of peace."[72] Whenever the communists parade with the word "peace," they have in view the subverting of the West through means little short of war.[73] It means that if the alleged aggressors were emasculated, conditions would prevail for the communists to rise and seize power.

Engaged in armed struggle in the name of peace, the communists deliberately spread confusion among the people. The 1960 Moscow declaration proclaimed that wars of national liberation would caponize the colonial powers and pledged to bolster such wars so as to extirpate the colonialists once and for all.[74] At the Stockholm World Peace Conference (December, 1961), the Chinese delegate Liu Ning-yi took exception to the disarmament proposal of the Soviet union, for he felt it would render nugatory the struggle for national liberation;[75] he declared vibrantly that it was through more and better arms that colonial insurrection could carry the day.[76]

World revolution has been neither disavowed nor deferred by the

---

[70] "Give full play to the revolutionary spirit of the 1957 Moscow declaration," *Sino-Soviet Dispute*, p. 172. Translation of "Fa yang i-chiu wu-ch'i mo-ssu-k'o...," *Jen-min jih-pao*, November 21, 1960.

[71] Michael Lindsay, *Annals of the American Academy of Political and Social Science*, 336 (July, 1961), 58.

[72] Report to the Eighth Plenary Session of the Chinese Communist Party, September 15, 1956, *Jen-min shou-ts'e* (People's handbook, 1957), p. 23.

[73] R. Hilsman, State Department, *Bulletin*, 47 (November 26, 1962), 808; Clarence A. Manning, *Ukrainian Quarterly*, 17 (Autumn, 1961), 262.

[74] "Zayavlenie soveshchaniya predistavitelei...," *Pravda*, December 6, 1960.

[75] To the Chinese charge that it minimized the importance of colonial struggle, the Soviet government countercharged that "the Chinese Party seeks to manipulate the national liberation movement to win, in the easiest way, popularity among the peoples of Asia, Africa and Latin America, even at the expense of the socialist camp." *See* "Oktrytoe pis'mo Tsentral'- nogo Komiteta Kommunisticheskoi Partii Sovetskogo Soiuza partiinym organizatsiyam, vsem kommunistam Sovetskogo Soiuza" (An open letter from the Central Committee of the CPSU, to the party apparatus and party members of the CPSU), *ibid.*, June 14, 1963. Further information can be found in Peter Tang, *Current History*, 45 (October, 1963), 227.

[76] William Griffith, *op. cit.*, p. 127.

communists; it is being executed in many ways and on many fronts.[77] Reinforced by proletarian revolts in the capitalist nations, the liberation war has been viewed as part and parcel of the international struggle. All military operations, national or proletarian, regular or irregular, are like the rivulets that converge to form the mighty channel of world revolution.[78] It ought to be noted that when the communists shout the slogan of "liberation of all mankind,"[79] they have in mind that if the imperialists be isolated by break-off of the colonies abroad and desertion of the workmen at home, a millennium will appear.[80] The November revolution is said to belong to the "general tidal wave of the world-wide struggle."[81] Civil wars in non-communist nations would stimulate the wars of national liberation by setting examples for the dependencies and demonstrating the fragility of the imperialist chain. Wars of national liberation, in turn, would stimulate civil wars,[82] for as Khrushchev said, the "success of the national liberation movement ... can strengthen" the socialist struggle inside the capitalist countries.[83] Hence the two types of war are unseverable in terms of aims and tactics. Kozlov stated that the "peoples of Asia, Africa and Latin America are taking an increasingly active part in international life and are making their contribution to the weakening of imperialism."[84] To the extent, he went on, that the movement grew mightier, the "positions of the working class would become stronger in the countries of monopoly capitalism."[85] As *Jen-min jih-pao* put it, the "national independence movements have greatly weakened the ... imperialist system," and the "October Revolution closely linked together" the proletarian movements at home and the national liberation movements abroad.[86]

---

[77] Chu-Hsin-min, "Between Moscow and Peiping," *Free China Review*, 10 (October, 1960), 16–17.

[78] K. Alexandrov, Institut zur Erforschung der UdSSR, *Bulletin*, 5 (October, 1958), 4; Tsou Tang, *Orbis*, 8 (Spring, 1964), 38.

[79] "The path of the great October revolution...," *Sino-Soviet Dispute*, pp. 159–61. Echoing the communists, Mme. Sun Yat-sen said: "We thank the Chinese Communist Party for its attempt to liberate mankind," *Jen-min shou-ts'e* (People's handbook, 1957), p. 35, in her address to the Eighth Plenary Session of the Chinese Communist Party as a guest speaker, September 26, 1956.

[80] "A proposal concerning the general line of the international communist movement, letter of the CCP in reply to the letter, dated March 30, 1963, of the CPSU," dated June 14, 1963, *Peking Review*, 25 (June 21, 1963), 14.

[81] "Zayavlenie soveshchaniya predstavitelei...," *Pravda*, December 6, 1960.

[82] *Voennaya strategiya* (Military strategy; 2nd ed.), p. 346.

[83] "Marksizm-leninizm...," *Izvestiya*, January 8, 1961; "Za novye pobedy...," *Pravda*, January 7, 1961; *Kommunist*, 1 (January, 1961), 34–35.

[84] F. P. Kozlov, "43-ya godoshchina velikoi...," (The 43rd anniversary of the great October socialist revolution), *Pravda*, November 7, 1960.

[85] *Ibid.*

[86] "Hold high the red banner of the October revolution, march from victory to victory,"

THE END OF THE COLONIAL SYSTEM

The Violent Overthrow of Colonial Authority

Is it possible for the colonies to dispense with war in the drive for independence? In answering this question, Moscow is more equivocal than Peking due perhaps to the fact that, if it held a brief for war, its alleged peace policy would be stultified.[87] Moscow's worry did not bother Mao whose jaundiced view on the Western world is near-proverbial. In an essay on democracy, he categorically insisted that there will be "either revolutionary war or colonial subordination; you have no third way."[88] Once the imperialists colonized a region, they would clench it without the faintest sign of quitting. During the later phase of the Algerian war, Peking demurred at Khrushchev's counsel of negotiations between France and the revolutionary leaders. In vitriolic terms, Peking ridiculed him as truly naive: "There has not been a single case in history in which the colonists withdrew ... of their own accord, nor will such a thing ever happen in the future."[89] Peking expected that the rebellion would evoke a chorus of war cries throughout the dependent world.[90] What was implicated in North Africa, emphasized the Chinese, concerned not the Algerian National Liberation Front alone, but the Olympian cause of proletarian internationalism. According to Mao, the masses in the colonies are "congenital revolutionists"[91] and to beguile them, as the Russians attempted to do, into seeking a compromise was preposterous.[92]

Providing miserly support to colonial wars against the imperialists, the Soviets were revolutionists in name only, charged Lu Ting-yi, the former propaganda chief of the Chinese Communist Party.[93] He said that all honorable Leninists must stand by the nationals of the colonies "without the slightest reservations."[94] He taunted the "son of the October revolution" (Khrushchev) that he had forgotten the teaching of Lenin, the founder of his own regime. Mao and company seemed to

---

Peking Review, 45 (November 8, 1960), 7–8; Sino-Soviet Dispute, pp. 161–62. Translation of "Kao-chu shih-yüeh ko-ming ti hung-ch'i...," Jen-min jih-pao, November 7, 1960.

[87] "The east wind," Economist, 20 (February, 1960), 695.

[88] "Lun hsin min-chu" (On new people's democracy), January, 1940, Mao Tse-tung hsüan-chi (Selected works), 1952, vol. 2, p. 652.

[89] "Victory belongs to the great African people," Hung-ch'i (March 6, 1960), 45.

[90] Donald S. Zagoria, The Sino-Soviet Conflict, 1956–1961, p. 213.

[91] Mao, "Lun hsin min-chu" (On new people's democracy), Mao Tse-tung hsüan-chi (Selected works), 1952, vol. 2, p. 652.

[92] "The Sino-Soviet Conflict," Royal Central Asian Journal, 50 (January, 1963), 61.

[93] "Unite under Lenin's revolutionary banner," Peking Review, 17 (April 26, 1960), 33.

[94] Ibid.

have little confidence in the victory of the national liberation war if left unaided. Such war is often pursued with insurmountable handicaps on the part of the insurgents. An article appeared in a well-known journal calling for brotherly concern with the revolutionists because of their odds against much stronger forces.[95] It said that without sacrificing thousands of lives independence can never be achieved. In addition, it drew attention to Lenin's precept that wars of national liberation must not be dismissed as a matter of no moment for the socialists. To the contrary, the journal continued, it was the late Russian statesman who spelled out, in no uncertain terms, the universality of wars of self-determination.[96] A conscionable internationalist cannot simply sit by and hear obdurately the wail of woe of the imperialist victims, it advised.[97] The toilers, no matter where they find themselves, should not only be oriented toward the communist goal, but ought to share the anxiety and tribulation of their fellow toilers. The failure of a revolution in any part of the world, the Chinese assumed, cannot but be accepted as a sorrow by the whole proletariat. On the contrary, the progress of a revolution brings so much closer the realization of the workers' paradise on earth.

The Soviets faced a quandary relative to wars of national liberation. As stated previously, they felt it impolitic to bless violence to achieve colonial independence. On the other hand, they were under a steady barrage by Peking, attacking their alleged indifference toward the grand aim of liberation. Particularly vulnerable was Khrushchev's avoidability doctrine discussed early in this work. Unable to straddle the fence for long, he chose to go over to the Chinese side, but not until the Algerian issue was nearing its settlement.[98] Reporting to the party conference early in 1961, he strove to emulate Mao by enunciating that wars of national liberation were just and that they ought to be propped by the bloc nations at the end of their tether.[99] So long as imperialism endures, colonies would have to fight for their freedom. "Just as tigers never feed on grass, colonialists never graciously take leave before being dagged out."[100] On March 6, 1962, only a few days prior to the

[95] *Kuo-chi wen t'i yen-chiu* (Studies in world politics), 5 (May 3, 1960), 1–10.
[96] Such war is a holy one, he stated; "Iz 'otkrytogo pis'ma Borisu Suvarinu'" (From an open letter to Boris Souvarine), December, 1916, *O voine, armii i voennoi nauke* (On war, army and military science; 2nd ed.), p. 320.
[97] *Kuo-chi wen-t'i yen-chiu* (Studies in world politics), 5 (May 3, 1960), 11.
[98] Tsou Tang, *Orbis*, 8 (Spring, 1964), 38; "Khrushchev manifesto," *Economist*, 200 (August 5, 1961), 525.
[99] "Marksizm-leninizm...," *Izvestiya*, January 8, 1961; "Za novye pobedy...," *Pravda*, January 7, 1961; *Kommunist*, 1 (January, 1961), 30–36.
[100] Khrushchev's speech to the welcome party given the President of the Republic of Mali,

Algerian cease-fire, Khrushchev told a Romanian audience that "we shall recognize and encourage national liberation wars. We salute those who snatch shovels to entomb the colonialists." Then he proceeded to name the following dependencies as those whose cause he championed: Algeria, Vietnam, West Irian, and the Congo.[101] "Together we combat colonialism," he stated.[102] Arms are the sole language to which imperialism would lend its ears when enjoined to vacate its dependencies.[103] "Our people take it upon themselves to assist those nations to get rid of the remnants of imperialism even after imperialists have left," Khrushchev told one of his African visitors in the Kremlin.[104]

It will be noted that when Khrushchev advanced his avoidability doctrine in 1956, he did not rule out colonial wars for independence. He felt that peaceful national liberation was only a possibility, not a sure matter.[105] This flexible stance indicates his awareness of the fact that after the Second World War, numerous colonies have become sovereign, not as a result of a bloody fight, but thanks to the voluntary retirement of the so-called bellicose imperialists. Treaty relations have been made, whereby aids of one kind or another were stipulated for the fledgling states.[106] Dub it neo-colonialism as the communists do, the stark reality seems to prove that revolutionary war is not a *sine qua non* for self-determination.[107] Having regard to this historical fact, the Moscow communique of the eighty-one communist parties including the CPSU and the CCP took no lopsided view with respect to the appropriate means to obtain national equality. "The peoples of the colonial countries win their independence both through armed struggle and by non-military methods, depending on the specific conditions in the country concerned."[108] In an attempt to make a concession to the Chinese, the statement runs: "The colonial powers never leave of their own free will the countries they are exploiting."[109] The Chinese

May 21, 1962, *Predotvratit' voinu, ostoyat' mir!* (Prevent war and defend peace!), p. 127.

[101] His speech in Obnova (Bulgaria), *ibid.*, p. 88.

[102] His speech to the welcome party given the President of the Republic of Mali, May 21 1962, *ibid.*, pp. 125–26.

[103] *Voennaya strategiya* (Military strategy; 2nd ed.), p. 27.

[104] Khrushchev's speech to the farewell party for the Prime Minister of the Republic of Senegal, June 15, 1962, *Predotvratit' voinu, otstoyat' mir!* (Prevent war and defend peace!), p. 174.

[105] "Otchetnyi doklad Tsentral'nogo Komiteta...," *Pravda*, February 15, 1956.

[106] Hugh Seton-Watson, *Neither War Nor Peace* (New York: Praeger, 1960), pp. 76–91, 270–96.

[107] Donald S. Zagoria, *The Sino-Soviet Conflict, 1956–1961*, p. 250.

[108] "Zayavlenie soveshchaniya predstavitelei...," *Pravda*, December 6, 1960.

[109] *Ibid.*

Ninth Plenum of the Eighth Central Committee (January 8, 1961) passed a resolution to underwrite the Moscow declaration with the warning that the socialist nations should never permit the imperialists "to strangle the liberation movement."[110] Lastly, we must mention that the Moscow pronouncement, even though sympathetic to the aspirations for national emancipation, pledged no all-out support for it. It seems to share Khrushchev's thought that such war might lead to broader conflict and that care should be taken so that things may not get out of control.

Coexistence and Wars of National Liberation

As we pointed out before, the Chinese view held that the policy of peaceful coexistence between states with different ideologies does not preclude aiding civil wars in the capitalist world. It is one thing to cultivate the comity of sovereignties; it is quite another to apologize for internal class peace.[111] The support of national-liberation as well as civil wars corrodes imperialist regimes and is not at variance with the support of coexistence.[112] The Chinese believed, if the colonies are incited to arms, this endangers no world peace.[113] Even should the West treat such action as a provocative, it dare not take vengeance because it is fearful of the Soviet nuclear power. This demonstrated, Peking maintained, that the breakthrough in science has virtually furnished the East with protection when it makes inroads into the enemy sphere.[114] Although not in so many words, Mao's theoreticians figured that the more developed the technology, the bolder the East should be in forcing the imperialists to retreat. On their part, the Russian communists concurred that the war of national liberation would prove as deadly

---

[110] "The resolution of the Chinese Communist Party on the Moscow declaration of December, 1960," Sino-Soviet Dispute, p. 222.

[111] "Forward along the path of the great Lenin," ibid., pp. 114–15; Peking Review, 17 (April 26, 1960), 23–32.

[112] "The resolution of the Chinese Communist Party on the Moscow declaration of December, 1960," Sino-Soviet Dispute, p. 223.

[113] The Chinese dismissed the escalation of a national liberation war to a world war as groundless: "In recent years, certain persons have been spreading the argument that a single spark from a war of national liberation or from a revolutionary people's war will lead to a world conflagration destroying the whole mankind ... Contrary to what those people say, the wars of national liberation and the revolutionary people's wars, that have occurred since World War II, have not led to a world war... The victory of these revolutionary wars has directly weakened the forces of imperialism and greatly strengthened the forces which prevent the imperialists from launching a world war and which defend peace," in "A proposal concerning the general line of the international communist movement, letter from the CCP in reply to the letter, dated March 30, 1963, of the CPSU," dated June 14, 1963, Peking Review, 25 (June 21, 1963), 14.

[114] Sino-Soviet Dispute, p. 91.

to the capitalist countries as civil war. But they did not feel it prudent
to aid the liberation front, nor did they think that the peace accent
in their diplomacy would "dull the vigilance of the proletariat."[115]
Kuusinen assured Peking of the unremitting communist militancy in
these words: "True to the behests of Lenin, our party has always backed
the liberation struggles of the oppressed people and their right of self-
determination."[116] The policy of peaceful coexistence cannot be allowed
to arrest the disintegration of capitalist states from inside as well as
from outside.

The problem of wars of national liberation was brought up for discussion in the 1957 Moscow conference of the ruling communist parties.[117]
Heading the Peking delegation, Mao was said to have insisted on putting
it on the agenda and defended it very hard.[118] His argument was that
by abetting revolts in the dependencies, the communist states could
hamstring the West and correspondingly improve their position.[119]
The Chinese assumed the effectiveness of a Soviet nuclear deterrence
from the time the Russians first put the artificial satellite into orbit.[120]
Mao's concept of the East wind prevailing over the West wind was
formulated at this very moment in a speech to a group of Chinese
students at Moscow University.[121] It appears that the strategy on
national liberation and the prevalence of the East over the West wind
are related, the first being conducive to the second. From 1957 on, the
categories of civil wars and wars of national liberation are always

[115] Iu. Frantsev, "Problemy voiny i mira...," *Pravda*, August 7, 1960.
[116] "Pretvorenie v zhizn' idei lenina" (To implement Lenin's ideas), *ibid.*, April 23, 1960.
[117] "Deklaratsiya soveshchaniya predstavitelei...," *ibid.*, November 22, 1957.
[118] *Sino-Soviet Dispute*, p. 41.
[119] A Chinese student made an excellent analysis of Mao's strategy in this way: "By 1937
Mao had developed a strategy of surrounding the cities from the countryside, because Kuomintang's hold on the cities was firm and incontestable while its control over the countryside
was weak and vulnerable. It is a new version of strategy which Mao proposes to use to defeat
the United States. Mao realizes that the power of the West in the developed areas cannot be
challenged successfully for the time being, but he believes its position in the underdeveloped
areas is weak and vulnerable. His strategy calls for the world communist movement to con-
centrate its energy and resources on the underdeveloped areas of Asia, Africa and Latin
America in order to promote national liberation movements and revolutionary wars," *see*
Tsou Tang, *Orbis*, 8 (Spring, 1964), 40. The same concept was propounded in an official
Peking medium, *see* "Holding high six revolutionary banners to smash revisionism: resolution
of the Second Plenum of the Central Committee of the Indonesian Communist Party concerning the political report of the Political Bureau," *Peking Review*, 13 (March 27, 1964), 17. *See
infra*, chap. VI, pp. 152–56.
[120] A. M. Halpern, *China Quarterly*, 3 (July–September, 1960), 20; K. S. Karol, *New Statesman*, 68 (November 13, 1964), 730. *See also Pravda*, October 10, 1957, for the "sputnik"
jubilee of the communists the world over.
[121] *Long live Leninism*, p. 9.

paired,[122] a further indication of their linkage. In spite of the fact that the 1960 Moscow declaration proposed variegated modes of struggle with the imperialists, it emphasized that "by giving a further powerful impetus to wars of national liberation, it [the bloc] exerted tremendous influence on the peoples, especially those of Asia, Africa, and Latin America."[123]

The Chinese felt anxious lest Khrushchev's diplomacy defer the revolutionary storm in the several colonies. Refuting Peking, E. Zhukov wrote that the "dogmatists and sectarians who fail to understand the laws of social development contend that the realization of . . . peaceful coexistence retards the unfurling of national liberation."[124] As a matter of fact, it was reasoned, coexistence and the liberation movement themselves coexist and complement each other,[125] for it is under the condition of coexistence that the movement can grow apace, on the one hand; and if the movement develops coexistence can be made smoother on the other. When national liberation war robs the imperialists of their overseas base of resource, they will be much less of a contender and not hard to deal with. Our time is one "of socialist revolution and national turmoil,"[126] and, in addition, the "armed muscle of socialism has again and again foiled the imperialists in their endeavor to stifle the socialist and national liberation struggles."[127] There seemed no ground to take fright at the Western competitors, the Russians believed. It would, therefore, be superfluous to goad national uprisings against the imperialist countries. The Chinese, however, thought that if the socialist camp poured just a tin of gasoline onto the colonial tinderbox, the framework of the Western house would be engulfed in a flame all at once.[128] Hence the present epoch remains one of war and revolution in both metropolis and dependencies.

[122] N. P. Mamai, "Predislovie" (Introduction), in Lenin, *O voine, armii i voennoi nauke* (On war, army and military science; 2nd ed.)k, pp. 4–10.

[123] "Zayavlenie soveshchaniya predstavitelei. . .,"*Pravda*, December 6, 1960.

[124] E. Zhukov, "Znamenatel'nyi faktor nashego vremeni" (Outstanding factor of our time), *ibid.*, August 26, 1960.

[125] It is claimed that neither the national liberation movement nor the class struggle against capitalists should be affected by the slogan of peaceful coexistence. *See* "Za edinstvo i splochnost' mezhdunarodnogo kommunisticheskogo dvizheniya" (For unity and solidarity in the international communist movement), *ibid.*, December 6, 1963.

[126] "Zayavlenie soveshchaniya predstavitelei. . .," *ibid.*, December 6, 1960.

[127] Khrushchev, "Nasushchnye voprosy razvitiya mirovoi sotsialisticheskikoi sistemy" (The essential problems of the development of the world socialist system), *Predotvratit' voinu, otstoyat' mir!* (Prevent war and defend peace!), p. 360.

[128] "A proposal concerning the general line of the international communist movement, letter of the CCP, in reply to the letter, dated March 30, 1963, of the CPSU," dated June 14, 1963, *Peking Review*, 25 (June 21, 1963), pp. 25–30.

Post-Liberation Non-Interference

To assist wars of liberation constitutes interference in the affairs of other sovereignties. Such actions would militate against the official line of coexistence. Therefore, the Kremlin leaders have to design a resilient policy toward the methods of achieving national independence, non-violent as well as violent. Rebutting Peking's stricture that the Soviets were cowardly, Kuusinen wrote that the CPSU has a broader understanding and saner judgment of world politics and that it is harmful to be lopsided in tackling liberation problems.[129] Especially after the ex-colonies achieve their statehood in the family of nations, it is inapposite to dictate their policy.[130] Peking was called "utopian" for its attempt to tell the former colonial nationals what to do with their economy.[131] It must be pointed out that the Chinese communists have persistently maintained that the neutral nations, i.e., former colonies, like Egypt and India, are not to be trusted, for they are ready to side with the West and have harshly persecuted their own communist citizens.[132] Both Nehru and Nasser were considered by Peking unworthy of assistance from the Soviet Union; it is regretted that the Soviet Union had not insisted, as a condition of its aid, on a freer life for the local communists.[133] The proletariat is still not liberated, in spite of the eviction of the imperialists, Peking held.[134] Such post-liberation bourgeois rule augurs ill for the populace. According to Peking's point of view, Soviet Russia should have long ago used its lever of the aid program to demand, on behalf of the toilers, concessions from the new government.[135]

The Soviets, however, felt that they could make more friends by

[129] "Pretvorenie v zhizn' idei lenina" (To implement Lenin's ideas), *Pravda*, April 23, 1960.

[130] E. Zhukov, "Znamenatel'nyi faktor nashego vremeni" (Outstanding factor of our time), *ibid.*, August 26, 1960.

[131] *Ibid.*

[132] Edward Crankshaw, *New York Times Magazine*, May 26, 1963, p. 90. On this point, the Soviets had once conceded to the Chinese stand. In the declaration of the Twenty-Second Congress of the CPSU it was said that communists were not to trust neutral leaders until they demonstrated their faith in socialism, "Novaya programma" (New program), *Pravda*, November 2, 1961; *Izvestiya* of the same date. *See* also Ernst Halperin, "Soviet-Chinese paradox," *Atlas*, 5 (September, 1963), 162.

[133] *Ibid.*, p. 163.

[134] Lenin once said: "The history of the 19th century taught that either you have proletarian dictatorship, or you have bourgeois dictatorship. There can be no third type of regime. Whoever overlooks this truism is a hopeless idiot." *See* "Pis'mo k rabochim i krest'yanam po povodu pobedy na Kolchakom" (Letter to the peasants and workers on the defeat of Kolchak), *O voine, armii i voennoi nauke* (On war, army and military science; 2nd ed.), p. 609.

[135] The Russians were interested in lining up the neutral nations against the West, or preventing them from falling into the imperialist camp. *See* Leonard Schapiro, *India Quarterly*, 18 (January–March, 1962), 9.

brushing aside the Chinese critique, for the communists were only a small fraction in the neutral countries. By goading on the Egyptian communist party to overthrow the Nasser government, for example, the Soviet Union would alienate itself from the "zone of peace."[136] Hence its resolve that from its help to the non-aligned nations it requires "no changes in their political and social structure ... neither changes in foreign policy nor ... favorable treatment for their communist parties."[137] As Khrushchev told a mass meeting in Sophia on May 19, 1962, "after the colonies obtained their liberation, we are not to restrain their course of action. They may or may not be socialist. But in the long pull, they all will go socialist."[138] The last point is worth noting, for by making it his confessed stand, the Russian leader hinted to the Chinese that he was not a man with a revisionist bent and was acceding to no imperialists.[139] As a matter of fact, Khrushchev still regarded the neutral nations to which the Soviet aid went as only semi-sovereign. "Many peoples in Africa, Asia and Latin America are truly colonial and have not yet become independent," he asserted.[140] To help them build up a viable economy would pave the way to real sovereignty. The bourgeois stage of the ex-colonies marked a transition to socialism during which the "Soviet Union never intends to prescribe for them a pattern of living."[141] Khrushchev's policy here is belied by the Soviet suppression of the national aspirations in the communist bloc. The brutal subjugation of popular revolts does not jibe with the line that "after throwing out the colonial power, people should determine their own destiny."[142]

In spite of the claim of non-interference, the policy of peaceful co-existence "means that the USSR wants to safeguard all it has" in its grip.[143] One may add that it seeks to expand into the "zone of peace." But how to achieve this objective without showing itself as meddle-some is the question. Patently, no country would concede that it has "poked its nose into another's garden," to use Stalin's well-known phrase. Even the 1956 Hungarian intervention was justified by the Soviet Government saying that it was merely an act of riot control and

---

[136] Madhu Limaye, *United Asia*, 12 (1960), 504; Harold C. Hinton, *Commonweal*, 79 (October 18, 1963), 92; Neal Stanford, *Foreign Policy Bulletin*, 40 (October 1, 1960), 11.

[137] Ernst Halperin, *Atlas*, 5 (September, 1963), 161.

[138] *Predotvratit' voinu, otstoyat' mir!* (Prevent war and defend peace!), p. 107.

[139] "Novaya programma" (New program), *Pravda*, November 2, 1961; *Izvestiya* of the same date.

[140] *Predotvratit' voinu, otstoyat' mir!* (Prevent war and defend peace!), p. 127.

[141] *Ibid.*, p. 129.

[142] *Ibid.*, p. 132.

[143] W. A. Kulski, *Peaceful Coexistence* (Chicago: Regnery, 1959), p. 136.

undertaken at the invitation of the Kadar regime.[144] The 1968 Czech invasion was defended by a theory of limited sovereignty, a point to be commented on in the next chapter. The Chinese have been very articulate in opposing interference in the affairs of the post-liberation as well as the pre-liberation peoples. It was written that "revolution is each nation's own business. We have always maintained that the working class can only depend on itself for its emancipation which in turn depends on its own awakening."[145] However, China's words are not borne out by her deeds. In the case of the struggle in Algeria, Peking was the first to extend official recognition to Ben Bella's insurgency. For the recent past, the Chinese were either ousted from or accused by Ghana, Burundi, the Republic of Indonesia, Dahomey, the Central African Republic and the Ivory Coast. Apparently Mao's overseas agents have overreached themselves in shoring up the local dissident groups to oppose the legitimate government. To Peking, the post-liberation regime in no way differs from their former selves. They bear no resemblance to people's democracies, and with the support of the imperialist nations, may prove brutish to the workers' movement.[146]

Neo-colonialism

As noted in the preceding chapter, the communists asserted that the metropolis has economically turned out to be the appendix of the distant possessions which are the source of supply and have strategic value. The assumption is: if the colonies leave the imperialist fold, the metropolitan people "will sink into an abyss of depression and civil strife, the most fertile soil for communism."[147] Has this become true? Facts show that the former colonial powers have continuously enhanced the people's livelihood. Minus the overseas territories which have since become independent and been admitted to the United Nations, the imperialist states have not gone from bad to worse and have compared favorably with the communist states in their standard

[144] D. T. Shepilov, "Voprosy mezhdunarodnogo polozheniya i vneshnei politiki Sovetskogo Soiuza" (The problems of international situation and the foreign policy of the Soviet Union), his address to the Supreme Soviet, *Pravda*, February 13, 1957.
[145] *Long Live Leninism*, p. 104. See also Lenin, "Sed'maya (aprel'skaya) vserossiiskaya konferentsiya RSDRP(B)" (The Seventh (April) All-Russian Conference of the RSDRP(B)), April, 1917, *O voine, armii i voennoi nauke* (On war, army and military science; 2nd ed.), p. 357. However, Lenin hastened to add that it was incumbent upon the revolutionaries to turn the popular "instinct" into "consciousness."
[146] Liu Shao-ch'i said that indiscriminate bloc economic and military assistance to the bourgeois leadership of a developing nation only served to consolidate the position to the middle class and make the proletarian struggle for power more difficult and even prolonged indefinitely. See his "Speech at Pyongyang," *Peking Review*, 39 (September 27, 1963), 10.
[147] Marvin L. Kalb, *op. cit.*, p. 241.

of living. Just what accounts for this phenomenon? In order to explain it, the Sino-Soviet media grinds out the word "neo-colonialism."[148] The term, of course, implies a re-emergence of colonial subordination after a brief span of time in which a constitution is drawn, elections are held and government comes into being. It is argued that the liberated peoples now enjoy political independence, but through their economic ties, they still make up a part of the mother country.[149] Even though the various levels of administration found themselves in the hands of the civil service staffed by natives, all the financial apparatus is dominated mainly by aliens, the former colonialists.[150] Since, as Lenin taught, political power derives from economic power,[151] the sovereignty of the new states is a mere show. Thus economic vassalage under the façade of political equality is the mark of neo-colonialism.

The semi-independence of certain new regimes is imputed to the fact that their wars of national liberation were not fought in the name of proletarian internationalism. The bourgeoisie took the lead in the pre-liberation struggle.[152] The capitalist monopolists refused to surrender the key enterprises in the former colonies; they sought to occupy new heights of the economic landscape.[153] During the initial phase of statehood, cadres to administer the several departments were lacking. Those who made themselves available happened to be the outmoded intelligentsia who proved unable to serve the true interests of the people. Since they found it impossible to sever their ties with their imperialist patrons, they could not be expected to undertake radical changes.

Nevertheless, this state of affairs is not to be deplored simply because of the bourgeoisie staying in power. E. Zhukov wrote that "under the flag of nationalism," those leaders guiding the emancipated people indubitably have played their "progressive and historical part" in the "breakthrough of the imperialist front" and that the "doctrinaires and leftists" should cease and desist from "sneering" at them.[154] He further

---

[148] Huang Chan-pen, "Underdeveloped economy: a new colonial theory," *Peking Review*, 44 (November 1, 1963), 16–18; translation of "Pu fa-ta ching-chi hsüeh shih hsin chih-min chu-i ti li-lun," *Hung-ch'i*, 18 (September 13, 1963), 25–29.

[149] *Marksizm-leninizm o voine i armii* (Marxism-Leninism on war and army; 4th ed.), p. 106.

[150] Yun Lun-kwei, "Ya-fei jen-min cheng-ch'ü che-ti ti ching-chi tu-li ti tao-lu" (The path toward complete economic independence movement of the Afro-Asian peoples), *Shih-chieh chih-shih* (World knowledge), 12 (June 25, 1965), 9–11; Hsiu Lieh-chün, "Ya-fei kuo-chia ching-chi k'uen-nan ti ken-pen yüan-yin" (The basic causes of economic troubles of the Afro-Asian nations), *ibid.*, 12–15.

[151] Lenin, *Sochineniya* (Collected works; 4th ed.), vol. 27, p. 373; vol. 1, p. 347.

[152] *Marksizm-leninizm o voine i armii* (Marxism-Leninism on war and army; 4th ed.), p. 107.

[153] *Ibid.*, pp 106–7.

[154] E. Zhukov, "Znamenatel'nyi faktor neshego vremeni" (Outstanding factor of our time), *Pravda*, August 26, 1960.

argued that there is no such thing as a "pure" revolutionary process, as the Chinese think. Khrushchev, even though having no love for the rulers of the neo-colonies, never counseled their ouster; he argued instead that the socialist nations should cooperate with them to build up their countries and to pursue a peace policy.[155] Khrushchev undoubtedly intended to woo them away from their association with the West. This is the technique designed to deprive the imperialists of their new economic base.

The former colonies have fallen into the hands of elements unrepresentative of the proletariat. But, according to the Russian communists, the situation is after all transient. "The imperialists have achieved temporary successes only in countries where they are given support by corrupt local reactionaries," wrote Kuusinen.[156] Sooner or later, the progressives will take over the reins of government, Yet, before that happens, neo-colonialism may assume a grotesque shape. Viewed through Soviet lenses, the international trade network in which the new nations are partners represents an intensified form of exploitation by the capitalist powers. It is through gathering together the one time colonies and placing them under the Western mercantile sway that neo-colonialism comes to pass.[157] Thus, the "common market will inundate Africa with European goods," envisioned Khrushchev.[158] The ulterior motive is none other than "economic strangling of the newly emerging regimes."[159] The best way to construct a popular economy is to put it on a self-reliance footing rather than gear it to the market of other countries. The Soviets declared that trade cooperation between the African and capitalist states would turn the former subservient people again into purveyors of raw materials, and convert the continent into an outpost of neo-imperialism.[160] Besides the common market and the Commonwealth,[161] the American Peace Corps is viewed as another contrivance to achieve neo-colonialism. Khrushchev sarcastically observed that Peace Corps juveniles are now replacing the gangs of the "Cross and Bible" as the talons of the imperialist beasts.[162] They are

[155] "Rech' t. N. S. Khrushcheva na III s'ezde...," (Khrushchev's speech to the Third Congress of the Romanian Workers' Party), *ibid.*, June 22, 1960; *Izvestiya*, June 23, 1960.
[156] "Pretvorenie v zhizn' idei lenina" (To implement Lenin's ideas), *Pravda*, April 23, 1960.
[157] "Khrushchev manifesto," *Economist*, 200 (August 5, 1961), p. 525.
[158] Khrushchev's speech at the Soviet-Mali friendship rally in Moscow, May 30, 1962, *Predotvratit' voinu, otstoyat' mir!* (Prevent war and defend peace!), p. 136.
[159] *Marksizm-leninizm o voine i armii* (Marxism-Leninism on war and army; 4th ed.), p. 107.
[160] Khrushchev's speech at the Soviet-Mali friendship rally in Moscow, May 30, 1962, *Predotvratit' voinu, otstoyat' mir!* (Prevent war and defend peace!), p. 137.
[161] J. D. B. Miller, *Australian Outlook*, 17, (April, 1963), 91.
[162] *Predotvratit' voinu, otstoyat' mir!* (Prevent war and defend peace!), p. 135.

to benumb the independent pathos of the natives. Along with the so-called "collective colonialism (the common market),"[163] the Alliance for Progress is deemed to be writing still a fresh chapter in the annals of Western aggression.[164] Imperialism, in fine, is the bloody enemy of the young nations, according to the communists.[165]

LOCAL WARS

The Danger of Escalation

"Local war" is frequently referred to as "limited war,"[166] and denotes armed conflict between Western powers and countries not already members of the Soviet bloc. While such war has not usually been treated at great length by either the Russians or the Chinese, it has not been totally overlooked.[167] The Sino-Soviet dialogue reveals that while China was little exercised about the risk of escalation from seemingly trivial incidents, Russia exhibited great concern.[168] As early as 1955, a Russian general wrote that our epoch was no longer one of local armed conflicts.[169] He assumed that the interests of the major powers would not tolerate the loss of a strategic spot anywhere on the globe without putting up a fight.[170] This view was shared two years later by the then Soviet premier. Writing President Eisenhower, Premier N. Bulganin conveyed the thought that the bifurcated world has virtually diminished the likelihood of limited hostilities on any continent.[171] In almost

---

[163] *Ibid.*, p. 139.

[164] *Ibid.*, p. 135.

[165] *Materialy XXII s'ezda KPSS* (Documentary materials of the Twenty-Second Congress of the CPSU) (Moskva: Gospolitizdat, 1961), p. 354.

[166] N. V. Pukhovskii, *op. cit.*, p. 182. Engels mentioned "local war" in Marx and Engels, *Werke*, vol. 36, pp. 525, 628; vol. 39, p. 27.

[167] S. Kozlov, "Tvorcheskii kharakter sovetskogo voennogo ucheniya" (The creative character of Soviet military doctrine), *Kommunist vooruzhennikh sil* (Communist of the armed forces), 11 (June, 1961), 55.

[168] "The dispute between China and Russia did not so much concern total wars as local wars," observed Obata Misao after he made a sample survey of opinion among the participants in a seminar on the Sino-Soviet dispute held in Japan (Lake Kawaguchi), September 19–24, 1960: *see* his previously cited article in *Japan Quarterly*, 8 (January–March, 1961), 29.

[169] Georgi Pokrovskii wrote: "The development of military techniques has reached a stage when reduction of armaments and prohibition of weapons of mass destruction is a pressing, burning problem. The age of local wars is over. Our generation has had ample demonstration of how local clashes develop into world conflicts involving the nations of every continent. What is more, those conflicts are not confined to the battlefront. The mass of the population, even in the most remote parts of the country, are drawn into the war and must work for it," in "The public must know the facts," *News, A Soviet Review of World Events*, 7 (April 1, 1955), 7. *See* also N. V. Pukhovskii, *loc. cit.*

[170] Georgi Pokrovskii, *News, A Soviet Review of World Events*, 7 (April, 1 1955), 7.

[171] "Poslanie Predsedatelya Soveta Ministrov SSSR, N. A. Bulganina, Prezidentu Soedin-nenykh Shtatov Ameriki, Duaitu D. Eizenkhauery" (A letter from the Chairman of the Coun-

identical terms, Khrushchev expressed the same idea to the British Labor Party in October 1957.[172] Interviewed by a group of newsmen from Brazil, he stated that in the present epoch "small wars"[173] could not remain small for long and that they would ultimately involve other nations and even coalitions of nations.[174] In 1960, Talenskii said that future wars would assume international dimension, in spite of their humble origin, i.e., arising from a tiny place.[175] In the past, he went on, fighting was limited geographically because of (1) the limited resources of both sides, (2) conventional weapons, (3) lack of ideological motivation and (4) pale pre-figuration of the present alliance complex.[176] All these have differed now, he stated.

The Soviets assumed that the Western powers would resort to local incidents to realize their global policies.[177] Such allegedly aggressive designs could lead to nuclear exchange, for it takes only the dart of a little fire to start a conflagration.[178] At Bucharest, Khrushchev warned candidly that local wars could be a prelude to an inter-state collison which would lay waste the East as well as the West.[179] It is also to be noted that in the same speech he refrained from lauding national liberation wars, as he did before, presumably because he felt they, too, might get out of control. In January, 1961, he told the meeting of party *apparatchiki* that the idea of so-called contained clashes as harbored by the NATO military brass was harebrained and that "these gentlemen" never bothered to think of the fire hazard of even an ember.[180] Meanwhile, he remonstrated the statemen of the democracies to be tractable and said he would seek to meet President Eisenhower's

cil of Ministers of the USSR, Bulganin, to the President of the United States, Dwight D. Eisenhower), *Pravda*, December 12, 1957.

[172] "[Pis'mo] k isponitel'nomu Komitetu Leiboristskoi Partii Velikobritanii [ot] TsK KPSS' (A letter from the Central Committee of the CPSU to the Executive Committee of the British Labor Party), *ibid.*, October 16, 1957.

[173] The term was once used by Lenin referring to limited colonial fight in which only a few Europeans were killed whereas the natives were destroyed by the hundreds of thousands. *See* his "Voina i revoliutsiya" (War and revolution), May, 1917, *O voine, armii i voennoi nauke* (On war, army and military science; 2nd ed.), p. 369.

[174] "Otvety N. S. Khrushcheva na voprosy brazil'skikh zhurnalistov Viktorio Martorelli i Tito Fleuri" (Khrushchev's answer to the Brazilian reporters, Messrs. Martorelli and Fleuri), *Mezhdunarodnye zhizn'* (International life), 12 (December, 1957), 6.

[175] N. Talenskii, "Sovremennaya voina: ee kharakter i sledstviya" (Modern war: its character and consequences), *ibid.*, 10 (October, 1960), 36.

[176] *Ibid.*

[177] "Novaya programma" (New program), *Pravda*, November 2, 1961; *Izvestiya* of the same date.

[178] *Marksizm-leninizm o voine i armii* (Marxism-Leninism on war and army; 4th ed.), p. 107.

[179] "Rech' t N. S. Khrushcheva na III s'ezde...," (Khrushchev's speech to the Third Congress of the Romanian Workers' Party), *Pravda*, June 22, 1960, *Izvestiya*, June 23, 1960.

[180] "Marksizm-leninizm...," *ibid.*, January 8, 1961; "Za novye pobedy....," *Pravda*, January 7, 1961; *Kommunist*, 1 (January, 1961), 4.

successor to take up the problem of wars, local as well as non-local. Sokolovskii and his associates made short shift of the whole concept of brush-fire wars and called it stupid: "Military theorists of the imperialist nations thought wrongfully that circumscribed hostilities are a possibility in the nuclear age, or that those hostilities could be localized."[181] The Anglo-French landing in the Suez Canal zone in October, 1956, was regarded as "pregnant with ominous fate to the world at large"[182] In a nutshell, regional war and general war cannot be strictly sundered.[183] "History has put such a question to mankind: coexistence or catastrophic war, not local or non-local war."[184]

Among the Russian military elites there existed a view on the escalation problem similar to that of the Chinese.[185] The dean of Soviet military philosophy, S. Krasil'nikov, wrote that even under modern conditions there could be limited, that is, local wars.[186] Another noted authority and contributor to the *Great Soviet Encyclopedia* (2nd ed.), I. S. Baz', deemed it erroneous to believe in the sure generality of future wars. There could be local ones as well, he emphasized.[187] It must be pointed out that the military men who thought small fightings inevitable did not answer the question whether they would escalate; their attention was rather rivetted on the possibility of the wars being started by the alleged aggressors. Such a possibility, however, was never minimized by the Russians. Khrushchev in 1961 warned that the imperialists could nonetheless be so idiotic as to play with fire and get themselves as well as others burned.[188] Sokolovskii and his fellow authors counseled that the "armed forces of the socialist countries must be ready at all times for local encounters which the imperialists would initiate."[189] It was further stated that in the period after the defeat of the fascists, many places have been the scenes of war without dragg-

---

[181] *Voennaya strategiya* (Military strategy; 2nd ed.), p. 61.

[182] *Marksizm-leninizm o voine i armii* (Marxism-Leninism on war and army; 4th ed.), p. 107.

[183] Lenin once spoke of the escalation of wars from local to world-wide scale; *see* his "Krakh II internatsionala" (Collapse of the Second International), July, 1915, *O voine, armii i voennoi nauke* (On war, army and military science; 2nd ed.), p. 236.

[184] *Voennaya strategiya* (Military strategy; 2nd ed.), p. 64.

[185] It is to be noted that Khrushchev's avoidability doctrine as propounded on February 15, 1956, was rejected by such military authorities as G. Fedorov, "O soderzhenie sovetskoi voennoi ideologii" (On the content of the Soviet military ideology), *Krasnaya zvezda* (Red star), March 22, 1957.

[186] "K voprosu o kharaktere sovremennoi voiny" (The problem of the character of modern war), *Marksizm-leninizm o voine i armii* (Marxism-Leninism on war and army; 1st ed.), p. 145.

[187] "Sovetskaya voennaya nauka o kharaktere sovremennoi voiny" (Soviet military science on the character of modern war), *Voen. vestn.* (Military herald), 6 (June, 1958), 24.

[188] "Marksizm-leninizm...," *Izvestiya*, January 8, 1961; "Za novye pobedy...," *Pravda*, January 7, 1961; *Kommunist*, 1 (January, 1961), 15.

[189] *Voennaya strategiya* (Military strategy; 2nd ed.), p. 234.

ing into it the bulk of humanity and that the bloc nations must therefore learn how to shape their military plan accordingly.[190] Because the imperialists may engage in limited action to achieve their limited objective, it is paramount to meet them with defensive measures.[191] Since China's inevitability doctrine refers to all kinds of armed struggle and since the Russians (with a few exceptions) think that limited conflicts are a possibility, the stands of the two parties differ very little.

Local Wars and Bloc Strength

Given the supposed hostile stripe of the imperialists, local, no less than world, war is threatening. In one way or another, it is accused, the ruling cliques of the West will seek to consolidate at the expense of the unprepared and weak nations, not necessarily those of the socialist bloc. The temptation of appropriating the fruit of others' labor is always irresistible and the imperialists have succumbed to it. This theme runs through the eighty-one-party Moscow statement.[192] Occasionally, however, the statement strikes such a sober note that limited local wars are less probable in the years ahead. This situation, it asserts, is attributable to the already familiar correlation of forces with the East steaming a-head.[193] But the declaration is not cockshure of the excludability of isolated fires that would be started by the enemy. The problem then is not one of doing away with such fires, but one of lessening the opportunities for the West to set them and add fuel to them. "There have been local wars in the past and they can break out again. But the chances of beginning them are dwindling," averred Khrushchev.[194] Yet he cautioned that the "imperialists are even making small-caliber atomic weapons" to take care of such eventualities.[195] If Khrushchev were to be trusted, the West had engaged in local fights by proxy; to support his assertion he adduced the alleged goading by Great Britain and the United States of Saudi Arabia and Jordan to invade Yemen in 1962.[196] However, he promised no material backing to Yemen, saying only that the imperialist design would somehow be abortive.

---

[190] *Ibid.*

[191] *Marksizm-leninizm o voine i armii* (Marxism-Leninism on war and army), 1958 ed., p. 44; 1961 (2nd ed.), p. 45.

[192] "Zayavlenie soveshchaniya predstavitelei...," *Pravda*, December 6, 1960.

[193] *Ibid.*

[194] "Marksizm-leninizm...," *Izvestiya*, January 8, 1961; "Za novye pobedy...," *Pravda*, January 7, 1961; *Kommunist*, 1 (January, 1961), 30.

[195] *Ibid.*

[196] "Sovremennoe mezhdunarodnoe polozhenie i vneshnyaya politika Sovetskogo Soiuza" (The contemporary international situation and the foreign policy of the Soviet Union), *Predotvratit' voinu otstoyat' mir!* (Prevent war and defend peace!), p. 406.

In spite of the imputed ambition of the West for discrete ventures, the Soviet leadership seemed quite certain of the "containability" so that a great war would not ensue. Perhaps the brightest hope was entertained by Khrushchev in his report to the Twenty-First Congress (January 27, 1959) that there has come into being a "real possibility that local wars could be avoided as well."[197] To substantiate this stand, he cited example after example. The 1956 Anglo-French-Israeli action in Egypt was said to have proved "how local wars were nipped in the bud by the intervention of the Soviet Union and the entire socialist camp."[198] As a consequence of the "stern warning" by the peace forces to Anthony Eden and Guy Mollet, he boasted, "the invasion of Egypt failed ignominiously."[199] Moreover, he went on, in 1957 "we prevented Syria from being attacked by Turkey which was prompted to an adventure by the United States imperialists."[200] As an additional instance of the Soviet deterrence, Khrushchev adduced the Middle-East crisis in July, 1958. "After the revolution in Bagdad, Washington and London landed their forces on the east Mediterranean and were ready to assault Iraq. Meanwhile Turkey, Iran and Pakistan were goaded into doing the same."[201] Again it was Russia which extinguished the portentous flame. Upon Khrushchev's varied examples Peking was in concurrence, as witnessed by an article in *Jen-min jih-pao* which, however, argued also that such conflicts as had happened in Korea and Indochina have not been completely stamped out, they are just momentarily stalemated.[202] It seems that China was not as reassuring as Russia of the chances of averting local wars. The sustenance of peace, however, the Russians thought to be the task of the people concerned who must bring pressure to bear upon their own government;[203] the bloc influence is only a supplementary factor.

The Russian deterrence has been deemed by Peking the preventor of local wars which are in one way or another instigated by the West,[204]

---

[197] "Dal'neishee ukreplenie mirovoi...," *Pravda*, January 28, 1959.
[198] "Marksizm-leninizm...," *Izvestiya*, January 8, 1961; "Za novye pobedy...," *Pravda*, January 7, 1961; *Kommunist*, 1 (January, 1961), 34–36.
[199] *Ibid.*
[200] "Rech' t. N. S. Khrushcheva na III s'ezde...," (Khrushchev's speech to the Third Congress of the Romanian Workers' Party), *Izvestiya*, June 23, 1960; *Pravda*, June 22, 1960.
[201] *Ibid.*
[202] "Chih yu chien chüeh tou-cheng, ts'ai-neng pao-wei ho-ping" (Only through resolute struggle may peace be defended), *Jen-min jih pao*,-August 8, 1958.
[203] "Rech' t. N. S. Khrushcheva na III s'ezde...," (Khrushchev's speech to the Third Congress of the Romanian Workers' Party), *Izvestiya*, June 23, 1960; *Pravda*, June 22, 1960.
[204] Hsiu Pan-han, "Hsüeh-hsi le-nin ti chan-tou ching-shen" (Learn Lenin's fighting spirit), *Jen-min jih-pao*, April 22, 1960.

and on this point both countries are in accord. Yet as to the apt response to such Western challenges, they could not sing in chorus. As one would expect, the bellicosity of Peking disposes it toward the view that the bloc must forcibly and timely repel any imperialist probe.[205] The Russian communists were exhorted that although peace is appetizing "it just cannot be begged for."[206] Without returning counterblows, the socialist countries would only coddle evil.[207] World peace hinges on the fortitude of the East to meet head-on any incidents.[208] The Chinese people have been indefatigably reminded that small wars will be more likely than ever before, since, it is asserted, the shrewd enemy would prefer petty gains to a Pyrrhic victory on a world-wide scale.[209] To the extent that the shadow of world war falls back, that of local war casts forward; or, to the extent that the bloc gets more powerful, the enemy is more driven to regional violence.[210] That the Chinese point of view was conceded by Khrushchev was attested to by his remark: "Some of the imperialist groups fear that a world war might end in complete destruction of capitalism, and for this reason they are banking on local moves."[211] However, Mao's tactics for responding to this kind of war are offensive as well as defensive.[212] To create for the enemy many unexpected troubles, no matter how small, is a good maneuver to pin him down and unnerve him; especially when the East "has not much to fear from Western strategic power, the bloc should feel free to ignite [brush-fire war]."[213]

[205] When Khrushchev took out his defensive missiles from Cuba in October, 1962, he was charged as cowardly and appeasing by Peking; see R. Hilsman, State Department, *Bulletin*, 47 (November 26, 1962), 807; Donald S. Zagoria, *Asian Survey*, 1 (April, 1961), 8.

[206] "Chih yu chien chüeh tou-cheng, ts'ai-neng pao-wei ho-ping" (Only through resolute struggle may peace be defended), *Jen-min jih-pao*, August 8, 1958. See also "Sino-Soviet conflict," *Royal Central Asian Journal*, 50 (January, 1963), 61.

[207] "The world cannot look on with folded arms." *Peking Review*, 22 (July 29, 1958), 5–6. Translation of "Pu-neng hsiu-shou pang-kuan," *Jen-min jih-pao*, July 20, 1958.

[208] John Gittings, *International Affairs* (London), 40 (January, 1964), 301.

[209] Chi Lung, "Mei-kuo ti chan-lüeh tsou-yu chiung tu" (The United States strategy is in a blind alley), *Shih-chien chih-shih* (World knowledge), 23 (December 5, 1957), 1–10.

[210] Yu Chao-li, "Ku-ba jen-min k'ang-mei ai-kuo tou-cheng sheng-li ti wei ta i-i" (The great significance of the Cuban People's patriotic struggle against U.S. imperialism), *Hung-ch'i* 9–10 (May 5, 1961), 11–17; Yang Yung, "The great victory in the struggle to resist U.S. aggression and aid Korea, "*Peking Review*, 44 (November 1, 1960), 12–14. Translation of "K'ang-mei yuan-chao tou-cheng ti wei ta sheng li, chi yen chung-kuo chih-yaun chün kang-mei yuan-chao ch'u kuo tso chan shih chou nien," *Jen-min jih-pao*, October 24, 1960. After Khrushchev withdrew his missiles from Cuba, the Chinese said that the "Russian revolution has run out of steam," *Jen min jih-pao*, November 7, 1962.

[211] "Marksizm-leninizm...," *Izvestiya*, January 8, 1961; "Za novye pobedy...," *Pravda*, January 7, 1961; *Kommunist*, 1 (January, 1961), 14–16.

[212] China preferred a war which "requires a small investment of resources in combat. She did not risk a large-scale Western military response," wrote David B. Borrow, *World Politics*, 16 (January, 1964), 287.

[213] Donald S. Zagoria, *The Sino-Soviet Conflict, 1956–1961*, p. 167.

Local War and World Communism

As has been emphasized throughout this work the inevitability of world war is Peking's persuasion. However, in a few instances, Russia's opposite theory is also echoed by Mao. Even in occasional deviation, his stress is on the epithet "world."[214] It is conceded that the bloc strength has sufficed to prevent a general conflict. But if global hostilities can be excluded, local ones cannot.[215] It is through such wars that the imperialists are likely to try to quell proletarian revolts; when this happens, the "countries and peoples of the world who love peace and freedom must not look on with folded arms."[216] The bloc help must be extended wherever the oppressed people cry for it. In July, 1958, when the Middle-East emergency flared up, Peking pleaded for a strong stand against the so-called "plot" by the North Atlantic Treaty Organization. It is interesting to note that Peking likened the bloc assistance to the Iraqi Government to the French assistance to the colonial revolt in North America in 1776–83.[217] Rhetorically the following question was asked: "Why are they (Iraqi people) not entitled to the sort of international aid the thirteen colonies received? Who dare say that the French who supported America's revolution in those days were aggressors?"[218] It is assumed that the Russians were derelict of their obligation because they refused to dispatch troops to Iraq.

Furthermore, the West has been thought to find it lucrative to fight tiny wars, since they are relatively cheap and of less danger in comparison with global involvement. The Soviet bloc, Peking believed, should follow suit and initiate similar engagements. There are so many loopholes along the imperialist lines, for example, the whole Middle-East, where Peking saw good opportunities to order an offensive. "If the imperialists were forced out of this area, their position in Africa would also be untenable," Peking stated.[219] This strategy was set forth in 1957, six months before the landing of Anglo-American troops in Lebanon and Jordan. Little wonder when the crisis did occur and when Khrushchev proposed only an emergency session of the United Nations to settle the issue, Mao showed his tenacious opposition, thus necessi-

---

[214] "A basic summing-up of experience...," *Sino-Soviet Dispute*, p. 167. Translation of "Chung-kuo Jen-min ko-ming...," *Hung-ch'i*, 20–21 (November 1, 1960), 1–13.

[215] *Sino-Soviet Dispute*, p. 88.

[216] "The world cannot look on with folded arms," *Peking Review*, 22 (July 29, 1958), 5–6; translation of "Pu-neng hsiu-shou pang-kuan," *Jen-min jih-pao*, July 20, 1958.

[217] "T'uan-chieh chiu-shih li-liang" (Solidarity is strength), *ibid.*, July 21, 1958.

[218] *Ibid.*

[219] *Shih-chieh chih-shih* (World knowledge), December 20, 1957, p. 8.

tating the Russian leader to make a hurried visit to him. The outcome of the visit was that the proposal of a UN meeting had to be dropped.[220] Suggesting an active policy in both defensive and offensive local wars, Mao felt that the East had much to gain and little to lose. On the one hand, with the Soviet nuclear umbrella the risk of Western retaliation is only minimal. On the other hand, as one media pointed out, the prospect of communization is the greatest when, as the result of a war, the Red armies must go to the other countries in hot pursuit of the enemy. Then the local authority can adopt the communist system and throw out their old regime.[221]

To the Russian contention that all local wars are to be avoided because nuclear arms might become involved, the Chinese rejoinder was that the imperialists could nevertheless avail themselves of old guns. "Even if those (local) wars are not fought with nuclear weapons, still do not wars using so-called conventional weapons count as wars?" the Chinese wished to know.[222] It is impolitic to preach regional peace simply because of the nuclear contingency, Peking criticized. Mao's view is that "brinkmanship should be answered in kind, otherwise the West would feel that it could get away with pocket adventures."[223] He also has argued that armed resistance by the peoples' democracies to the imperialist pressure upon non-aligned nations would have the salutary effect of both cultivating the proletarian morale everywhere in the world and forcing the Western militarists to call a general halt in front of the mighty East.[224] In this regard, Kozlov seemed to have spoken the Chinese mind: "The socialist camp backed by all the peace forces has in recent years more than once cut short attempts by the imperialist aggressors to foment insulated troubles."[225] Reporting to the Supreme Soviet on December 12, 1962, Khrushchev stated that the West has sought to re-impose its overlordship through sporadic armed

[220] This interpretation was shared among most students: Klaus Mehnert, "Soviet-Chinese relations." *International Affairs* (London), 35 (October, 1959), 423; "The Sino-Soviet conflict,' *Royal Central Asian Journal*, 50 (January, 1963), 61; Harrison Salisbury, *Foreign Policy Bulletin*, 39 (June 15, 1960) 36; John Gittings, *International Affairs* (London), 40 (January, 1964), 71. A different view was taken by Herbert Ritvo, *Problems of Communism*, 7 (September–October, 1958), 47–48. He argued that there was a coordination of Sino-Soviet policy in the 1958 Middle-East crisis.
[221] *Shih-chieh chih-shih* (World knowledge), December 20, 1957, p. 8.
[222] *Sino-Soviet Dispute*, p. 88.
[223] "Chan tsai pao-wei ho-ping ti tsui chien-hsien" (Stand on the foremost peace front), *Jen-min jih-pao*, August 4, 1958.
[224] "Chih yu chien-chüeh tou-cheng, ts'ai-neng pao-wei ho-ping" (Only through resolute struggle may peace be defended), *ibid*, August 8, 1958.
[225] "43-ya godovshchina velikoi...," *Pravda*, November 7, 1960.

probes.[226] What has taken place in the Congo, Vietnam, South Korea, North Borneo and many other areas, all testifies to the outrages of imperialists and shocks the conscience of the socialist camp.[227] However, his position is in profound contrast with Mao's, for the Chinese leader taught that local war be aided and goaded so as to enable the communists to seize power and form peoples' democracies.[228] To him, local war is world war written small, and world war is local war written large.

---

[226] "Sovremennoe mezhdunarodnoe polozhenie...," *Predotvratit' voinu, otstoyat' mir!* (Prevent war and defend peace!), p. 406.

[227] *Ibid.*

[228] *Jen-min jih-pao,* April 25, 1960.

CHAPTER VI

SINO-SOVIET DIALOGUE
DURING THE VIETNAM WAR[1]

THE PROBLEM OF AIDING HANOI

The Change of Soviet Leadership

During the second half of Khrushchev's rule, the Moscow-Peking duel rapidly approached its decrescendo, leaving all the disputed points in abeyance.[2] Upon the heels of his departure, the Vietnam crisis took a turn for the worse. For the nonce, both sides sought to play down their differences in the hope that by burying the hatchet they could easily face the new development. At first, Peking guardedly welcomed the Kremlin shift by firing a last savlo at the outgoing premier and urging his successors to reverse the line of detente. On their part, Russia's duumvirate also hinted at their readiness to readjust the China policy. It looked as if the leadership change was for the better. Noticeably, the propaganda mills had slowed down grinding out obloquies against each other, and there were some revival of cultural intercourse and official tourism between the two capitals.

However, all the outward cordiality could not paper over the inveterate enmity which had been pent-up. As a matter of fact, a round of *sub rosa* talks still failed to harmonize their views on many problems, especially the evolving war in Vietnam.[3] Even so, the highly skilled

---

[1] A recent Moscow publication of the Sino-Soviet dispute makes a historical survey from roughly the time of the October Revolution (1917) to 1967. This is a collected work, the post-1949 development being written by O. Borisov and P. Koloskov, under the chapter title: Politika Sovetskogo Soiuza v otnoschenii KNR – sotsialisticheskii internatsializm v deistvii (sovetsko-kitaiskie otnosheniya, 1948–1967 gg.) (Policy of the Soviet Union toward China – socialist internationalism in action (Sino-Soviet relations, 1948–1967), in *Politika SSSR v otnoshenii Kitaya* (Policy of the USSR toward China) (Moskva: Izd-vo "Nauka," 1968), pp. 159–256. The introduction by M. I. Sladkovskii presents a good account of the latest happenings, pp. 3–19. For a critical examination of the book by the present author, *see* the book review section of *New Review*, 10 (March, 1970), 64–6.

[2] T. S. An, "Sino-Soviet dispute and Vietnam," *Orbis*, 9 (Summer, 1956), 426.

[3] K. L. London, "Vietnam: a Sino-Soviet dilemma," *Russian Review*, 26 (January, 1967), 26.

diplomacy had kept the chasm from the general public until well into 1966 when a major article appeared in a Soviet media formally re-opening the battle against the Chinese on-and-off attacks.[4] The 4,500-word editorial decried Mao Tse-tung for abandoning the principles and policy as embodied in the 1957 Declaration and the 1960 Statement. From these polemics we know that all post-Khrushchev attempts at conciliation were in vain, that Peking had long been skeptical of the intended policy-change by Kosygin and Brezhnev and that the dispute was definitely compounded by the raging war. Early in 1966 the CPSU extended an invitation to the CCP to attend its 23rd Congress in the following May, only to be spurned curtly.[5] In a fraternal tone, Peking chided the would-be host that they "have not shown the slightest repentance" despite the fact that "we have advised (them) ... on a number of occasions to make a first start" in shaping *de novo* their foreign policy. The most interesting remark the CCP made at this time is that Russia's new rulers "told us (the CCP) to our face that there was not a shade of difference between Khrushchev and yourselves on the question of the international communist movement or of relation with China."[6] Worth noting also is that the CCP showed its bitter resentment against the degrading of Stalin. "In attacking Stalin, you were attacking Marxism-Leninism, the Soviet Union, communist parties, China, the people and all the Marxist-Leninists of the world."[7] To Peking, Stalin just represents the entirety of its value system, and de-Stalinization is the epitome of sacrilege. Thus, the Sino-Soviet dissonance remained, in spite of a change of Russian leadership.[8]

The Vietnam War – A Gaping Divide

The war has widened immeasurably the differences between the two parties. On the surface, both agreed on underwriting the Liberation Front and castigating the United States. This is not to be unexpected,

[4] The attack by the Chinese appeared as early as March, 1965, *see* the 20,000-word editorial in *Hung-ch'i*, March 22, 1965. Nearly the entire issue was devoted to the theme of betrayal of Vietnamese communists by the new leaders of Russia. For Russia's answer, see "Po povodu sobytii v kitae" (Events in China), *Pravda*, Movember 27, 1966. An excerpt in English can be found in *New York Times*, November 27, 1966, p. 18.

[5] For the Russian communication to Peking, *see* "Letter of CC of CPSU, dated February 24, 1966," *Peking Review*, 13 (March 25, 1966), 6; for China's reply, *see* "Chinese Communist Party cannot send delegation to CPSU 23rd Congress," *ibid.*, pp. 5–6. For Western comment, *see* "Fight of the tigers," *Time*, 87 (April 1, 1966), 82; "Dirty deal, Chinese boycott of the 23rd Congress of the Soviet Communist Party," *Senior Scholastic* (teacher ed.), 88 (April 22, 1966), 13.

[6] *Peking Review*, 13 (March 25, 1966), 5–6.

[7] *Ibid.*, p. 6.

[8] T. S. An, *Orbis*, 9 (Summer, 1965), 426.

since from the viewpoint of the communists the fight against the so-called exploiters, indigenous and foreign, is part and parcel of the goal of proletarian internationalism and people's democracy.[9] Neither Moscow nor Peking can escape being stigmatized among the communists if it should stay mute in the matter, let alone pursuing a moderate course. Yet there are practical reasons counseling for prudence toward the war, reasons which underlie the basic policy of the Soviets. The latter have long felt that local wars can get bigger and that the dire consequences are the destruction of millions of lives. It stands to reason that the Soviets must have advised their Chinese comrades that a precipitate response to the allied action in Vietnam would possibly have uncontrollable results. Although no such advice is publicly known, the mutual critiques leave no doubt that this is the case. Peking once clearly stated that Moscow had not done all it could to provide the necessities for Hanoi. The shipment which had been made was described as too little to do any good.[10] A pusillanimous aid, Peking asserted, amounted to remission by the leading socialist state of its international duties to the victims of imperialism. What the Soviets should do is to bring in all materiel by massive air and sea transshipping; it is within the capacity of Moscow so to do, Peking believed.[11]

Due to this self-indignation over the Soviet lack of help commensurate to its ability, the Chinese regime may have wilfully impeded the progress of transit of aid through its territory, leaving aside the possibility that its domestic convulsion has caused necessary delay. From time to time, the Soviets filed protests with Peking for its alleged detention of carriers bound for Vietnam.[12] Meanwhile the non-cooperation of Peking was censured by the pro-Soviet parties of the world. A French communist leader, Waldeck Rochet, for example, on January 4, 1967 accused China of supporting the United States by blocking the transport to North Vietnam. In a more than four hours' speech to the 18th Congress of the Communist Party of France, Rochet said the Chinese policy caused the supplies to be sent by longer and slower routes.[13] It has also

[9] Lenin, *Sochineniya* (Collected works), 5th ed., vol. 41, p. 245. *See* also V. S. Semenov, "Razvitie Leninym idei proletarskogo internatsionalizma" (Development of proletarian internationalism by Lenin), in *V. I. Lenin – velikii teoretik* (V. I. Lenin, a great theorist), p. 426.

[10] K. L. London, *Russian Review*, 26 (January, 1967), 37.

[11] "Joint statement of China and Albania," *Peking Review*, 21 (May 20, 1966), 5–12.

[12] For example, the Soviet news agency, TASS, reported (April 3, 1968) that the Soviet Government assailed the "illicit embargo starting March 27, 1968, in Port Whampoo (near Canton) of the Soviet tanker, Komsomolets Ukrainy, carrying a cargo for embattled Vietnam," *Facts on File*, 1968, p. 260.

[13] *Le monde*, 951 (January 5–11, 1967), 6.

been reported that Mao has relabeled the cargo from Russian to Chinese makes, thus to convince Hanoi that Peking, not Moscow, was its friend and to draw North Vietnam into his orbit.[14]

China's Maneuver?

Just what moves Peking to halt the Soviet aid to Ho Chi-minh? The Russians asserted that Mao Tse-tung was attempting to manipulate the situation.[15] In 1966, the Kremlin was urged by China to exert every ounce of effort to fight the Americans to the same extent as it fought the Nazis during the last war. Such a course, however, the Russians would not take.[16] True, they can dispatch hundreds of supply planes and vessels to Vietnam. But the Soviets feared such an all-out endeavor would lead to direct encounter with America. "There is every reason to assert that it is one of the goals of the policy of the Chinese leadership in the Vietnam question to originate a military conflict between the USSR and the United States," wrote the Soviets. Mao's intent was crystal clear. "They (Chinese) want a conflict of this kind, so that they may, as they say themselves, 'sit on the mountain and watch the fight of the tigers.'"[17] It appears more than likely that should the Chinese counsel prevail, the local war would swiftly escalate. The upshot, felt the Soviets, is a calamity to both superpowers with China alone among the big nations intact. *Pravda* editorialized that the Maoist regime was "pursuing a course that would aggravate the already charged international atmosphere and ultimately pave the way to inter-bloc war, allegedly in the name of world revolution."[18]

The purpose of Peking in retarding the flow of Vietnam-bound material is probably to force the Russians to use air and ocean navigation, thus, increasing the possibility of collision with the United

[14] T. S. An, *Orbis*, 9 (Summer, 1965), 427. *See* also E. O'Ballance, "Sino-Soviet influence on the war in Vietnam," *Contemporary Review*, 210 (February, 1967), 70.

[15] O. L'vov, "Politicheskie manevry Mao Tsze-duna" (Political maneuvers of Mao Tsetung), *Pravda*, January 11, 1969.

[16] T. S. An, *Orbis*, 9 (Summer, 1965), 434.

[17] The quotation is from a letter reportedly written by the Central Committee of the CPSU and addressed to the communist parties of East Europe. A copy of the letter was published in *Die Welt* of Hamburg. The paper said it had received the letter from "qualified sources." The existence of the document had been reported in West-Berlin, March 17, 1966 by RIAS (Radio in the American Sector). *Le monde* of Paris, February 15, 1966, p. 3 has reported that an anti-Chinese circular authorized by the Soviet Central Committee was distributed to the Hungarian communist partisans. "Peking plant den Weltkrieg" – Moskau fasst seine massiven Vorwürfe in einen 'Dokument der Anklage' zusammen (Der geheime Brief der KPdSU über den Konflikt mit China), *Die Welt*, March 21, 1966, p. 6. The authenticity of the letter is no longer in doubt for all the charges and phrases appear in *Korni nyneshnikh sobytii v Kitae* (The roots of the current events in China) (Moskva: Gos. izd-vo polit. lit-ry, 1968).

[18] "Po povodu sobytii v Kitae" (Events in China), *Pravda*, November 27, 1966.

States.[19] Repudiating China, the Kremlin leaders reminded her that she herself is very careful to avoid direct grappling with the imperialists, while she goads others to do just that.[20] This is the sort of double standard, the Soviets charged, Peking has set for the diplomatic behavior of the bloc nations.[21] What specifically Russia refers to is that Mao has flinched from provocation in re-annexing Hong Kong, Macao, and Taiwan, territories to which he has strong claims. Yet he does nothing of that kind for fear of involvement.[22] By brushing aside Peking's suggestion to embark upon a vast aid program to Ho Chi-minh and limiting, instead, to less than a total commitment,[23] the leadership of the Soviet Union simultaneously contrives both to localize the war and to fulfill its obligation to the liberation cause.[24]

Mao's Refusal of Coordination of Efforts and Hanoi's Stance

On the ground that China's hindrance of the overland routing of aid to Hanoi impairs the position of the Vietcong, the Russian leaders charged that Peking has contributed to the success of the United States.[25] Many calls were made by the Kremlin upon China to coordinate their efforts in dealing with the war question. But they were rebuffed with insult: "The Soviet demand for unified action by all communist parties against United States in Vietnam was a propaganda sham to deceive the revolutionary people of the world."[26] The Chinese were in no mood for a conciliation. "Let us tell the Moscow gentlemen sternly: under no circumstances will we take 'united action' with you who are a pack of rank traitors to the Vietnam revolution ... and no. 1 accomplices to the US gangsters."[27] Certainly such a haughty demeanor functions only to rile Moscow. Brezhnev excoriated the "chauvinist, great power course of the Mao Tse-tung group" for undermining the solidarity of the world socialist movement. On the other hand, he

[19] K. L. London, *Russian Review*, 26 (January, 1967), 36; T. S. An, *Orbis*, 9 (Summer, 1965), 428–29.

[20] It was written that while assiduously shunning away from scrimmage with her avowed foe, China at the same time tried every means to conjure up a war situation to entrap others. I. Aleksandrov, "Vopreki interesam Kitaiskogo naroda (In spite of the interests of the Chinese people), *Pravda*, August 16, 1967.

[21] *Ibid.*

[22] From a speech by Khrushchev at a meeting of the Supreme Soviet, December 12, 1962, Moscow Domestic Service Broadcast, December 12, 1962, An edited text could be located in *New York Times*, Western ed., December 13, 1962, p. 2. *See* also *Jen-min jih-pao*, March 8, 1963, for a comment on the statement of the Communist Party of the USA.

[23] K. L. London, *Russian Review*, 26 (January, 1967), 37.

[24] T. S. An, *Orbis*, 9 (Summer, 1965), 433.

[25] *Izvestiya*, August 30, 1967.

[26] *Peking Review*, 13 (March 25, 1966), 3–6.

[27] *Jen-min jih-pao*, April 30, 1967.

lauded the "best sons of the Chinese Communist Party" who are currently fighting Maoists.[28]

Such discord between Moscow and Peking has enormously baffled Hanoi which can hardly afford to take sides. On December 21, 1968, the Commander-in-Chief of North Vietnam, Vo Nguyen Giap, emphasized, in a speech, his country's sovereignty in words chosen to please both Mao and Brezhnev. Expressing a veiled warning to the first to keep hands off his regime's domestic affairs, he sought to propitiate him by iterating the usual line that the war was directed at the total defeat of the United States.[29] Perhaps because of Hanoi's ambiguity, Sino-Vietnam diplomacy has been cooling off considerably since 1968.[30] For example, on the 1967 national day (October 1), Lin Piao pledged China's succor to North Vietnam, and Chou En-lai spoke in the same vein. In 1968, on the same occasion, the defense chief referred to no Vietnam at all, while the premier tuned his keynote to the alleged U.S.-Soviet deal, and promised Chinese support only if it was requested.[31] The Vietnam peace talks were opposed by the Peking regime which felt that Mao's guerilla tactics and "people's war" must be vindicated by complete allied defeat.[32] With Russia's tacit endorsement, however, the Paris negotiations were started.[33]

LIN PIAO'S GEOPOLITICS

Guerilla Tactics Internationalized

In September, 1965, a politico-military doctrine of supreme importance

---

[28] *Pravda*, November 7, 1967.

[29] *Facts on File*, 1968, p. 605; E. O'Ballance, *Contemporary Review*, 210 (February, 1967), 74.

[30] T. S. An, *Orbis*, 9 (Summer, 1965), 430–31. The North Vietnamese have little love for the Chinese who were historically their oppressors. If Ho called in the Chinese "volunteers," they would be hard to get rid of. That is why he did not want to widen the war in order to preclude that necessity. The Sino-Vietnam relations were treated historically in King C. Chen, *Vietnam and China, 1938–1954* (Princeton, N. J.: Princeton University press, 1969). For a critical examination of the book, *see* the present author's book review in *Journal of Asian Studies*, 29 (August, 1970), 925–26.

[31] *Facts on File*, 1968, p. 489.

[32] E. O'Ballance, *Contemporary Review*, 210 (February, 1967), 76; *Jen-min jih-pao*, March 17, 1965, took a hard line equating peace talks to total capitulation to the US.

[33] W. Averrel Harriman, former US chief negotiator, took pains "during TV interview to more than hint at the role played by the Soviet Union in getting these talks started. The Soviet Union, Mr. Harriman was convinced, is sincerely interested in 'peaceful, neutral' Southeast Asia that would serve to block Chinese communist expansionism," *America*, 120 (February 8, 1969), 154. *See* also T. S. An, *Orbis*, 9 (Summer, 1965), 534–35. As of this writing (October, 1970), Prince Sihanouk's exile government has not been recognized by the Soviet Union which wanted Cambodia to remain neutral, *Pravda*, May 26, 1970. *See* also "Chinas Gesetz der Geschichte" (China's law of history), *Der Spiegel*, July 6, 1970, p. 75.

was formulated by a rising Chinese general, Lin Piao. His treatise, entitled "Long live the victory of people's war," reminds one of a little noticed sentence in the "Communist manifesto" that "the communists disdain to conceal their view and aims";[34] and to all intents and purposes, it lays down the ideological ground for China's diplomacy. It is a blend of theory and lines of action in world revolution. Writing with an eye on Vietnam, but mainly mapping a grand strategy for the future Armageddon of the communist and non-communist forces, Lin explains well Peking's world outlook.

Building on Mao's guerrilla tactics, Lin seeks to apply them from the intra- to the inter-national sphere. It will be recalled that in maneuvering with his mobile bands during the insurrection, Mao felt constrained to infiltrate the environs of a city and, by holding onto it, to deny sources of provision and conscription to the enemy. Such a maneuver stood him in good stead in the civil war. The basic assumption could be stated in a neat formula following H. J. Mackinder: whoever controls the rural areas will control the nation, or, whoever loses them will lose the nation. The eclat of the tactics was fairly patent at certain stages in the rise of Mao to power; however, truth requires one to append that toward the later years of the civil strife in China, the reverse was the case. Frequently the hugger-mugger retreat of the National troops from towns forced the Reds to fill in the urban void first and then fan out to the countryside. Be that as it may, Lin seized on the idea and managed to universalize it. The capitalist redoubts in North America and Western Europe, he said, are cities of the world, with rural areas in Asia, Africa and Latin America.[35] The latter continents which now form a tight-knit trio in the communist propaganda vintage are the "main battlefield of the fierce struggle between the people of the world on the one hand and U.S. imperialism on the other."[36] It is said to be the intent of American diplomacy to impose a sway upon the people in those regions, a sway which has become more vulnerable. The countermeasure, according to Mao's heir apparent, is to deny those intermediate zones to the United States by fomenting people's wars and by holding down the U.S. foot soldiers sent in for pacification. He drew the conclusion that the forces which dominate the continental trio would do-

---

[34] President Lyndon B. Johnson must have had this declaration in mind when he addressed the American Legion convention on August 6, 1966, regarding Peking's avowed intent to foment revolutionary wars in other countries. He said: "The United States must assume every word they (Chinese) utter about encouraging liberation war," *New York Times*, August 31, 1966, p. 1.

[35] *China after Mao*, p. 242.

[36] *Ibid.*, p. 247.

minate the entirety of our planet. When socialism prevails in these rural parts of the world, the urban parts would fall as a matter of course. There is nothing the United States can do to stop such a process.

The Balance of Geopolitical Forces

Lin moved on to examine the correlation of forces on the geopolitical checkerboard. In the first place, South Vietnam is a laboratory for his theme, and the battle over there is for a sector in the world rurality. Without expressly stating it, Lin conveys the idea that the struggle on the Indochinese peninsula becomes all the more vital in the race for the three continents, because it lies at the threshold of the rural hub of the world, viz., China. With Russia having counted herself out of the socialist camp, China assumes the command of the urban encirclement. This explains partly why Peking is fond of equating the Sino-Vietnam relation with the relation of teeth and lips, an oriental metaphor connoting the inseparability of any existing pair. A non-communist half of Vietnam would pose an urban threat in the mind of Lin. In the second place, having proved effective in either driving out the allies, or in engaging the mass soldiery of the imperialists,[37] the people's war will become an invincible means to storm the capitalist fortress one after another until North America and Western Europe come in for the final assault.[38] If the United States seeks to stem the tide whenever the people's war erupts, its power has to be so diffused that it lies beyond its ability to hold on forever.[39] The Chinese leader has obviously in mind the dismantling of the mutual security system of the United States,[40] whose failure to honor its commitment in one instance will be followed in rapid succession by many others. This is the Chinese domino strategy, a strategy not of the West's making.

[37] "Brilliant example of resisting to U.S. imperialist aggression: unparalleled victories of people's war in South Vietnam," *Peking Review*, 1 (January 3, 1968), 21-4.

[38] "If South Vietnam should fall to the communists, Mao Tse-tung will be able to use the victory as evidence that 'wars of national liberation' can safely be supported and even multiplied in other parts of the noncommunist underdeveloped world without danger of courting a nuclear war," T. S. An, *Orbis*, 9 (Summer, 1965), 428.

It is interesting to note the following statement by one of the leaders of the Second International during the First World War: "Der europäische Sozialismus nicht selbstzufrieden auf das automatische Ende des Kapitalismus warten dürfe, dass stillstand Rückschritt bedeute und dass die deutsche Partie ihre Stärke dazu benutzen müsse, ein Bastion des Kapitalismus nach der anderen zu stürmen (European socialism will not complacently wait for the automatic collapse of capitalism, that would mean a quiet retreat. The German party must utilize its strength to storm one capitalist fortress after another), Winfried B. Scharlan and Zbynek A. Zeman, *Freibeuter der Revolution* (A privateer of revolution) (Köln: Verlag Wissenschaft und Politik, 1964), p. 45.

[39] *China after Mao*, pp. 248–49.

[40] T. S. An, *Orbis*, 9 (Summer, 1965), 428.

In the third place, Lin must dispose of America's nuclear might in order to make cogent his argument for pushing toward the world metropolis. Here he makes a distinction between the mere possessing of thermonuclear weapons and the discretion of using them. In his strategical calculus, to possess such arms is one thing, but to be able to apply them is another. No matter how well-stocked an enemy is with mass destructive means, he can be weak nonetheless simply because the objective circumstances inhibit him from delivering them. The paper-tiger analogy refers to an America which is seen beset by dilemmas in its attempt to unleash an atomic attack. "Nuclear weapons cannot be used lightly. U.S. imperialism has been condemned by the people of the whole world for its towering crime of dropping two atom bombs on Japan. If it uses nuclear weapons again, it will become isolated in the extreme," reasoned Lin.[41] Incidentically he is the one who reverses the Chinese view on the imperialist nature. Whereas previously Peking held that America's aggressive policy would be translated into real action despite the objective handicaps, now Lin felt U.S. imperialism has been and will be deterred by the unsurmountable world public opinion. It appears as if the paper tiger has cut atomic teeth but is transplanted with a chicken heart. Furthermore, Lin asserted that Washington's self-limitation is partly attributed to the fear of retaliation. Here we see another reversal of China's pre-1965 position which predicated on the assumption that no such fear could ever exist in the minds of the Americans since belli-cosity is precipitated by the imperious urge of rapacity.

In the fourth place, the blighted world urbanity and the bright world rurality has by and large predetermined the outcome of the geopolitical scuffle. This part of Lin's theory is not new for the communist propa-ganda along that line is a familiar one. He envisions the "broadest possible united front" currently being formed against America on his rural continents in reaction to her blatant "policy of seeking domina-tion."[42] Such policy is seen instrumental in rallying up the downtrodden to oppose the U.S. Short of the aggressive course taken by Washington, in other words, there would be a slower consolidation of the millions. Thus, the progressive elements of the continental trio have taken a "big leap forward," they are taking up arms and embarking on violent revolt, shouting the battle cry: "Long live the victory of people's war," à la comrade Lin, let it be added.[43] In the last place, the world urban unrest

---

[41] *China after Mao*, p. 250.
[42] *Ibid.*, p. 247.
[43] *Ibid.*, p. 262.

and disorder is portrayed as ominous and going beyond any nostrum such as the anti-poverty and other remedial programs. Mao thinks now that the "imperialists are plunged into deep gloom."[44] The trade war is sharpening between the imperialist powers who are unable to escape perdition;[45] "economic crisis [is] looming large in capitalist world."[46] The success of people's armed forces led by the Communist Party of Burma,[47] and the "aggravation of economic crisis and intensification of class contradictions in France,"[48] all eloquently testify to the urban debacle of the imperialists. North America and Western Europe, the lands of the desperate reactionaries, have witnessed "raging waves of strikes."[49] Early in 1969, President Nixon was characterized as a frightened man assuming the reigns of a government plagued by financial stresses.[50] All in all, "a storm is shaking the backyard" of the imperialist house.[51] Sooner rather than later, the revolutionary masses will finish up with the imperialists.[52] The bourgeois society, lastly, cannot be saved by such other "gimmicks" as the "new strategy of NATO."[53]

Russia's Refutation of Lin

Lin's doctrine we have just outlined was underwritten as a state policy by the Eleventh Central Committee of the CCP on August 12, 1966. It was beatified as the truly genial contribution to, and derivation from, Chairman Mao's thought.[54] The Chinese cadres hailed it a lodestar of their revolutionary Weltanschauung. However, in contrast to the fulsome lauds inside China are the indirect and disagreeable references to it in the Soviet press. To a certain extent, this tactic of the Kremlin's holds true with Maoism, a Maoism deified in one country, but decried in another. A secretly circulated letter of the CPSU cited above treated Lin's disquisition with scorn and derision. As the Russians understood it, the focal point of the doctrine was to sprint toward world war to universalize communism.[55] In doing so, the Peking regime mistakenly relegated the role of the working class to the background. Instead, such

[44] *Peking Review*, 46 (November 19, 1968), 30.
[45] *Ibid.*, pp. 23–5.
[46] *Ibid.*, 15 (April 12, 1968), 24–6, 28.
[47] *Ibid.*, 35 (August 30, 1968), 19–20.
[48] *Ibid.*, 23 (June 7, 1968), 27–8.
[49] *Ibid.*, 19 (May 10, 1968), 23–5.
[50] *Jen-min jih-pao*, and *Hung-ch'i*, joint editorial, January 27, 1969.
[51] *Peking Review*, 42 (October 18, 1968), 21–2.
[52] *Ibid.*, 52 (December 27, 1968), 20.
[53] *Ibid.*, 1 (January 1, 1968), 48–9.
[54] *China after Mao*, pp. 277–87, at 283.
[55] *Die Welt*, March 21, 1966, p. 6.

shibbolethes as armed revolt, conspiracy, export of revolution received their highest premium in the Maoist stock of ideology. Peking, taxed Moscow, does not know that there must be multi-methods of proletarian struggle, depending on the circumstances. The Soviets quoted Lenin that it is silly, and criminal as well, to dive into a revolution for which the broad masses of people are unprepared.[56] An uprising by the working class during the ebb of a revolutionary tide merely ends in extermination of the cadres and in loss of influence of the communist party among the workers.[57] It is stated in effect that an explosive situation exists neither in North America, nor in Western Europe, nor in the continental trio as Peking pretends to have seen. Noteworthy is the fact that the dismal picture drawn of the non-communist society is conspicuous by its absence in the Russian media after 1965. A sane appreciation of the standard of life in the Western countries seems to disabuse the Russian elites of Peking's persuasion that only the grass on this side of the fence is green and disinclines them to bank on and abet the internal revolts of other nations.

In August, 1967, *Izvestiya* challenged that "if the present Chinese statesmen had the courage to speak up openly about the results of their activities," they would have to "admit their responsibility for the situation that had developed in Indonesia and in certain other parts of Asia where the struggle against imperialism has been accomplished."[58] Peking's interloping with Burmese affairs in 1967 was most caustically impugned in the Soviet press.[59] The pace of history is said to move in a zigzag way and revolution has its snags; such circumstances call for constant shift of tactics on the part of the vanguard.[60] To maintain that only "armed struggle is the road to liberation"[61] proves futile and "is tantamount to negating ... socialism and communism." The attempt of the CCP hierarchy to call on all workers' parties of the non-socialist states to rise up to overthrow the governments "in effect means to force upon the communist movement *putschist* tactics."[62] The Chinese are reminded of the ABC of Leninism: one must pay the utmost attention to the changing conditions and peculiarities of each country, as

---

[56] N. V. Tropkin, "Strategiya i taktika leninizma" (Strategy and tactics of Leninism), in *V. I. Lenin – velikii teoretik* (V. I. Lenin, a great theorist), p. 189.
[57] *Ibid.*, p. 198.
[58] *Izvestiya*, August 30, 1967.
[59] A. Shchetinkin, "Proval aventiury Pekina v Birme" (The fiasco of Peking's adventurism in Burma), *Agitator*, 19 (1967), 59–60.
[60] N. V. Tropkin, *op. cit.*, p. 199.
[61] *Peking Review*, 33 (August, 16, 1968), 10–14.
[62] *Die Welt*, March 21, 1966, p. 6.

far as revolution goes.[63] Thus, Lin's urge to storm the metropolitan heartland from the rural fringe is traduced as out-Trotskying Trotsky.[64] It betrays fully the harebrained scheme of the Maoist groups.[65] The policy-makers in Peking are catcalled by the Russians as Marxist misfit with insidious mind and heinous deportment.[66] In short, "the concept of revolution as the struggle of the world village against the world city is an outright rejection of the important part of the working people" and is thus tossing Marxism-Leninism to the winds.[67]

Change of Sides on the Nuclear-war Issue

Lastly, the Soviets take exception to the Chinese stand on the thermo-missile war. In this instance, the two parties changed sides. At the inception of the Sino-Soviet polemics, it will be recalled, Moscow stated that the balance of forces weighed so much in the East's favor that the enemy had been deterred from enkindling a war, nuclear or otherwise. Repudiating such view, Peking elected to believe in the undeterrability of the imperialists. Consequently, on the publication of Lin's article, the two disputants withdrew from their original positions. Now it is Russia which feels that nuclear war becomes more probable than ever before. Writing in an American media, a member of the Soviet Academy of Sciences, A. D. Sakharov, asserts that from an economic point of view, the fissionary arms are becoming more attractive because an advanced technology now costs less to design and manufacture them. It is, then, more tempting to rely upon these arms.[68] In essence, he suggests that countries are less inclined to produce the more expensive old weapons. In contrast, the Chinese, as we mentioned above, have all but ruled out the possibility of the imperialists' use of the nuclear bombs.

[63] S. L. Vygodskii, "Razvitie leninym politicheskoi ekonomii kapitalizma" (Lenin's elaboration of political economy of capitalism), in *V. I. Lenin – velikii teoretik* (V. I. Lenin, a great theorist), p. 80; also N. V. Tropkin, *loc. cit.* This very concept is treated in the following sources: N. V. Medvede, "Soderzhanie i forma" (Substance and form), in M. M. Rozental' and G. M. Shtraks (eds.), *Kategorii materialisticheskoi dialektiki* (Categories of materialist dialectics) (Moskva: Gos. izd-vo polit. lit-ry, 1956) p. 299; M. I. Zaozërov, "Yavlenie i sushchnost'" (Phenomenon and essence), *ibid.*, p. 78; M. M. Rozental', "O kategoriyakh materialisticheskoi dialektiki" (On the categories of materialist dialectics), *ibid.*, p. 54.

[64] *Pravda*, September 18, 1966, reprinted an editorial published in North Korea's *Rodoong shinmoon* (Labor news) of September 17, 1966.

[65] G. Apalin, "Ideologicheskie osnovy vneshnei politiki gruppy Mao Tsze-duna" (Ideological bases of the foreign policy of the Mao Tse-tung group), *Mezhdunarodnaya zhizn'* (International life), 6 (1968), 60–70, at 69.

[66] "O politicheskom kurse Mao Tsze-duna na mezhdunarodnoi arene" (On the political course of Mao Tse-tung on the international arena), *Kommunist*, 8 (May, 1968), 95–108, at 97, 98, 102.

[67] *Die Welt*, March 21, 1966, p. 6.

[68] "A thought about progress, peaceful coexistence and intellectual freedom," *New York Times*, July 22, 1968, pp. 15–16.

Other than this difference, their views on the tolls of war remain unchanged, with Russia continually deploring the high sacrifices to advance socialism.[69] A Soviet novel by Konstantin Simonov evolves around the moral that revolutionary war is a tragedy. Almost immediately, the book drew fire from Peking which dubbed it anti-revolutionary poison.[70] It was reported in a Moscow media that in an interview by a foreign newsman, the Chinese Foreign Minister, Ch'en Yi, said: "If the United States imperialists decided to force a war of aggression upon us, then we would welcome it, if they can, even earlier. We would welcome it if they come as early as tomorrow." This, the Soviets remarked, was bad enough, for he was plainly provocative. But "what should one think ... of the statement of the same Ch'en Yi: 'With the help of the atom bomb one may destroy one or two generations of people. But the third generation will rise to offer resistance and peace will be restored.'" The Mao Tse-tung man, went on the Soviets, did not know that in a world conflict, there would be no third generation who could "rise." "Such a disparaging approach to the lives of millions of people, to the fate of entire nation only compromises the ideology and goal of communism," it is lamented.[71]

SINO-SOVIET NON-COEXISTENCE

Peking: The Non-coexistence of Capitalist and Socialist States

In the post-Khrushchev altercation, the problem of peaceful coexistence, which he first brought up in 1956 to support his line of detente, has taken a fresh import.[72] Whereas previously coexistence referred to states of the East and West blocs, now intra-East bloc coexistence becomes problematical. It will be recalled that the former premier realized that a new epoch is dawning, an epoch in which states

[69] N. V. Tropkin, *op. cit.*, p. 196; see also *V. I. Lenin, kratkii biograficheskii ocherk* (V. I. Lenin, a short biographical sketch; 4th ed.), (Moskva: Gos. izd-vo polit. lit-ry, 1966), p. 116.

[70] The novel is called *Days and nights*, see Hsieh Sheng-wen, "Poisonous specimen of revisionist days and nights," *Peking Review*, 13 March(29, 1968), 35–7.

[71] *Die Welt*, March 21, 1966, p. 6. The interview with Ch'en Yi to which the Russians referred was made by an Uruguayan reporter, Carlos M. Gutierrez. It was originally published in *Marcha* of Montevideo, and translated in: "Hidden tiger," *Atlas*, 12 (October, 1966), 10–15, at 10.

[72] For a reaffirmation of coexistence by Brezhnev, *see* an editorial: "Vernost' geroicheskim traditsiyam" (Faithful to the heroic traditions), *Pravda*, May 9, 1969; by Kosygin, *see* "Poslanie Predsedatelya Soveta Ministrov SSSR, A. N. Kosygina, Preredentu SSHA, Prezidentu Frantsii, Prem'eru Ministru Velikobritanii, v svyazi s 25-letiem Potsdamskogo soglasheniya" (The message of the Chairman of the Council of Ministers of the USSR, A. N. Kosygin, to the President of the United States, the President of France, and the Prime-Minister of Great-Britain on the occasion of the 25th anniversary of the Potsdam Declaration), *Pravda*, August 2, 1970.

having different social systems will live side by side peaceably. In Peking's view, the proponents of the slogan are visionary and fail to answer the question with whom to coexist. The Russians, however, feel that the alternative is war and that coexistence is a necessity. Apropos of the issue at stake, Leninism is indecisive and, as a matter of fact, provides each side with grounds from which to attack the other. It is well known that Lenin once spoke of coexistence in the belief that such was the practical way,[73] and another time of the impossibility of it.[74] This complexity of Lenin's mind lies beyond the scope of the present work; we shall, instead, confine ourselves to the current argument between China and Russia regarding this very issue, and try to find out if they can live together themselves. To begin with, capitalism is not deemed by the Chinese as a worthy social system as it symbolized the intolerable oppression of the workers.[75] To pair it with socialism is a lack of good sense. Moreover, since one system is to supplant the other

[73] Peaceful coexistence was first brought out during the 1922 Genoa conference, see Lenin, *Sochineniya* (Collected works; 4th ed.), vol. 27, p. 49; vol. 30, pp. 20–21. For a contemporary discussion on that historical event, see Kuusinen, "Pretvorenie v zhizn' idei lenina" (To implement Lenin's ideas), *Pravda*, April 23, 1960; N. Inozemtsev, "Velichie leninskoi politiki mira" (The great Leninist policy of peace), *Kommunist*, 6 (April, 1964), 28–38; *idem*, "Mirnoe sosuchestvovanie i mirovoi revoliutsionnyi protsess" (Peaceful coexistence and world revolutionary process), *Pravda*, July 28, 1963. For an English material, see Lazar M. Pistrak, "Lenin and peaceful coexistence," *Problems of communism*, 8 (November–December, 1959), 53–6.

[74] The impossibility of peaceful coexistence was suggested by Lenin on three different occasions. The first time was in 1915. "O lozunge soedinennykh shtatov evropy" (On the slogan of the United States of Europe), August, 1915, in *O voine, armii i voennoi nauke* (On war, army and military science; 2nd ed.), p. 273. The second time was in 1916. "Voennaya programma proletarskoi revoliutsii" (The military program of the proletarian revolution), September, 1916, *ibid.*, p. 303. Here Lenin attributed the idea of non-coexistence to Engels. See Marx and Engels, *Sochineniya* (Collected works; 2nd ed.), vol. 35, pp. 296–98; as quoted in *ibid.*, p. 303. The third time was when Lenin addressed the Eighth Party Congress in March 18, 1919. This statement can be found in any one of the following sources: (1) *ibid.*, 1st ed., vol. 2, p. 373; (2) *idem*, *Sochineniya* (Collected works; 4th ed.), (Moskva: Gos. izd-vo polit. lit-ry, 1914–57, vol. 29, pp. 131–36; (3) *idem*, *Selected Works* (London: Lawrence and Wishart, 1936), vol. 8, p. 33.

It is of some interest to note that the concept of life-and-death struggle was not widely cited by the Soviets. Stalin spoke of it twice: once in his "Pis'mo t. Ivanova i otvest t. Stalina" (The letter of comrade Ivanov and comrade Stalin's reply), *Bol'shevik*, 4 (February 15, 1938), 14. This letter does not appear in his *Sochineniya* (Collected works; 13 vols., published from 1946 to 1951, covering his writings up to 1934); another time in his famous "Osnovy leninizma" (The foundations of Leninizm), in his *Sochineniya*, vol. 7, pp. 95–6.

The present writer can only find two other references to the concept at issue. One appears in M. V. Frunze, "Soedinnenoe uchenie i Krasnaya Armiya" (A unified military doctrine and the Red Army), *Voennaya nauka i revoliutsiya* (military science and revolution), 1 (1921), 39. Elsewhere Frunze said that coexistence was only a temporary affair, see his *Izbrannye proizvedeniya* (Selected works), vol. 2, p. 316.

Another appears in L. Leont'ev, *Leninskaya teoriya imperializma* (Lenin's theory of imperialism), p. 124. Even the militant M. Tukhavcheskii did not adduce Lenin's slogan of a struggle for existence between the Soviets and their opponents in his article in the first ed. of the *Bol'shaya sovetskaya entsiklopedia* (The great Soviet encyclopedia), vol. 12.

[75] *Sino-Soviet Dispute*, p. 92.

as the only way of human life, it is an obvious *non sequitur* to propound their coexistence. Peking believes it axiomatic that vice and virtue cannot coexist, nor can god and demon, wolf and lamb, Buddha and butcher, horse and its rider, and, of course, capitalist and socialist states. Nearly thirty years ago, Mao Tse-tung discussed this same problem, using the simile of dark-and-light to signify the absurdity of the functioning of two antithetics at one given time.[76]

Moscow: The Non-coexistence of Capitalist and Socialist Ideologies

Put on the defensive, the Soviets have cudgeled their brains to explain their stand by pointing to the ideological non-coexistence on the one side, and to the business-like and merely "correct" relations between West and East, on the other.[77] To live with the capitalist nations implied no laxity of principle struggle. "The contemporary world is in a hell of a fight between hostile patterns of life and world views," wrote L. F. Il'ichev.[78] "Ideological coexistence," enunciated the Central Committee of the CPSU, "is a high treason to Marxism-Leninism."[79] Nevertheless, the very being of the capitalist regime is a fact itself; one may frown upon, but not ignore, it altogether.[80] Philosophical struggle is rendered that much easier if states with different systems cease and desist from estrangement and if chances are there for the socialist states to demonstrate their superiority in practice as well as in principle. Such chances are bright in the milieux of international comity, but evaporate in a tense world.[81] Therefore, peaceful coexistence does not import an approbation of the despicable capitalism, dilutes no Marxism-Leninism, and only accedes to the "objective necessity and historical regularity."[82]

[76] Mao Tse-tung, "Tsai yen-an wen-i tso-t'an hui shong ti t'an-hua" (A talk at the literary table in Yenan), May 2, 1942, in *Mao Tse-tung hsüan-ch'i* (Collected Works), 1953, vol. 3, p. 849.
[77] Iu. Krasin, *Filosofskie nauki* (Philosophical sciences), 5 (1963), 11; *V. I. Lenin, kratkii biograficheskii ocherk* (V. I. Lenin, a short biographical sketch), pp. 202–03.
[78] *Ocherednye zadachi ideologischekoi raboti partii* (The next task of Part's ideological work) (Moskva: Gos. izd-vo polit. lit-ry, 1963), p. 4.
[79] *Postanovleniya plenuma Tsk KPSS* (The decisions of the plenum of the Central Committee of the CPSU, June, 1963) (Moskva: Gos. izd-vo polit. lit-ry, 1963), p. 4.
[80] *Leninskaya diplomatiya mira i sotrudnichstva* (Lenin's diplomacy of peace and cooperation) (Moskva: Izd-vo "Nauka," 1965), p. 4. V. G. Smolyanskii, *Mirovaya sotsialisticheskaya sistema i antikommunizma* (World socialist system and anticommunism), p. 82.
[81] V. V. Platkovskii wrote: "The transition from capitalism to socialism can undoubtedly be shortened, provided there will be no war, a war which diverts our attention away from peaceful construction and makes us to continue proletarian dictatorship," *see* his "Leninskoe uchenie o diktature proletariata i sotsialisticheskom gosudarstve" (Lenin's doctrine of proletarian dictatorship and socialist state), in *V. I. Lenin – velikii teoretik* (V. I. Lenin, a great theorist), p. 272. The Soviets say they have passed the period of proletarian dictatorship and entered the all-people's democracy; any war would force them to slide back.
[82] N. V. Pilippenko, "Neobkhodimost' i sluchainost'" (Inevitability and fortuity), in M. M.

In addition, coexistence precludes no propaganda aimed at cultivating class hatred and debars no support of the liberation movement.[83]

Lack of A Basis of Coexistence Between Moscow And Peking

However, there is a common ground on which both disputants stand in the problem at issue, namely, to coexist with the people concerned, not necessarily their governments. The Chinese express no enmity against the working masses in capitalist nations and attack only the ruling cliques whom they deem as unrepresentative of those masses. For example, Peking media vociferously cheered the "American people' in their refuting of the Johnson administration's policy in Vietnam.[84] The Soviets, while continuing their long tradition in assailing the power wielders of the West, have a different view on the relation between, say, the White House and the American public. The latter are said to like their way of live. Such an identification of the ruled and the rulers by the Russians makes them empathetic with the capitalist regime; it surely inclines them toward a policy of cooperation. There is little doubt that Brezhnev and company feel that the imperialists stand for their people just as much as they theirs and that Russia is dealing with regimes not just isolated from, inimical to, and universally refuted by, the peasants and workers. Therefore, the people and their governments in the West are worth coexisting with. How have the Kremlin leaders sized up their counterpart in Peking? As it will be discussed in the following pages, the CCP is asserted to have declared war on the Chinese masses and would have been forced out of office save for the punitive arms at its disposal. Hence coexistence with that sort of regime is not what can be inferred from the Soviet view of the problem. The same can be said from the Chinese stance, for Peking also regards the CPSU as an illegitimate authority. The CCP has frankly made it known that it cannot deal with such traitors as Brezhnev and company.

Besides, coexistence premises on the all too clear assumption that one's fellow-states hatch no plot to destroy himself. Were such a plot seen in the making, coexistence is a deceit. In that event, elimination of a state or its government, instead of keeping it at arm's length, has to be the logical result. Viewed from this angle, Sino-Soviet coexistence

Rozental' and G. M. Shtraks (eds.), *Kategorii materialisticheskoi dialektiki* (Categories of materialist dialectics), p. 143.

[83] Iu. Krasin, *Filosofiskie nauki*, pp. 10–12; Pukhovskii, *op. cit.*, pp. 136–42. *See* also M. I. Kolesnikova, *Mirnoe sosushchestvovanie i voprosy voiny i mira* (Peaceful coexistence and the problems of peace and war) (Moskva: Izd-vo Moskovskogo Universiteta, 1968), p. 26.

[84] "Salute to the American people for their struggle against U.S. aggression in Vietnam," *Peking Review*, 14 (April 1, 1966), 9–11.

lacks foundation, for each has accused the other of forming a hostile alignment with the avowed purpose to attack and annihilate it. A related point of the issue pertains to the basic character of government. Since the Chinese have long professed their inability to exist with an imperialist regime, and since the Russian regime is imperialist, co-existence is certainly out of the question. On its side, the CPSU has sworn its non-coexistence with an ideology alien to Marxism-Leninism, and now that Mao and his followers have betrayed that lofty principle, coexistence à la russe loses its meaning too. Thus from either Peking's or Moscow's viewpoint, living side by side between them is impossible. Let us examine the respective charges bearing on this issue.

Russo-American Alignment

One of the most remarkable developments in the Peking and Moscow rift concerns what even the most audacious speculators could not have foreseen toward the end of the Khrushchev era. It is again the Vietnam war that is accountable for this new phase. Throughout 1965 their mass media intermittently alluded to the help allegedly given the United States by either side. Nothing substantial, however, has ever been divulged. Definite charges of conspiracy began to emerge during the 20th plenary session of the United Nations, a session watched attentively by Peking. On January 1, 1966, the Chinese press for the first time formally came out with the allegation of the Russo-American swindle in the world body under the headline: "The UN – a market place for U.S.-Soviet political deals."[85] Thenceforth, similar assertives have become the daily food for the Chinese masses; their repetitious monotony is only matched by their vibrant loquacity. Now a modern dark age is opened in the eternal battle between progress and reaction, Peking warned. Coming in for flaying was the regime of the world's first social-ist state, it looked as if the beacon lights of yesteryear turn out to be the evil genii of today. Peking's fulmination is multi-pronged, all zero-ing in on the putative Janus-faced men of the Kremlin. First, there is the indictment of a USSR-US protocol to maintain the status quo. Each party is said to have had enough sphere of influence and agreed not to be disgorged by the other. Mindful of America's paper strength, the Chinese leaders are literally nauseous of this cowardly policy of the Soviets.[86] Mutually accomodating, both refrained from stirring up in-

[85] *Peking Review*, 1 (January 1, 1966), 13.
[86] *Jen-min jih-pao*, August 30, 1966.

cidents and from treading on each other's toes, the Chinese charged.[87]

To the Maoists, the political world has entered an ice age with the frozen poles at Washington and Moscow.[88] The cunning rivalry is assuaged by a repartition of the world, a phrase reminding one of Lenin's scoffing at the imperialists during the First World War days.[89] Further reaching out from the duo-fortress, North America and Eurasia, would be undertaken with tacit consent and connivance. Such attempt, Peking is confident, will meet timely and stout repulsion from the people. No matter what is being done to check the historical wheel by the amalgam of the two forces, the effort will not succeed. It takes a miracle to "block the triumphant advance of Marxism, Leninism, and Mao Tse-tung's thought," asserted the Chinese.[90] Foreign Minister Ch'en Yi officially condemned the United States and Soviet Governments for collaboration to redivide the globe.[91]

Second, the alignment has been responsible for the Kremlin's tolerance of American aggression in Vietnam. *Jen-min jih-pao* berated the Soviet Union as an accomplice of U.S. gangsters in a campaign to extinguish the fire of the Vietnam national liberation.[92] After President Johnson delivered a speech on October 7, 1966, and alluded to a somewhat amenable Russian stand toward given problems, a Chinese press suspected: "Soviet-United States alliance was already in existence, but it was simply inconvenient for both countries to make it public."[93] Ostentatiously supporting the victims of U.S. imperialism, the Soviet rulers are out-and-out traitors to them.[94] Unable to put a finger on any specific instrument embodying the imputed Russo-American deal, Peking rationalized that it was only after being assured that the Soviet Union would not disturb the balance of power in Europe that Washington moved to transfer "part of its armed forces, artillery and munition from Europe to South Vietnam."[95] Russia, therefore, was held by Peking directly responsible for bringing U.S. power to bear upon the rebels. Third, there is said to be a cordon sanitaire around China. Mao's spokesmen saw in the making a U.S.-USSR-Chiang alliance as a result

---

[87] *Peking Review*, 1 (January 1, 1966), 13.
[88] *Jen-min jih-pao*, August 30, 1966.
[89] *Ibid.*, and *Hung-ch'i*, joint editorial, January 27, 1969.
[90] *Ibid.*
[91] *Peking Review*, 37 (September 13, 1968), 31.
[92] *Jen-min jih-pao*, April 30, 1967.
[93] *Ibid.*, October 16, 1966.
[94] *Peking Review*, 1 (January 1, 1966), 13; *Jen-min jih-pao*, August 30, 1966.
[95] *Ibid.*; *Peking Review*, 1 (January 1, 1966), 13.

of a suspected two-China policy of the Soviet leaders.[96] Also a Japan-Soviet amity was said to have been rivetted against none other than Peking.[97] Further, China viewed the treaty between Russia and West Germany, signed on August 12, 1970, with alarm, alleging its "sell-out of the interests" of the Chinese, German and other European peoples.[98] The future of world revolution would suffer greatly, she exclaimed.

Fourth and last, America and Russia have built a joint "force de frappe" threatening the lives of millions upon millions. It called the attention of the entire world to the "grave step in forming a U.S.-Soviet counterrevolution nuclear-military alliance."[99] Hsinhua, the Chinese news agency, sought to justify Mao's effort at atomic armament in these words: "China's purpose in developing nuclear weapons is precisely to oppose the nuclear monopoly and nuclear blackmail by the United States and the Soviet Union acting in collusion."[100] It has been Peking's belief that there came into being a "holy alliance" in the tandem of Soviet revisionism and U.S. imperialism.[101] The mouthpiece of Mao cited evidence after evidence to prove the existence of such an alliance, the latest one being the "Rogers plan" for the peace in the Middle East.[102] In view of Peking's implacable attitude toward its former ally, Western writers have gradually come to hold that the Soviet Union has begun to replace the United States as China's chief adversary.[103]

[96] *Ibid.; Jen-min jih-pao*, August 30, 1966; also August 30, 1970. *Peking Review*, 3 (January 16, 1970), 4.

[97] *Ibid.*, 6 (February 4, 1966), 10–13. *See* also *Toronto Courier* (in German), October 8, 1970, p. 4.

[98] *Jen-min jih-pao*, September 18, 1970; *Peking Review*, 38 (September 18, 1970), 7–12. A denunciatory editorial of *Zeri i popullit* (an Albanian paper) was reprinted in *ibid.*, pp. 12–16.

[99] *Peking Review*, 12 (March 22, 1968), 31–2.

[100] *Facts on File*, 1966, p. 411. The non-proliferation treaty was characterized as "another big exposure of U.S.-Soviet counterrevolution collaboration," *Peking Review*, 28 (July 12, 1968), 5–6; "Nuclear fraud jointly hatched by the big two," *ibid.*, 25 (June 21, 1968), 17–18.

[101] *Ibid.*, 12 (March 12, 1969), 25.

[102] "U.S. imperialism ... [is] forcibly pushing the 'Rogers plan' ... in collusion with another 'superpower'," *ibid.*, 38 (September 25, 1970), 18. *See* also "Confessions concerning the line of Soviet-U.S. collaboration pursued by the new leaders of the CPSU," *ibid.*, 8 (February 18, 1966), 6–12.

[103] For example, L. Abegg, "Hass und Hassliebe" (Hate and love of hate), *Die Weltwoche*, March 21, 1969, p. 1. The author wrote: "Manche Beobachter der Geschehnisse in China waren seit langens der Meinung, dass sich schliesslich die Sowjetrussen und nicht die Amerikaner als Hauptfeinde dieses Landes entpuppen würden" (Many observers of the events in China have long arrived at the conclusion that finally Russia, not America, turns out to be China's main enemy). *See* also H. E. Salisbury, "Aircraft ready all over Siberia; China now treats Russia as the enemy," *New York Times*, August 17, 1966, p. 6; E. Brownlow, "Chinese threat seen focused on Soviets," *Aviation Weekly*, 85 (November 14, 1966), 29.

China Is a Partner to Imperialists

To this array of charges, the Russian did not answer seriatim. The allegation of encirclement and collusion between various states seems to be clearly unfounded; the nuclear deal is scarcely less so, although the non-proliferation treaty may be viewed as disadvantageous to the non-nuclear states in terms of power and prestige. The matter of the division of the world is implausible for there can hardly be a mutual understanding concerning the respective domains of the two great powers. Even though there is a Russian share of the world in the eastern part of Europe, the concept of an American share is hazy and undefinable. Indeed, the Chinese never attempted to draw on a map the suspect spheres of America and Russia. The very slogan of division of the world provides an apt example showing how the Peking rulers find it hard to modify their Leninist vocabulary. Regarding the Vietnam war, the CPSU turned the table round, so to speak, against the CCP. Its official media regarded Mao as being instrumental in America's continued domination in southeast Asia. He has trivialized the platform embraced by the world communist conferences in previous years and hampered Ho Chi-minh's war effort by refusing to forward the aid promptly to him. It is clearly implied that such refusal was close to courting the imperialist advance.[104]

Izvestiya sought to bring the Chinese to task for their part in escalating the conflict. It asserted: "For nearly ten years after the Geneva conference, the United States had refrained from large-scale intervention there. It is only after China flatly rejected the call by the Soviet Union ... for unity of action and began to pursue its ... anti-Soviet line, did the U.S. step up its involvement."[105] Such an attitude of Peking's was critized by scores of workers' parties with a pro-CPSU cast of mind, and was linked to communist setbacks in many areas of the world. D. Vol'skii collected all of these criticisms and put them out in one of the Soviet media with the heading: "Expansion of the United States and Peking's policy, from foreign press."[106] The Russian suspicion of an agreement between China and the United States appeared in 1967. V. Matveyev wrote that China made it clear that she would not intervene in Vietnam unless she herself is attacked by the United States. This the author took to mean a Sino-American understanding that China would

[104] "Po povodu sobytii v kitae" (Events in China) *Pravda*, November 27, 1966.
[105] *Izvestiya*, August 30, 1967.
[106] "Ekspansiya SSHA i politika Pekina, po stranitsam zarubezhnoi pechati," *Novoe vremya* (New time), 47 (1967), 11–13.

refrain from rendering help to Hanoi in return for immunity from United States invasion.[107] This is the diplomatic speculation made in Moscow to counter the one made in Peking.

The existence of Washington and Peking rapprochement in opposition to Russia herself is also suggested in the Soviet press. In an article titled "Peking and Washington: a new round," B. Bulatov professed to have discerned an increasingly favorite stand of the "United States monopoly toward Peking's proposal of a February, 1969 talk," a talk which was later cancelled due to the Liao Ho-shu affair.[108] The feature writer quoted from the *Weekly Tribune of Ceylon* that the United States instructed all its Information Agencies to support Mao against the USSR. He related this to steady assault of the Chinese media upon the Soviet Government and drew the inference that the reactionaries in the U.S. had joined forces in the struggle with Russia and that Mao directed his main efforts against her by counting on the silent prop of the U.S. The Sino-American pact, he went on, was merely a hypocritical cover for planned collaboration on an anti-Soviet basis.[109] The same conclusion was reached by B. Olginskii. In an article titled "In expectation of a fine day," he answered his own oratorial question, "How are the Sino-U.S. relations to be improved?" by stating: "Needless to say, Russophobia unites them."[110] The alleged detente of Peking and Washington is no more true than that of Moscow and Washington.[111] Their lack of factual basis and credibility makes further comment superfluous.

BOURGEOIS COMMUNISM

A new recrimination made its appearance in the oral war between Moscow and Peking during the past several years. In every respect, it is not foreseen, especially when one recollects the rather mawkish love of the two parties in the early fifties. Their fraternity was once saluted as inexhaustible as the currents in the Volga and Yangtse, and as towering as the Urals and Tienshan. Mao even wrote into the Constitution of the Chinese People's Republic the good relations in these words: "Our country has already built an indestructible friend-

---

[107] *Izvestiya*, March 29, 1967.
[108] *Free China Weekly*, 9 (February 23, 1969), 1.
[109] *Literaturnaya gazeta*, 50 (December 11, 1968), 9.
[110] *Ibid.*, 4 (January 22, 1969), 10.
[111] For a Russian denial of the Moscow-Washington detente, *see* M. I. Sladskovskii's introduction to *Leninskaya politika SSSR v otnoshenii Kitaya* (Lenin's policy of USSR toward China), p. 18. For a Western comment, *see* K. L. London, *Russian Review*, 26 (January, 1967), 35.

ship with the Union of Soviet Socialist Republics."[112] Now that a state's constitution is the law of laws, such comradeship of China toward Russia, enshrined in that law, has to be the policy of policies. From this propitious start to the present day, their diplomacy of affection has traveled its longest way and reached its sourest end.[113] The perigee is the imperialism charge, there being no more vicious epithet left as far as the communist war of words goes. Further than this has to be a war of swords which has already been described as within the realm of likelihood after the Damanskii (in Chinese geography, Chen-pao) incidents in March, 1969.[114] In logical terms, the allegations enumerated in the preceding section would lead to name-calling each other as imperialist, a charge patently implied in such phrases as division of the world, encirclement of China, etc. Because of their recitative way of learning (a way of millennial standing) and their alacrity to transfer the learning, the Chinese quickly apply Leninism to denigrate Lenin's compatriot progeny. This we shall see in the following pages.

Origins of Soviet Embourgeoisement

The Chinese launched a three-flanked offensive on social-imperialism, colonial exploitation and bourgeois communism. In their imprecatory stock, there are also such other articles as social fascism, neo-mercantilism, new-Czarism, war-lordly Bolshevism, and the like; but they can be subsumed under one of the three main categories. Building on Lenin's theory of capitalist imperialism, the CCP leaders sought to account for what they referred to as social imperialism by an economic dissection of the Russian polity. In good Leninist methodology, they set out to posit that Russian economy has waned bourgeois.[115] If this viewpoint is substantiated, they just fall back on Lenin's words with little supererogation. That Stalin left the Soviet Union a full-fledged socialist state

[112] The Soviets charged the unfriendly policy of Peking toward them as unconstitutional, see *Korni nyneshnikh sobytii v Kitae* (The roots of the present events in China), p. 17.

[113] "Red romance that went sour," *Life*, 60 (April 8, 1966), 20–25.

[114] Konstantin Simonov, "Mysli v skukh" (Thoughts in ears), *Pravda*, May 4, 1969. He wrote: "We know from history that war cannot always be stopped; we are obligated to know this." On the 24th anniversary of Soviet victory over the Nazis, Defense Minister, A. Grechko, stated: "Soviet troops are on guard and ready for action." He lashed at the adventurist and provocative policy of Mao Tse-tung, "Velikaya pobeda" (The great victory), *ibid.*, May 9, 1969. For an early Western speculation along the same line, see Victor Zorza, "Russia hints at war risk with China," *Guardian*, February 16, 1967, pp. 1, 16.

[115] The Soviets have discerned such an attempt of the Chinese and stated the Chinese just parroted what the imperialists have long chattered about Russia, see R. I. Kosokarov, "Politicheskie vzaimootnosheniya sotsialisticheskikh stran interpretatsii ideologov imperializma" (Political relations of socialist states in the interpretation of the imperialist ideologues), in *Mirovaya sotsialisticheskaya sistema i antikommunizm* (World socialist system and anti-communism), p. 131.

is readily conceded by Peking. In fact, it was accentuated merely to dramatize the alleged degeneracy of that ex-land of socialism. Following the death of Stalin, however, his country has begun to veer to the capitalist road, commencing with Malenkov's emphasis on consumer industry. After his downfall, the bourgeois come-back goes apace in every facet of life.[116]

Oblivious of the revolutionary vocation, and entranced by the charms of luxury, the CPSU elites set highest esteem on mundane comfort. Things characteristic of the declining West have become ubiquitous in their country. It is deplored by Peking that the young people, "the most active and vital force in history,"[117] have been deflowered. "The Soviet revisionist Komsomol [is the] tool for restoring capitalism," wrote an organ of the Central Committee of the CCP.[118] Compared with the Chinese counterpart tempered and hardened in a crucible of the Great Proletarian Cultural Revolution, the Russian teenagers are being nurtured as a swarm of locusts. Unworthy of the land of Lenin, Russia's Mao Tse-tung, those adolescents are living off the hard labor of the masses. Who are those parasites, after all? Are they scions of workers and peasants? "No!" answered the Chinese. They are the "pampered sons and daughters of the privileged class," the name Komsomol has been modified by the Chinese with the epithetic "so-called."[119]

A Society of Namby and Pamby

It is abominable to the puritan Chinese to observe, in the Soviet state, "wedding ceremonies with revived antiquities," instead of taking a vow citing the Chairman's quotations, as is done in China now. Besides, the films, music, vaudevilles, jamborees, and festivals of many sorts are all eaten into by bourgeois erosives.[120] When the future builders of communism are moulded this way, the Soviet body politic has lost all its nutrients. The studied cultivation of capitalist esthetics goes on in the academic circles. Scholars in the several disciplines are hungry for bookish romanticism. Particularly angering Peking is the "convergence theory" of Sakharov, prognosticating a gradual intershading of capital-

[116] The Soviets invariably blamed the imperialists for "sending ideological poison into our country," *Robitnycha hazeta*, February 21, 1968, p. 1. They charged the Chinese of falsely depicting life in the Soviet Union, "Anti-sovetskaya deyatel'nost' kitaiskikh diplomatov" (Anti-Soviet activity of Chinese diplomats), *Izvestiya*, January 12, 1969.
[117] Mao Tse-tung, *Quotations from Chairman Mao-Tse-tung* (Peking: Foreign Languages press, 1966), p. 290.
[118] *Peking Review*, 51 (December 20, 1968), 27.
[119] "Glimpses into the Soviet revisionist renegade clique's restoration of capitalism," *ibid.*, (March 10, 1968), 28.
[120] *Ibid.*

ist and socialist economies. Ridiculous talks like this, asserted the CCP, have sown the seeds of destruction of the Soviet structure.[121] These professional aristocrats are said to have misplaced their "isms." Resolute not to crack down on such putrid elements, the Kremlin has pursued a policy of laissez-faire. By all accounts, "Soviet institutes of higher learning [have] turned into tools for all-round exploitation," regretted Peking.[122] Further, Russian writers and cinematics have produced nothing of socialistic redemption, seeking only to gratify the vulgar fondness of the pseudo-communists, and have hired themselves out as the "sordid salesmen of reactionary Western cultures," it was averred.[123] There cannot be sifted one Marxist-Leninist grain out of the immense chaff of plays, novels, scenarios, and what not. Yet those men of letters received the highest rewards and, thus, constituted a caste set apart from the mass of toilers. Worse yet are the bureaucrats, the party pen-pushers, the military elites, the managerial slave-drivers, the trade-unionists and other ill-sorted *apparatchiki* who all give their own interests precedence over the interests of the proletariat. Having lost communication with the people, they immerse themselves in a world of their own, a world that becomes ever more petty and piteous.

Corrupted Officialdom

The rampant defalcation, mutual protection and patronage, doctoring of reports, fabrication of figures, red-tape, brutality, profiteering, and black marketing are the order of an average Soviet day. "The unbridled activities of the bourgeoisie against the proletariat are widespread ... in the sphere of production as well as the sphere of circulation ... all the way ... from the grass-roots to the higher leading bodies."[124] Since the new rulership took over in 1964, the Soviet state has become more capitalistic than even under Khrushchev. Now Brezhnev and company have taken measures to retool industry and agriculture so as to blur altogether the distinction between socialism and free enterprise.[125] Look, Peking cries out, at such stuffs as private incentive,

---

[121] The convergence theory and its critiques could be found in: V. Cheprakov, "Problemy poslednei treti veka" (The problems of the last thirty years of the century), *Izvestiya*, August 11, 1968.

[122] *Peking Review*, 31 (August 2, 1968), 27–8.

[123] *See* the article by Hung Tsin-ta and Nan Hsueh-lin, *ibid.*, 44 (November 1, 1968), 25 –6, 28. Now and then, the Russian press sounded the alarm of the arrival of Western ideas, *Radyanska Ukraina*, June 6, 1968, pp. 3–4.

[124] *China after Mao*, p. 145.

[125] "Soviet revisionist renegades step up capitalist reorganization of economy," *Peking Review*, 44 (November 1, 1968), 23–5.

hodgepodge of advertisement, surplus-sharing, etc.[126] What do all these lead to and what do all these signify? The Chinese proceed to examine. They point to the swindle of the men of the Kremlin and held in contempt the slogan of "welfare for the whole people," a slogan designed to give the people a bit of psychological sop. In reality, the people get nothing from it, they are as miserably exploited as their brethren in the imperialist countries. The true beneficiaries, Peking goes on, are not those who have been shedding sweat, tears and blood (the toilers), but the revisionists elites. Upon the broad backs of the former, the latter shamelessly ride.[127]

Peking sees the "capitalized" Soviet regime as the prime reasons for this state of sorrow. It says free economy has shown its ugly face in the West and has fathered nothing but penury, stagnation, depression, privilege for the few, and privation for the many. A similar fate is seen befalling the Soviet masses. The pervasive corruption denoted a hard life which forces the cadres to roam for extra pelves. Basically, should the whole system be built on the socialist tenet, there would be abundance, for all. The scandal, then, would be healed at its roots. But, alas! the Chinese sigh, such is not the case in Russia now. There they see a replica of what is happening in a capitalist country. A nominally egalitarian society has generated the most blatant cleavage; there is the gaping hiatus in the distribution of wealth between the common men at the bottom and the handful at the apex. The rich are grinding the face of the poor and they are doing so under the exalted verbalism of commonwealth or people's well-being. "Soviet workers in abyss of suffering" heads an article in a Peking journal.[128] After fifty years of socialism and countless promises to heighten the people's standard of life, what has actually come to pass is "ruthless exploitation and enslavement" of the little men by the bosses.[129] The latter sleep on the socialist bed, but chase the capitalist dream.[130] Year in and year out, Brezhnev and company make fantastic claims of bumper harvest; but, Peking is elated to say, this represents an array of white lies.[131] The Soviet agriculture has irreparably gone from bad to worse, and, short of magic, will come to the brink of total collapse. No matter how saga-

---

[126] *Ibid.*, 19 (May 10, 1968), 28.
[127] "Capitalist restoration in the Soviet Union, the true picture of so-called welfare for the whole people," *ibid.*, 7 (January 16, 1968), 36–7.
[128] *Ibid.*, 42 (October 18, 1967), 20–24.
[129] *Ibid.*
[130] *Ibid.*, 44 (November 1, 1968), 20–21.
[131] *Ibid.*, 4 (January 24, 1969), 27–8; 18 (April 30, 1970), 23–6.

cious the propaganda is, the true plight may never be concealed for long. The people always keep their eyes open, rarely letting themselves be deluded. In short, "sophistry cannot cover up reality in the Soviet Union," declared Peking.[132]

SOCIAL IMPERIALISM

Embarking Upon Foreign Adventurism

In view of such a tragic picture, the Peking regime has manifested its regret and at the same time professed to descry a gleam of hope. Seeming to share with J. J. Rousseau a kind of universal sympathy for the suffering of men, the Chinese are standing with the Russian masses. "The Soviet revisionist perverse action promotes further awakening of Soviet people," Mao and his associates are glad to observe.[133] Like the capitalist regime in the West, the Soviet regime has no popular base and will be smashed to pieces in a general uprising of the oppressed. All the anti-people's forces, whether socialist or capitalist, have been doomed; before the people's court, they will soon be brought to justice and made to pay for their crimes.[134] Until such a court pronounces its verdict, the repressive and anti-socialist Kremlin leaders have to cast about for ways to secure their positions in the same fashion as any unhappy governing côtérie is wont to do. Now that the CPSU "revisionist renegade clique [is] riddled with contradictions," the alternative is either to submit to the workers' mandate, that is, return the power to them, or to resort to colonial adventure. Since they have refused to do the former, only the latter remains, an old method which resembles the straw snatched by a drowning man. The line of reasoning used by Peking is not unlike that used by Lenin. On account of the forlorn state of affairs at home, the Soviet Government has to turn abroad to seek raw materials and markets. The outcome is the economic strangulation of other nations which may even be more developed than the Soviet Union.

Colonial Exploitation – Soviet Style

The major step in economic imperialism is to create the CMEA (Council for Mutual Economic Aid). Behind such screens as reciprocal trade,

---

[132] *Ibid.*, 32 (August 9, 1968), 25–6.

[133] *Ibid.*, 4 (January 24, 1969), 27–8.

[134] "Soviet revisionist clique cannot escape the punishment of history," *ibid.*, 10 (March 8, 1968), 23–3; "The days of imperialism, modern revisionism and reaction of all countries are numbered," *Jen-min jih-pao*, November 28, 1966; "Revolutionary Soviet people will rise to overthrow reactionary Kremlin's new Czars," *Peking Review*, 6 (February 9, 1968), 21–3.

exchange of technique, and the like, this body helps the Soviet "plunder and exploit East European people."[135] The supposed mutuality has turned out to be lopsided, with benefit accruing to Russia alone.[136] Other partners are no more than financial yeomen under the legal obligation to pay tribute to, and underwrite credit for, the Soviet companies. Thus the economy of the junior partners has been mobilized to rescue the collapsing industry and agriculture of the senior partner of the organization. It is bad luck to those satellites which are impelled to adopt pastoralism, thus perpetuating their dependence on Russia. With economic sovereignty gone, political sovereignty goes too. Yung Chung-tung saw in "Soviet revisionism the new Czar lording it over the East European people."[137] Along the same line was a charge hurled by M. Shehu of Albania that the "Warsaw Treaty has become an instrument for Soviet revisionists' . . . enslavement of member states."[138] Commenting on the Moscow-Delhi trade deal in 1968, a Peking media believes "Soviet revisionism carried out . . . economic exploitation in India."[139] Besides those specific instances adduced to document the Kremlin's design to deceive others, China visualizes a broader schema with a similar intent but with less instrusiveness. The economic relations established by Russia with many countries are depicted as another squeezing action undertaken jointly by Russia and the native "Asian, African and Latin American reactionaries."[140] Premier Chou En-lai attributed financial motives to the alleged Russo-American division of the globe with Russia having exclusive rights in East Europe, and America in the Middle East and Southeast Asia.[141] Although the term social-colonialism has not yet acquired a great vogue in Chinese literature, the implied effect cannot be missing in all the polemics. From colonial expansion to imperialist aggression is a short step. In

[135] *Ibid.*, 48 (November 29, 1968), 24.

[136] The Soviets say that economic cooperation among the several socialist states benefits them all and stems from the "very nature of socialism," *see* V. I. Gorbach, "Kommunizm – svetloe budushchee vsego chelovechstva" (Communism, bright future for all humanity), in *Ot sotsializma k kommunizmu* (From socialism to communism) (Minsk: Izd-vo Akademii Nauk, BSSR, 1963), p. 363–437, at 374; *see* also M. N. Rosenko, "Ekonomicheskie osnovy sotrud-nichestva i sblizheniya sotsialisticheskikh natsii v protsesse stroitel'stva kommunizma v SSSR" (Economic bases of cooperation and affinity of socialist nations in the process of building up communism in the USSR), in *Problemy nauchnogo kommunizma* (The problems of scientific communism) (Leningrad: Izd-vo Leningradskogo Universiteta, 1968), p. 52.

[137] *Ibid.*, p. 23.

[138] "Speech by comrade Shehu at session of Albanian People's Assembly," *ibid.*, 38 (September 10, 1968), 8–14.

[139] *Ibid.*, 45 (November 8, 1968), 26.

[140] *Ibid.*, 20 (May 17, 1968), 24–6.

[141] Speech by the Premier in honoring the North Vietnamese national day, December 2, 1968, *Facts on File*, 1968, p. 489.

fact, the two concepts may not easily be differentiated, for there can never be imperialism without domination over an unwilling people. However, the term "imperialism" strongly points to military move to pacify a rebelling dependency, while colonialism has less of that effect.[142]

Russia on the Defensive

The Soviet Government professed its tireless effort to achieve global peace and accused the Chinese of blocking this effort. Peking has practiced its imperialism, it said, by helping subversive and dissident groups in ex-colonies.[143] States like Mongolia, India, Nepal, Cambodia and Indonesia have all been the targets of the Maoists;[144] and the fraternal parties are forced to accept a Sinicized Leninism.[145] To justify its own action in Czechoslovakia, now known as the Brezhnev Doctrine, the Russian leadership set forth an array of reasons. Apart from the ready allegation of the Czech people's consent, it propounds a "limited sovereignty" of a state in an alliance like the Warsaw Treaty organization.[146] Mazurov, a Politburo member, said that dictatorship of the proletariat will no longer be the concern of one bloc-nation alone.[147] Since that dictatorship now has a universal front, no hostile force is tolerated to penetrate in it. Then there is said to be a socialist community, a community which has provided the political bond.[148] When the ominous counterrevolution takes place, other socialist nations ought to lend

[142] Lenin, "Itogi diskussii o samoopredelenii" (The results of the discussion of self-determination), in his *Voprosy natsional'noi politiki i proletarskogo internatsionalizma* (Problems of nationality policy and proletarian internationalism) (Moskva: Gos. izd-vo polit. lit-ry, 1965), 124–63, at 135, 139.

[143] I. Aleksandrov, "Vopreki interesam Kitaiskogo naroda" (In spite of the interests of the Chinese people), *Pravda*, August 16, 1967, and "Po povodu sobytiĭ v Kitae" (Events in China), *ibid.*, November 27, 1966; *Izvestiya*, August 30, 1967.

[144] K. Nevskii and L. Davydov, "Politika shovinizma i voinstvuiushchego natsionalizma [o provokatskii kampanii KNR protiv MNR]" (The policy of chauvinism and militant nationalism, on the provocation of the campaign by the Chinese People's Republic against the Mongolian People's Republic), *Aziya i Afrika segodnya* (Asia and Africa of today), 1 (1968), 6–8; "O politicheskom kurse Mao Tsze-duna na mezhdunarodnoi arene" (The policy of Mao Tsetung on international arena), *Kommunist*, 8 (May, 1968), 103.

[145] G. D. Obichkin, "Osnovy leninskogo ucheniya o partii" (The bases of Lenin's doctrine of party), in *V. I. Lenin – velikii teoritik* (V. I. Lenin, a great theorist), p. 241.

[146] Sergei Kovalev, "Suverenitet internatsional'nogo obyazannosti sotsialisticheskikh stran" (Souvereignty of international obligation of socialist states), *Pravda*, September 26, 1968.

[147] K. T. Mazurov, "Pyat'desyat pervaya godovshchina velikoi oktyaber'skoi sotsialisticheskoi revoliutsii" (The fifty-first anniversary of the great October Socialist Revolution), *Izvestiya*, November 7, 1968.

[148] V. Truchanovskii, "Proletarian internationalism and peaceful coexistence – foundation of the Leninist foreign policy," *International Affairs* (Moscow), 11 (November, 1968), 55, 60, 61. A. Sovetov, "The present stage in the struggle between socialism and imperialism," *ibid.*, p. 9.

their selfless hands to eliminate it.[149] "World socialism is indivisible," declared Korev.[150] Furthermore, in the communist bloc, there is a division of labor and specialization of produce which make the bloc an economic union,[151] a union of free and voluntary states.[152] It is of great interest to note that the Soviets minced no words in conceding that their own interests were also at stake in the domestic turmoil of Czechoslovakia.[153] Strongly implied is the assertion that Russia is entitled to expel a Czech regime hostile to Russia herself because during the Second World War the Red Army suffered 144,000 casualities in driving out the enemy troops from Czechoslovakia.[154]

Peking's Refutation

In the Sino-Soviet dialogue it appears to be Premier Chou En-lai who first applied the epithets of social-imperialist and social-fascist to the Soviets, when he exclaimed against the Czech invasion in a speech given at the Romanian Embassy in Peking. "The Soviet revisionist renegade clique has long since degenerated into a gang of social-imperialists and social-fascists," he asserted.[155] As the Brezhnev Doctrine grows finer, so is the Chinese criticism. On Lenin's centennial birthday, a joint editorial of three papers of the government analyzed that Doctrine into five points and refuted them one by one.[156] First the idea of "limited sovereignty" is said to imply the unlimited sovereignty of the Kremlin over fellow socialist states, in spite of the Russian propaganda that those states' independence is not impaired. Second, the "transformation of national proletarian dictatorship into an international one" means nothing but the subjection of others to the "new Czar." Third, Brezhnev's "socialist community" is labeled synonymous for his colonial empire. Fourth, Peking sees in the slogan "international division of labor" a Soviet pretext to exploit the East bloc. If Czecho-

---

[149] Sergei Kovalev, "Suverenitet internatsional'nogo...," *Pravda*, September 26, 1968.
[150] *Ibid.*
[151] V. G. Smolyanskii, "Sotsial'no-ekonomicheskie osnovy novogo tipa mazhdunarodnikh otnoshenii i fal'sifikatorskie teorii antikommunizma" (Socio-economic bases of the new type of international relations and the false theories of anticommunism), in *Mirovaya sotsialisticheskaya sistema i antikommunizma* (World socialist system and anticommunism), p. 23.
[152] *Ibid.*
[153] A. Gromyko, "Voprosy mezhdunarodnogo polozheniya i vneshnei politiki Sovetskogo Soiuza" (The problems of international situation and the foreign policy of the Soviet Union), *Pravda*, July 10, 1969. He addressed the Supreme Soviet.
[154] V. Truchanovskii, *International Affairs* (Moscow), 11 (November, 1968), 58.
[155] "Chinese Government and people strongly condemn Soviet revisionist clique's armed occupation of Czechoslovakia," *Peking Review*, 34 (August 23, 1968, supplement), 3–8.
[156] "Le-nin chu-i huan shih she-hui t'i-kuo chu-i?" (Leninism or social-imperialism?) *Jenmin jih-pao, Hung-ch'i*, and *Chieh-fang chün-pao*, April 22, 1970. The editorial is available in English: *Leninism or Social-Imperialism?* (Peking: Foreign languages press, 1970).

slovakia be allowed to break away, the supplies on the Russian revision-ist markets are getting short. Lastly, to the assertion that "our interests are involved," the Chinese retorted: "Can a country regard all parts of the world as areas affecting its interests and lay its hands on them? Can a country send its gunboats everywhere to carry out intimi-dation?"[157] Besides Czechoslovakia, the Soviets are said to have a sinister design on China as evidenced by the Damanskii incident.[158] The Chinese are firmly convinced that "only by resolutely opposing Soviet revisionism can the world's people carry the struggle against U.S. imperialism through to the end."[159] Reading the arguments of the Chinese and Russian governments one is wondering whether they have not redefined imperialism as the highest development of socialism.

China – A "Demonarchy"

In regard to the charge of deviation from socialism, the Soviet spokes-men bandied back the same charge which is more telling because of China's internal chaos. Brezhnev unceremoniously declared: "Mao Tse-tung can no longer be called a communist. His policy is diametrically opposed to the world socialist movement. He is in communion with imperialism."[160] A *Pravda* article asserted that Mao openly sold out Marxism-Leninsim.[161] The crime committed by him is that he set out to corrupt the proletarian minds and vitiate the very philosophy on which the world's progressive people repose their hopes and which illuminates the path of mankind. Hanging out the shingle of people's democracy, he lines himself up with the bestial tyrants in whom China's history abounds.[162] The Chinese ruler was described as being seized by devils and thoroughly dehumanized. This being the case, a deviation from the right path is the very thing to be expected.[163] Now that the CCP top echelon has trampled on Leninism, whither is it going except toward an economic debacle? No stone is left unturned by the Soviets in detailing the plight of the Chinese agonizing under the heavy feet

---

[157] All quotations are from *Jen-min jih-pao*, April 22, 1970. The Chinese charges of Russian economic exploitation were almost an echo of A. Uschakow, *Der Rat für gegenseitige Wirt-schaftshilfe COMECON* (Köln: Verlag Wissenschaft und Politik, 1962), p. 35.

[158] *Peking Review*, 12 (March 12, 1969), 18.

[159] *Ibid.*, 38 (September 20, 1968), 35.

[160] *Pravda*, September 7, 1967.

[161] I. Aleksandrov, "Vopreki interesam Kitaiskogo naroda" (In spite of the interests of the Chinese people), *ibid.*, August 16, 1967.

[162] I. Gavrilov, "Fal'shivyi flag, k sobytiyam v Kitae" (The false flag, the events in China), *Sovety deputatov trudyashchikhsya* (Councils of working people's deputies), 4 (1968), 108–10, at 109.

[163] "Korni nyneshnikh sobytii v Kitae" (The roots of the current events in China), *Kom-munist*, 6 (March, 1968), 103–03.

of Mao Tse-tung. Impoverishment has overtaken them. This was caused not so much by the four elements of nature as by the blunders and fumblings of the leadership of "demonarchy."[164] The proletarian cultural revolution, mocked the Soviets, is neither proletarian, nor cultural, nor a revolution.[165] It is engineered to get rid of anti-Maoist cadres and senselessly to harass the populace.[166] The Chinese achievements during the preceding two decades are puny in the first place, now the cutthroat styled Red Guard has totally wiped out what had been started through Soviet aid.[167] With the foundation of industry ruined, transport interrupted, agricultural work neglected, China is coming home to her feudal past.[168]

Using eyewitness accounts, the Kremlin blasted Mao and his supporters for making themselves "enemies of the people," a term from the Soviet Constitution (Article 131).[169] They ganged up with the rightist Kuomintang men by subsidizing their agencies in places like Hong Kong.[170] Conscionable Marxists and Leninists, the Russians hold, inevitably address themselves to securing an orderly society, and to improving the lot of the common people, whereas the Peking elites go the other way by setting fire to their own houses.[171] Having led the juvenile delinquents to play havoc with the all too shaky state fundament, the CCP has lost its sense of direction and not known how to cope with the aftermath.[172] The internal convulsion can only be accounted

[164] L. K. Sergeev, "Sobytiya v Kitae" (Events in China), *Agitator*, 9 (1968), 57–9.
[165] "O kharaktere kul'turnoi revoliutsii v Kitae" (The character of the cultural revolution in China), *Kommunist*, 7 (May, 1968), 106–07.
[166] I. Aleksandrov, "Vopreki interesam Kitaiskogo naroda" (In spite of the interests of the Chinese people), *Pravda*, August 16, 1967.
[167] E. Savadskaya, "Dni razrusheniya, o kul'turnoi revoliutskii v Kitae" (The days of destruction, on the cultural revolution in China), *Inostrannaya literatura* (Foreign literature), 6 (1968), 268–71.
[168] A. Ter-Grigoryan, "Tragediya Kitaya, o politike gruppy Mao Tsze-duna" (The tragedy of China, on the policy of the Mao Tse-tung group), *Novoe vremya* (New Time), 10 (1967), 9–12.
[169] V. Pasenchuk and V. Viktorov, "Antinarodnyi kurs Pekinskikh pravitelei" (The anti-people's policy of the Peking rulers), *Pravda*, June 22, 1968.
[170] I. Gavrilov, "Fakti razoblachaiut reveransy gomintanovtsu" (Facts expose the obeisanc to a Kuomintangite), *Izvestiya*, February 4, 1969. The article takes issue with CCP high officials paying tribute to an ex-Vice President of the Chinese Republic, General Li Tsung-jen, who returned to Peking after some 14 years' stay in America and died there on February 2, 1969.
[171] A. Snegirtsev, "Pekinskii dnevnik, ob unichtozhenii i razruzhenii pamyatnikov kul'tury v Kitae, vyderzhki iz dnevkika sovetskogo literaturoveda stazhirovavshegosya v KNR" (Peking diaries, on the destruction of cultural monuments in China, excerpts from diaries of Soviet literary workers in China), *Vokrug sveta* (Round the world), 12 (1967), 49–52.
[172] A. Rumyantsev and A. Strebaleva, "Sotsialo ekonomicheskii kurs gruppy Mao Tsze-duna i rabochii klass Kitaya" (The socio-economic course of the Mao Tse-tung group and the Chinese working class), *Mirovaya ekonomiya i mezhdunarodnye otnosheniya* (World economy and international relations), 6 (1967), 30–44, at 35.

for by the demented resolve of Mao that it is through economic setbacks and the power of poverty that the revolutionary elan can be sustained and the proletarians put where they used to be.[173] The difficulty of the people's life moves no Peking mandarins to shed their crocodile tears.[174] However, the leaders themselves are free from want, although the majority of them are not free from being purged for anti-Maoism.[175] There has developed an acute contradiction between the masses and the officialdom as a result of the dilapidated economy which emanates, in turn, from the cultural revolution and the Saturnalia of the "hung-wei-ping" (Red Guard).[176] China's anarchism has given rise to a mad and reckless diplomacy. So indicted the Soviets.[177]

The Military Dictatorship of Mao

As the Russians claimed, Mao Tse-tung has proceeded from visiting miseries on the people to building up his personal control. The term "military bureaucratic dictatorship" appeared in the Soviet press as early as 1967, a dictatorship first directed against his party cadres, then against other social groups.[178] Mao is said to substitute a "dictator-

---

[173] Iu. Kosiukov, "Ekonomika Kitaya pod udarami kul'turnoi revoliutsii" (Chinese economy under the blows of the cultural revolution), *Novoe vremya* (New time), 3 (1967), 18–20; *idem*, "Posle antrakta v Pekine, k kharakteristike vnutri polit. obstanovki v KNR (After an interval in Peking, characteristics of internal political situation in China), *ibid.*, 11 (1968), 14–15; "O kharaktere kul'turnoi revoliutsii v Kitae, red. stat'ya" (The characteristics of the cultural revolution in China, an editorial), *Kommunist*, 7 (May, 1968, 104–13; A. Zhelokhodt-sev, "Kul'turnaya revoliutsiya v Kitae s blizkogo rasstoyaniya, zapiski ochevidtsa" (The cultural revolution in China at a close look, from the notes of an eye-witness), *Novoi mir* (New world), 3 (1968), 181–213; "Maoistskaya panatseya" (Maoist panacea), *Izvestiya*, December 19, 1968.

[174] "Sobytie v Kitae – tsitatniki vmesto vrachei" (Events in China – quoters instead of physicians), *ibid.*, February 12, 1969.

[175] The Soviets reported that two thirds of the CCP Central Committee and a majority of the Politburo have been attacked and ousted, *Pravda*, August 16, 1967. The same media reprinted an editorial of a Polish paper *Tribyna liudu* which said that a great majority of the central and provincial party cadres had been eliminated during the cultural revolution, "S'ezd partii Mao" (Mao's party congress), *Pravda*, May 8, 1969.

[176] Vidal'zhan-Emil', "20 mesyatsev kul'turnoi revoliutsii v Kitae, stat'i iz frantsuzskii gaz. *Iiumanite*, napech. v. sokr." (20 months' cultural revolution in China, articles from the French paper *Humanite*, abbreviated version), *Kommunist Estonii*, 4 (1968), 98–113; "*Ekonomist* o polozhenii v Kitae, po materialam stat'i opubl. v angl. ezhenedel'nike ot 17–23 iiunya, 1967g." (The London *Economist* on the situation in China, materials gathered from articles during the week, June 17–23, 1967), *Novoe vremya* (New time), 27 (1967), 11.

[177] N. Kapchenko, "Kul'turnaya revoliutsia vneshnaya politika gruppy Mao Tsze-duna" (The cultural revolution and foreign policy of the Mao Tse-tung group), *Mezhdunarodnaya zhizn'* (International life), 2 (1968), 19–31; G. Apalin, "Ideologicheskie osnovy vneshnei politiki gruppy Mao Tsze-duna" (Ideological bases of the foreign policy of the Mao Tse-tung group), *ibid.*, 6 (1968), 70–72.

[178] I. Aleksandrov, "Vopreki interesam Kitaiskogo naroda" (In spite of the interests of the Chinese people), *Pravda*. August, 16, 1967.

ship devoted to himself" for the "accepted principle of communism."[179] Such an individualized sovereignty is Caesarism at its best and combines warlordism and bureaucratism of the typical Chinese kind. It shares nothing with the "true ideas of socialism and democracy, and vital interests of the working people."[180] Brezhnev characterized Mao's conduct as veritable counterrevolution.[181] The sinews and bones which go into the making of Maoism are "inhuman suppression, fanaticism of the youth and terror in general."[182] Under his stifling hands, all reasonable criticisms are throttled and the CCP summit throws overboard democratic centralism. Every public action is subjected to the imperative that "politics takes command."[183] It is observed that objective conditions which are requisite for the successful operation of socialism ought to be bypassed so that the personal dictatorship of Mao Tse-tung, instead of the proletarian dictatorship of the multitude, is to obtain. Such flagrant violation of the rule of dialectical law will "be doomed to failure."[184] Marxism has been sullied at the hands of the Chinese, just as it has been sullied at the hands of others like pseudo-Leninists, adventurists, splitters, Trotskyites, nationalists, great power chauvinists, dogmatists, etc.[185] A freakish socialism is foisted upon the Chinese people. Truly speaking, Moscow declared, Cathay has neither the substance, nor the trappings, of popular democracy; hers is a juggernaut, a grotesque autarchy.[186] Basing itself on hatred against both genuine Marxist-Leninists and the mass people, Maoism has cranked back the historical clock.[187] The Russians urged the Chinese people to "break with the hopeless course of Mao and renew the fraternal relations between them and the Soviet Union and other socialist countries for the sake of world socialism and, above all, for China herself."[188] Mincing

---

[179] O. L'vov. "Politicheskie manevry Mao Tsze-duna" (Political maneuvers of Mao Tse-tung), *ibid.*, January 11, 1969.

[180] *Ibid.*

[181] *Ibid.*, September 7, 1967; *see* also V. Fetov, "Kul'turnaya revoliutsiya – 69 v Kitae" (The cultural revolution in China, 1969), *Literaturnaya gazeta*, 6 (February 6, 1969), 5.

[182] *Pravda*, September 7, 1967.

[183] *Pukhovskii*, op. cit., p. 53.

[184] S. Tikhvinskii, "Politika, obrechenaya na proval" (Policy doomed to failure), *Pravda*, March 12, 1969. D. N. Kukin wrote: "Collective leadership is the core of democratic centralism and basically militates against the personality cult. The latter proves alien to Marxism-Leninism and the very nature of the communist party," *see* his "Leninskie printsipy partii-nogo i gosudarsrvennogo rukovodstva" (Lenin's principles of party and state leadership), in *V. I. Lenin – velikii teoretik* (V. I. Lenin, a great theorist), p. 297.

[185] "Letter of CC of CPSU, dated February 24, 1966," *Peking Review*, 13 March 25, 1966), 6; "CCP cannot send delegation to CPSU 23rd Congress," *ibid.*, p. 5.

[186] B. Stolpovskii, "Politicheskii avantiurizm gruppy Mao Tsze-duna" (Political adventurism of the Mao Tse-tung group), *Trud*, March 13, 1969, p. 1.

[187] "Sobytiya v Kitae" (Events in China), *Pravda*, March 15, 1969.

[188] *Ibid.*; *see* also an interview with Kosygin by Japanese newsmen, *Mainichi* (Daily news),

no words, Kosygin and Brezhnev appealed to the true communists in China to dump the Maoists group, before it becomes too late to keep her from being lost as a workers' polity.[189] It is interesting to note that Canada's diplomatic recognition of the Peking regime on October 13, 1970, was barely mentioned in the Soviet media.[190]

PEKING – THE HEADQUARTERS OF WORLD REVOLUTION

Mao Dons Lenin's Toga

From what has been analyzed above, one is led to ask where is the Mecca of socialism, for each disputant has excommunicated the other as a turncoat and usurper of the people's power. Mindful of an old tradition, the CCP cautioned the CPSU that it has long exhausted the mandate of heaven. In positive terms, the dispute boils down to: Who is the real master of world communism? On its side, the Kremlin group finds it unnecessary to put in a claim.[191] It simply rests content that the majority of the world's communist and workers' parties have deferred to it and demurred at China. It is rather the Chinese who have to bestir themselves to establish their heirship to Lenin. This is indeed what they have tried to do ever since the cultural revolution. After the sellout of the "fruits of socialism to U.S. imperialism," the Soviets have degraded their personality, or the quality of man, as the Chinese are prone to say.[192] They forfeited the first place in the East bloc; and onto that spot, Peking has moved itself. In the Chinese literature, Mao comes to make up a species of Siamese triplet with Marx and Lenin, occasionally, the Siamese quintuplet, by hooking up Engels and Stalin. In the mentality of Maoists, Leninism literally escapes from Russia to China and Lenin himself has been reincarnated in Mao, or Mao prefigured in Lenin. It is asserted that the "world has entered the era with Mao Tsetung's thought as the great banner; socialist China has become the

January 3, 1969. The interview is carried in: Kosygin, "Politika dobrososestva, ovtety Predsedatelya Soveta Ministrov SSSR, A. N. Kosygin, na voprosy gazety *Mainichi*" (Goodneighbor policy, answers of the Chairman of the Council of Ministers of the USSR to questions put to him by the *Mainichi* newsmen), *Pravda*, January 5, 1969.

[189] A. A. Fedossev, "O formakh diktatury proletariata" (On the forms of proletarian dictatorship), in *Problemy nauchnogo kommunizma* (Problems of scientific communism) (Leningrad: Leningradskogo Universiteta, 1968), 13–21, at 13. *See also Pravda*, March 15, 1969, November 7, 1967.

[190] *Ibid.*, October 14, 1970; *Izvestiya* made no mention at all.

[191] "As the first major party it (CPSU) considered it has divine right to dictate and interpret the gospel according to Marx and Lenin to the whole world as it has been trying to do for years through first of all the Comintern and then the Cominform," *see* E. O'Ballance, *Contemporary Review*, 210 (February, 1967), 71.

[192] *Jen-min jih-pao*, August 23, 1968.

impregnable redoubt of world revolution."[193] The logical implication is that China's leader has assumed the role of generalissimo in that revolution.

A Prophet and Guiding Star

In order to make good their claim, Peking media reproduced a large number of encomia made by communist parties all over the world. One of these reads: "Mao Tse-tung's thought brings world revolution into a new triumphant era."[194] Another runs like this: "China, under the leadership of Chairman Mao, is the vanguard of world revolution."[195] Jacques Jacquet, a French communist leader, enunciated that "Mao Tse-tung's thought guides the people of the world to advance triumphantly."[196] Similarly eulogizing the Chinese leader was the Italian Communist Party.[197] Grateful for his moral support of the Czech liberal regime, *Mlada Fronta* of Prague writes of him as the "last living true revolutionary."[198] It seems as if the Chairman were really on the top of the socialist world; his is the legacy of Marx and Lenin, and championship of the international liberation cause. The aim of the liberation is not only to storm the "world city" of North America and Western Europe, but to storm the "world village" of Eurasia as well. Currently, the Chairman's thought has been credited with victories in many revolutionary wars. His teachings on guerilla warfare were acquainting the people of Indonesia with the correct way of smashing the "Suharto-Nasution fascist military regime" and building up the people's democratic power in that island state.[199] "Solidly united under the great red banner of Mao Tse-tung's thought, the PKI is leading the Indonesian people to march onward on the road to people's war," officially stated

[193] "Situation of world revolution is excellent," *Peking Review*, 42 (October 18, 1966), 14–18

[194] "Statement by the Political Commission of the Central Committee of the Communist Party of Peru," *ibid.*, 32 (August 9, 1968), 10–17.

[195] "*Espartaco*, organ of the revolutionary Communist Party of Chile praises China for its tremendous contribution to the defense of Marxism-Leninism," *ibid.*, 3 (January 19, 1968), 31.

[196] "Jacques Jacquet calls on entire French Communist Party to study and master Mao Tse-tung's thought," *ibid.*, 22 (May 31, 1968), 21–22.

[197] "Chairman Mao's thought is powerful encouragement to world people's struggle, Italian Communist Party organ hails Chairman Mao's statement supporting Afro-American struggle," *ibid.*, p. 21.

[198] A Russian media carried the Czech praises for the sole purpose of attacking Mao, *see* V. Smirnov, "*Mlada Fronta* i Mao Tsze-dun," *Literaturnaya gazeta*, 1 (January, 1969), 9.

[199] "Comrade Mao-Tse-tung's teachings on people's war are Indonesian people's powerful weapon for smashing Suharto-Nasution fascist military regime and establishing people's democratic power in Indonesia, hailing the publication of the Indonesian version of the *Selected Military Writings of Mao Tse-tung* by the delegation of the Central Committee of Communist Party of Indonesia," *Peking Review*, 30 (July 26, 1968), 8–11.

the Indonesian Communist Party.[200] In Vietnam, as one would expect, it is his very thought which wins the fight and in Thailand its application has begun to have a good result. Before long, the Thai revolution will be crowned with a signal success.[201] As far as America, the struggle of the Negro is indebted to him for its vigorous and rapid tempo. It will turn out to be a hurricane to blow off the imperialist regime, Peking predicted.[202]

Russia's Tactics of Refutation

The Soviet press takes little notice of such dramatic pretensions and does not even bother to refute.[203] Instead, it seeks to dramatize Peking's alleged failures and ignore its achievement such as the orbiting satellite.[204] It is felt that this is the best disabuser of the legend of Mao. When one can prove that a giant's feet are clay, nothing else need be said to stultify the web of mystique. This the Russians have done with ease, for no outraged country can boast of a saintly statesman. The pandemonium throughout China is the prima facie evidence of misgovernment. Such a tactic has been largely followed by communist parties with Moscow orientation. Now and then, these parties did resort to frontal disclaimer of Peking's assertion. For instance, in a rebuttal of China's charges on January 22, 1967, that the Japanese Communist Party pursued a revisionist line, *Akahata*, the Party's organ, in an editorial on "smashing anti-party elements blindly following Red Guards," declared that there had been no such thing as the "universality of Mao's thought."[205] The Japanese accused the CCP as wrongfully construing Marxism-Leninism and "attempting to disseminate its ideology abroad with contumely." Thus, Mao's trumpeted hegemony of the international liberation is not generally accepted. Certainly, it will be harder to get accepted after he is gone. Unlike Lenin, Mao Tse-tung is apotheosized to such a degree in his lifetime that an application of his writings and behests, euphemistically called creative, would smell of

---

200 *Ibid.*, 22 (May 31, 1968), 17–19, on the occasion of the 48th anniversary of the Indonesian Communist Party.

201 *Ibid.*, 42 (October 18, 1968), 20–21.

202 "Afro-American struggle against violent repression developing vigorously, Chairman Mao's great statement points out direction of struggle for the black people in the United States," *ibid.*, 33 (August 16, 1968), 10–14.

203 "O politicheskom kurse Mao Tzse-duna na mezhdunarodnoi arene" (Political course of Mao Tse-tung on the international scene), *Kommunist*, 8 (May, 1968), 96.

204 B. Zanegin, "Proval vneshnepoliticheskogo kursa Pekina" (Failure of Peking's foreign policy), *Izvestiya*, May 22, 1968. China's man-made satellite was launched on April 24, 1970. Both *Pravda* and *Izvestiya* kept strangely silent on the event.

205 *Akahata*, February 9, 1967.

peccancy. Internationally, his halo building has so far failed. Domestically, the Chinese elites have been forced to memorize arid quotations,
and made to believe that the Cathay headed by him has acquired the
leadership of world revolution, a leadership Soviet Russia loses simply
by default. How long do those quotations stick after the nine days'
wonder is over, provided they are absorbed in the first place, let the
future be the traditional oracle.

CHAPTER VII

CONCLUSION

Having made an analysis of the Sino-Soviet dispute on war, the author will set forth his conclusion in the following pages. To begin with, we have seen that both disputants are in agreement that monopoly capitalism sow the seeds of armed conflict. The exploitative class has waged wars internally with the workers and peasants, and externally with the colonies. Both agree in attributing all aggression to the system of private ownership of the means of production; the prevention of war, therefore, can be achieved by the takeover in public hands of those means, or, in other words, the "substitution of socialism for capitalism" as a way of life. A world community without class exploitation would be one in which all men enjoy the fruits of their common labor. Admittedly this is a communist ideal. Can war be averted before the realization of that ideal? The Chinese professed their unswerving faith in Leninism and answered the question negatively. A universal peace, they believed, would not reign until the establishment of what Lenin called the "international workers' republic." By its very nature, imperialism is aggressive; and it would be contradictory to equate a harmonious world with one in which imperialism exists. This principle, the Chinese asserted, always remains true. It is plainly nugatory for one to try to revise it in view of such irrelevant factors as "scientific discoveries." Allegedly tampering with Marxism-Leninism by propounding the avoidability doctrine, the Soviets were said to be doing a disservice to proletarian internationalism.

Not entirely refuting Peking's contention, Moscow stated that although up until now war has been inevitable, it is no longer so. During the time of Lenin, diplomatic relations were such that wars frequently erupted. The reasons were, first, that it was the imperialists who made up the whole cast of political drama, and second that it was they who could unleash attacks at will. Further, the effect of armed conflict proved limited in two aspects. A hostile action was usually engaged in by only a few states and never threatened to spread far and wide. More important, the techniques of fighting were not mass destructive, although casualties sometimes ran high. Thus, the small scale of the theater of operations, plus the use of conventional arms, made past wars comparatively mild. But the situation changed vastly with the dawning of the nuclear age. There came into being two great military powers each having its allies. Should an armed contest take place, it would assume global dimensions. Literally millions upon millions of people would be affected. Cities with their teeming populace would be turned into ashes in a matter of minutes. A future world war is unthinkably terrible. Fortunately, the Soviets asserted, such an eventuality is being rendered less likely, due to the growing power of the socialist nations which have played an increasing role in settling world issues. With the shrinkage of the imperialist sphere of influence, the pro-war forces are retreating before the pro-peace forces. Hence, armed conflict proves not inevitable. Ours is the socialist era, not the imperialist era in which Lenin once lived.

In propounding the theory of the avoidability of war, the Soviets did not consider themselves un-Leninist. The policy of peaceful coexistence, they explained, was prescribed by the late Russian leader himself as early as 1922. Further, he also envisaged the impact of new weapons on the probability of war in the future. Regarding the correlation of forces which can ward off imperialist assault, Moscow argued that a flexible course of action in the light of such developments as the formation and growth of the socialist system is actually required by the spirit of Leninism. Lenin himself warned against dogmatism. To hold onto the precept of the inevitability of a life-and-death struggle between the socialist and capitalist states would prove inimical to the interests of the people.

To all these arguments, the Peking theorists replied that, since the imperialists are as unreasonable as beasts of prey, the struggle Lenin forecast is only a matter of time. However, one must not take this to mean that the Chinese leaders plan to start a world war in order to overthrow the capitalist regimes of the West. They have made it crystal clear that they have no such plans and have no intention of encroaching on one inch of the territory of others. Their concept of the inevitability of war is unmistakably caused by a fear of being attacked. In fine, since Peking believes that the socialist camp is the earmarked victim of imperialist aggression, it is wishful thinking to bank on the avoidability of war.

With regard to civil war, both sides concurred that it emanates from the aggravation of class enmity within a national community. There is said to be no need for outsiders to promote such wars; in fact outsiders are likely to misjudge the situation, because the intensity of class struggle varies from country to country and because the revolutionary pace cannot be prematurely hastened. On a few occasions, both sides abandoned this view in favor of promoting class war by way of aid to the proletarian instigators. Yet, there were differences between Moscow and Peking. First of all, the latter was more daring than the former regarding advocacy of assistance to rebels who were fighting for national independence. The reason was that China did not feel, as Russia did, that by doing so she might offend the leadership of the metropolitan states. The Russians, in addition, feared that civil war with foreign involvement could be escalated. Therefore, any such move on the part of the bloc nations should be taken in such a way as to evoke no general conflict. However, the divisive issue concerning civil war was the problem of the parliamentary avenue to socialism versus revolution. The Chinese felt the bourgeois legislative process could not be employed to achieve the socialist objective. The seizure of power has to be through violence; and to preach peace in the presence of the exploitation of man by man is to lower the revolutionary standard of the proletarians. The capitalist class, Peking argued, would not willingly step out of history; it has to be forced out. Therefore, arms are the only means whereby the toilers can get themselves enthroned. Yet it is to be noted that Khrushchev's parliamentarianism was far from being peaceful because it included such action as shattering the military and bureaucratic machinery of a bourgeois state. The Chinese chose to ignore this facet of Khrushchev's argument and, instead, concentrated their criticism on the peaceful procedures implied by the term "parliamentarianism."

Wars of national liberation were defined as those fought to expel the imperialists from the colonies. Such wars should have the full support of the socialist states. Both the dependent peoples and the proletariat in the metropolises were said to be the objects of oppression by the capitalists who ought to be opposed by all conscionable Leninists. The best way to bury the exploiters is to bring about the decomposition of their body politic. Since for raw materials, markets and inexpensive labor, the Western nations rely upon the colonies, the latter's liberation would deprive these nations of their very sustenance. Hence it is to the advantage of the socialist camp to render help to the colonies which revolt against their mother country. It is when internal turmoil like workers' uprisings are coupled with insurgence in the dependencies that the east wind is irretrievably prevailing over the west wind. This theoretical analysis is generally agreed to by both Moscow and Peking. However, due to the fact that Khrushchev sought to establish broad personal contacts with the capitalist statesmen, he found it impolitic to espouse wars of national liberation. The Algerian war, for instance, put the Soviet leadership in a peculiar position, for they could not support the insurgents without vitiating the Franco-Russian detente created by Khrushchev's visit with de Gaulle in 1960. If the Russian ruler could get the French President to break off from the Western alliance, he could not afford to champion the cause of the rebels in one of France's overseas departments. This maneuvering explains why the Soviets never actively aided the Algerian National Liberation Front. By way of contrast, the Chinese found it to their interest to recognize the insurrection led by Ben Bella; in doing so, they hoped to draw his forces under their infleunce.

With reference to local wars, such as the Anglo-French invasion of Egypt in 1956, Peking and Moscow also formulated divergent policy lines. It was China's belief that the West would invariably start incident after incident on a small scale to subdue various communist movements. The bloc, she felt, must take up the challenge energetically to check Western expansion and foster proletarian internationalism. The Soviets rebutted that local clashes could easily lead to a world-wide collision. Besides, they argued that the bloc was already powerful enough to deter the West from precipitating limited crisis. After the Suez event of October, 1956, they claimed, the West was repeatedly thwarted in its attempt to encroach on the non-communist nations. Thus, the necessity of fighting local wars is disappearing. The waging of the cold war by the imperialist nations was regarded as indicating how they have not dared to go over to a shooting war of either the small or big variety. Russia's assumption was that the imperialists have sufficient sense to refrain from plunging the globe into a conflagration through playing with brush fires. To Peking, which maintained that the imperialists are warlike and cannot be scared away from aggression, the Soviet argument was not convincing. Pocket wars will happen more frequently even though a possible world war gets more ruinous. Further, Mao thought, the East must also take the initiative with tactical probes to harass the imperialist frontier. These probes could be taken with relative impunity, since the Soviet nuclear superiority provided safety against possible Western retaliation. At any rate, if local wars are started and won by the West, the proletarian cause will be set back, Peking cautioned. Hence the necessity to fight such wars offensively no less than defensively.

The Vietnam war separates the disputants still further. Mao Tse-tung wanted to see the fullest engagement of the Soviets in the conflict. But they objected and charged that he has desired and actually maneuvered a Russo-American war so that he could, to use his own words, "sit on the mountain and watch the fight of the tigers." Further, Lin Piao's geopolitics was to prove that the communist struggle for Asia, Africa and Latin America which he termed the "world village" calls for a victorious people's war in Vietnam. According to his global strategy, the communist final assault is aimed at North America and Western Europe which he termed the "world city." The socialist nations will destroy the world city by seizing control of the surrounding "world village." Then the whole world is theirs. In formulating this plan, he sought to internationalize the guerilla tactic of first taking the environs and then taking the town, a tactic employed by Mao Tse-tung during his rebellion. Reversing China's former view on the nature of the imperialists, Lin came to hold that they dare not use thermonuclear arms for fear of world public opinion and for fear of retaliation in kind.

For the past several years, each country has excommunicated the other from the East bloc by denouncing it as an enemy and a traitor to Marxism-Leninism. Nowadays, all the shopworn curses the communists leveled at the old capitalist nations have been bandied back and forth between Moscow and Peking. A real basis for them to live side by side in view of the meaning both China and Russia chose to read into the slogan of peaceful coexistence is disappearing. Particularly notable in this connection is the mutual incrimination of scheming hostile alignment to destroy each other. Indeed, the possibility of Sino-Soviet war has been openly and incessantly voiced by either side after the Damanskii episode in March, 1969. Of course, such a war will not be considered one between socialist countries, since China and Russia do not treat each other as socialist, but one, so the charge goes, between a socialist and an imperialist country. Does this not lead one to revise Lenin that uneven development of communism, instead of capitalism, is the cause of international war?

BIBLIOGRAPHY

I. CLASSICAL WORKS

1. Lenin

"Bor'ba partii v Kitae" (The struggle of the Communist Party in China), originally appearing in *Pravda*, May 3, 1913, now in *Kommunist*, 6 (March, 1960), 10–12.

Clausewitz' Werk "Vom Kriege"; Auszüge und Randglossen (Clausewitz's book on war; extracts and annotations). Berlin: Verlag der Ministerium für National Verteidigung, 1957.

Collected Works. Moscow: Foreign languages publishing house, 1960. 28 vols.

O voine, armii i voennoi nauke (On war, army and military science). 1st ed. Moskva: Voen. izd-vo, 1957. 2nd. ed 1965.

"Rech'na IV konferentsii gubernskikh chrezvychainykh komissii, fr. 6, 1920 g." (Speech to the fourth conference of the provincial extraordinary commissions, February 6, 1920), *Kommunist*, 5 (April, 1957), 19–23.

Selected Works. London: Lawrence and Wishart, 1936. 12 vols.

Sobrannie sochineniya (Selected works). 2nd ed. Moskva: Gosizdat, 1926–29. 32 vols.

Sochinenyia (Collected Works). 3rd ed. Moskva: Gosizdat, 1932. 32 vols. 4th ed. Moskva: Gos. izd-vo polit. lit-ry, 1941–57. 42 vols. 5th ed. With a different title: *Polnoe sobrannie sochinenii*. 1958–1965. 55 vols.

Voprosy natsional'noi politiki i proletarskogo internatsionalizma (The problems of nationality policy and proletarian internationalism). Moskva: Gos. izd-vo poliyt. lit-ry, 1965. Compiled by Ts. Beilina.

Zamechaniya na knigu Klausevitza o voine i vedenii voiny (Notes on the book of Clausewitz on war and its prosecution). Moskva: Gosizdat, 1933. A Russian translation from the German text listed above.

2. Mao

Basic Tactics. New York: Praeger, 1966.

Chung-kuo ko-ming chan-cheng ti chan-lüeh wen-t'i (Strategical problems of the Chinese revolutionary war). 2nd ed. Hong Kong: New Democracy publishing house, 1949.

Chung-kuo ko-ming yü chung-kuo kung-ch'an-tang (The Chinese revolution and the Chinese Communist Party). 2nd ed. Chi-chung, Han-tan: North China hsin-hua shu chiu, 1949.

Ho mei-kuo chi-che an-na lu-i-ssu sse-le-lang ti t'an-hua (Talk with the American correspondent, Anna Louise Strong). Peking: People's publishers, 1960.

Imperialism and All Reactionaries Are Paper Tigers. Peking: Foreign languages press, 1958.

Kuan-yü mu-ch'ien tang ti cheng-ts'e chung ti chi-ko chung-yao wen-t'i (On some important problems of the party's present policy). Peking: People's publishers, 1961.

Lun jen-min min-chu chuan-cheng (On people's democratic dictatorship). Peking: People's publishers, 1960.

Mao chu-hsi tsai su-lien ti yen-lun (Speeches of Chairman Mao in the Soviet Union). Peking: People's publishers, 1957.

Mao Tse-tung hsüan-chi (Selected works). Peking: People's publishers, 1951–53. 3 vols.

Mu-ch'ien hsing-shih ho wo men-ti jen-wu (The current situation and our tasks). Peking: People's publishers, 1960.

On Guerrilla Warfare. Translated with an introduction by Samuel Griffith. New York: Praeger, 1961.

On People's War. English ed. Peking: Guozi Shudian [1970].

People of the World, Unite and Defeat the U.S. Aggressors and All Their Running Dogs! (statement of May 30, 1970). Peking: Foreign languages press, 1970. Also in *Peking Review*, Special issue (May 23, 1970), 8–9.

Quotations from Chairman Mao Tse-tung. Peking: Foreign languages press, 1966.

Selected Military Writings. New York: Universal Distributors, 1963.

Selected Works. New York: International publishers, 1945–49. 5 vols.
  1st ed. Peking: Foreign languages press, 1961–67. 4 vols.
  British ed. London: Lawrence and Wishart, 1954–56. 5 vols.

Strategical Problems of China's Revolutionary War. 1st ed. Peking: Foreign languages press, 1954.

3. Marx/Engels/Lenin

a. Marx

Der Bürgerkrieg in Frankreich (Civil war in France). Moskau: Verlagsgenossenschaft ausländischer Arbeiter in der UdSSR, 1937.

b. Engels

Anti-Dühring. Moskva: Gos. izd-vo polit. lit-ry, 1948.

Izbrannye voennye proizvedeniya (Selected military writings). Moskva: Gospolitizdat, 1937.

Der Ursprung der Familie, des Privateigentums und des Staates (The origin of family, private property and state). Hotting-Zürich: Verlag der Schweizerischen Volksbuchhandlung, 1884.

Zametki o voine (Notes on war). Moskva: Gospolitizdat, 1941.

c. Marx/Engels (collected works by two)

Izbrannye proizvedeniya (Selected works). Moskva: Gospolitizdat, 1952. 20 vols. 2-volume ed. 1948.

Manifesto kommunisticheskoi partii (Communist manifesto). Moskva: Gos. izd-vo polit. lit-ry, 1952.
  English ed: *Communist Manifesto.* Toronto: Vanguard publication [n.d.]

Selected Works. Prepared by the Institute of Marxism-Leninism. Moscow: Foreign languages publishing house, 1962. 2 vols.
Werke. Berlin: Dietz, 1967. 39 vols.

d. Marx/Engels/Lenin (collected works by three)

O dialekticheskom materializme (Dialectical materialism). Moskva: Gos. izd-vo polit. lit-ry, 1966.
O proletarskom internatsionalizme (Proletarian internationalism). Moskva: Gos. izd-vo polit. lit-ry, 1968.

4. Stalin

Beseda s korrespondentom "Pravdy" (Interview with the "Pravda" correspondent). Moskva: Gos. izd-vo polit. lit-ry, 1951.
Ekonomicheskie problemy sotsializma v SSSR. Moskva: Gos- izd.vo polit. lit-ry, 1952. English edition: *Economic Problems of Socialism in the USSR*. New York: International publishers, 1952.
Mastering Bolshevism. New York: Workers' library publishers, 1937.
Mezhdunarodnoi kharakter oktyabr'skoi revoliutsii (The international character of the October Revolution). Moskva: Gos. izd-vo polit. lit-ry, 1953.
O dialekticheskom i istorichekom materializma (Dialectical and historical materialism). Moskva: Gospolitizdat, 1941.
O Lenin i leninizme (Lenin and Leninism). Moskva: Gospolitizdat, 1924.
O trekh osobennostyakh Krasnoi Armii (The three peculiar characters of the Red Army). Moskva: Gos. izd-vo polit. lit-ry, 1939.
Ob oktyabr'skoi revoliutsii; sbornik statei i rechi (The October Revolution; a collection of articles and speeches). Moskva: Partiinoe izd-vo, 1932.
Oktyabor'skaya revoliutsiya i taktika russkikh kommunistov (The October Revolution and the tactic of the Russian communists). Moskva: Gos. izd-vo polit. lit-ry, 1954.
Rech' na predvybornom sobranii izbiratelei stalinskogo izbiratel'nogo okruga g. Moskvy, 9 fevr. 1946 g. (Election speech in the Stalin district of the city of Moscow, February 9, 1946). Moskva: Gos. izd-vo polit. lit-ry, 1946.
Sochineniya (Collectde Works). Moskva: Gos. izd-vo polit. lit-ry, 1946–51. 13 vols. Containing his works up to and including 1934. English edition: *Works*. Moscow: Foreign languages publishing house, 1952–55. 13 vols.
War of National Liberation. New York: International publishers, 1942.

II. CHINESE POLEMIC LITERATURE

5. Official party and government statements

"Apologists of neo-colonialism: comment on the open letter of the Central Committee of the CPSU (B), by the Editorial Departments of *Renmin ribao* and *Hongqi*," *Peking Review*, 43 (October 25, 1963), 6–15.
"Chinese Communist Party cannot send delegation to CPSU 23rd Congress," *Peking Review*, 13 (March 25, 1966), 5–6.
"Chinese Foreign Ministry strongly protests against unreasonable Soviet demand," *Peking Review*, 27 (July 5, 1963), 7–8.
"Chinese Government and people strongly condemn Soviet revisionist clique's

armed occupation of Czechoslovakia," *Peking Review*, 34 (August 23, 1968, supplement), 3–8. A policy speech by Chou En-lai.

Communique of the Eleventh Plenary Session of the Eighth Central Committee of the Communist Party of China. Peking: Foreign languages press, 1970.

Communique of the Enlarged Twelfth Plenary Session of the Eighth Central Committee of the Communist Party of China. Peking: Foreign languages press, 1970.

"Five proposals for settlement of the differences and attainment of unity contained in the letter of the Central Committee of the CCP in reply to the letter of information of the Central Committee of the CPSU, September 10, 1960), *Peking Review*, 37 (September 13, 1963), 23.

"Is Yugoslavia a socialist country? comment on the open letter of the Central Committee of the CPSU (B), by the Editorial Departments of *Renmin ribao* and *Hongqi*," *Peking Review*, 39 (September 27, 1963), 14–27.

"Joint statement of China and Albania," *Peking Review*, 21 (May 20, 1966), 5–12.

"Message of greeting from the Central Committee of the Chinese Communist Party," *Peking Review*, 26 (June 28, 1960), 5.

"On the question of Stalin, comment on the open letter of the Central Committee of the CPSU, by the Editorial Departments of *Renmin ribao* and *Hongqi*," *Peking Review*, 38 (September 20, 1963), 8–14. Taken from *Hung-ch'i*, 18 (September 13, 1963), 1–12.

"The origin and development of the differences between the leadership of the CPSU and ourselves, comment on the open letter of the Central Committee of the CPSU, by the Editorial Departments of *Renmin ribao* and *Hongqi*," *Peking Review*, 37 (September 13, 1963), 6–20.

"Peaceful coexistence – two diametrically opposed policies, comment on the open letter of the Central Committee of the CPSU (B), by the Editorial Departments of *Renmin ribao* and *Hongqi*," *Peking Review*, 51 (December 20, 1963), 6–18.

"Pis'mo TsK KPK Tsentral'monu Komitetu KPSS, ot 7 maya 1964 g." (A letter from the Central Committee of the CCP to the Central Committee of the CPSU, dated May 7, 1964), *Kommunist*, 10 (July, 1964), 20–24.

Press Communique of the Secretariat of the Presidium of the Ninth National Congress of the Communist Party of China. Peking: Foreign languages press, 1970.

"A proposal concerning the general line of the international communist movement, the letter of the Central Committee of the CCP in reply to the letter of the Central Committee of the CPSU of March 30, 1963)," *Peking Review*, 25 (June 21, 1963), 6–33; 30 (July 26, 1963), 10–26.

"Statement by a spokesman of the Central Committee of the Communist Party of China, July 19, 1963," *Peking Review*, 30 (July 26, 1963), 9.

"Statement by the spokesman of the Chinese Government, a comment on the Soviet Governments' statement of August 21, 1963," *Peking Review*, 36 (September 6, 1963), 7–16.

"Statement by the spokesman of the Chinese Government, a comment on the Soviet Government's statement of August 3, 1963," *Peking Review*, 33 (August 16, 1963), 7–15.

"Statement of the Central Committee of the Communist Party of China, July 1 and 5, 1963," *Peking Review*, 27 (July 5, 1963), 5–6.

"Statement of the Chinese Government advocating the complete, thorough, total and resolute prohibition and destruction of nuclear weapons, proposing a conference of the government heads of all countries of the world," *Peking Review*, 31 (August 2, 1963), 7–8.

"Statement of the delegation of the CCP at the Bucharest meeting of the fraternal parties, June 26, 1960," *Peking Review*, 37 (September 13, 1963), 22–3.
"Two different lines on the question of war and peace, comment on the open letter of the Central Committee of the CPSU, by the Editorial Departments of *Renmin ribao* and *Hongqi*," *Peking Review*, 47 (November 22, 1963), 6–16.
"The truth about how the leaders of the CPSU have allied themselves with India against China," *Peking Review*, 45 (November 8, 1963), 18–29.

6. Unsigned articles

"Afro-American struggle against violent repression developing vigorously – Chairman Mao's great statement points out direction of struggle for the black people in the United States," *Peking Review*, 33 (August 16, 1968), 10–14.
"Aggravation of economic crisis and intensification of class contradictions in France," *Peking Review*, 23 (June 7, 1968), 27–8.
"Ai-sen-hao-ewi-erh ti ch'i-chih chiu-shih hai-tao ti ch'i-chih" (The banner of Eisenhower is the banner of pirates), *Jen-min jih-pao*, July 21, 1958.
"Another big exposure of US-Soviet counterrevolution collaboration," *Peking Review*, 26 (July 12, 1968), 5–6. Taken from *Jen-min jih-pao*.
"A basic summing up of experience gained in the victory of the Chinese people's revolution," in *Sino-Soviet Dispute* (edited by George F. Hudson, Richard Lowenthal and Roderick MacFarquhar; New York: Praeger, 1961, pp. 162–67). Translated of "Chung-kuo jen-min ko-ming sheng-li ching-yen ti chi-pen tsung-chieh," written in celebrating the publication of the fourth volume of Mao's works, *Hung-ch'i*, 20–21 (November 1, 1960), 1–13.
"A betrayal of the Soviet people," *Peking Review*, 32 (August 9, 1963), 10–11. Translation of "Che shih tui su-lien jen-min ti pei-p'an," *Jen-min jih-pao*, August 3, 1963.
"Brilliant example of resistance to US imperialist aggression, unparalleled victories of people's war in South Vietnam," *Peking Review*, 1 (January 3, 1968), 21–4.
"Capitalist restoration in Soviet Union, privileged strata brutally oppress and exploit working people," *Peking Review*, 17 (April 26, 1968), 28–9.
"Chan tsai pao-wei ho-ping ti tsui ch'ien-hsien" (Stand on the foremost peace front), *Jen-min hji-pao*, August 4, 1958.
"Chih yu chien-chüeh tou-cheng, ts'ai-neng pao-wei ho-ping" (Only through resolute struggle may peace be defended), *Jen-min jih-pao*, August 8, 1958.
"Ch'ing-k'an su-lien pao-k'an shih tsen-mo-yang fei-pang ho kung-chi chung-kuo ti" (Look! how the Soviet media slander and attack China), *Jen-min jih-pao*, September 3, 1963.
"Ch'ü-mai chung-kuo yin-mou ti chin i pu puh-lu ken-nai-ti tao-lu san-kuo t'iao-yeo chu-yao shih ho-huo tui-fu chung-kuo" (The tripartite treaty of Russia, England and America is designed to hurt China's interests), *Jen-min jih-pao*, August 3, 1963.
"Chung-a liang kuo jen-min ti chan-cheng yu-i wan sui" (Long live the Sino-Albanian military friendship), *Jen-min jih-pao*, October 6, 1960.
"Confessions concerning the line of Soviet-US collaboration pursued by the new leaders of the CPSU," *Peking Review*, 8 (February 18, 1966), 6–12. Taken from *Hung-ch'i*.
"Confusion in an impasse, Nixon is resolved to recklessly pursue the beaten path of Truman, Eisenhower, Kennedy and Johnson," *Peking Review*, 6 (February 7, 1969), 15.

"Counterrevolutionary collusion between Soviet revisionist renegade and Japanese reactionaries." *Peking Review*, 51 (December 20, 1968), 22,

"Counterrevolution holy alliance, Soviet revisionism is US imperialism's no. 1 accomplice," *Peking Review*, 12, 1969), 25.

"Czechoslovak people demonstrate against military occupation by Soviet revisionist renegade clique," *Peking Review*, 6 (February 7, 1969), 15.

"Economic crisis looming large in capitalism world, the imperialist system heads fast for total collapse," *Peking Review*, 15 (April 12, 1968), 24–6, 28.

"Evils of capitalist restoration in the Soviet country," *Peking Review*, 30 (July 26, 1968), 21–2.

"Fa yang mo-ssu-k'o hsüan-yen ho mo-ssu-k'o shen-ming ti ko-ming ching-shen" (Carry forward the revolutionary spirit of the Moscow declaration and the Moscow statement), *Jen-min jih-pao*, November 15, 1961.

"Forward along the path of the great Lenin," *Peking Review*, 17 (Aptril 26, 1960), 23–32. Translation of "Yüan-cho wei-ta le-nin ti tao-lu ch'ien-chin," *Jen-min jih-pao*, April 22, 1960.

"Give full play to the revolutionary spirit of the 1957 Moscow declaration," *Peking Review*, 48 (November 29, 1960), 6–8. Translation of "Fa yang i-chiu wu-ch'i mo-ssu-k'o hsüan-yen ti ko-ming ching-shen," *Jen-min hji-pao*, November 21, 1960.

"Glimpses into the Soviet revisionist renegade clique's restoration of capitalism," *Peking Review*, 19 (May 10, 1968), p. 28.

"Great financial crisis grips capitalist world," *Peking Review*, 49 (December 6, 1968), 26.

"Heroes' blood and renegades' fear, how the Khrushchev-Brezhnev renegades have tried to erase from people's memory the meritorious services of Chinese volunteer heroes who fell in battle in defense of Soviet power during civil war [in Russia]," *Peking Review*, 3 (January 17, 1969), 11.

"Hold high the red banner of the October Revolution, march from victory to victory," *Peking Review*, 45 (November 8, 1960), 7–8. Translation of "Kao-chu shih-yüeh ko-ming ti hung-ch'i, ts'ung sheng-li tsou hsiang sheng-li," *Jen-min jih-pao*, November 7, 1960.

"How Soviet revisionists use the CMEA to plunder and exploit East European people," *Peking Review*, 48 (November 29, 1968), 24.

"Hsiang ying-hsiung ti ku-ba jen-min chih-ching, ko-ming ti ku-ba wan sui" (Greeting the heroic Cuban people, long live the revolutionary Cuba), *Jen-min jih-pao*, November 2, 1962.

"Hsiang kung-ch'an chu-i chin-chün ti hao-chiao" (The clarion-call of armed march toward communism), *Hung-ch'i*, 4 (February 16, 1959), 1–8.

"Inextricable crisis hit capitalist world," *Peking Review*, 51 (December 20, 1968), 27.

"Integrating Mao Tse-tung's thought with the revolutionary practice in Thailand is decisive factor for winning Thai revolution," *Peking Review*, 42 (October 18, 1968), 20–21.

"Kao-chu mo-ssu-k'o hsüan-yen ti ma-k'e-ssu le-nin chu-i ko-ming ti ch'i-chih" (Hold high the revolutionary standard of Marxism-Leninism as expressed in the Moscow declaration), *Jen-min jih-pao*, June 29, 1960.

"Kuan-yü wu-ch'an chieh-chih chuan-cheng ti li-shih chin-yen" (On the historical experience of the dictatorship of the proletariat), *Jen-min jih-pao*, April 5, 1956. Also in *Jen-min shou-ts'e*, 1957, pp. 148–51.

"Leaders of the CPSU are betrayers of the Declaration (1957) and the Statement (1960)," *Peking Review*, 1 (January 1, 1966), 9–12.

"Le-nin chu-i huan shih she-hui t'i-kuo chu-i?" (Leninism or social-imperialism?)

Jen-min jih-pao, Hung-ch'i and *Chieh-fang chün-pao*, April 22, 1970. Joint editorial.

"Long live Leninism," *Peking Review*, 17 (April 26, 1960), 6–22. Translation of "Le-nin chu-i wan sui," *Hung-ch'i*, 8 (April 16, 1960), 1–29.

"New criminal evidence of Soviet revisionists' collusion with US imperialism to boost Chiang Kai-shek gang," *Peking Review*, 13 (March 29, 1968), 31–2.

"New era with Mao Tse-tung's thought as its great banner acclaimed," *Peking Review*, 2 (January 12, 1968), 12–14, 27.

"New strategy cannot save NATO from disintegration," *Peking Review*, 1 (January 1, 1968), 48–9. Taken from *Jen-min jih-pao*.

"Not even by fascist tyranny can Soviet revisionists save themselves," *Peking Review*, 3 (January 17, 1969), 28.

"Nuclear fraud jointly hatched by the United States and the Soviet Union," *Peking Review*, 25 (June 21, 1968), 17–18. Taken from *Jen-min jih-pao*.

"Outline of views on the questions of peaceful coexistence," *Peking Review*, 37 (September 13, 1963), 21–2.

"Pao-wei ma-k'e-ssu le-nin chu-i ti shun chieh hsing" (Defending the purity of Marxism-Leninism), *Hung-ch'i*, 22 (November 16, 1962), 1–6.

"Paper-tiger US imperialism frustrated at home and abroad," *Peking Review*, 2 (January 10, 1969), 20.

"The path of the great October Revolution is the common path of the liberation of mankind," *Peking Review*, 45 (November 8, 1960), 5–7. Translation of "Wei-ta shih-yüeh ko-ming ti tao-lu shih chuan jen-lei chieh-fang ti kung-t'ung tao-lu," *Hung-ch'i*, 20–21 (November 1, 1960), 14–17.

"Peking rally backs Tokyo conference," *Peking Review*, 35 (August 31, 1962), 7–9. The conference was organized by the leftists calling for world peace.

"Peking rally greets American people's struggle against US aggression in Vietnam," *Peking Review*, 14 (April 1, 1966), 9–11.

"People's armed forces led by Communist Party of Burma score major victories," *Peking Review*, 35 (August 30, 1968), 20.

"Pu kan-tsou mei-kuo ch'iang-tao, pu chieh-fang tai-wan, shih pu kan hsiu" (Struggle forever until the ouster of the United States from Taiwan), *Jen-min jih-pao*, June 29, 1960.

"Pu yao wang-chi shih-chieh shong huan-yu san-fen-chih-erh ti pei ya-pe jen-min" (Don't forget the oppressed two-thirds of the world's people), *Shih-chieh chih-shih*, 5 (May 10, 1966), reverse side of the title page.

"Raging waves of strikes sweeps North America and Western Europe," *Peking Review*, 19 (May 10, 1968), 23–5.

"Revolutionary mass movement surges forward in Western Europe and North America, new awakening of proletariat and broad sections of the people in capitalist countries," *Peking Review*, 52 (December 27, 1968), 20.

"Revolutionary Soviet people will rise up to overthrow reactionary rule of Kremlin's new Czars," *Peking Review*, 6 (February 9, 1968), 21–3.

"Situation of world revolution is excellent," *Peking Review*, 44 (November 1, 1968), 14–18.

"Sophistry cannot cover up reality in the Soviet Union," *Peking Review*, 32 (August 3, 1968), 25–6.

"Soviet institutes of higher learning turned into tools for all-round restoration," *Peking Review*, 31 (August 31, 1968), 27–8.

"Soviet leadership exposed itself as accomplice of US imperialism," *Peking Review*, 16 (April 15, 1966), 22.

"Soviet revisionism carries out social-imperialist economic exploitation in India," *Peking Review*, 45 (November 8, 1968), 26.

"Soviet revisionism, no. 1 accomplice of US imperialism in suppression of Afro-American struggle," *Peking Review*, 20 (May 17, 1968), 26–7.

"Soviet revisionist clique cannot escape the punishment of history," *Peking Review*, 10 (March 8, 1968), 22–5.

"Soviet revisionist clique is the vicious enemy of the Asian people," *Peking Review*, 8 (February 23, 1968), 28–9. Taken from *Jen-min jih-pao*.

"Soviet revisionist komsomol, tool for restoring capitalism," *Peking Review*, 51 (December 20, 1968), 27.

"Soviet revisionist renegade clique is a new pack of vampires," *Peking Review*, 19 (May 10, 1968), 25–6.

"Soviet revisionist renegade clique riddled with contradictions," *Peking Review*, 2 (January 10, 1969), 23.

"Soviet revisionist renegades step up capitalist reorganization of economy," *Peking Review*, 44 (November 1, 1968), 23–5.

"Soviet revisionists insist on armed occupation of Czechoslovakia," *Peking Review*, 36 (September 6, 1968), 9–12.

"Soviet revisionists intensify collaboration with Asian, African and Latin American reactionaries," *Peking Review*, 20 (May 17, 1968), 24–6.

"Soviet revisionists' towering crimes against the Indonesian revolution, Soviet revisionist renegade group is the no. 1 accomplice of US imperialism in its enslavement of the Indonesian people," *Peking Review*, 11 (March 15, 1968), 30–31.

"Soviet workers in abyss of suffering," *Peking Review*, 42 (October 18, 1968), 20–24.

"A storm is shaking the 'backyard' of US imperialism," *Peking Review*, 42 (October 18, 1968), 21–2.

"Su-lien pao-k'an tui chung-kung ti kung-chi yü lai yü pu hsiang yang-tsu, k'o pi ho yü-ch'un ti ch'i-t'an kuai-lun" (The Russian publications getting ever worse in their laughable and lamentable criticism of the Chinese Communist Party), *Jen-min jih-pao*, August 3, 1963.

"Supplies on Soviet revisionist market were getting short, Soviet revisionists' perverse action promotes further awakening of Soviet people," *Peking Review*, 4 (January 24, 1969), 27–8.

"Thoroughly crush the rabid aggressive ambitions of Soviet revisionist social-imperialism," *Peking Review*, 12 (March 21, 1969), 18.

"T'i-kuo chu-i, shen tai shiu-chen chu-i ho chuan shih-chieh ti fan-tun fen-tsu tso-yu chiung-tu" (The days of imperialism, modern revisionism and reaction of all countries are numbered), *Jen-min jih-pao*, November 28, 1966.

"Trade war between imperialist powers sharpening," *Peking Review*, 32 (August 9, 1968), 23–5.

"True picture of socalled 'welfare for the whole people'," *Peking Review*, 7 (February 16, 1968), 36–7.

"Ts'ai-lun kuan-yü wu-ch'an chieh-chih chuan-cheng ti li-shih chin-yen" (Once more on the historical experience of the dictatorship of the proletariat), *Jen-min jih-pao*, December 29, 1956. Also in *Jen-min shou-ts'e*, 1957, pp. 151–58.

"Ts'ien-wan pu-yao wang-chi chieh-chih tou-cheng" (Never forget class struggle), *Chieh-fang chün-pao*, May 4, 1960. Also in *Shih-chieh chih-shih*, 10 (May 25, 1960), 18–21; *Jen-min jih-pao*, August 3, 1963 (a reprint).

"T'uan-chieh chiu shih li-liang" (Solidarity is strength), *Jen-min jih-pao*, July 21, 1958.

"UN, a market-place for US-Soviet political deals," *Peking Review*, 1 (January 1, 1966), 13.

"US-Soviet collaboration: new crime," *Peking Review*, 30 (July 26, 1968), 19–20.

"Usher in the great 1970's," *NCNA*, January 1, 1970. Taken from *Jen-min jih-pao*, *Hung-ch'i* and *Chieh-fang chün-pao*, January 1, 1970. Also in *Peking Review*, 1 (January 2, 1970), 5–7.

"Washington and Moscow collaborate as well contend over Czechoslovakia," *Peking Review*, 35 (August 30, 1968), 19–20.

"We want unity, not a split," *Peking Review*, 39 (July 19, 1963), 7–9. Translation of "Wo-men yao t'uan-chieh, pu yao fen-lieh," *Jen-min jih-pao*, July 13, 1963.

"Whom is the Soviet leadership taking united action with?" *Peking Review*, 6 (February 4, 1966), 10–13.

"The World cannot look on with folded arms," *Peking Review*, 22 (July 29, 1958), 5–6. Translation of "Pu-neng hsiu-shou pang-kuan," *Jen-min jih-pao*, July 20, 1958.

7. Signed articles and books

Ai, Ssu-ch'i. *Chin i pu hsüeh-hsi "chang-wu wu-ch'an chieh-chi shih-chieh kuan"* (To further our learning how to master proletarian Weltanschauung). Hong Kong: Hsin-ho ... publishing house, 1961.

――. *She-hui fa-chan shih chiang-hsüeh t'i kang* (On the history of social development). Rev. ed. Shee-an: North-west Hsin-hua shu-shiu, 1949.

Chang, Ho-sun. "An example of modern revisionism in art – a critique of the films and statements of Grigori Chukhrai," *Peking Review*, 50 (December 13, 1963), 6–13.

Chang, Hsiang-shan. "Hsüeh-hsi Mao chu-hsi lun chih-min t'i pan chih-min t'i kuo-chia min-tsu min-chu ko-ming wen-t'i ti i-hsieh t'i -hui"(Study Chairman Mao's theory of national democratic revolution in the colonies and semi-colonies), *Chung-kuo ch'ing-nien*, 9 (May 1, 1960), 10–14.

Chang-chiang jih-pao. *Chung-kuo ko-ming ken-pen wen-t't* (The fundamental problems of the Chinese revolution). Rev. ed. Hang-ko: Chung-nan people's publishers, 1951. 2nd ed. rev. 1957.

Chao, Shin. "Lung-tuan tsu-pen ti chüh-shih li-Yun" (Monopoly profit as a result of militarism), *Shih-chieh chih-shih*, 8 (April 25, 1966), 18–20.

Chen, Chi-wu. *Lun wen-hua ko-ming ho ssu-hsiang ko-ming* (Cultural revolution and ideological revolution). Shanghai: People's publishers, 1958.

Ch'en, Yi. "Shih-yüeh ko-ming ti kuang-mang chao-yao cho i-chieh cheng-ch'ü chieh-fang ti jen-min" (The glory of the October Revolution shines upon all the peoples struggling for liberation), *Jen-min jih-pao*, November 7, 1960.

――. "Sino-Soviet alliance is the mighty bulwark of world peace," *Peking Review*, 5 (February 2, 1960), 6–9. Translation of "Chung-su t'ung-meng shih shih-chieh ho-ping ch'iang-ta pao-lui), *Hung-ch'i*, 3 (February 1, 1960), 1–6.

――. "Vice-Premier Ch'en yi condemns US imperialism and Soviet revisionism for collaboration in vain effort to redivide the world," *Peking Review*, 37 September 13, 1968), 31.

Chi, Lung. "Mei-kuo ti chan-lüeh tsou-yu chiung-tu" (The United States strategy is in a blind alley), *Shih-chieh chih-shih*, 23 (December 5, 1957), 1–10.

Chinese People's Institute of Foreign Affairs. *Two Tactics, One Aim: an Exposure of the Peace Tricks of US Imperialism*. Peking: The Institute, 1960.

Chou, En-lai. "Speech at the national day reception," *Peking Review*, 40 (October 4, 1963), 5–6.

――. "Speech at the send-off ceremony at Pyongyang airport" (April 7, 1970), in *Premier Chou En-lai Visits the Democratic People's Republic of Korea*. Peking: Foreign languages press, 1970. pp. 95–7.

——. "Speech at the welcoming banquet given by Comrade Kim Il Sung, Premier of the Cabinet of the Democratic People's Republic of Korea" (April 5, 1970). *Ibid.*, pp. 38–50.

——. "Speech at the welcoming mass rally held by the People's Committee of Pyongyang City" (April 7, 1970). *Ibid.*, pp. 71–91.

Chou, Mou-yang. *Lun wo-kuo jen-min nei-pu mao-tun ti ko-kuan ken-yüan* (The objective origins of the internal contradictions of our people). Shanghai: People's publishers, 1957.

Chung, Hsin-ching. "Two sources of war threatening world peace," *Peking Review*, 25 (June 21, 1960), 22–7. Translation of "Wei-sheh shih-chieh ho-ping ti liang-ko chan-cheng tse-yüan t'i," *Hung-ch'i*, 21 (June 1, 1960), 8–15.

Chung-kuo ch'ing-nien. *Cha hung-ch'i pa pai-ch'i pa tsu-ch'an chieh-chi tsui-hou ti chen-t'i to-ch'ü kuo-lai* (Hoist the red flag, drag down the white flag and storm the final fortress of the capitalists). Peking: Chung-kuo ch'ing-nien sh'ü pan-she, 1958.

——. *Lun ko-ming jen-hsing kuan* (On revolutionary Weltanschauung). Peking: Chung-kuo ch'ing-nien ch'ü pan-she, 1952.

——. *Jen-hsing, tang-hsing, ko-hsing* (The nature of men, the party and individuals). Peking: Chung-kuo ch'ing-nien ch'ü pan-she, 1957.

Commentator. "The 'new holy alliance' will end in no better way than the old," *Peking Review*, 41 (October 11, 1963), 12–15.

Fang, Ko-yu. "Le-nin lun chung-kuo ko-ming" (Lenin on the revolution in China), *Hung-ch'i*, 8 (April 16, 1960), 30–34.

Fu, Chung. "Mao Tse-tung chün-shih p'ien-cheng fa ti wei-ta sheng-li" (The great victory of Mao Tse-tung's military dialectics), *Jen-min jih-pao*, October 6–7, 1960.

Hsieh, Sheng-wen. "Poisonous specimens of revisionist war literature – a rebuttal of Konstantin Simonov's 'Days and nights,'" *Peking Review*, 13 (March 29, 1968), 35–7.

Hsiu, Lieh-chün. "Ya-fei kuo-chia ching-chi k'uen-nan ti ken-pen yüan-yin" (The basic causes of economic troubles of the Afro-Asian nations), *Shih-chieh chih shih* 12 (June 25, 1965), 12–15.

Hsiu, Pan-han. "Hsüeh-hsi le-nin ti chan-tou ching-shen" (Learn Lenin's fighting spirit), *Jen-min jih-pao*, April 22, 1960.

Hu, Shih-kuen. "Le-nin kuan-yü ho-ping yü chan-cheng ti li-lun" (Lenin's doctrine of peace and war), *Jen-min jih-pao*, April 25, 1960.

Huang, Chan-peng. "Underdeveloped economy; a neo-colonial theory," *Peking Review*, 44 (November 1, 1963), 16–18. Translation of "Pu fa-ta ching-chi-hsüeh shih hsin chih-min chu-i ti li-lun," *Hung-ch'i*, 18 (September 13, 1963), 25–9.

Hung, Tsin-ta, and Nan Hsüeh-lin. "Soviet revisionists: sordid salesmen of reactionary Western cultures," *Peking Review*, 44 (November 1, 1968), 25–6, 28.

K'ang, Sheng. "On the current international situation," *Peking Review*, 6 (February 5, 1960), 6–9.

Kao, Ko. "The victorious road of national-liberation war," *Peking Review*, 46 (November 15, 1963), 6–14.

Leninism or Social-Imperialism? Peking: Foreign languages press, 1970. Also in *Peking Review*, 17 (April 24, 1970), 5–15.

Liao, Ch'eng-chi. "Thoroughly expose the reactionary nature of the tripartite treaty," *Peking Review*, 32 (August 9, 1963), 12–16.

——. "The world council of peace must return to the correct path; speech at the

Warsaw Session of WCP, November 28, 1963," *Peking Review*, 49 (December 6, 1963), 12–16.

Lin, Piao. "Letter to members of the Standing Committee of the Military Commission of the Party Central Committee" (March 22, 1966), in *Summary of the Forum on the Work in Literature and Art in the Armed Forces with Which Comrade Lin Piao Entrusted Comrade Chiang Ching*. Peking: Foreign languages press, 1970.

——. "Lin Piao's speech at the celebration rally," in *Forward along the High Road of Mao Tse-tung's Thought*. Peking: Foreign languages press, 1970.

——. *Report to the Ninth National Congress of the Communist Party of China*. Peking: Foreign languages press, 1970.

——. "Speech at the Peking mass rally to receive revolutionary teachers and students from all over China, in" *The Great Proletarian Cultural Revolution in China*. Peking: Foreign languages press, 1970. Book 8.

Liu, Ch'ang-sheng. "On the question of war and peace," *Peking Review*, 24 (June 14, 1960), 13–14.

Liu, Shao-ch'i. "Speech at Pyongyang," *Peking Review*, 39 (September 27, 1963), 8–14.

——. "The world's people's must persist in struggle to isolate US imperialism to maximum; speech at the state banquet in honor of Chairman Haxhi Lleshi," *Peking Review*, 23 (June 7, 1960), 6.

Liu, Ta-nien. "T'i-kuo chu-i tui chung-kuo ti ch'in-lüeh yu chung-kuo jen-min fan-tui t'i-kuo chu-i tou-cheng, i-pa-ssu-ling nien chung-ying ya-pien chan-cheng chih i-chiu-ssu-chiu chung-hua jen-min kung-ho-kuo ch'ing-li" (Imperialist aggregation against China and the anti-imperialist struggle of the Chinese people, from the Sino-English opium war of 1840 to the founding of the People's Republic of China in 1949), *Li-shih yen-chiu*, 4 (July 20, 1964), 101–18.

Long Live Leninism. Peking: Foreign languages press, 1961.

Lu, Ting-yi. "Unite under Lenin's revolutionary banner," *Peking Review*, 17 (April 26, 1960), 33–9.

Mao, Tun. "The way to general disarmament and world peace," *Peking Review*, 29 (July 10, 1962), 5–13.

P'eng, Chen. "The Chinese Communist Party greets the Third Congress of the Romanian Workers' Party," *Peking Review*, 26 (June 28, 1960), 4–6; also printed in *Pravda*, June 22, 1960.

——. "Speech at the national day celebration," *Peking Review*, 40 (October 4, 1963), 7–9.

Shieh, Fang. "T'i-kuo chu-i chen-ying nei-pu ti ta hun-chan" (The pell-mell inside the imperialist camp), *Shih-chieh chih-shih*, 6 (March 25, 1966), 6–11.

——. "T'i-kuo chu-i kuo-chia chih chien mao-tun chin i pu chien jui hua" (Further aggravation of the inter-imperialist conflicts), *Shih-chieh chih-shih*, 5 (May 10, 1965), 9–12.

Shih, Chieh. "Wei-chi ssu-fu ti mei kuo ching-chi" (The crisis-laden American economy), *Shih-chieh chih-shih*, 7 (April 10, 1966), 8–11.

Shih, Tung-hsiang. "Chieh-chih tou-cheng kuei-lu shih pu-neng wang-chi ti" (One may not forget the class struggle), *Hung-ch'i*, 22 (November 16, 1962), 12–22.

——. "Lenin and Stalin on the road of the October Revolution," *Peking Review*, 45 (November 8, 1963), 7–15. Translation of "Le-nin ssu-ta-lin lun shih yüeh ko-ming ti tao-lu," *Hung-ch'i*, 21 (November 7, 1963), 1–12.

——. "Refuting the fallacy that the nature of imperialism has changed," *Peking Review*, 25 (June 21, 1960), 11–13. Translation of "P'o t'i-kuo chu-i pen-hsing i pien ti miu-lun," *Hung-ch'i*, 12 (June 16, 1960), 1–4.

Sung, Ch'ing-ling. "Chung-kuo ti chieh-fang, chung-su yu-i, jen-lei hsiang wei-lai ti yao-chin" (The liberation of China and the Sino-Soviet friendship leap forward incessantly), *Hung-ch'i*, 18 (September 16, 1959), 1–8.

Tu, Ching. "Chin fang chia-mao" (Beware of falsification), *Hung-ch'i*, 17 (September 6, 1963), 44–8.

Wan, Kuong. "Mei-kuo t'i-kuo chu-i shih tsui ta ti kuo-chieh po-hsüeh che" (American imperialism is the greatest exploiter on the international plane), *Hung-ch'i*, 21 (November 21, 1963), 13–22.

Wen, Yi-chin. "Khrushchev's fairy tales about the 'ruins of imperialism,'" *Peking Review*, 38 (September 20, 1963), 15–18. Translation of "K'e-lu-hsiao-fu wei shen-mo yao tsai 't'i-kuo chu-i ssu-wang ti fei hsü' che tien shong ta tsou yao-yen," *Hung-ch'i*, 17 (September 6, 1963), 38–43.

Yang, Yung. "The great victory in the struggle to resist US aggression and aid Korea," *Peking Review*, 44 (November 1, 1960), 12–14. Translation of "K'ang-mei yüan-chao tou-cheng ti wei ta sheng-li, chi yen chung-kuo chih-yüan chün k'ang-mei yüan-chao ch'u kuo tso cheng shih chou nien," *Jen-min jih pao*, October 24, 1960.

Yao, Wen-yuan. *The Working Class Must Exercise Leadership in Everything*, Peking: Foreign language press, 1970.

Yu, Chao-li. "The Chinese people's great victory in the fight against imperialism," *Peking Review*, 38 (September 22, 1959), 6–11. Translation of "Chung-kuo jen-min fan-tui t'i-kuo chu-i tou-cheng ti wei-ta sheng-li shih chou nien," *Hung-ch'i*, 18 (September 16, 1959), 9–16.

——. "Excellent situation for the struggle for peace," *Peking Review*, 1 (January 5, 1960), 15–19. Translation of "Cheng ch'ü ho-ping tou-cheng ti ta-hao hsing-shih," *Hung-ch'i*, 1 (January 1, 1960), 33–9.

——. "The forces of the new are bound to defeat the forces of decay," *Peking Review*, 25 (August 19, 1958), 8–11. Translation of "Hsin-sheng li-liang i ting chan sheng fu-hsiu li-liang," *Hung-ch'i*, 6 (August 6, 1958), 1–6.

——. "Ku-ba jen-min k'ang-mei ai-kuo tou-cheng sheng-li ti wei-ta i-i" (The great significance of the Cuban people's patriotic struggle against US imperialism), *Hung-ch'i*, 9–10 (May 5, 1961), 11–17.

——. "A new upsurge of national revolution," *Peking Review*, 26 (August 26, 1958), 8–9. Translation of "Min-tsu ko-ming ti hsin kao-chang," *Hung-ch'i*, 5 (August 1, 1958), 9–11.

——. "On imperialism as a source of war in modern times; and the path of people's struggle for peace," *Peking Review*, 15 (April 12, 1960), 17–24. Translation of "Lun t'i-kuo chu-i shih hsien-tai chan-cheng ti ken-yüan; pen lun ko-kuo jen-min cheng-ch'ü ho-ping ti tao-lu," *Hung-ch'i*, 7 (April 1, 1960), 1–12.

——. "Peaceful competition; an inevitable trend," *Peking Review*, 33 (August 16, 1959), 6–8. Translation of "Ho-ping ching-sai shih ta shih so ch'ü," *Hung-ch'i*, (August 16, 1959), 24–7.

Yun, Lun-kuei. "Ya-fei jen-min cheng-ch'ü che-ti ti ching-chi tu-li ti tao-lu" (The path toward complete economic independence movement of the Afro-Asian peoples), *Shih-chieh chih-shih*, 12 (June 25, 1965), 9–11.

Yung, Chung-tung. "Soviet revisionism, new Czar lording it over the East European people," *Peking Review*, 48 (November 29, 1968), 23.

8. Non-Chinese literature reprinted in Chinese media

Aidit, D. N. "Making a momentous choice," *Peking Review*, 41 (October 11, 1963), 17–19. Excerpts from a speech by D. N. Aidit, Chairman of the Central Committee of the Indonesian Communist Party at a meeting held at the Party Headquarters in Djakarta on September 29, 1963 to welcome the return of the Party's delegation from weeks' tour abroad.

"Albanian Government's statement: the partial test-ban treaty is a public document of betrayal and capitulation by Khrushchev group to US imperialism," *Peking Review*, 34 (August 23, 1963), 13–15. Excerpts from the Albanian Government's statement of August 15, 1963.

"Carry the revolution through to the end: commemorating the 45th anniversary of the founding of the Third International," *Peking Review*, 13 (March 267, 1964), 18–20. Reprint of an editorial of the march 2, 1964 issue of *Rodoong shinmoon* (Labor news, North Korea).

"Chairman Mao's statement is powerful encouragement to world people's struggle, Italian Communist Party hails Chairman Mao's statement supporting Afro-American struggle," *Peking Review*, 22 (May 31, 1968), 21.

"China, under the leadership of Chairman Mao, is the vanguard of world revolution, *Espartaco*, organ of the revolutionary Communist Party of Chile praises China for its tremendous contribution to the defense of Marxism-Leninism," *Peking Review*, 3 (January 19, 1968), 21.

"Comrade Mao Tse-tung's teachings on people's war are Indonesian people's powerful weapon for smashing Suharto-Nasution fascist military regime and establishing people's democratic power in Indonesia, hailing the publication of the Indonesian version of the *Selected Military Writings of Mao Tse-tung*, by the delegation of the Central Committee of the Communist Party of Indonesia," *Peking Review*, 30 (July 26, 1968), 8–11.

"Declaration of the Australian Marxist-Leninists," *Peking Review*, 49 (December 6, 1963), 20–25; also in *Jen-min jih-pao*, November 28, 1963. The declaration was issued on November 11, 1963 by E. F. Hill (a leader of the Australian Communist Party) and other Marxist-Leninist parties.

"Holding high six revolutionary banners to smash revisionism," *Peking Review*, 13 (March 27, 1964), 16–8. Resolution of the Second Plenum of the Central Committee of the Indonesian Communist Party regarding the political report of the Politburo.

"Mao Tse-tung's thought brings world revolution into a new triumphant era – Political Commission of the Central Committee of the Communist Party of Peru acclaims Chairman Mao's statement supporting the Afro-American struggle against violent repression as a brilliant document," *Peking Review*, 32 (August 6, 1968), 10–17.

"Mao Tse-tung's thought guides the people of the world to advance triumphantly – Jacques Jacquet calls on entire French Communist Party to study and master Mao Tse-tung's thought," *Peking Review*, 22 (May 31, 1968), 21–2.

Njoto. "Safeguarding the unity of the international communist movement," *Peking Review*, 29 (July 19, 1963), 21–2.

"Peace can only be won through struggle," *Peking Review*, 34 (August 23, 1963), 19–30. Excerpts from an editorial in the 14th issue of *Keunroja*, journal of the Central Committee of the North Korean Workers' Party.

"Peace or violence," *Peking Review*, 42 (October 18, 1963), 17–24. Reprint of an article from the 9th issue of *Hoc tap* (Study), the theoretical organ of the North Vietnam Workers' Party.

"Protesting the revisionist leadership of the Ceylon Communist Party," *Peking Review*, 48 (November 29, 1963), 17.

"Refutation of revisionists' calumnies against national-liberation war," *Peking Review*, 29 (July 19, 1963), 19–21. Excerpts from an article entitled "A just and patriotic war in commemoration of the 15th anniversary of the Malayan people armed struggle for national-liberation," *Malayan Monitor* (London), June 30, 1963.

"Reply to Khrushchev, resolution of the Central Committee of the Communist Party of Brazil," *Peking Review*, 37 (September 13, 1963), 39–43. Excerpts from a resolution of July 27, 1963 published in the August (15) issue of the Brazilian fortnighly *A classe operaria*.

"Resolutions of the National Committee of the Communist Party of New Zealand reaffirm that revisionism is the main danger in the world communist movement," *Peking Review*, 49 (December 6, 1963), 25–8.

"Solidly united under the great red banner of Mao Tse-tung's thought, the PKI is leading the Indonesian people to march onward on the road to people's war – statement of the delegation of the Central Committee of the Communist Party of Indonesia in commemoration of the 48th anniversary of the founding of the Party," *Peking Review*, 22 (May 31, 1968), 17–19.

"Soviet revisionists are agents of US imperialism, says N. Sanmugathasan, a member of the Political Bureau of the Communist Party of Ceylon," *Peking Review*, 8 (February 18, 1966), 20–21.

"Soviet revisionists' crime of savage aggression against Czechoslovakia most strongly condemned – statement by the delegation of the Central Committee of the Indonesian Communist Party," *Peking Review*, 44 (November 1, 1968), 18–20.

"Soviet revisionists' fascist crime of armed aggression against Czechoslovakia strongly condemned – statement by Central Committee of the Malayan Communist Party," *Peking Review*, 38 (September 20, 1968), 35.

"Soviet revisionists have degenerated into imperialists waving the signboard of socialism – statement by the Central Committee of the Communist Party of Brazil condemns Soviet revisionists for their crime of aggression against Czechoslovakia," *Peking Review*, 44 (November 1, 1968), 20–21.

"Soviet revisionists' plot to call counterrevolutionary international meeting can only speed their own doom, excerpts from an article by the Editorial Department of the Albanian paper *Zeri i popullit*," *Peking Review*, 2 (January 12, 1968), 25–7.

"Soviet-Czechoslovak treaty legalizes transformation of Czechoslovakia into Soviet revisionist colony, excerpts from an editorial in the Albanian peper *Zeri i popullit*," *Peking Review*, 44 (November 1, 1968), 17.

"Statement by N. Sanmugathasan, General Secretary of the Communist Party of Ceylon, expressing the hope that the revolutionary forces of Czechoslovakia will rise to beat back the aggression by the Soviet revisionist ruling clique in their own country and return to the path of socialism," *Peking Review*, 38 (September 10, 1968), 36.

"Statement of ten Central Committee members of the Ceylon Communist Party," *Peking Review*, 48 (November 29, 1963), 9–16. The statement was issued on October 27, 1963, in reply to the party leadership's statement of September 26, 1963, upholding revisionism.

"Warsaw treaty has become instrument for Soviet revisionists' aggression and enslavement of the people of member states, speech by comrade Shehu at session of Albania's Assembly," *Peking Review*, 38 (September 10, 1968), 8–14.

Wilcox, V. G. "The leadership of the CPSU has taken the revisionist path,"

Peking Review, 52 (December 27, 1963), 16–20. V. G. Wilcox, General Secretary of the New Zealand Communist Party, addressed the students of the Aliarcham Academy of Social Sciences in Djakarta, Indonesia, on September 9, 1963. The address was printed in the November, 1963 issue of the New Zealand *Communist Review*, under the title: "The nature of social democracy."

Yuchi, A. and Iu Aribari. "Feng-k'uang ti fan-ma-k'e-ssu chu-i che ho chan-cheng fan-tsu ti tsou-kou, lüeh-lun cha-de-ehr ti 'she-hui chu-i yü chan-cheng' i shu" (The crazy anti-Marxist and warmonger's running dog, a critique on the book *Socialism and War* of Edward Kardelj), *Jen-min jih-pao*, October 6, 1960. The two authors are Albanians.

III. SOVIET POLEMIC LITERATURE

9. *Official party and government statements*

"Deklaratsiya soveshchaniya predstavitelei kommunisticheskikh i rabochikh partii sotsialisticheskikh stran" (Declaration of the conference of the representatives of the communist and workers' parties of the socialist countries), *Pravda*, November 22, 1957.

"Kommiunike o soveshchanii politicheskogo konsul'tativnogo komiteta gosudarstv, uchastnikov varshavskogo dogovora o druzhbe, sotrudnichestve i vzaimnoi pomoshchi" (Communique of the Political Consultative Conference of the Warsaw Organization), *Pravda*, February 5, 1960.

KPSS v rezoliutsiyakh i resheniyakh s'ezdov, konferentsii i plehumov Tsk (Collection of resolutions and decisions taken by the CPSU congresses, conferences and plenary sessions of the Central Committee), 7th ed. Moskva: Gospolitizdat, 1953.

"Letter of the Central Committee of CPSU, dated February 24, 1966), *Peking Review*, 13 (March 25, 1966), 6.

Materialy XXII s'ezda KPSS (Documentary materials of the 22nd Congress of the CPSU). Moskva: Gospolitizdat, 1961.

"Novaya programma" (New program), *Pravda*, and *Izvestiya*, November 2, 1961.

"Open letter of the Central Committee of the Communist Party of the Soviet Union to its party organizations at all levels and to all its party members," *Peking Review*, 30 (July 26, 1963), 27–46.

"Otkrytoe pis'mo Tsentral'nogo Komiteta Kommunisticheskoi Partii Sovetskogo Soiuza partiiym organizatsiyam, vsem kommunistam Sovetskogo Soiuza" (An open letter from the Central Committee of the CPSU to the party apparatus and party members of the CPSU), *Pravda*, July 14, 1963.

"Pis'mo ispolnitel'nomu Komitetu Leiboristskoi Partii Velikobritanii [ot] Tsk KPSS" (A letter from the Central Committee of the CPSU to the Executive Committee of the British Labor Party), *Pravda*, October 16, 1957.

"Pis'mo Tsentral'nogo Komiteta KPSS Kompartii Kitaya, ot 15 iiunya 1964 g." (A letter from the Central Committee of the CPSU to the Central Committee of the CCP, dated June 15, 1964), *Kommunist*, 10 (July, 1964), 9–20. Also published as a booklet: Moskva: Gos. izd-vo polit. lit-ry, 1964. 30 pp.

Postanovleniya plenum TsK KPSS (The decisions of the plenium of the Central Committee of the CPSU), Moskva: Gos. izd-vo polit. lit-ry, 1963.

Programmye dokumenty bor'by za mir, demokratiiu i sotsializm (The programs of the struggle for peace, democracy and socialism). Moskva: Gospolitizdat, 1963.

"Reshitel'nyi otpor raskol'nicheskomu kursu Pekina, po materialam mezhduna-

rodnikh soveshchaniya kommunisticheskikh i rabochikh partii [v Moskve]"
(A decisive refusal of the dissident course of Peking, materials of international
conferences of communist and workers' parties held in Moscow), *Kommunist*,
10 (May, 1969), 95–100.

"Statement of the Soviet Government", *Peking Review*, 33 (August 16, 1963),
16–24; also in *Jen-min jih-pao*, August 15, 1963.

"Zayavlenie pravitel'stva SSSR ot 13 iiunya 1969 goda, peredannoe pravitel'stvu
Kitaiskoi Narodnoi Respubliki [o normalizatsii obstanovka na Sovetsko-
Kitaiskoi granitse]" (Statement of the Soviet Government of June 13, 1969,
to the Chinese Government, on the normalization of the situation along the
Sino-Soviet boundaries), *Novoe vremya*, 25 (1969), 35–40.

"Zayavlenie soveshchaniya predstavitelei kommunisticheskikh i rabochikh
partii" (Statement of the conference of the representatives of the communist
and workers' parties), *Pravda*, December 6, 1960; also in *Izvestiya*, December 7,
1960; *Kommunist*, 17 (November, 1960), 3–32; *Peking Review*, 49–50 (December 13, 1960), 6–22.

"Zayavlenie sovetskogo pravitel'stva, zayavlenie predstavitelya Kitaiskogo
pravitel'stva peredanno agenstvom sinkhua" (Statement of the Soviet Government in reply to the Chinese declaration as contained in the *NCNA*), *Izvestiya*,
August 22, 1963; *Pravda*, August 21, 1963.

XXII s'ezd Kommunisticheskoi Partii Sovetskogo Soiuza, stenograficheskii otchet
(Report of the 22nd Congress of the CPSU). Moskva: Gos. izd-vo polit. lit-ry,
1962.

XXIII s'ezd Kommunisticheskoi Partii Sovetskogo Soiuza, stenograficheskii otchet
(Report of the 23rd Congress of the CPSU). Moskva: Gos. izd-vo polit. lit-ry,
1966.

10. Unsigned articles and books

"Aktivno formirovat' marksistsko-leninskoe mirovozzrenie kommunistov" (To
formulate dynamically the Marxist-Leninist Weltanschauung of the communists), *Kommunist*, 13 (September, 1965), 3–11.

"Amerikano-Saigonskie voiska dolzhny vyvedeny iz Kambodzhi" (American
and Saigon troops must be withdrawn from Cambodia), *Izvestiya*, and *Pravda*,
May 20, 1970.

"Antisovetskaya deyatel'nost' Kitaiskikh diplomatov (Anti-Soviet activity of
the Chinese diplomats), *Izvestiya*, January 12, 1969.

"Avantiuristicheskim kursom" (An adventurist course), *Izvestiya*, March 6, 1970.

"Beschest'e Pekina, o provokats. deistviyakh Pekinskikh rukovoditelei protiv
ofits. predstavitelei SSSR v Kitae, red. stat'ya" (Disgrace of Peking, provocation of Peking leadership against official representatives of the USSR in
China, an editorial), *Novoe vremya*, 7 (1967), 2–3.

"Boevoe znamya tvorcheskogo marksizma-leninizma" (The fighting banner of
creative Marxism-Leninism), *Kommunist*, 16 (November, 1962), 3–12.

"Dal'neishee ukreplenie mirovoi sotsialisticheskoi sistemy" (Further strengthening of the world socialist system), *Pravda*, January 28, 1959.

"12-ya godovshchina Kitaiskoi Narodnoi Respubliki" (The 12th anniversary of
the Chinese People's Republic), *Kommunist*, 14 (September, 1961), 9–13.

"Ekonomika – glavnoe pole bor'by za kommunizm" (Economy is the main field
of struggle for communism), *Kommunist*, 17 (November, 1963), 3–14.

"*Ekonomist* o polozhenii v Kitae, po materialam stat'i opubl. v ezhenedel'nike
ot 17–23 iiunya 1967 g." (The London *Economist* on the situation in China,

Materials gathered from articles during the week, June 17–23, 1967), *Novoe vremya*, 27 (1967), 11.

"Fal'shivye lozungi" (False slogans), *Izvestiya*, and *Pravda*, February 18, 1970.

Fundamentals of Marxism-Leninism. Moscow: Foreign languages publishing house, 1961. (In Russian: *Osnovy Marksizma-leninizma* Moskva: Gos. izd-vo polit. lit-ry, 1961).

"General'naya liniya mezhdunarodnogo kommunisticheskogo dvizheniya i raskol'nicheskaya platforma Kitaiskogo rukovostva" (The general line of international communist movement and the split platform of the Chinese leadership), *Kommunist*, 14 (September, 1963), 3–38.

"Glavnoe napravlenie istoricheskogo razvitiya" (The major direction of historical development), *Kommunist*, 18 (December, 1960), 3–24.

"Glavnoe zveno sluzhby byta" (Main work of life), *Pravda*, April 11, 1969.

"Ideinoe oruzhie partii" (The ideological weapon of the party), *Kommunist*, 4 (March, 1965), 3–14.

"Istorya uchit" (History teaches), *Pravda*, May 11, 1969.

"Izbavit' chelovechestvo ot ugrozy atomnoi voiny" (To save mankind from atomic war), *Pravda*, October 16, 1958.

"Izuchat' marksizm-leninizm, ovladevat' kommunisticheskim mirovozzreniem" (To study Marxism-Leninism and to hold onto communist Weltanschauung), *Kommunist*, 13 (September, 1960), 3–9.

"Izuchenie revoliutsionnei teorii i stroitel'stvo kommunizma" (The study of revolutionary theory and building of communism), *Kommunist*, 14 (September, 1964), 3–10.

"Kak byt' s universitetami i shkolami?" (What is to be done with the universities and schools?) *Izvestiya*, and *Pravda*, January 25, 1970.

"Kommunisticheskaya Partiya Kitaya prevrashchaetsya v votchinu Mao" (Communist Party of China turned into a patrimony of Mao), *Pravda*, May 17, 1969.

"Komu eto vygodno?" (Who benefits from this?) *Pravda*, March 14, 1970.

"Korennaya problema mirovoi politiki" (The basic problem of world politics), *Mezhdunarodnaya zhizn'*, 12 (December, 1957), 8–13.

"Korni nyneshnikh sobytii v Kitae" (Roots of the current events in China), *Kommunist*, 6 (March, 1968), 102–13.

"KPSS – partiya leninizma" (The CPSU is the party of Leninism), *Kommunist*, 6 (April, 1964), 3–13.

"KPSS tvorcheski razvivaet marksistsko-leninskuiu teoriiu" (The CPSU creatively develops Marxist-Leninist theory), *Kommunist*, 12 (August, 1963), 3–11.

"Krepnet bratskoe sotrudnichestvo" (Strengthen the fraternal solidarity), *Pravda*, April 28, 1969.

"Krepnet solidarnost' trudyashchikhsya vsekh stran" (Strengthen the solidarity of working people of all nations), *Kommunist*, 6 (March, 1960), 3–8.

"Krepnet splochennost' kommunisticheskikh ryadov" (Strengthen the solidarity of the communist ranks), *Pravda*, November 25, 1968.

"Krovnoe delo vsekh narodov" (Vital interests of all peoples), *Pravda*, April 7, 1969.

"Latinskaya Amerika boretsya" (Latin America fights on), *Pravda*, May 15, 1969.

"Lenin – nashe znamya! tozhestvennoe posvyashchenoe 99-i godovshchine so dnya rozhdeniya V. I. Lenina" (Lenin is our banner! in commemoration of the 99th birthday of V. I. Lenin), *Izvestiya*, April 23, 1969.

"Lenin – znamya nashei epokh" (Lenin is the banner of our epoch), *Kommunist*, 5 (March, 1961), 3–12.

"Leninizm i aktual'nye zadachi bor'by protiv antikommunizma" (Leninism and

the urgent tasks of the struggle against anti-communism), *Voprosy filosofii*, 2 (February, 1970), 3–8.
"Leninizm sozdannaya, leninizmu vernaya" (Be faithful to the creative Leninism), *Kransnaya zvezda*, July 30, 1963.
"Leninizm – znamya nashikh pobed" (Leninism is the banner of our victories), *Kommunist*, 5 (May, 1964), 3–12.
"Leninskaya traditsiya" (Leninist tradition), *Pravda*, April 8, 1969.
Leninskaya diplomatiya mira i sotrudnichestva (Leninist diplomacy of peace and cooperation). Moskva: Izd-vo "Nauka," 1965.
"Leninskim kursom – k pobede kommunizma" (Lenin's course leads to the victory of communism), *Kommunist*, 2 (January, 1964), 3–10.
"Likvidirovat' agressivnyi blok NATO, trebuiut miroliubivye narody" (Peace-loving people demand liquidation of the aggressive bloc of NATO), *Pravda*, April 11, 1969.
"Maoistskaya panatseya" (Maoist panacea), *Izvestiya*, December 19, 1968.
"Maoistskii kinopaskvil'" (Maoist squib), *Pravda*, April 23, 1969.
"Maoizm i imperialisticheskie derzhavy" (Maoism and the imperialist powers), *Mirovaya ekonomika i mezhdunarodnye otnosheniya*, 6 (1969), 61–71.
"Maoizm i mirovaya reaktsiya" (Maoism and world reaction), *Mirovaya ekonomika i mezhdunarodnye otnosheniya*, 7 (1969), 56–65.
"Marksizm-leninizm – osnova edinstva kommunisticheskogo dvizheniya" (Marxism-Leninism is the cornerstone of the unity of communist movement), *Kommunist*, 15 (October, 1963), 13–47.
"Marksistsko-leninskaya programma kommunisticheskogo dvizheniya" (Marxist-Leninist program of communist movement), *Kommunist*, 17 (November, 1963), 12–13.
"Marksistsko-leninskoe uchenie i sovremennyi mir" (Marxist-Leninist teaching and the present world), *Kommunist*, 14 (September, 1965), 3–16.
"Mirnoe sosushchestvovannie v deistvii" (Peaceful coexistence in action), *Kommunist*, 10 (July, 1964), 3–8.
"Mirovaya pechat' ob avantiurizme Pekina" (World press about the adventurism of Peking), *Novoe vremya*, 8 (1967), 3–4.
"Moguchii shchit mira i progressa" (Powerful shield of peace and progress), *Izvestiya*, May 15, 1969.
Nabliudatel' (Observer). "Chernye ochki Pekinskikh gazet" (Dark glasses of Peking newspapers), *Izvestiya*, August 14, 1963.
"Nashe pobedonosnoe znamya" (Our victorious banner), *Pravda*, April 13, 1960.
"Natsional'no-osvoboditel'noe dvizhenie i sotsial'nyi progress" (National-liberation movement and social progress), *Kommunist*, 13 (September, 1965), 23–34.
"Nerushimaya druzhba Sovetskogo i Kitaiskogo narodov" (The indestructible friendship of the Soviet and Chinese peoples), *Kommunist*, 3 (February, 1961), 10–13.
"O kharaktere kul'turnoi revoliutsii v Kitae" (The character of the cultural revolution in China), *Kommunist*, 7 (April, 1968), 103–14.
"O kul'turnoi revoliutsii v NKR, obzor zarubezhnoi pechati" (The cultural revolution in China, a survey of foreign press), *Aziya i Afrika segodnya*, 11 (1966), 25–6.
"O kul'turnoi revoliutsii v KNR, otryvki iz statei opubl. v zarubezhnoi pechati" (The cultural revolution in China, excerpts from articles published in foreign press), *Aziya i Afrika segodnya*, 12 (1966), 16–17.
"O nekotorykh storonakh partiinoi zhizni v Kompartii Kitaya" (On several aspects of the life of the CCP), *Kommunist*, 7 (May, 1964), 10–24.
"O politicheskom kurse Mao Tsze-duna na mezhdunarodnoi arene, red. stat'ya"

(Political course of Mao Tse-tung on the international arena: an editorial), *Kommunist*, 8 (April, 1968), 95–108.

"O Sovetsko-Kitaiskikh otnosheniyakh" (Sino-Soviet relations), *Novoe vremya*, 25 (1969), 6–7.

"Ob antisovetskoi politike Mao Tsze-duna i ego gruppy" (Anti-Soviet policy of Mao Tse-tung and his group), *Novoe vremya*, 9 (1967), 35–40; *Pravda*, February 16, 1967.

"Oplot mira i progressa" (The pillar of peace and progress), *Pravda*, May 18, 1969.

"Ot dogmatizma v istorii i opportunizmu v praktike" (From historical dogmatism to practical opportunism), *Krasnaya zvezda*, July 21, 1963. The Chinese attacked this article in: "Su-lien pao-k'ang tui chung-kung ti kung-chi yü lai yü pu hsiang-yang-tsu, k'o pi ho yü-ch'un ti ch'i-t'an kuai-lun" (The Russian publications getting ever worse in their laughable and lamentable criticism of the Chinese Communist Party), *Jen-min jih-pao*, August 3, 1963.

"Otkaz Kitaiskikh vlastei" (Refusal by Chinese authorities), *Pravda*, and *Izvestiya*, February 24, 1970.

"Partiya vedet k kommunismu" (The party leads to communism), *Pravda*, July 30, 1963.

"Peretryakhivanie voennykh kadrov v Kitae" (Shake-up of military personnel in China), *Pravda*, April 5, 1970.

"Plechom k plechy" (Shoulder by shoulder), *Izvestiya*, May 1, 1969.

"Po leninskomu puti" (On the Leninist path), *Krasnaya zvezda*, July 21, 1963.

"Po povodu besedy Mao Tsze-duna s gruppoi yaponskikh sotsialistov" (In connection with Mao Tse-tung's conversation with a group of Japanese socialists), *Pravda*, September 2, 1964.

"Politicheskii boetz partii" (Political fighter of the party), *Pravda*, May 8, 1969.

"Programma bor'by za mir i mezhdunarodnuiu bezopasnost'" (The program of struggle for peace and international security), *Kommunist*, 1 (January, 1964), 11–22.

"Proiski maoistov" (The intrigues of the Maoists), *Pravda*, April 9, 1969.

"Proletarskii internatsionalizm i maoistskii shovinizm" (Proletarian internationalism and Maoist chauvinism), *Pravda*, April 27, 1969. Reprint of an article from a Bulgarian paper *Rabotnichesko delo* (Workers' affairs).

"Propagandistskaya fal'shivka i real'naya deistvitel'nost'" (Propaganda falsification and true reality), *Pravda*, August 4, 1963.

"Provokatsiya Kitaiskikh vlastei na Sovetsko-Kitaiskoi granitse" (The provocation of the Chinese authority on the Sino-Soviet boundaries), *Pravda*, March 3, 1970.

"Reshitel'no povernut' rul' sobytii s puti voiny na put' mira!" (The wheel is decidedly turning from the path of war to the path of peace!) *Pravda*, July 21, 1958.

"Ser'eznyi ochag napryazhennost' v Azii" (The storm center of Asia), *Pravda*, September 19, 1963; also translated into Chinese, *Jen-min jih-pao*, September 25, 1963.

"Severoatlantischeskii blok – istochnik napyazhennost'" (North Atlantic bloc is the source of tension), *Pravda*, April 12, 1969.

"S'ezd partii Mao" (Mao's party congress), *Pravda*, May 8, 1969.

"Shkoly perevospitaniya – po maoistski" (Maoist-style: schools for re-education), *Pravda*, June 4, 1970.

"Slovo partii k millionam" (A word of the party to the millions), *Pravda*, April 20, 1969.

"Smysl Pekinskikh provokatsii" (The meaning of Peking's provocations), *Novoe vremya*, 34 (1967), 16.

"Sobytie v Kitae – tsitatniki vmesto vrachei" (Events in China, quoters instead of physicians), *Izvestiya*, February 12, 1969.
"Sobytie v Kitae" (Events in China), *Pravda*, January 12, 1969.
"Soiuz sil sotsializma i natsional'no-osvoboditel'nogo dvizheniya" (The merging of forces of socialism and national-liberation movement), *Kommunist*, 8 (May, 1964), 3–10.
"Sotsializm, mir, blagosostoyanie" (Socialism, peace and welfare), *Kommunist*, 8 (May, 1960), 3–12.
"Sovetskii Soiuz – glavnaya opora miroliubivogo chelochestva" (The Soviet Union is the main stronghold of peace-inclined peoples), *Kommunist*, 8 (May, 1960), 13–23.
"Splochenie pod znamenem marksizma-leninizma" (United under the banner of Marxism-Leninism), *Pravda*, November 23, 1960.
"Sudy na stadionakh" (Trials in stadium), *Izvestiya*. and *Pravda*, February 24, 1970.
"Svet velikikh idei" (The world of great ideas), *Izvestiya*, April 22, 1969. Devoted to Lenin's 99th birthday.
"Svidetel'stvuet pressa, zakupaiut strategicheskie materialy" (Press testimony: buying up strategic materials), *Izvestiya*, January 29, 1970.
"Terror i zapugivanie" (Terror and intimidation), *Izvestiya*, March 29, 1970; *Pravda*, March 28, 1970.
"Tragediya intelligentsii" (The tragedy of the intelligentsia), *Teatr*, 7 (1969), 163–64.
"Triumf teorii i praktiki leninizma" (Triumph of the theory and practice of Leninism), *Kommunist*, 15 (October, 1960), 3–10.
"Tyazhelye vremena Kitaiskoi derevni" (Hard times for the Chinese countries), *Izvestiya*, March 24, 1970.
"V avangarde sil progresse" (In the vanguard of forces of progress), *Pravda*, April 21, 1969.
"Velichie leninskikh idei" (The greatness of Lenin's ideas), *Kommunist*, 6 (April, 1961), 3–10.
"Velikii oktyabr' – putevodnaya zvezda" (The great October is the lodestar), *Kommunist*, 16 (November, 1960), 3–11.
"Velikoe sotrudnichestvo po povodu mira" (Great Cooperation in the interest of peace), *Pravda*, August 6, 1958.
"Vernost' geroicheskim traditsiyam" (Faithful to the heroical tradition), *Pravda*, May 9, 1969.
"Vernost' velikim traditsiyam" (Faithful to the great traditions), *Pravda*, April 12, 1969.
"Vo imya bezopasnosti bratskikh narodov, nikom i nikomu ne budet posvoleno vyrvat ni odnogo zvena iz sodruzhestva sotsialisticheskikh gosudarstv" (In the name of security, no one is permitted to knock away one circle from the solidity of the socialist states), *Izvestiya*, August 22, 1968.
"Vo imya kommunizma i mira" (In the name of communism and peace), *Kommunist*, 1 (January, 1963), 3–9.
"Voennyi psikhoz v Kitae" (War psychosis in China), *Izvestiya*, January 10, 1970.
"Yarmarka v Guanchzhou i politika Mao" (The fair in Kwangchow and Mao's policy), *Pravda*, April 17, 1970.
"Za edinstvo i splochennost' mezhdunarodnogo kommunisticheskogo dvizheniya (For the unity and solidarity of international communist movement), *Pravda*, December 6, 1963.
"Za mir, za razoruzhenie, za svobodu narodov" (For peace, disarmament and freedom of the peoples), *Kommunist*, 14 (September, 1960), 3–12.

"Za postroenie razvitogo sotsialisticheskogo obshchestvo" (For building up a developed socialist society), *Pravda*, April 14, 1969. Reprint of an article from a Bulgarian paper *Stanko todorova*.

"Za torzhestvo tvorcheskogo marksizma-leninizma, protiv revisii kursa mirovogo kommunisticheskogo dvizheniya" (For victorious and creative Marxism-Leninism in opposition to revisionism of world communist movement), *Kommunist*, 11 (May, 1963), 3–36.

Zhizn' lenina – velikii podvig (The life of Lenin, a great career). Edited by P. N. Pospelov, including an introduction and thirteen articles by different authors. Moskva: Gos. izd-vo polit. lit-ry, 1960.

"Znamya epokh" (The banner of the epoch), *Kommunist*, 6 (April, 1963), 9–10.

"Znamya peredovykh sil chelovechstva" (The banner of the progressive forces of mankind), *Kommunist*, 6 (April, 1965), 8–10.

11. Works by post-1953 Soviet leaders (including here only the several Chairmen of the Council of Ministers and the CPSU's General Secretaries)

a. Khrushchev, N. S.

"Beseda N. S. Khrushcheva s glavnym redaktorom yaponskoi gazety 'assakhi simbun' g-nom Tomoo Shrooki" (Interview with the chief editor of the Japanese paper, *Asahi Shimbun*, Tomo Shroki), *Krasnaya zvezda*, June 30, 1957.

Conquest without War. Edited by N. H. Mager and Jacques Katel. New York: Simon and Schuster, 1961.

"Marksizm-leninizm, znamya nashkikh pobed" (Marxism-Leninism is the standard of our victories), *Izvestiya*, January 8, 1961.

Mir bez oruzhiya, mir bez voiny (Peace without arms, peace without war). Moskva: Gos. izd-vo polit. lit-ry, 1960. 2 vols.

Nasushchnye voprosy razvitiya mirovoi sotsialisticheskoi sistemy (The pressing problems of the development of the world socialist system). Moskva: Gos. izd-vo polit. lit-ry, 1962; *Kommunist*, 12 (August, 1962), 3–28.

"O mezhdunarodnom polozhenii i vneshnei politike Sovetskogo Soiuza" (International situation and foreign policy of the Soviet Union), *Pravda*, November 1, 1959.

"O mire i mirnom sosushchestvovanie" (On peace and peaceful coexistence), *Kommunist*, 7 (May, 1964), 3–9.

On Peaceful Coexistence. Moscow: Foreign languages pubilishing house, 1961.

"Otchetnyi doklad Tsentral'nogo Komiteta Kommunisticheskoi Partii Sovetskogo Soiuza XX s'ezdu Partii, doklad pervogo sekretarya TsK KPSS, t. N. S. Khrushcheva" (Khrushchev's report to the Twentieth Congress of the CPSU), *Pravda*, and *Izvestiya*, February 15, 1956.

"Otvety N. S. Khrushcheva na voprosy brazil'skikh zhurnalistov Viktorio Martorelli i Tito Fleuri" (An interview with the Brazilian newsmen, Messrs. Martorelli and Fleuri), *Mezhdunarodnaya zhizn'*, 12 (December 1957), 3–7.

"Otvety N. S. Khrushcheva na voprosy glavnogo korrespondenta amerikanskogo agenstva iuunaited press internatsional v Moskve, g. Shapiro" (An answer to the questions put by the chief correspondent of United Press International in Moscow, Mr. Shapiro), *Pravda*, December 31, 1963.

"Poslanie Predsedatelya Soveta Ministrov SSSR, N. S. Khrushcheva, Prezidentu SSHA, Dzhonu Kennedi" (A letter from the Chairman of the Council of Ministers of the Soviet Union, N. S. Khrushchev, to the President of the United States, John Kennedy), *Pravda*, and *Izvestiya*, February 24, 1962. In

English it appears in: State Department, *Bulletin*, 47 (October-December 1962) 741–43.

Predotvratit' voinu, otstoyat' mir! (To prevent war and defend peace!) Moskva: Gos. izd-vo polit. lit-ry, 1963.

"Priem v posol'stve Pol'skii Narodnoi Respubliki, rech' t. N. S. Khrushcheva" (Speech at the reception of the Polish Embassy on the 14th anniversary of national renascence), *Pravda*, July 23, 1958.

"Razoruzhenie – put' k uprochenii mira i obesprecheniiu druzhby mezhdu narodami" (Disarmament is the key to peace and international comity), *Pravda*, January 15, 1960.

"Rech' na mitinge sovetsko-vengerskoi druzhby" (Speech at the Soviet-Hungarian friendship rally), *Pravda*, July 20, 1963.

"Rech' t. N. S. Khrushcheva na mitinge trudyashchkhsya goroda Novosibirska" (Speech to a mass meeting in the city of Novosibirsk), *Pravda*, October 11, 1959.

"Rech' t. N. S. Khrushcheva na III s'ezde Rumynskii Rabochei Partii" (Speech of Khrushchev to the Third Congress of the Romanian Workers' Party), *Izvestiya*, 23 and *Pravda*, June 22, 1960.

"Rech' t. N. S. Khrushcheva na torzhestvernnom zasedanii smolenskogo obkoma KPSS i oblastnogo soveta deputatov trudyashchikhsya, posvyashchennom vruchniiu oblasti ordena lenina 13 avgusta 1958 goda" (Khrushchev's speech at a mass meeting in the district of Smolensk), *Pravda*, August 24, 1958.

"Rech' t. N. S. Khrushcheva" (Khrushchev's speech [in Krasnodar District]), *Pravda*, October 16, 1958.

Stroitel'stvo kommunizma v SSSR i razvitie sel'skogo khozyaistva (The building of communism and development of agricultural economy in the Soviet Union). Moskva: Gos. izd-vo polit. lit-ry, 1966. 8 vols.

"T. N. S. Khrushshev v primor'e mnogotysyachnie miting trudyashchikhsya Vladivostoka" (Speech at a mass meeting in Vladivostok), *Pravda*, October 7, 1959.

"Ukrepim edinstvo kommunisticheskogo dvizheniya vo imya torzhestva mira i sotsializma" (Let us strengthen the unity of communist movement for the sake of peace and socialism), *Pravda*, January 7, 1963.

"Za novye pobedy mirovoi kommunisticheskogo dvizheniya" (For new victories of the world communist movement), *Pravda*, January 7, 1961; *Kommunist*, 1 (January, 1961), 3–37.

b. *Malenkov, G. M.*

"Rech' Predsedatel'ya Soveta Ministrov SSSR, deputatov G. M. Malenkov" (Speech of the Chairman of the Council of Ministers, G. M. Malenkov), *Pravda*, April 27, 1954.

"Rech' t. G. M. Malenkova na sobranii izbiratelei leningradskogo izbiratel'nogo okruga g. Moskvy 12 marta 1954 g." (Election speech in the Leningrad constituency, Moscow, March 12, 1954), *Pravda*, March 13, 1954.

c. *Bulganin, N.*

"Poslanie Predsedatelya Soveta Ministrov SSSR, N. Bulganina, Prezidentu Soedinnenykh Shtatov Ameriki, Duaitu D. Eizenkhauery" (A letter from the Chairman of the Council of Ministers of the USSR, N. Bulganin, to the President of the United States of America, Dwight D. Eisenhower), *Pravda*, December 12, 1957.

d. Brezhnev, L. I.

Fifty Years of Great Achievements of Socialism: a Report. Moscow: Novosti press agency publishing house, 1967. The Russian edition listed below.

Leninskii kurs (Leninist course). Moskva: Gos. izd-vo polit. lit-ry, 1970. 2 vols. Vol. 1 covers the period from 1964 to 1967; vol. 2 from 1967 to 1970.

"Pod voditel'stvom partii – leninskim kursom, rech' tovarishcha L. I. Brezhneva" (Under the leadership of the party, the Leninist course, a speech by comrade L. I. Brezhnev), *Pravda,* and *Izvestiya,* May 2, 1969.

Pyat' desyat let velikikh pobed sotsializma; doklad i zakliuchit. rech' na sovmestnom torzhestv. zasedanii TsK KPSS, Verkhovnogo Soveta SSR i Verkhovnogo Soveta RSFSR v kremlevskom dvortse s'ezdov 3–4 noyabrya 1967 g. (Fifty years of great achievements of socialism; a report and concluding speech on the joint victory-celebrating session of the Central Committee of the CPSU, the Supreme Soviet of the USSR, and the Supreme Soviet of the RSFSR, November, 3–4, 1967), Moskva: Gospolitizdat, 1967.

Rech' na XV s'ezde VLKSM (Vsesoiuznyi leninskii kommunisticheskii soiuz molodezhi). Privetstvie TsK KPSS XV s'ezdu VLKSM. (Speech to the 15th Congress of the Young Communist League). Moskva: Molodaya gvardiya, 1966.

Rech' na plenume TsK KPSS 29 sentyabrya, 1965 g. (Speech on the plenary session of the Central Committee of the CPSU, September 29, 1965). Moskva: Gos. izd-vo polit. lit-ry, 1965.

Socialism's First Century; a Report. Sydney: Novosti press agency, 1968.

Soviet View of NATO; speech on April 24, 1967; prepared for the use of the Subcommittee on National Security and International Operation (pursuant to S. Res. 54, 90th Congress) of the Committee of Government Operations, United States Senate. Washington: Government Printing Office, 1967.

Unsere Zeit im Zeichen des wachsenden Einflusses des Sozialismus; Rechenschaftsbericht des ZK der KPdSU an den 23. Parteitag, 29 März–8 April, 1966 (Our time, the sign of growing influence of socialism; a report of the Central Committee to the party congress of the CPSU, March 29–April 8, 1966). Berlin: Diez, 1966.

Za ukreplenie splochennosti kommunistov, za novyi pod'em antiimperialisticheskoi bor'by (For strengthening the solidarity of communists, for new growth of anti-imperialist struggle), *Izvestiya,* June 8, 1969.

e. Kosygin, A. N.

Doklad na plenume TsK KPSS 27 sentyabrya 1965 g. (Report on the plenary session of the Central Committee of the CPSU, September 27, 1965). Moskva: Gos. izd-vo polit. lit-ry, 1965.

"Politika dobrososedstva, otvety Predsedatelya Soveta Ministrov SSSR, A. N. Kosygin, na voprosy gazety *Mainichi*" (Good-neighbor policy, answers of the Chairman of the Council of Ministers of the USSR to questions put to him by the *Mainichi* newsmen), *Pravda,* January 5, 1969.

"Poslanie Predsedatelya Soveta Ministrov SSSR, A. N. Kosygina, Prezidentu SSHA, Prezidentu Frantsii, i Prem'er-Ministru Velikobritanii, v svyazi s 25-letiem Potsdamskhogo sogloseniya" (The message of the Chairman of the Council of Ministers of the USSR, A. N. Kosygin, to the President of the United States, the President of France, and the Prime-Minister of Great Britain on occasion of the 25th anniversary of the Potsdam Declaration), *Pravda,* August 2, 1970.

Über den Entwurf der Direktiven zum Fünfjahrplan 1966 bis 1970; Schlusswort. Direktiven des XXIII. Parteitages der KPdSU für den Fünfjahrplan zur

Entwicklung der Volkswirtschaft der UdSSR in den Jahren 1966 bis 1970. Berlin: Dietz, 1966. Translation of "Direktivy dvattsat' tret'ego s'ezda KPSS po pyatiletnemu planu" (Directives of the 23rd Congress of the CPSU on the five-year-plan).

Zayavlenie pravitel'stva SSSR ob osnovnykh voprosakh vnutrennei i vneshnei politiki; vystuplenie predsedatelya Soveta Ministrov Soveta SSR sed'mogo soiuza, 3 avgusta 1966 goda (The declaration of the Government of the USSR on its domestic and foreign policy; a report of the Chairman of the Council of Ministers of the USSR, August 3, 1966). Moskva: Gos. izd-vo polit. lit-ry, 1966. The English version is listed in the following entry.

The USSR Government Statement on Principal Questions of Home and Foreign Policy; speech by the Chairman of the USSR Council of Ministers, A. N. Kosygin, at the session of the USSR Supreme Soviet on August 3, 1966. Statement of the USSR Supreme Soviet in connection with the intensification of the American imperialist aggression in Vietnam. Moscow: Novosti press agency publishing house, 1966.

12. Works by other writers in the Soviet Union

Akatova, T. "Rabochii klass Kitaya i ego bor'ba" (The working class of China and its struggle), *Aziya i Arfika segodnya*, 6 (1967), 20–22.

Aleksandrov, L. "V odnoi upryazhke s imperialisticheskoi reaktsei [ob antisovetskikh provokatsiyakh kliki Mao Tsze-duna] po materialam inostr. pechati" (In one time with the imperialist reaction, the anti-Soviet provocation of the clique of Mao Tse-tung as seen through foreign press), *Kommunist vooruzhennikh sil*, 9 (1969), 81–4.

Andropov, Iu. "Bezumie Pekina, o velikoi proletarskoi kul'turnoi revoliutsii v Kitae" (Peking's folly, the great proletarian cultural revolution), *Novoe vremya*, 15 (1966), 12–15.

——. "Kitai etoi osen'iu, o politikoi proletarskoi kul'turnoi revoliutsii" (China in this autumn, politics of the proletarian cultural revolution), *Novoe vremya*, 48 (1966), 12–14.

——. "Proletarskii internatsionalizm – boennoe znamya kommunistov" (Proletarian internationalism is the fighting banner of communists), *Kommunist*, 14 (September, 1964), 11–18.

——. "Za kulisami Kitaiskoi kul'turnoi revoliutsii" (Behind the Chinese cultural revolution), *Novoe vremya*, 50 (1966), 11–13.

Apalin, G. "Ideologicheskie osnovy vneshnei politiki gruppy Mao Tsze-duna" (Ideological bases of the foreign policy of the Mao Tse-tung group), *Mezhdunarodnaya zhizn'*, 6 (1968), 20–22.

——. "Maoizm – reserv imperialisticheskoi reaktsii" (Maoism – the reserve of imperialist reaction), *Mezhdunarodnaya zhizn'*, 7 (1969), 27–36.

Arzumanyan, A. i V. Korionov. "Noveishie otkroveniya revizionizma" (The latest revelations of revisionism), *Pravda*, September 2, 1960.

Bagramov, E. "Natsional'nyi vopros v ideologicheskoi bor'be" (Nationality problem in ideological struggle), *Pravda*, April 1, 1969.

Beleliubskii, F. "Velikie idei oktyabrya i kitaya" (Great ideas of October and China), *Mirovaya ekonomika i mezhdunarodnye otnosheniya*, 10 (1967), 134–41.

Belyakov, A. i F. Burlatskii. "Leninskaya teoriya sotsialisticheskoi revoliutsii i sovremennost'" (Lenin's theory of socialist revolution in present conditions), *Kommunist*, 13 (September, 1960), 10–27.

Bodyanskii, V. "Slova i dela ... k voprosy o politike gruppe Mao Tsze-duna v stranakh Arab Vostoka" (Words and deeds ... the policy of the Mao Tse-tung group in the Arab nations), *Sovetskie profsoiuzy*, 11 (1969), 43-4.

Burlatskii, F. "Konkretnyi analiz – vazhneishee trebovanie leninizma" (Concrete analysis is a major requirement of Leninism), *Pravda*, July 25, 1963.

Butenko, A. i V. Pchelin. "Sovremennaya epokha i tvorcheskoe razvitie marksizma-leninizma" (Contemporary epoch and creative development of Marxism-Leninism), *Kommunist*, 12 (August, 1960), 8–20.

Checknarin, E. "Proletarskii internatsionalizm i zashchita zavoevanii sotsializma" (Proletarian internationalism and defense of the achievement of socialism), *Pravda*, April 20, 1969.

Chernyayev, A. "Sotsializm – glavnaya sila mirovogo revoliutsionnogo razvitiya" (Socialism is the main force of world revolutionary development), *Pravda*, August 3, 1963.

Dalin, S. "Leninskaya teoriya imperializma i osobennost' tsiklicheskogo razvitiya sovremennogo kapitalizma" (Lenin's theory of imperialism and the peculiarity of cyclic development of modern capitalism), *Kommunist*, 1 (January, 1969), 48–60.

Datt, R. "Kuda idet Kitai?" (Where is China going?) *Novoe vremya*, 24 (1967), 27–30.

Davilov, D. "Kitaiskie provokatory i zapadnogermanskii militarizm" (The Chinese provocations and West German militarism), *Mirovaya ekonomika i mezhdunarodnye otnosheniya*, 8 (1969), 61–71.

D'enkos, E. K. "Problema natsionalykh men'shistov v Kitae" (The problem of national minorities in China), *Novoe vremya*, 15 (1967), 23–30.

Dymkov, A. "O sobytiyakh v Ukhan, vosstanie armeiskoi organizatsii 'Baivan' siunshi protiv gruppy Mao Tsze-duna" (Events in Wuhan, revolt of army organization against the Mao-Tse-tung group), *Novoe vremya*, 33 (1967), 23.

Dzhenkins, Devid. "Poezdka v maoistskii rai [ocherk avstral. publitsista, posetivshego Kitai v 1968 g.]" (Traveling to the Maoist realm, eye-witness account of an Australian publicist visiting China in 1968), *Vokrug sveta*, 6 (1969), 64–9.

Efimov, G. "Tam, za Kitaiskoi stenoi, o kul'turnoi revoliutsii v KNR" (Outside the Great Wall, the cultural revolution in China), *Neva*, 3 (1967), 145–47.

Fedorov, G. "O soderzhenie sovetskoi voennoi ideologii" (On the content of the Soviet military ideology), *Krasnaya zvezda*, March 22, 1957.

Fedoseev, P. "Materialistskoi ponemanie istorii i 'teoriya nasiliya'" (The materialist understanding of history and the 'theory of violence'), *Kommunist*, 7 (May, 1964), 51–66.

Fedosev, P. "V. I. Lenin – velikii teoritik kommunizma" (V. I. Lenin – a great theorist of communism), *Kommunist*, 1 (January, 1969), 13–20.

Fetov, V. "Kul'turnaya revolitsiya – 69 v Kitae" (The cultural revolution in China, 1969), *Literaturnaya gazeta*, 6 (February 5, 1969), 5.

Franstev, Iu. "Problemy voiny i mira sovremennikh usloviyakh" (The problems of war and peace in present-day conditions), *Pravda*, August 7, 1960.

Garushyants, Iu. "Stranitsa istorii, dlya chego maoisty izvrashchaiut fakty" (Pages of history, for what the Maoists distort the facts), *Izvestiya*, May 8, 1969.

Garuzner, N. "Rabochii klass kapitalisticheskikh stran v usloviyakh nauchno-tekhnicheskoi revoliutsii" (The working class of the capitalist countries in the conditions of scientific, technological revolution), *Kommunist*, 2 (January, 1969), 24–36.

Gavrilov, I. "Fakti razoblachaiut reveransy gomintanovtsu" (Facts exposes the obeisance to a Kuomintangite), *Izvestiya*, February 4, 1969.

——. "Fal'shivyi flag, k sobytiyam v Kitae" (The false flag, the events in China), *Sovety deputatov trudyashchikhsya*, 4 (1968), 108–10.

——. "Gruppa Mao Tsze-duna – vrag druzhby narodov Kitaya i Sovetskogo Soiuza" (The Mao Tse-tung group is the enemy of the peoples of China and the Soviet Union), *Agitator*, 9 (1969), 19–21.

——. "Orudie despoticheskoi vlasti Maoistov" (The instrument of despotic rule of the Maoists), *Sovety deputatov trudyashchikhsya*, 6 (1969), 108–10.

——. "Za fasadom kul'turnoi revoliutsii v Kitae" (Behind the facade of the cultural revolution), *Dal'nii vostok*, 2 (1967), 152–60.

Gel'bras, V. G. "Antimarksistskaya sushchnost' sotsional'noekonomicheskoi politiki gruppy Mao Tsze-duna" (The anti-Marxist essence of socio-economic policy of the Mao-Tse-tung group), *Politicheskoe samoobrazovanie*, 5 (1969), 28–37.

——. "K voprosu o stanovlenie voenno-biurokraticheskoi diktatury v Kitae, o politike gruppy Mao Tsze-duna" (The problem of formation of military bureaucratic dictatorship in China, the policy of the Mao Tse-tung group), *Narody Azii i Afriki*, 1 (1968), 21–34.

——. "Nekotorye cherty politicheskoi bor'by bv Kitae" (Some lines of the political struggle in China), *Narody Azii i Afriki*, 3 (1969), 17–31.

Glezerman, G. "Entering communism", *East Europe*, 9 (May, 1960), 22–4. Translation from *Sovetskaya aviatsiya*, March 24, 1960.

Glotov, I. "O narodnykh kommunakh Kitaya" (The people's communes in China), *Ekonomika sel. khoz-va*, 7 (1969), 113–18.

Golikov, A. "Kak eto bylo, o politike diskriminatsii v otnoshenii Kazakhov i Uigurov v KNR" (How was it? the policy of discrimination against Kazaks and Uighurs in China), *Ogonek*, 26 (1967), 30–31,

Grechko, A. "Velikaya pobeda" (The great victory), *Pravda*, May 9, 1969.

——. "V. I. Lenin i stroitelstvo sovetskikh vooruzhennikh sil" (V. I. Lenin and the build-up of Soviet military forces), *Kommunist*, 3 (February, 1969), 15–26.

Grigor'ev, I. "Put' k miru – cherez razoruzhenie" (The path to peace is through disarmament), *Mezhdunarodnaya zhizn'*, 12 (November, 1960), 76–80.

Gromyko, A. "Nashi sympatii na storone tekh kto vosstaet protiv kolonizatorov" (Our sympathy for the colonial struggle), *Pravda*, August 31, 1960.

——. "Voprosy mezhdunarodnogo polozheniya i vneshnei politiki Sovetskogo Doiuza" (The problems of international situation and the foreign policy of the Soviet Union), *Pravda*, July 10, 1969.

Guber, A. "Obostrenie krizisa kolonial'noi sistemy" (The infuriation of colonial crisis), *Mezhdunarodnaya zhizn'*, 12 (December, 1957), 23–31.

Gudoshnikov, L. M. i Topornin, B. N. "Krizis politiko-pravovogo razvitiya v Kitae" (The crisis of politico-legal development in China), *Sovetskoe gosudarstvo i pravo*, 5 (1969), 11–20.

Il'ichev, I. "Revoliutsionnaya nauka i sovremennost', protiv antileninskogo kursa Kitaiskikh rukovoditelei" (The revolutionary science in the present-day conditions, against anti-Leninist course of the Chinese ruling circles), *Kommunist*, 11 (May, 1964), 12–36.

Il'inskii, M. "Nash kommentarii: dobrovol'tsy ponevole" (Our commentary: volunteers afainst their will), *Izvestiya*, June 7, 1970.

Inozemtsev, N. "Mirnoe sosushchestvovanie i mirovoi revolutsionnyi protsess" (Peaceful coexistence and world revolutionary process), *Pravda*, July 28, 1963. The Chinese attacked this article in "Su-lien pao-k'ang tui chung-kung ti kung-chi yü lai yü pu hsiang-yang-tsu, k'o-pi ho yü-ch'un ti ch'i-t'an kuai-lun" (The Russian publications getting ever worse in their laughable and lamentable criticism of the Chinese Communist Party), *Jen-min jih-pao*, August 3, 1963.

——. "Velichie leninskoi politiki mire" (The great Leninist policy of peace), *Kommunist*, 6 (April, 1964), 28–38.

Kagramov, Iu. "Tainy Kitaiskoi mafii [o kontrabandnoi torgovle narkotikami]" (The secret of Chinese mafia, the contraband narcotic traffics), *Aziya i Afrika segodnya*, 6 (1969), 10–11.

Kapchenko, N. "Kul'turnaya revoliutsiya i vneshnaya politika gruppy Mao Tsze-duna" (The cultural revolution and foreign policy of the Mao Tse-tung group), *Mezhdunarodnaya zhizn'*, 2 (1968), 19–31.

——. "Sushchnost' i politika maoizma" (The essence and policy of Maoism), *Mezhdunarodnaya zhizn'*, 5 (1969), 12–22.

Kapitonov, I. V. "Vernost' leninizmu, istochnik vsekh nashikh pobed; na torzhestvennom zasedanii, posvyashchennom 99-i godoshchine so dnya rozhdeniya V. I. Lenina" (Be truthful to Leninism, the source of all our victories; speech given at the victory-celebrating session devoted to the 99th birthday anniversary of Lenin), *Pravda*, and *Izvestiya*, April 23, 1969.

Kapitsa, M. S. "Antiimperializm na slovakh i flirt s imperialistam na dele" (Anti-imperialism in words, but flirt with the imperialists in deeds), *Morskoi sbornik*, 6 (1969), 13–18.

Kolesnichensko, Tomas, "Velikoe protivoborstvo" (Great antagonism), *Pravda*, January 11, 1970.

Konstantinov, F. "Filosofiya nashei epokhi" (The philosophy of our epoch), *Kommunist*, 6 (April, 1964), 18–28.

——. "I. V. Stalin i voprosy kommunisticheskogo stroitel'stva" (J. V. Stalin and the problems of building of communism), *Pravda*, March 5, 1955.

——. "Lenin i sovremennost' – 90 letiiu so dnya rozhdeniya V. I. Lenina" (Lenin and the present-day conditions, in commemoration of the 90th anniversary of Lenin's birth), *Kommunist*, 5 (March, 1960), 10–27.

——. i Kh. Momdzhyan. "Dialektika i sovremennye usloviya" (Dialectics and present-day conditions), *Kommunist*, 10 (July, 1960), 35–50.

Korinov, I. "Solidarnost' – kliuch k pobede" (Solidarity is the key to victory), *Pravda*, May 4, 1969.

Korolev, B. i A. Golota. "Sovetskaya intelligentsiya v period razvernuto-stroitel'stva kommunizma" (The Soviet intelligentsia during the period of progressing build-up of communism), *Kommunist*, 10 (May, 1963), 15–25.

Kosiukov, Iu. "Ekonomika Kitaya pod udarami kul'turnoi revoliutsii" (Chinese economy under the blows of the cultural revolution), *Novoe vremya*, 3 (1967), 18–20.

——. "Posle antrakta v Pekine, k kharakteristike vnutripolit. obstanovki v KNR" (After an interval in Peking, the characteristics of internal political situation in China), *Novoe vremya*, 11 (1968), 14–15.

Kozlov, F. R. "43-ya godovshchina velikoi oktyabr'skoi sotsialisticheskoi revoliutsii" (The 43th anniversary of the great October Socialist Revolution), *Pravda*, November 7, 1960.

Kozlov, S. "Tvorcheskii kharakter sovetskogo voennogo ucheniya" (The creative character of the Soviet military doctrine), *Kommunist vooruzhennikh sil*, 11 (June, 1961), 55–9.

Krasin, Iu. "Marksistsko-leninskaya dialektika i problemy mirnogo sosushchestvovanie" (Marxist-Leninist dialectic and the problems of peaceful coexistence), *Filosofskie nauki*, 55 (1963), 3–12.

Krupskaya N. D., *O Lenine* (On Lenin). Moskva: Gospolitizdat, 1960.

Krushanov, A. I. "Territorial'nye pretenzii maoistov i pravda istorii" (The Maoists' territorial claims and historical truth), *Morskoi sbornik*, 8 (1969), 18–24.

Kuusinen, Otto. "Pretvorenie v zhizn' idei lenina" (To implement Lenin's ideas), *Pravda*, April 23, 1960.

Kuz'min, V. i G. Ovsyannikov. "Koloniya, kotoraya nuzhna Mao [Gonkong v torg.-ekon. politike Kitaya]" (The colony which Mao needs; Hong Kong in the trade and economic policy of China), *Mezhdunarodnaya zhizn'*, 6 (1969), 99–103.

Kuz'minov, I. "Ob ekonomicheskom polozhenii kapitalisticheskogo mira" (On the economic situation of the capitalist world), *Mezhdunarodnaya zhizn'*, 10 (October, 1960), 48–56.

Leninskaya diplomatiya mira i sotrudnichestva (Lenin's diplomacy of peace and cooperation). Moskva: Izd-vo "Nauka," 1965.

Litoshko, E. i E. Strel'nikov. "Mir – glavnaya zadacha OON" (Peace is the main task of the UN), *Pravda*, October 24, 1958.

Lukin, Iu. "Kul'turnaya revoliutsiya: leninskaya kontseptsiya i maoistskaya praktika" (The cultural revolution: Leninist concept and Maoist practice), *Filosofiya*, 2 (1969), 15–24.

L'vov, O. "Politicheskie manevry Mao Tsze-duna" (Political maneuvers of Mao Tse-tung), *Pravda*, January 11, 1969.

Maevskii, Viktor. "Ob odnom dne v Kitae" (One day's stay in China), *Ogonek*, 15 (1966), 22–3.

Malyavin, P. "O vneshnepoliticheskom kurse kliki Mao Tsze-duna" (The foreign policy of the Mao Tse-tung clique), *Voen. vestn.*, 6 (1969), 15–18.

Matkovskii, N. "Ideinoe oruzhie kommunizma" (The ideological weapon of communism), *Pravda*, June 12, 1960.

Mayakovskii, V. "Torzhestvo velikikh idei leninizma" (The triumph of the great ideas of Leninism), *Pravda*, April 18, 1960.

Mazurov, K. T. "Pyat'desyat pervaya godovshchina velikoi oktyabr'skoi sotsialisticheskoi revoliutsii" (The fifty-first anniversary of the great October Socialist Revolution), *Izvestiya*, November 7, 1968.

Medvedev, M. "Kurs na voinu i blokirovanie s imperializmom" (On the warpath and alliance with imperialism), *Mirovaya ekonomika i mezhdunarodnye otnosheniya*, 7 (1969), 56–65.

Migolat'ev, A. "Kurs vrazhdebnyi interesam narodov [o raskol'nicheskoi politike gruppy Mao Tsze-duna]" (The course inimical to the interests of the people, on the divisive policy of the Mao-Tse tung group), *Kommunist vooruzhennikh sil*, 13 (1969), 33–9.

Mikhailov, A. "Klika Mao – razruzhitel' Kompartii Kitaya" (The clique of Mao – the destroyer of Chinese Communist Party), *Kommunist vooruzhennikh sil*, 16 (1969), 78–83.

——. "Maoisty v Efire [ob antisovetskoi propagande Pekinskogo radio]" (The Maoists in the Ivory Coast, the anti-Soviet propaganda of Peking radio), *Radio*, 7 (1969), 54–5.

Mikhailov, M. i N. Polyanov. "Printsipy, kotorya dolzhny torzhestvovat'" (The principles which must succeed), *Izvestiya*, August 14, 1960.

Mikhailov, S. "Cuban revolution and Latin America," *International Affairs* (Moscow), 12 (December, 1963), 44–9.

Mil'yas, Orlando. "Splachivat' antiimperialisticheskikh sily" (Unite the anti-imperialist forces), *Pravda*, May 19, 1969.

Mironov, A. i Ya. Mikhailov. "Kul'turnaya revoliutsiya v Kitae" (The cultural revolution in China), *Politicheskoe samoobrazovanie*, 4 (1967), 60–70.

Modrzhinskaya, E. "Serediny tut net, Lenin o printsipakh ideologicheskoi bor'by" (There is no middle way, Lenin's principles of ideological struggle), *Izvestiya*, April 5, 1969.

Mologoev, A. "Leninskii put' k sotsializmu" (Lenin's way toward socialism), *Kommunist*, 2 (January, 1969), 13–23.

Nekrasov, A. "Ot bol'shogo skachka k kul'turnoi revoliutsii, ob ekon. polozhenii v KNR" (From the great leap forward to the cultural revolution, the economic situation in China), *Mezhdunarodnaya zhizn'*, 5 (1967), 28–37.

Nekrasov, V. i E. Grigor'ev. "Pod znamenem proletarskogo internatsionalizma" (Under the banner of proletarian internationalism), *Pravda*, April 15, 1969.

Nekrysov, L. "Vneshneekonomicheskii kurs gruppy Mao Tsze-duna" (Foreign economic policy of the Mao Tse-tung group), *Mirovaya ekonomika i mezhdunarodnye otnosheniya*, 2 (1968), 29–40.

Nevskii, K. i L. Davidov. "Politika shovinizma i voinstvuiushchego natsionalizma, o provokatsii kampanii KNR protiv MNR (Policy of chauvinism and militant nationalism, on the provocation of campaign by the Chinese People's Republic against the Mongolian People's Republic), *Aziya i Afrika segodnya*, 1 (1968), 6–8.

Nikanorov, O. "Gruppa Mao i Amerikanskii imperializm" (The group of Mao and American imperialism), *Mirovaya ekonomika i mezhdunarodnye otnosheniya*, 7 (1969), 56–65.

Oizerman, T. I. "Leninskie printispy nauchnoi kritiki idealizma" (Leninist principles of scientific critique of idealism), *Voprosy filosofii*, 2 (February, 1970), 9–20.

Oleshchuk, F. *Is War Inevitable?* Moscow: Foreign languages publishing house, 1958.

Ostroumov, G. E. "Politico-pravovaya ideologiya i krizis politicheskoi vlasti v Kitae" (Politico-legal ideology and crisis of political power in China), *Sovetskoe gosudarstvo i pravo*, 6 (1967), 59–66.

Ovcharenko, A. "Tragicheskii Kitai, vpechatleniya chlena sovetskoi delegatsii o poezdke po strane" (Tragedy of China, the impression of the members of Soviet delegation on their arrival in the country), *Druzhba narodov*, 10 (1967), 201–26.

Pasenchuk, V. "Pekinskie otraviteli [ob antisovstskoi progadande]" (The poisoners of Peking, the anti-Soviet Maoist propaganda), *Zhurnalist*, 5 (1969), 64–6.

———, i V. Viktorov. "Antinarodnyi kurs Pekinskikh pravitelei" (The anti-people policy of the Peking leadership), *Pravda*, June 22, 1968.

Petrov, I. "Sem'ya v sovremennoi Kitae" (Family in present China), *Dal'nii vostok*, 5 (1969), 138–43.

Pokrovskii, Georgi. "The public must know the fact," *News, a Soviet Review of the World Events*, 7 (April 1, 1955), 7.

Ponomarev, B. "Leninizm – nashe znamya i vsepobezhdaiushchee oruzhie" Leninism is our victorious standard and invincible weapon), *Pravda*, April 23, 1963.

———. "Mirnoe sosushchestvovanie zhiznennaya neobkhodimost'" (Peaceful coexistence is a vital necessity), *Pravda*, August 12, 1960.

———. F. Konstantinov, i Iu. Andropov. "Na starykh revizionistskikh positsiyakh (On the old revisionist positions), *Kommunist*, 8 (May, 1960), 24–8.

Pospelov, P. "Istoricheskoe znachenie vtorogo s'ezda RSDRP" (The historical significance of the Second Congress of the Russian Social Democratic Labor Party), *Pravda*, July 30, 1963. The Chinese attacked this article in *Jen-min jih-pao*, August 3, 1963.

Pozhitnov, L. i B. Shragin. "Kul'turnaya revoliutsiya i kul'tura" (The cultural revolution and culture), *Teatr*, 1 (1968), 135–47.

Pukhovskii, N. V. *O mire i voine* (On peace and war). Moskva: Izd-vo "Mysl'," 1965.

Rachkov, A. "Bonnskoe napravlenie Pekina, ob ekon. i polit. sblizhenii Kitaya s

FRG" (Peking's Bonn orientation, the economic and political affinity of China and West Germany), *Aziya i Afrika segodnya*, 7 (1967), 35–7.

Rakhimov, T. "Velikoderzhavnyaya politika Mao Tsze-duna i ego gruppy v natsional'nom voprose" (Great power politics of the Mao Tse-tung group in nationality problem), *Kommunist*, 7 (April, 1967), 114–19.

——, i V. Bogoslovskii. "Velikoderzhavnyi shovinizm Mao Tsze-duna" (Great power chauvinism of Mao Tse-tung), *Aziya i Arfika segodnya*, 7 (1969), 28–30.

Ratiani, Georgii. "Put' mira i zigzagi global'noi strategii" (The path of peace and the zigzags of global strategy), *Pravda*, January 25, 1970.

Ravisov, I. "Nepopulyannaya politika, o vneshnepolit. kurs gruppy Mao Tsze-duna, po materialam pressu arab. stran" (Unpopular policy, the foreign political course of the Mao Tse-tung group, according to the Arab press), *Aziya i Afrika segodnya*, 9 (1967), 12–13.

Rumyantsev, A. "Maoizm i antimarksistskaya sushchnost' ego 'filosofii'" (Maoism and anti-Marxist essence of its 'philosophy'), *Kommunist*, 2 (January, 1969), 91–106.

——, i A. Strebaleva. "Sotsialo ekonomicheskoi kurs gruppy Mao Tsze-duna i rabochii klass Kitaya" (Socio-economic course of the Mao Tse-tung group and the Chinese working class), *Mirovaya ekonomika i mezhdunarodnye otnosheniya*, 6 (1967), 30–44.

Samailenko, V. "Velikokhan'skii natsionalizm Mao Tsze-duna" (The great-Han natsionalism of Mao Tse-tung), *Voen. vestn.*, 7 (1969), 22–6.

Sanakoev, S. "The basis of the relations between the socialist countries," *International Affairs* (Moscow), 7 (July, 1958), 21–33.

Saradskaya, E. "Dni razrusheniya, o kul'turnoi revoliutsii v Kitae" (The days of destruction, on the cultural revolution in China), *Inostrannaya literatura*, 6 (1968), 268–71.

Sergeev, L. "Novye zigzagi v kul'turnoi revoliutsii" (New zigzags in the cultural revolution), *Agitator*, 7 (1967), 52–4.

——. "Natsional'nyi vopros v KNR i ego shovinistcheskoe izvrashchenie" (Nationality problem in China and its chauvinist perversion), *Agitator*, 11 (1967) 55–8.

——. "Pochemu Mao Tsze-dunu prikhoditsya zakhvatyvat' vlast" (Why Mao Tse-tung has to seize power), *Agitatgoer*, 4 (1967), 50–52.

——. "Shto oznachaiut' novye ustanovki v Kitae" (What does the new arrangement mean in China), *Agitator*, 1 (1967), 47–9.

——. "Sobytiya v Kitae" (Events in China), *Agitator*, 9 (1968), 57–9.

——. "Tragediya Kitaiskogo komsomola" (Tragedy of the Chinese komsomol), *Molodoi kommunist*, 6 (1967), 108–15.

——. "Tragediya Kitaya, o politike gruppy Mao Tsze-duna" (Tragedy of China, the policy of the Mao Tse-tung group), *Novoe vremya*, 10 (1967), 9–12.

——. "Vneshnyaya politika KNR: zamysly i deistvitelnost'" (Foreign policy of China: designs and reality), *Agitator*, 3 (1967), 53–5.

——. "Voinstvuiushchie kapitulyanty iz Pekina, zametki obozrevatelya" (Militant capitulators from Peking, notes of an observer), *Agitator*, 18 (1967), 57–9.

Sergeev, S. "Britanskii partner" (British partner), *Mirovaya ekonomika i mezhdunarodnye otnosheniya*, 8 (1969), 61–71.

Shchetinkin, A. "Proval avantury Pekina v Birme" (The fiasco of Peking's adventurism in Burma), *Agitator*, 19 (1967), 59–60.

Shakhnazarov, G. "Kul'turnaya revoliutsiya v Kitae i melkoburzhuarznyi avanturizm" (The cultural revolution in China and small bourgeois adventurism), *Kommunist*, 3 (February, 1967), 104–13.

Shelepin, V. "Intrigi maoistov v tret'em mire" (The intrigues of the Maoists in the third world), *Novoe vremya*, 26 (1969), 6–8.

Shepilov, D. T. "Voprosy mezhdunarodnogo polozheniya i vneshnei politiki Sovetskogo Soiuza" (The problems of international situation and the foreign policy of the Soviet Union), *Pravda*, February 13, 1957.

Sheremetyv, A. "Sobytiya v Kitae i raschety imperialistov, po zarubezhnoi pechati" (Events in China and calculation of the imperialists, according to foreign press), *Agitator*, 23 (1967), 58–60.

Shiryaev, S. L. "Kul'turnaya revoliutsiya i sostoyanie zheleznodorozhnogo transporta Kitaya" (The cultural revolution and the state of railway transport), *Zheleznodorozhnyi transport*, 6 (1969), 84–5.

Sidikhmenov, V. "Maoisti revisiiut general'nuiu liniiu KPK" (The Maoists revise the general line of the Chinese Communist Party), *Kommunist*, 3 (February, 1969), 96–106.

Simonov, Konstantin. "Kak eto nachalos' [o voorzh. provokatsii Kitaiskikh vlastei na Sovetsko-Kitaiskoi granitse v raione O. Damanskii na R. Ussuri]" (How did this begin? the armed provocation of the Chinese authority on the Sino-Soviet border in the region of Damanskii in the River Ussuri), *Novoe vremya*, 20 (1969), 14–15.

———. "Mysli v skukh" (Thoughts in ears), *Pravda*, May 4, 1969.

Sklyarevskii, Ya. "Mao gvetsya v Afriku" (Mao rushes into Africa), *Sovetskie profsoiuzy*, 13 (1969), 44–6.

Sladkovskii, M. "Podryv maoistami sotsial'no-ekonomicheskoi struktury KNR" (Undermining of social-economic structure of China by the Maoists), *Voprosy ekonomiki*, 6 (1969), 76–87.

Slepov, V. "Neodolimaya sila marsizma-leninizma" (The indomitable force of Marxism-Leninism), *Pravda*, April 22, 1969.

Smirnov, S. "Kommunizm – delo kazhdogo" (Communism is each one's affair), *Kommunist*, 7 (May, 1961), 22–23.

Smirnov, V. "*Mlada Fronta* i Mao Tsze-dun" (*Mlada Fronta* and Mao Tse-tung), *Literaturnaya gazeta*, 1 (January, 1969), 9. The Czech paper extolled Mao for his opposing the Russian incursion of August, 1968.

Snegirtsev, A. "Pekinskii dnevnik, ob unichtozhenii i razruzhenii pamyatnikov kul'tury v Kitae, vyderzhki iz dnevnika sovetskogo literaturoveda stazhirovavshegosya v KNR" (Peking diaries on the destruction of cultural monuments in China, excerpts from diaries of Soviet literary workers in China), *Vokrug sveta*, 12 (1967), 49–52.

———. "Renegaty vremen kul'turnoi revoliutsii v Kitae" (Renegades of the cultural revolution in China," *Inostrannaya literatura*, 11 (1967), 245–47.

———. "Stupeni predatel'stva, antisovetskii kurs politiki Mao – izmena interesam Kitaiskogo naroda" (The steps of treachery, the anti-Soviet course of the policy of Mao – betrayal to the interests of the Chinese people), *Molodoi kommunist*, 5 (1969), 36–41.

———. "Zhestokaya tsena politiki 'velikogo kormchego'" (The bitter price of the policy of the 'great helmsman'), *Molodoi kommunist*, 3 (1969), 42–8.

Sovetov, A. "The present stage in the struggle between socialism and imperialism," *International Affairs* (Moscow), 11 (November, 1968), 3–9.

Stepanov, L. "Vazhnaya sostavnaya chast' mirovogo revoliutsionnogo protsessiya" (The important component of world revolutionary procession), *Pravda*, July 8, 1963. The Chinese attacked this article in *Jen-min jih-pao*, August 3, 1963.

Stepanov, V. "Kommunizm – nasha vysshaya tsel'" (Communism is our highest objective), *Pravda*, August 24, 1963.

Stolpovskii, B. "Politicheskii avantiurizm gruppy Mao Tsze-duna" (Political adventurism of the Mao Tse-tung group), *Trud*, March 13, 1969.

Taipov, Z. "Beschinstva maoistov na Uigurskoi zemle" (The excesses of the Maoists in the Uigur land), *Novoe vremya*, 7 (1969), 11–12.

Talenskii, N. "Sovremennaya voina: kharakter i sledstviya" (Modern war: its character and consequences), *Mezhdunarodnaya zhizn'*, 10 (October, 1960), 31–7.

Ter-Grigorya, A. "Korni shovinizma v Kitae" (The roots of chauvinism in China), *Novoe vremya*, 34 (1969), 8–10.

——. "Otvet na nekotorye voprosy o sobytiyam v Kitae" (Answer to several questions concerning the events in China), *Novoe vremya*, 42 (1967), 23–5.

——. "Pas'yans Mao, obzor sobytii v Kitae" (Patience of Mao, observation of events in China), *Novoe vremya*, 2 (1968), 21–2.

——. "Razmyshleniya o polozhenii v Kitae" (Reflections on the situation in China), *Novoe vremya*, 20 (1969), 11–13.

——. "Tragediya Kitaya, o politike gruppy Mao Tsze-duna" (The tragedy of China, on the policy of the Mao Tse-tung group), *Novoe vremya*, 10 (1967), 9–12.

Tikhvinskii, S. "Politika obrechenaya na proval" (The policy doomed to failure), *Pravda*, March 12, 1969.

Titarenko, S. "Leninskie uchenie po povodu sotsializma i sovremennost'" (Lenin's teaching on the victory of socialism and the present-day conditions), *Pravda vostoka*, August 23, 1960.

——. "Voprosy voiny i mira v sovremennikh usloviyakh" (Problems of war and peace in present-day conditions), *Sovetskaya Latvia*, August 16, 1960.

Trifonov, V. "Maoisty – vragi edinstva" (The Maoists are the enemy of unity), *Sovetskie profsoiuzy*, 9 (1969), 40–42.

Trukhanovskii, V. "Proletarian internationalism and peaceful coexistence – foundation of the Leninist foreign policy," *International Affairs* (Moscow), 11 (November, 1968), 54–62.

Tunkin, G. "Granitsy gosudarstvo i mirnoe susushchestvovanie" (The limits of state sovereignty and peaceful coexistence), *Pravda*, August 27, 1963.

Ul'yanov, V. "Nedostoinye priemy" (The unworthy methods), *Pravda*, August 9, 1963.

Usanov, P. "Okrylennaya iiunost'" (Inspired youth), *Izvestiya*, April 22, 1969. Devoted to Lenin's 99th birthday anniversary.

Valtin-Boris. "Neskol'ko dnei v Kitae, vpechatleniya o poezdke po strane v period kul'turnoi revoliutsii" (Several days in China, impression on a trip to China during the cultural revolution), *Zhurnalist*, 1 (1967), 66–7, 70–71.

Vasilev, D. "Politika Pekina v otnoshneii yaponii" (The policy of Peking toward Japan), *Mirovaya ekonomika i mezhdunarodnye otnosheniya*, 8 (1969), 61–71.

Vidal-Zhan, Emil. "20 mesyatsev kul'turnoi revoliutsii v Kitae, stat'i iz frantsuzskii gaz. *Iumanite*, napech. s sokr." (20 months' cultural revolution in China, articles from the French paper *Humanité*, abbreviated version), *Kommunist Estonii*, 4 (1968), 98–113.

Vladimirov, Iu. V. "K voprosu o sovetskogo-Kitaiskikh ekonomicheskikh otnosheniyakh v 1950–1966 godakh" (The problem of Sino-Soviet economic relations from 1950 to 1966), *Voprosy istorii*, 6 (1969), 46–62.

Vol'skii, D. "Ekspansiya SSHA i politika Pekina, po stranitsam zarubezhnoi pechati" (United States expansion and the policy of Peking, from foreign press), *Novoe vremya*, 47 (1967), 11–13.

——. "Komu sluzhit politika Pekina?" (Who benefits from the policy of Peking?) *Novoe vremya*, 32 (1969), 65–7.

Vont, Florimon. "Avantiuristichestkaya politika Kitaiskikh rukovoditelei" (The

risky policy of the Chinese leaders), *Kommunist*, 14 (September, 1963), 39–43.
The author is a French communist and has lived in the Soviet Union all his life.
Yakolev, A. "Tverdnaya i neizmennaya pozitsiya [o zayavlenii pravitel'stva
SSSR po voprosy o normalizatsii obstanovki na Sovetsko-Kitaiskoi graniste]"
(The firm and immutable position, the statement of the Government of the
USSR on the problems of normalization on the Sino-Soviet boundaries),
Agitator, 13 (1969), 36–8.
Zanegin, B. "Proval vneshnapoliticheskogo kursa Pekina" (The failure of Peking's
foreign policy), *Izvestiya*, May 22, 1968.
Zavadskaya, E. "Dni razrusheniya, o kul'turnoi revoliutsii v Kitae" (Days of
destruction, on the cultural revolution in China), *Inostrannaya literatura*, 6
(1968), 268–71.
Zhelekhovtsev, A. "Drama Kitaiskogo krest'yanstva" (The drama of the Chinese
peasantry), *Aziya i Afrika segodnya*, 5 (1969), 22–6.
——. "Kul'turnaya revoliutsiya v Kitae s blizkogo rasstoyaniya, zapiski
ochvidtsa" (The cultural revolution in China at a close look, notes from an eye-
witness), *Novyi mir*, 3 (1968), 181–213.
Zhirovov, R. "Trotskyizm, nepriyatel' leninizma" (Trotskyism is the enemy of
Leninism), *Partinaya zhizn'*, 3 (Febryuar 1969), 77–9.
Zhukov, E. "Znamenatel'nyi faktor nashego vremeni" (Outstanding factor of our
time), *Pravda*, August 26, 1960.
Zhukov, Iu. "Razgovory o voine i mire" (Talks about war and peace), *Pravda*,
April 8, 1969.
Zorin, V. "Vazhneishii vopros sovremennoi mezhdunarodnoi politiki, o vseobsh-
chem i polnom razoruzhenii" (The most significant problem in the current
international politics, the general and complete disarmament), *Kommunist*, 2
(January, 1960), 6–21.

IV. PERIODICAL ARTICLES IN ENGLISH PUBLISHED OUTSIDE RUSSIA AND CHINA

13. The dispute treated as a whole

Alexandrov, K. "Regulating factors in the current Sino-Soviet relations,"
Institut fur Erforschung der UdSSR, *Bulletin*, 5 (October, 1958), 3–9.
Barnett, A. D. "Tension on the China-Soviet border," *Look*, 31 (October 3, 1967),
40–42ff.
Bloodworth, Dennis. "The explosive frontier," *Observer* (February 12, 1967), 11.
Boynton, John. "Sino-Soviet dispute and international congresses," *World Today*,
19 (August, 1963), 323–26.
Brooke-Shepherd, Gordon. "Red rivalry in the black continent," *Reporter*, 26
(January 18, 1962), 33–5.
Burnham, James (ed.) "Bear and dragon: what is the relations between Moscow
and Peking?" a symposium, *National Review*, 9 (November 5, 1960), S5–S45.
——. "History à la Deutscher," *National Review*, 11 (August 12, 1961), 78–9.
——. "Sino-Soviet sense and nonsense," *National Review*, 14 (January 15, 1963),
16.
Burton, R. A. "Parting the veils over red rifles," *Saturday Review*, 45 (June 2,
1962), 29–30.
Carlisle, D. S. "Sino-Soviet schism," *Orbis*, 8 (Winter, 1965), 790–815.
Chamberlain, William Henry. "The quarrel of the communist giants," *Russian
Review*, 23 (July, 1964), 215–22.

Cheng, Chu-yuan. "Moscow's hungry ally: the Sino-Soviet rift," *New Leader*, 44 (July–August, 1961), 18–20.

Chow, S. K. "Significance of the rift between the Chinese communist regime and the Soviet Union," *Annals of the American Academy of Political and Social Science*, 372 (July, 1967), 64–71.

Chu, Hsin-min. "Between Moscow and Peiping," *Free China Review*, 10 (October, 1960), 15–18.

"Closer to a final split," *Time*, 89 (February 17, 1967), 26.

Conquest, Robert. "Cracks in the carapace," *Spectator*, 211 (July 19, 1963), 73.

——. "Two pikes in a pond," *Spectator*, 207 (September 8, 1961), 311–13.

Crankshaw, Edward. "Why Peking baits the Kremlin," *Observer* (September 4, 1966), 10.

Critchlow, J. "Bear and the dragon at war over science," *Commonweal*, 91 (February 27, 1970), 572–73.

Davis, J. P. "Sino-Soviet rift, an old, old story," *Reporter*, 29 (August, 1963), 32–4.

Dean, William. "Communism's grim struggle," *Spectator*, 212 (April 10, 1964), 468.

——. "The unknown border," *Spectator*, 212 (September 11, 1964), 333, 335.

Deutscher, Isaac. "Khrushchev, Mao and the wolf of Chung-shan," *Reporter*, 23 (August 4, 1960), 29ff.

"The east wind," *Economist*, 199 (February 20, 1960), 695–96.

Erickson, John. "Sino-Soviet relations," *Journal of Royal United Services Institute*, vol. 105, no. 618, pp. 234–52.

Falls, C. "Dictators in conference," *Illustrated London News*, 235 (October 10, 1959), 390.

——. "Soviet Russia, China and Romania," *Illustrated London News*, 243 (July 13, 1963), 44.

Fischer, L. "Russian bear and the Chinese tiger," *Virginia Quarterly Review*, 36 (Fall, 1960), 550–68.

Frayn, M. "Kremlinological inexactitudes," *National Review*, 12 (May 8, 1962), 323.

Freeberne, M. 'Racial issues and the Sino-Soviet dispute," *Asian Survey*, 5 (August, 1965), 408–16.

Gordon, Max. "The Sino-Soviet conflict," *Monthly Review*, 15 (December, 1963), 432–42.

Halperin, E. "Soviet-Chinese paradox," *Atlas*, 6 (September, 1963), 159–63.

Harriman, W. A. "Sino-Soviet conflict," in: Academy of Political Science, *The Soviet Union since Khrushchev, New Trends and Old Problems*, New York, 1965, pp. 101–11.

Harris, Richard. "Sino-Soviet dispute," *Political Quarterly*, 35 (July–September, 1964), 324–41.

Heyst, Axel. "The Moscow-Peking tangle," *Contemporary Review*, 204 (August, 1963), 76–9.

"Hidden tiger," *Atlas*, 12 (October, 1966), 10–15.

"High invective," *Time*, 89 (February 3, 1967), 25.

Huang, T. C. "Rift between Moscow and Peiping," *Free China and Asia*, 7 (October, 1960), 3–7.

Hugh, Richard. "Duel of communism's big two," *New York Times Magazine*, April 1, 1962, pp. 9. 116–19,

James, F. "For every vice there is a versa," *Atlas*, 18 (September, 1969), 23.

Kalb, M. L. "Agitprop goes to work," *Reporter*, 24 (January 5, 1961), 32–3.

——. "One time the Soviets wish they could be uncommitted too," *Reporter*, 27 (November 22, 1962), 26–7.

Kennedy, W. V. "Reporting the communist rift," *America* 104 (November 19, 1960), 255.

Koo, E. "Russian-Chinese relations today," *Carroll Russian Bulletin*, 6 (Spring, 1962), 59–65.

"Let's stand idly by," *Economist*, 232 (September 20, 1969), 13–14.

Lisann, M. "Moscow and the Chinese power struggle," *Problems of Communism*, 18 (November, 1969), 32–41.

McLane, Charles B. "The Moscow-Peking alliance: the first decade," *Current History*, 37 (December, 1959), 326–32.

McNeal, Robert H. "The exhaustion of diplomatic technique in the Sino-Soviet dispute," *International Journal*, 18 (Autumn, 1963), 513–19.

"Mao bites the Russian bear," *Newsweek*, 69 (February 13, 1967), 47–8.

Mauny, Erik de, and Anthony Lawrence. "The Sino-Soviet dispute," *Listener*, 70 (October 10, 1963), 527.

Maxwell, Neville. "Simmering dispute along the Sino-Soviet border," *New York Times*, September 30, 1968, p. 9.

Mehnert, Klaus. "Soviet-Chinese relations," *International Affairs* (London), 35 (October, 1959), 417–26.

Metaxas, Alexandre. "China versus Russia," *Nation*, 191 (July 2, 1960), 12–13.

——. "Moscow vs Peking: reasons for the rift," *Nation*, 194 (April 14, 1962), 332–33, 340.

——. "The Soviet Union and foreign policy," *Listener*, 44 (September, 1960), 369–71.

Michael, F. "Moscow and the current Chinese crisis," *Current History*, 53 (September, 1967), 141–47.

Misao, Obata. "The Sino-Soviet dispute," *Japan Quarterly*, 8 (January–March, 1961), 25–32. Report of a seminar held at Lake Kawaguchi, Yamanashi Prefecture, Japan, September 19–24, 1960, attented by scholars and government officials of eleven countries. Neither Peking nor Taipei was represented.

Monerot, Jules. "What about the Sino-Soviet split?" *National Review*, 15 (June 4, 1963), 447–49, and (July 2, 1963), 541.

"Moscow-Peking conflicts viewed from Mao's reply in *People's daily* editorial of December 15, 1962," *Free China and Asia*, 10 (January, 1963), 13–17.

Mosley, Philip E. "The Chinese-Soviet rift: origins and portents," *Foreign Affairs*, 42 (October, 1963), 11–24.

Murarka, Dev. "Border troubles," *Spectator*, (April 1, 1966), 398.

"No war, maybe, but no love," *Economist*, 233 (October 25, 1969), 33ff.

O'Gara, James. "Battle of the giants," *Commonweal*, 77 (March 22, 1963), 654.

"Out sick," *Economist*, 234 (January 10, 1970), 32–3.

Parta, R. Eugene, and Robert Farrell. "Vietnam and the Sino-Soviet dispute," *Analysis of Current Developments in the Soviet Union*, 37 (1965–66), 1–9.

Peltier, Rear Admiral. "Fathers and sons," *Military Review*, 30 (April, 1960), 82–91.

"Poor Mr. Kuznetsov must just keep on talking," *Economist*, 234 (January 3, 1970), 26.

Portisch, H. "Chinese-Soviet gap widens," *Saturday Review*, 49 (July 2, 1966), 8–12.

Prybyla, J. S. "Unsettled issues in the Sino-Soviet dispute," *Virginia Quarterly Review*, 41 (Autumn, 1965), 510–24.

"Quick bash of Sinkiang won't solve their problems," *Economist*, 232 (September 6, 1969), 22.

Reshetar, John. "Sino-Soviet relations: past and future," *Western Political Quarterly*, 14 (September, 1961, supplement), 73–5.

Roucek, Joseph S. "Racial elements in the Sino-Soviet dispute," *Contemporary Review*, 210 (February, 1967), 77–84.

Rowe, David Nelson. "Fallacy of the Sino-Soviet rift," *New Leader*, 43 (November 14, 1960), 12–14.

"Sabbath of witches, a canceling of Chirstmas," *Time*, 89 (February 10, 1967), 31.

Salisbury, H. E. "Russia vs China: global conflict," *Antioch Review*, 27 (Winter, 1967–68), 425–39.

Scalapino, R. A. "Sino-Soviet conflict in perspective," *Annals of the American Academy of Political and Social Science*, 351 (January, 1964), 1–14.

Schlesinger, Rudolf. "Observation on the Sino-Soviet dispute," *Science and Society*, 27 (Summer, 1963), 257–82.

Seton-Watson, Hugh. "The great schism on Sino-Soviet conflict," *Encounter*, 20 (May, 1963), 61–70.

Simon, S. W. "Kashmir dispute in Sino-Soviet perspective," *Asian Survey*, 7 (March, 1967), 176–87.

"Sino-Soviet conflict," *Royal Central Asian Journal*, 50 (January, 1963), 60–63.

St. John, Andrian. "Russia and red China – mutual nemesis," *U.S. Naval Institute Proceedings*, 87 (August, 1961), 48–57.

Stern, Geoffrey. "The dragon versus the Kremlin," *Listener*, 76 (September 29, 1966), 443–48.

Stevens, F. S. "Russia vs red China: what's actually going on," *U.S. New and World Report*, 62 (February 20, 1967), 36–40.

Swearingen, Rodger. "Russo-Chinese alliance," *Current History*, 43 (October, 1962), 229–33, 246.

Tang, Peter. "Sino-Soviet tension," *Current History*, 45 (October, 1963), 223–29.

——. "Sino-Soviet territorial disputes: past and present," *Russian Review*, 28 (October, 1969), 403–15.

Tao, Hsi-sheng. "Khrushchev-Mao conflict and reconciliation: Peking-Moscow rift," *Free China and Asia*, 10 (May, 1963), 10–17.

Ting, K. H. "An analysis of the rumoured Moscow-Peiping clash," *Free China and Asia*, 8 (October, 1961), 3–8.

Tsiang, T. F. "Moscow and Peiping, before and after the split," *Vital Speeches*, 29 (October 1, 1963), 760–63.

——. "Moscow-Peking rift?" *New Leader*, 42 (March 23, 1959), 16–18.

Wheeler, G. "Russia and China in central Asia," *World Today*, 23 (March, 1967), 89–92.

"When comrades fall out," *Economist*, 234 (January 24, 1970), 9–10.

Whiting, Allen S. "An analysis of Sino-Soviet stresses and strains," *New Leader*, 42 (October 19, 1959), 13–17.

——. "Contradictions in the Moscow-Peking axis," *Journal of Politics*, 20 (February, 1958), 127–61.

——. "Dynamics of the Moscow-Peking axis," *Annals of the American Academy of Political and Social Science*, 321 (January, 1959), 100–111.

Wiles, Peter. "China's road to the summit," *Western World*, 18 (October, 1958), 25–8.

Yapp, K. E. "Where Russia and China meet?" *New Society*, 4 (September 24, 1964), 27–8.

Zagoria, Donald S. "Sino-Soviet conflict, 1956–61," *Reporter*, 27 (March 29, 1962), 44–6.

——. "Strains in the Sino-Soviet alliance," *Problems of Communism*, 9 (May–June, 1960), 1–11.

Zorza, Victor. "Moscow sniping at China's grip in Sinkiang," *Guardian*, February 14, 1967, p. 9.
——. "Threat of explosion on Sino-Soviet border," *Guardian*, February 17, 1967, p. 13.

14. The dispute viewed from the angle of ideology

Alexandrov, K. "Contradiction between Moscow and Peiping," Institut zur Erforschung der UdSSR, *Bulletin*, 6 (December, 1959), 21–9.
Bialer, Seweryn. "Moscow vs Belgrade: a key to Soviet policy," *Problems of Communism*, 7 (July–August, 1958), 1–8.
Brien, Alan. "Afterthought," *Spectator*, 211 (November 8, 1963), 610–11.
Damien, G. D. "On the philosophy of contradiction: the Sino-Soviet dispute as a case study in communist conflict thinking," *Orbis*, 11 (Winter, 1968), 1208–32.
"East is not so red," *Economist*, 222 (September 24, 1966), 1222–23.
Fisher, H. S. "Communist solidarity and Sino-Soviet rivalry," *Current History*, 41 (September, 1961), 129–35.
Garden, M. "Russia vs China: the end of revolutionary communism," *U.S. News and World Report*, 661 (November 7, 1966), 50.
Ho, Ming. "Chopsticks in Albania," *Commonweal*, 76 (May 25, 1962), 223–26.
Hook, Sidney. "Revisionism at bay," *Encounter*, 19 (September, 1962), 63–7.
"How communism splits: communism divided or multiplied?" *Senior Scholastic* (teacher ed.), 89 (November 11, 1966), 9–10.
Hudson, G. F. "Mao, Marx and Moscow," *Foreign Affairs*, 37 (July, 1959), 561–72.
Karol, K. S. "Chou in Moscow," *New Statesman*, 68 (November 13, 1964), 729–30.
——. "Fidel, Mao and Nikita," *New Statesman*, 65 (March 22, 1963), 414–16.
——. "Mao's lament for Stalin," *New Statesman*, 66 (September 20, 1963), 346–48.
——. "Showdown in Moscow," *New Statesman*, 66 (July 12, 1963), 38.
Kashin, A. "Moscow claims leadership and unity of world communist movement," *Analysis of Current Developments in the Soviet Union*, 35 (1965–66), 1–7.
——. "New Soviet polemics with communist China," Institut zur Erforschung der UdSSR, *Bulletin*, 7 (August, 1960), 36–44.
——. "The Soviet and Chinese paths to communism: are they essentially different?" Institut zur Erforschung der UdSSR, *Bulletin*, 8 (May, 1961), 40–44.
Kovner, Milton. "The Sino-Soviet dispute: communism at the crossroads," *Current History*, 47 (September, 1964), 129–35, 179.
Limaye, Madhu. "The Sino-Russian conflict within international communism," *United Asia*, 12 (1960), 499–506.
Lowenthal, Richard. "Cracks in the communist monolith," *New York Times Magazine*, February 25, 1962, pp. 9ff.
——. "Shifts and rifts in the Russo-Chinese alliance," *Problems of Communism*, 8 (January–February, 1959), 14–25.
——. "Khrushchev's flexible communism," *Commentary*, 27 (April, 1959), 277–84.
——. "Sino-Soviet dispute," *Commentary*, 31 (May, 1961), 379–94.
Malamuth, Charles. "Mao's theory of intermediate zones," *Communist Affairs*, 4 (July–September, 1964), 3–8.

Mayer, P. "International fraternity vs national power, a contradiction in the communist world," *Review of Politics*, 28 (April, 1966), 193–209.

Michael, F. "Struggle for power," *Problems of Communism*, 16 (May, 1967), 12–21.

Miller, J. D. B. "A commonwealth for communists," *Australian Outlook*, 17 (April, 1963), 85–91.

O'Brien, Conor Cruise. "Varieties of anti-communism," *New Statesman*, 66 (September 13, 1963), 319–21.

"Pass the theodolite, comrade," *Economist*, 233 (October 11, 1969), 31.

"Profile of the Sino-Soviet split," *Senior Scholastic* (teacher ed.) 89 (September 23, 1966), pt. 2, pp. 5–6.

"Red romance that went sour, with reports," *Life*, 60 (April 8, 1966), 20–35.

"Ridicule and bullets widen the great rift," *Life*, 62 (February 24, 1967), 30–31.

Rush, Myron. "Esoteric communication in Soviet politics," *World Politics*, 11 (July, 1959), 614–20.

Schlesinger, Rudolf. "The CPSU program: the concept of communism," *Soviet Studies*, 13 (April, 1962), 383–402.

Shram, S. R. "What makes Mao a Maoist?" *New York Times Magazine*, March 8, 1970, pp. 36–7ff.

"Sino-Soviet conflict and the crisis of the international communist movement," *World Socialist Review*, 27 (Spring, 1966), 76–85.

Steiner, H. A. "China to the left of Russia," *Asian Studies*, 4 (January, 1964), 625–37.

Sweezy, Paul M. "A Marxist view of imperialism," *Monthly Review*, 4 (March, 1953), 414–25.

"When comrades fall out," *Problems of Communism*, 25 (September, 1966), 57–9.

Wohl, P. "Debate within communism," *Nation*, 191 (September 10, 1966), 130–31.

Zagoria, Donald S. (ed.) "Communist China and the Soviet bloc: symposium," *Annals of the American Academy of Political and Social Science*, 349 (September, 1963), 1–162.

——. "The 1957 Moscow conference and the Sino-Soviet dispute," *China Quarterly*, 7 (July–September, 1961), 17–34.

Zorza, Victor. "Choice before world's Marxists: survival or revolution," *Guardian*, January 7, 1963, p. 7.

15. Differences regarding war

An, T. S. "Sino-Soviet dispute and Vietnam," *Orbis*, 9 (Summer, 1965), 426–36.

Borrow, David B. "Peking's military calculus," *World Politics*, 16 (January, 1964), 287–301.

Burin, Frederic S. "Communist doctrine of the inevitability of war," *American Political Science Review*, 57 (June, 1963), 334–54.

Crankshaw, Edward. "Cold war of the communisms," *New York Times Magazine*, May 26, 1963, pp. 25, 89–90, 92.

——. "Khrushchev and China," *Atlantic Monthly*, 207 (May, 1961), 43–7.

——. "Split between Russia and China," *Atlantic Monthly*, 211 (May, 1963), 60–65.

Dutt, D. Som. "Chinese political and military thinking on guerrilla warfare," *Journal of Royal United Services Institute*, 92 (July–September, 1962), 225–29.

Galay, Nikolai. "The Soviet armed forces and the Twenty-Second Party Congress, Institut zur Erforschung der UdSSR, *Bulletin*, 9 (January, 1962), 3–16; also in a digested form in *Military Review*, 42 (September, 1962), 78–91.

Guelzo, Carl M. "The communist long war," *Military Review*, 11 (December, 1960) 14–22.

Hsieh, A. L. "The Sino-Soviet nuclear dialogue," *Journal of Conflict Resolution*, 8 (June, 1964), 99–115.

Defever, Ernest, W. "The just war doctrine: is it relevant to nuclear war: *World View*, 4 (October, 1961), 6–10.

London, K. L. "Vietnam: a Sino-Soviet dilemma," *Russian Review*, 26 (January, 1967), 26–7.

Lorine, G. "Russia, China and Vietnam," *New Statesman*, 69 (May 14, 1965), 754.

MacFarquhar, R. "Sino-Soviet brinkmanship," *New Statesman*, 78 (September 19, 1969), 360–61.

Michael, F. "Strategy of guerrilla warfare in the intra-communist conflict," *Orbis*, 9 (Summer, 1967), 418–25.

"Nyet means da? concerted communist action in Indochina," *New Republic*, 162 (June 13, 1970), 9.

O'Ballance, E. "Sino-Soviet influence on the war in Vietnam," *Contemporary Review*, 210 (February, 1967), 70–76.

"Revisionists betray Vietnam," *World Revolution*, 2 (January–March, 1969), 60. Originally in "Revisionist treachery against Vietnamese," *Vanguard*, December 17, 1968.

Rhee, T. C. "Sino-Soviet military conflict and the global balance of power," *World Today*, 26 (January, 1970), 29–37.

Royle, P. "Historical inevitability and the Sino-Soviet debate," *Political Quarterly*, 34 (July–September, 1963), 292–99.

Schneider, Joseph. "Is war a social problem?" *Journal of Conflict Resolution*, 3 (December, 1959), 535–60.

Set, A. "Behind the iron curtain: China means war?" *American Mercury*, 80 (May, 1955), 121–24.

Stewart, Charles T. "Nuclear stalemate and simulated war," *Military Review*, 42 (January, 1962), 78–89.

Tang, Peter. "Moscow and Peking: the question of war and peace," *Orbis*, 5 (Spring, 1961), 15–30.

Thornton, Thomas Perry. "Communist China and nuclear weapons," *Military Review*, 44 (September, 1964), 31–8.

"Three-way international sparring match," *America*, 120 (February 8, 1969), 154.

Tsou, Tang. "Mao's limited war in the Taiwan Strait," *Orbis*, 3 (Fall, 1959), 332–50.

Wolfe, Bertram D. "Lenin and the class war," *Orbis*, 3 (Winter, 1960), 443–57.

Wu, Y. L. "Can communist China afford war?" *Orbis*, 6 (October, 1962), 453–64.

Zagoria, D. S. "Who's afraid of the domino theory?" *New York Times Magazine*, April 21, 1968, pp. 28–9ff; reply with rejoinder by J. E. McSherry, *ibid.*, May 12, 1968, pp. 22ff.

Zorza, Victor. "Moscow and Peking step up struggle to win Hanoi's allegiance," *Guardian*, July 26, 1967, p. 9.

16. The dispute and its impact on the West

Brzezinsky, Zbigniew. "Pattern and limits of the Sino-Soviet dispute," *Problems of Communism*, 9 (September–October, 1960), 1–7; also printed with slight variations in *New Leader*, 43 (September 19, 1960), 5–8.

Cousin, N. "When one danger is greater than two," *Saturday Review*, 44 (October 14, 1961), 38.

Crozier, Brian. "The struggle for the third world," *International Affairs* (London), 40 (July, 1964), 440–52.

Davids, J. "Sino-Soviet conflict and the Far East," in *The United States in World Affairs*. New York: Harper, 1965.

Dean, Vera Michelas. "Red China on the march, what U.S. action?" *Foreign Policy Bulletin*, 39 (January 15, 1960), 71–2.

Devlin, K. "Which side are you on?" *Problems of Communism*, 16 (January, 1967), 52–9.

"Fanning the red flames," *Far Eastern Economic Review*, 44 (May 14, 1964), 339–41.

Frankel, M. "Russian-Chinese struggle over who will bury us?" *Saturday Evening Post*, 236 (April 13, 1963), 30ff; same with the title: "Bitter feud that splits the communist world," *Reader's Digest*, 83 (August, 1963), 138–44.

Goldstein, Walter, and S. M. Miller. "Accident war," *New Left Review*, 15 (June, 1962), 21–33.

Horowitz, Irving Louis. "Latin America and the Sino-Soviet split," *Liberation*, 8 (May, 1963), 11–15.

Kennan, George F. "Can we deal with Moscow?" *Saturday Evening Post*, 236 (October 5, 1963), 38, 40–43.

Levi, Werner. "China and the two great powers," *Current History*, 39 (December, 1960), 321–26.

Mackintosh, M. "Implication of the Sino-Soviet dispute," in *The Military-technical Revolution*, edited by J. Erickson. New York: Praeger, 1966.

Ritvo, Herbert. "Sino-Soviet relations and the summit," *Problems of Communism*, 7 (September–October, 1958), 7–9.

Soviet-Asian Relations Conference, University of Southern California. *Conference Report:* no. 1–8, 10–15. Los Angeles: School of International Relations, University of Southern California, 1959.

Stebbins, R. P. "Facing the communist world," in *The United States in World Affairs*. New York: Harper, 1965.

Thornton, Thomas Perry. "Peking, Moscow and the underdeveloped areas," *World Politics*, 13 (July, 1961), 491–504.

Warner, Denis. "China fans the fires," *Reporter*, 32 (January 14, 1965), 16–20.

Whetten, L. L. "Moscow's anti-China pact," *World Today*, 25 (September, 1969), 385–93.

Zagoria, D. S. "Sino-Soviet conflict and the West," *Foreign Affairs*, 41 (October, 1962), 171–90.

Zorza, Victor. "How we can profit from the China-Soviet break?" *Look*, 27 (November 19, 1963), 49–50.

17. From the Soviet side of the dispute

Achiminov, H. F. "Crisis in Mao's realm and Moscow's China policy," *Orbis*, 11 (Winter, 1968), 1179–92.

"And the Russians too," *Economist*, 224 (August 26, 1967), 706.

Bartok, Leszlo. "Political evaluation of the 22nd Soviet Communist Party Congress," *East-Central European Papers*, 5 (March, 1962), 73–91.

Bialer, Seweryn. "The 21st Congress and Soviet policy," *Problems of Communism*, 8 (March–April, 1959), 1–9.

"Chance for Moscow," *Economist*, 222 (January 14, 1967), 103.

"China defies Russia – and muddles on at home," *Economist*, 233 (October 4, 1969), 21–2.

"China's yellow peril," *U.S. News and World Report*, 64 (January 22, 1968), 8.

Cliff, Tony. "The 22nd Congress of the Russian Communist Party," *New Politics*, 1 (Winter, 1962), 51–65.

Conolly, Violet. "Sino-Soviet conflict and the Soviet Far Eastern regions," *Royal Central Asian Journal*, 54 (June, 1967), 146–50.

Daniels, Robert V. "Toward a definition of Soviet socialism," *New Politics*, 1 (Winter, 1962), 111–18.

Folliard, E. T. "Meaning of the Peking-Moscow feud," *America*, 106 (March 31, 1962), 850.

"Khrushchev manifesto," *Economist*, 200 (August, 5 1961), 524–26.

Kohler, F. D. "Mideast outlook: why Russia shuns a showdown," *U.S. News and World Report*, 68 (June, 22 1970), 25–6.

Lippmann, Walter. "Dealing with the Soviet Union," *Newsweek*, 62 (July 22, 1963), 17.

McGovern, R. L. "Moscow and Hanoi," *Problems of Communism*, 16 (May, 1967), 64–71.

Manning, Clarence A. "Khrushchev's new communist program," *Ukrainian Quarterly*, 17 (Autumn, 1961), 259–67.

Marabini, J. "Russia's magic Moslems – new dam for a Chinese flood," *Atlas*, 18 (September, 1969), 20–22.

Murarka, D. "Russia asks for talks on China," *Observer*, (November 26, 1967), 2.

Pistrak, Lazar M. "Lenin and peaceful coexistence," *Problems of Communism*, 8 (November–December, 1959), 53–6.

Rothstein, Andrew. "The Twenty-First Congress," *Labour Monthly*, 41 (March, 1959), 131–38.

"Russia on the eve," *Economist*, 222 (January 21, 1967), 218.

"Russian charge: Peking is hijacking Soviet jets," *U.S. News and World Report*, 62 (March 6, 1967), 12.

Schapiro, Leonard. "The Sino-Soviet dispute and the Twenty-Second Congress," *India Quarterly*, 18 (January–March, 1962), 3–8.

Schlesinger, Rudolf. "The CPSU programme: historical and international aspects," *Soviet Studies*, 13 (January, 1962), 303–17.

Spector, Ivar. "Soviet policy in Asia: a reappraisal," *Current History*, 43 (November, 1962), 257–62.

Thomas, J. R. "Soviet Russia and southeast Asia," *Current History*, 55 (November, 1968), 275–80.

Tidmarch, Kuril. "How Russians view the East," *New York Times*, January 24, 1967, p. 13.

Todd, Oliver. "Mao's thoughts find few buyers in Hanoi," *Observer*, (December 16, 1967), 5.

Weeks, A. "Khrushchev's new radicalism," *New Leader*, 44 (April 3, 1961), 15–17.

Wertin, A. "Recriminations in Moscow: Sino-Soviet logger-heads," *Nation*, 197 (July 27, 1963), 43–6.

——. "Walkout in Moscow: Twenty-Second Congress," *Nation*, 193 (November 11, 1961), 370–72.

"Your problems too, Alexei," *Economist*, 222 (February 11, 1967), 489–90.

Zilliacus, Koni. "What do the Russians want?" *Monthly Review*, 14 (December, 1963), 443–7ff.

Zorza, Victor. "Mr. K. fails to move against China," *Guardian*, October 30, 1963, pp. 1, 9.

——. "Mr. K. speaks of Chinese service to imperialists," *Guardian*, September 5, 1964, p. 9.

——. "Russia hints at war with China," *Guardian*, February 16, 1967, pp. 1, 16.

18. From the Chinese side of the dispute

Adie, W. A. C. "Mao on the warpath?" *Spectator*, 209 (November 9, 1962), 701.
——. "Oil, aid and ideology," *Spectator*, 210 (June 28, 1963), 829.
Alexandrov, K. "China's independent policy," Institut zur Erforschung der UdSSR, *Bulletin*, 7 (May, 1960), 30–34.
Alsop, J. "How red China shook the Kremlin?" *Reader's Digest*, 83 (October, 1963), 129–30.
Alsop, S. "Madness of Mao Tse-tung," *Saturday Evening Post*, 236 (October 26, 1963), 12.
"Anti-Russian tirades," *New Statesman*, 69 (March 19, 1965), 427.
"As the turmoil in China keeps growing," *U.S. News and World Report*, 62 (February 6, 1967), 6.
Barnett, A. D. "The inclusion of communist China in arms control program," *Daedalus*, 89 (Fall, 1960), 831–45.
——. "What Chou En-lai's words mean to us?" *Look*, 25 (January, 1961), 105.
Beecher, William. "Gaging China's will," *Wall Street Journal*, 165 (March 5, 1965), 1–5.
Brownlow, O. "Chinese threat seems focused on Soviets," *Australian Weekly*, 85 (November 14, 1966), 29.
Caroe, O. "China in Central Asia: a challenge to Russia's empire," *Round Table*, 56 (October, 1966), 379–86.
Charles, David A. "The dismissal of Marshal Peng Teh-huai," *China Quarterly*, 8 (October–December, 1961), 63–76.
Chen, Chien-chung. "The Chinese communist position in the light of the Khrushchev-Mao struggle," *Free China and Asia*, 10 (August, 1963), 4–8.
"Dirty deal, Chinese boycott of the 23rd Congress of the Soviet Communist Party," *Senior Scholastic* (teacher ed.), 88 (April 22, 1966), 13.
Donnelly, D. "Mr. K's Chinese dragon," *Reporter*, 205 (September 2, 1960), 330–31.
Elegant, Robert S. "The view from Peking," *New Leader*, 43 (December 12, 1960), 8–11.
"Fight of tigers, concerning the letter of Chinese Central Committee to Russians," *Time*, 87 (April 1, 1966), 28.
Halperin, A. M. "Communist China and peaceful coexistence," *China Quarterly*, 3 (July–Sptember, 1960), 16–31.
Hinton, Harold C. "China: a dragon rampant," *Commonweal*, 77 (February 15, 1963), 531–34.
——. "Peculiar partnership," *Commonweal*, 79 (October 18, 1963), 91–4.
Hudson, G. F. "Admonitions from comrade Mao," *New Leader*, 46 (July 22, 1963), 3–5.
——. "Mao and Moscow," *Foreign Affairs*, 36 (October, 1957), 78–90.
——. "The Peking -Moscow axis," *Commentary*, 26 (October, 1958), 492–98.
"Invitation refused," *Economist*, 218 (March 26, 1966), 1221.
MacKenzie, Norman. "Chinese crackers," *New Statesman*, 65 (February 1, 1963), 144.
McWilliams, W. C. "Will China intervene? the stakes in Vietnam," *Commonweal*, 85 (February 17, 1967), 553–55.
Marlow, James, "Peking maps U.S. destruction," *Los Angeles Herald-Examiner*, September 6, 1966, p. A–6.
North, Robert C. "China: a tiger by the tail," *Reporter*, 20 (March 5, 1959), 23–5.

Obja, I. C. "China and North Vietnam : the limits of the alliance," *Current History*, 54 (January, 1968), 42–7.

Pavlov, K. "Communist China: a reluctant dragon," Institut zur Erforschung der UdSSR, *Bulletin*, 9 (March, 1962), 3–14; and 9 (April, 1962), 3–12.

Quested, R. "Further light on the expansion of Russia in East Asia, 1792–1860," *Journal of Asian Studies*, 29 (February, 1970), 327–45.

Sacks, W. M. "Borders of China," *New Republic*, 148 (May 4, 1963), 38–9.

Salisbury, H. E. "Aircraft ready all over Siberia: China now treats Russia as the enemy," *New York Times*, August 17, 1966, p. 6.

———. "Haunting enigma of Red China," *New York Times Magazine*, June 12, 1960), pp. 11–13.

———. "Red China against Russia," *Saturday Evening Post*, 232 (March 19, 1960), 91–2, 94.

———. "U.S. and U.S.S.R.: the dangers ahead," *Foreign Policy Bulletin*, 39 (June 15, 1960), 145–47, 150.

Schwartz, B. "Repercussion in China," *New Republic*, 134 (June 11, 1956), 30–32.

Snow, Edgar. "Red China's leaders talk peace in their terms," *Look*, 25 (January, 1961), 86–104.

Stephens, Robert. "Fight on, says China," *Observer*, (April 7, 1968), 4.

Tang, Yen-pin. "Powder keg of Central Asia: Sinkiang," *Free China Review*, 14 (July, 1964), 38–43.

Thornton, Thomas Perry. "On the correct handling of contradiction," *World Politics*, 25 (October, 1962), 151–52.

Tsai, P. Y. "Mao Tse-tung's application of dialectics: his strategy and tactics," *Free China and Asia*, 9 (September, 1962), 6–10.

Wainwright, L. "Break through in R.S.V.P.'ism: Chinese reply to the Russian invitation to attend Soviet Congress," *Life*, 60 (April 8, 1966), 25.

Zorza, Victor. "China charges Mr. K. with racism," *Guardian*, October 22, 1963, p. 9.

———. "China may be advising Hanoi to reduce or end aid to Vietcong," *Guardian*, July 15, 1966, p. 8.

———. "Hanoi breaks away from Chinese tutelage," *Guardian*, October 14, 1966, p. 11.

———. "When Peking and Hanoi fall out," *Guardian*, September 1, 1966, op. 1.

19. The future of the dispute

"Chinas Gesetz der Geschichte" (China's law of history), *Der Spiegel*, July 6, 1970, pp. 75ff.

Chubb, C. Edmund. "Patchwork on the Sino-Soviet alliance," *Military Review*, 42 (August, 1962), 2–12.

Clemens, W. C. "Nuclear test ban and Sino-Soviet relations," *Orbis*, 10 (Spring, 1966), 152–53.

Dallin, Alexander. "The tie that binds two giants," *Saturday Review*, 44 (May 20, 1961), 39–40.

Dallin, Davis J. "The future of the Sino-Soviet alliance," *Orbis*, 1 (October, 1957), 315–25.

Dedjer, Vladimir. "Early Sino-Soviet break unlikely," *New York Times*, January 11, 1961, p. 6.

Gittings, John. "Cooperation and conflict in the Sino-Soviet relations," *International Affairs* (London), 40 (January, 1964), 60–75.

——. "Political control of the Chinese army," *World Affairs*, 19 (August, 1963), 327–36.
Harrington, Michael. "China-Soviet conflict?" *Commonweal*, 71 (January 8, 1960), 411–14.
Hilsman, R. "How real is the break between Russia and China?" State Department, *Bulletin*, 47 (November 26, 1962), 807–11; also in *U.S. News and World Report*, 53 (November 26, 1962), 74–5.
Labedz, Leopold. "The growing Sino-Soviet dispute," *New Leader*, 43 (September 12, 1960), 3–5.
——. "Ideology: the fourth stage," *Problems of Communism*, 8 (November–December, 1959), 1–10.
Laqueur, W. Z. "Russia and China, uneasy allies," *New Republic*, 143 (August 15, 1960), 10–11.
Lindsay, Michael. "Is cleavage between Russia and China inevitable?" *Annals of the American Academy of Political and Social Science*, 336 (July, 1961), 53–61.
McCabe, Robert Karr. "China burns its bridges: the Sino-Soviet dispute will never be the same," *New Leader*, 45 (December 24, 1962), 8–10.
Martin, Robert P. "How real is the split between China and Russia?" *U.S. News and World Report*, 50 (June 26, 1961), 42–3.
"Moscow-Peking feud: rift grows wider," *U.S. News and World Report*, 60 (April 4, 1966), 6.
Portisch, H. "Worry for red empire on another front," *U.S. News and World Report*, 65 (September 9, 1968), 83–4.
Pu, Jen. "Is there any possibility for reconciliation between Moscow and Peiping? *Free China and Asia*, 11 (November, 1964), 8–10.
"Sino-Soviet rift: complication of world reaction to dispute," *Senior Scholastic* (teacher ed.), 88 (April 15, 1966), 24.
Stanford, Neal. "Moscow-Peiping feud grows," *Foreign Policy Bulletin*, 40 (October 1, 1960), 11.
Taylor, George E. "Can the Moscow-Peking front endure?" *Western World*, 3 (March, 1960), 27–37.
"This is the third world war," *Economist*, 220 (August 20, 1966), 709–10.
"Who'll break first?" *Economist*, 222 (February 11, 1967), 494.
Yuriev, Grigory. "The sharpening of the Soviet-Chinese conflict," *Analysis of Current Developments in the Soviet Union*, 20 (1962–63), 1–5.
Zagoria, D. S. "The future of Sino-Soviet relations," *Asian Survey*, 1 (April, 1961), 3–14.
——. "Widening gulf between Mao and Khrushchev," *Reporter*, 28 (April 25, 1963), 38–40.

V. WORKS ON MILITARY MATTERS

Berchin, Michael and Eliahu Ben-Horin. *The Red Army*. 1st ed. New York: Norton, 1942.
Bernard, L. *War and Its Causes*. Chicago: Regnery, 1944.
"China will die Weltrevolution nur mit gewaltsame Mitteln" (China seeks to use violence to carry out world revolution), *California Staats-Zeitung*, June 28, 1963.
Fedotoff, White Dimitri. "Soviet philosophy of war," *Political Science Quarterly*, 51 (1936), 321–53.
Frunze, M. V. "Soedinnenoe voennoe uchenie i Krasnaya Armiya" (A unified

military doctrine and the Red Army), *Voennaya nauka i revoliutsiya*, 1 (1921), 3–40.

Garlick, Gerald S. "Communist interpretation of the causes of war." Unpublished doctoral dissertation, University of Iowa, 1955. Excerpted in *Dissertation Abstract*, 1955, pt. II, pp. 2275–76.

Garthoff, Raymond, *Soviet Military Doctrine*. Glencoe, Illinois: Free Press, 1953.

——, (ed.) *Sino-Soviet Military Relations*. New York: Praeger, 1966.

Griffith, Samuel. *Peking and People's Wars*. New York: Praeger, 1966.

Jeffe, Ellis. *The PLA in Politics and Politics in the PLA, 1965–66*. Columbia University Seminar on Modern China, November 30, 1966.

Lin, Piao, "Long live the victory of people's war," in *China after Mao*, edited by A. D. Barnett. Princeton, N.J.: Princeton University press, 1967.

McDougall, William. *Janus: the Concept of War*. London: Kegan Paul [n.d.]

Marksizm-leninizm o voine i armii (Marxism-Leninism on war and army). 4th ed. Moskva: Voen. izd-vo, 1965. 1st ed. 1956. 5th ed. 1968.

Porrit, Arthur (ed.) *The Causes of War*. New York: Macmillan, 1932.

Prokof'ev, E. A. *Voennye vzglyady dekabristov* (The military ideologies of the Decembrists). Moskva: Voen. izd-vo, 1953.

Shifman, M. J. *Voina i ekonomika* (War and economy). Moskva: Voen. izd-vo, 1964.

Theory and Research on the Causes of War. Edited by Dean G. Pruitt, and Richard C. Snyder. Englewood Cliffs, N.J.: Prentice-Hall, 1969.

Trotskii, L. "Voennye spetsialisty i Krasnaya Armiya" (Military specialists and the Red Army), *Izvestiya*, January 10, 1919.

Voennaya strategiya (Military strategy). 2nd ed. Moskva: Voen. izd-vo, 1963.

Voina i voennoe iskusstvo v svete istoricheskogo materializma (War and military art in the light of historical materialism). Moskva: Gosizdat, 1927.

W. I. Lenin als Militärwissenschaftler (Lenin as a military scientist). Berlin: Verlag des Ministerium für National Verteidigung, 1956. Published by the Defense Department of East Germany, articles are translated from the Russian text.

Welton, H. *The Third World War*. London: Pall Mall press, 1959.

Wollenberg Erich. *The Red Army: a Study of the Growth of Soviet Imperialism*. London: Secker and Warburg, 1940. Translated from an MS which was written in German.

Yin, J. "Soviet theory of war." Unpublished Master's thesis, University of Southern California, 1964.

VI. WORKS ON CAPITALISM AND COMMUNISM

Antikommunizm – orudie imperialisticheskoi reaktsii (Anti-communism, the weapon of imperialist reaction). Moskva: Gos. izd-vo polit. lit-ry, 1967.

Bauer, Otto. *Die Nationalitätenfrage und die Sozialdemokratie* (The nationality problems and Social Democracy). Wien: Verlag der Wiener Volksbuchhandlung, 1924.

Carew-Hunt, R. N. *Theory and Practice of Communism*. London: Bles, 1950.

Chambre, Henri. *De Karl Marx à Mao Tse-tung*. Paris: Spes, 1958.

Cheprakov, V. "Problemy poslednei treti veka" (The problems of the last thirty years of the century), *Izvestiya*, August 11, 1968.

Diversity in International Communism. Edited by A. Dallin. New York: Columbia University Press, 1964.

Duverger, Maurice. *Les parties politiques.* 4th ed. Paris: Librarie Armand Colin, 1961.

Essential Works of Chinese Communism. Edited by W. Chai. [N.p.] Pica press, 1969.

Fainsod, Merle. *How Russia is Ruled.* Rev. ed. Cambridge, Mass: Harvard University press, 1960.

Germanskii militarizm i imperializm (German militarism and imperialism). Moskva: Gos. izd-vo polit. lit-ry, 1965.

Griffith, William. *World Communism Divided.* Nesw York: Foreign Policy Association, 1964.

Guesde, Jules. *En garde! contre les contrefaçon, les mirages et la fausse monnaie des reformes bourgeoises; polemique* (On guard against the counterfeit coinage of the bourgeois reform). Paris: J. Rouff, 1911.

Hilferding, Rudolf. *Das Finanzkapital; eine Studie über die jüngste Entwicklung des Kapitalismus* (The finance capital; a study of the latest development of capitalism). Berlin: Diez, 1947.

Hobson, John. *Imperialism.* London: Allen and Unwin, 1938.

Il'ichev, L. F. *Ocherednye zadachi ideologicheskoi raboty partii* (The next task of the party's ideological work). Moskva: Gos. izd-vo polit. lit-ry, 1963.

Kautsky, Karl. "Krisentheorien" (The crisis theory), *Die Neue Zeit,* 2 (1901–02), 133–35.

Kennan, George F. *On Dealing With the Communist World.* New York: Harper and Row, 1964.

Kolarz, Walter. *Communism and Colonialism.* London: Macmillan; New York: St. Martin's press, 1964.

Kovalez, Sergei. "Suverenitet internatsional'nogo obyazannosti sotsialisticheskikh stran" (Sovereignty of international obligation of socialist states), *Pravda,* September 26, 1968.

Krasin, Iu. *Lenin, revoliutsiya i sovremennost' – problemy leninskoi teorii sotsialisticheskoi revoliutsii* (Lenin, revolution in the modern time – problems of Lenin's theory of socialist revolution). Moskva: Gos. izd-vo polit. lit-ry, 1967.

KPSS v bor'be za osushchestvlenie programmy stroitel'stva kommunizma (CPSU in the struggle for realization of the programmatic structure of communism). Edited by V. L. Ignat'ev and P. I. Kotel'nikov. Moskva: Izd-vo "Mysl'," 1968.

KPSS v period zaversheniya stroitel'stva sotsializma i perekhoda k kommunizmu (CPSU in the period of building-up of socialism and transition to communism). Moskva: Gos. izd-vo polit. lit-ry, 1967.

Leont'ev, L. *Leninskaya teoriya imperializma* (Lenin's theory of imperialism). Moskva: Moskovskii rabochii, 1954.

Luxemburg, Rosa. *Die Akkumulation des Kapitals: ein Beitrag zur ökonomischen Erklärung des Imperialismus* (The accumulation of capital; an economic explanation of imperialism). Berlin: Vorwarts P. Singer, 1913.

Mayo, Henry B. *Introduction to Marxist Theory.* 1st ed. New York: Oxford University press, 1960.

Meyer, Alfred G. *Leninism.* 3rd ed. New York: Random house, 1967.

New Communism. Edited by D. N. Jacobs. New York: Harper and Row, 1969.

Mirovaya ekonomika (World economy). Moskva: Gos. izd-vo polit. lit-ry, 1965.

Mirovaya sotsialisticheskaya sistema i antikommunizm (World socialist system and anti-communism). Edited by A. B. Butenko. Moskva: Izd-vo "Nauka," 1968.

Modelski, George. *The Communist International System.* Research monograph no. 9. Princeton, N.J.: Princeton University press for Center of International Studies, 1960.

Ot sotsializma k kommunizmu (From socialism to communism). Minsk: Izd-vo Akademii Nauk BSSR, 1963.

Perfil'ev, M. N. *Kritika burzhuaznykh teorii o sovetskoi politicheskoi sisteme* (Critique of bourgeois theories on Soviet political system). Leningrad: Izd-vo "Nauka," 1968.

Razin, V. I. *Marksistsko-leninskoe uchenie o gosudarstve* (Marxist-Leninist doctrine on state). Moskva: Gos. izd-vo polit. lit-ry, 1966.

The Road to Communism: China since 1912. Edited by D. J. Li. New York: Van Nostrand-Rheinhold, 1970.

Rozental', M. M. and G. M. Shtraks (eds.) *Kategorii materialisticheskoi dialektiki* (The categories of materialist dialectics). Moskva: Gos. izd-vo polit. lit-ry, 1956.

Sakharov, A. D. "Thoughts about progress, peaceful coexistence and intellectual freedom," *New York Times,* July 22, 1968, pp. 15–16.

Scharlan, W. H. and Z. A. Zeman. *Freibeuter der Revolution: Parvus-Helphand, eine politische Biographie* (A privateer of revolution; a political profile of Parvus-Helphand). Köln: Verlag Wissenschaft und Politik, 1964.

Schumpeter, Joseph A. *Capitalism, Socialism and Democracy.* New York: Harper, 1950.

Stewart-Smith, D. G. *The Defeat of Communism.* 1st ed. London: Lugdate press, 1964.

Sudarikov, A. *Klassy i klassovaya bor'ba sotsial'nye revoliutsii* (Classes and class struggle, social revolution). Moskva: Gos. izd-vo polit. lit-ry, 1966.

Swearingen, Rodger. *Focus: World Communism.* Boston: Houghton, 1965.

——. *The World of Communism.* Rev. ed. Boston: Houghton, 1966.

Tang, Peter. *The Twenty-Second Congress of the Communist Party of the Soviet Union and Moscow-Tirana-Peking.* Washington: Research Institute on the Sino-Soviet Bloc, 1962.

Teoriya gosudarstva i prava (Theory of state and law). Moskva: Gos. izd-vo iuridicheskoi lit-ry, 1959.

Triska, Jan F. (ed.) *Soviet Communism: Programs and Rules.* San Francisco: Chandler publishing company, 1962.

Uschakow, A. *Der Rat für gegenseitige wirtschaftshilfe COMECON.* Köln: Verlag Wissenschaft und Politik, 1962.

U.S. Congress. House. Committee on Un-American Activities. *Facts on Communism,* vol. I: *The Communist Ideology; vol.* II: *The Soviet Union, from Lenin to Khrushchev.* Washington: Government Printing Office, 1960.

V. I. Lenin – velikii teoretik (V. I. Lenin, a great theorist). Moskva: Gos. izd-vo polit. lit-ry, 1966.

Varga, Eugene. *Osnovye voprosy ekonomiki i politiki imperializma posle vtoroi mirovoi voiny* (The fundamental problems of imperialist economy and politics after the Second World War). Moskva: Gos. izd-vo polit. lit-ry, 1953.

Vygodskii, S., *et al. Istoriya diplomatii* (Diplomatic history), vol. 3: *Diplomatiya na pervom etape obshchego krizisa kapitalisticheskoi sistemy* (Diplomacy on the first stage of the general crisis of the capitalist system). 2nd ed. Moskva: Gos. izd-vo polit. lit-ry, 1965.

Voprosy sovetskogo gosudarstva i prava (Problems of the Soviet government and law). "Seriya iuridicheskii nauk" (Series of judicial science), no. 7. Moskva: Izd-vo Liningradskogo Universiteta, 1955.

"Vozzvanie ispolnitel'nogo komiteta kommunisticheskoi internatsionale" (Appeal of the Executive Committee of the Communist International), *Kommunisticheskii internatisonal,* 8–9 (1939), 3–4.

VIII. WORKS ON THE SINO-SOVIET DISPUTE (MAINLY BOOKS)

Abegg, L. "Hass und Hassliebe" (Hate and love of hate), *Die Weltwoche*, March 21, 1969, p. 1.

"Die Absetsung des Rektors der Universität Peking, Ma Jing-tschus Kritik am 'Grossen Sprung'" (Dismissal of Ma Yin-ch'u, President of Peking University, for his criticism of the 'Great leap forward'), *Neue Zürcher Zeitung*, April 20, 1960, p. 12.

Barcata, Louis. *China geht nicht Russlands Weg* (China is not going Russia's way). Stuttgart: Diez, 1959.

Barnett, Robert W. *Quemoy: the Use and Consequence of Nuclear Deterrence.* Cambridge, Mass.: Harvard University press, 1960.

Brandt, Conrad. *Stalin's Failure in China, 1924–1927.* Cambridge, Mass.: Harvard University press, 1958.

Cecil, V. Crabb. *Nations in a Multi-polar World.* New York: Harper and Row, 1968.

Chen, King C. *Vietnam and China, 1938–1954.* Princeton, N.J.: Princeton University press, 1969.

Chin, Ssu-kai. *Communist China's Relations with the Soviet Union, 1949–1957.* Hong Kong: Union Research Institute, 1961.

China after Mao. Edited by A. D. Barnett. Princeton, N.J.: Princeton University press, 1967.

Chrepanov, A. I. *Severnyi pokhod natsional'no-revoliutsionnoi armii Kitaya* (The Northern Expedition of the national revolutionary army of China). Moskva: Izd-vo "Nauka," 1968.

Clemens, W. C. *The Arms Race and Sino-Soviet Relations.* Stanford, California: Stanford University press, 1968.

Communist Struggles in Asia; a Comparative Analysis of Government and Parties. Edited by A. D. Barnett. London: Pall Mall press, 1964.

Crankshaw, Edward. *The New Cold War: Moscow v Peking.* Harmonds-Worth, England: Penguin, 1963.

Dedjer, Vladimir. *Tito.* New York: Simon and Schuster, 1961.

Floyd, David. *Mao against Khrushchev.* New York: Praeger, 1964.

George, A. L. *The Chinese Communist Party in Action.* New York: Columbia University press, 1967.

Ghosh, M. *China's Conflict with India and the Soviet Union.* Calcutta: World press, 1969.

Griffith, William. *Albania and the Sino-Soviet Rift.* Cambridge, Mass.: MIT press, 1963.

Gurtov, M. *The First Vietnam Crisis.* New York: Columbia University press, 1967.

Hsieh, A. L. *The Chinese Genie: Peking's Role in the Nuclear Ban Negotiation.* Santa Monica: California, Rand Corp., 1960.

Isaacs, Harold. *The Tragedy of the Chinese Revolution.* Rev. ed. Stanford, California: Stanford University press, 1951.

Iur'ev, M. F. *Revoliutsiya, 1925–1927, v Kitae* (The Revolution in China, 1925–1927). Moskva: Izd-vo "Nauka," 1968.

Kalb, M. L. *Dragon in the Kremlin.* New York: Dutton, 1961.

Kulski, W. A. *Peaceful Coexistence.* Chicago: Regnery, 1959.

Levesque, Jacques. *Le Conflict Sino-Sovietique et l'Europe de l'est.* Montreal, Canada: Les press de l'Universite de Montreal, 1970.

Mayer, Peter. *Sino-Soviet Relations since the Death of Stalin.* Hong Kong: Union Research Institute, 1962.

Mendie, Ribor. *China and Her Shadow.* New York: Coward McCann, 1962.

Michael, F. and George Taylor. *The Far East in the Modern World.* Rev. ed. New York: Holt, 1964.

Morison, David. *The U.S.S.R. and Africa.* London: Oxford University press, 1964.

North, Robert C. *Moscow and Chinese Communists.* 2nd ed. Stanford, California: Stanford University press, 1963.

Overstreet, Harry and Bonaro Overstreet. *The War Called Peace: Khrushchev's Communism.* New York: Norton, 1961.

Payne, Robert. *Portrait of a Revolutionary: Mao Tse-tung.* Rev. ed. New York: Alebard-Schuman, 1962.

Politika SSSR v Otniosheni Kitaya (Policy of the USSR toward China), Moskva: Izd-vo "Nauka," 1968.

Quested, R. K. I. *The Expansion of Russia in East Asia, 1857-1860.* New York: Oxford University press, 1969.

Rauch, George von. *A History of Soviet Russia.* Rev. ed. New York: Praeger, 1959.

Russian-Chinese Rift. Edited by I. Isenberg. New York: Wilson, 1966.

Salisbury, H. E. *Orbit of China.* New York: Harper and Row, 1967.

——. *War between Russia and China.* New York: Norton, 1969.

Schwartz, Harry. *Tsars, Mandarins and Commissars.* Philadelphia: Lippincott, 1964.

Seton-Watson, Hugh. *Neither War Nor Peace.* New York: Praeger, 1960.

Shih, Yuan-ching. *The Relations between Moscow and Peiping.* Taipei: Asian People's Anti-communist League, 1961.

Sino-Soviet Dispute; documented and analyzed by George F. Hudson, Richard Lowenthal, and Roderick MacFarquhar. New York: Praeger, 1961.

Sino-Soviet Relations and Arms Control. Edited by M. H. Halperin. Cambridge, Mass.: MIT press, 1967.

Soviet and Chinese Communist Power in the World War Today. Edited by Rodger Swearingen. New York: Basic Books, 1966.

Survey of the Sino-Soviet Dispute; a commentary and extract from the recent polemics. Edited by John Gittings. Toronto: Oxford University press, 1968. Especially pp. 254–70.

Swearingen, Rodger. "The political and ideological relationship between the Chinese Communist Party and the Soviet Union." UnpublishedMaster's thesis, University of Southern California, 1948.

Tashjean, John E. "Where China meets Russia: an analysis of Wilhelm Starlinger's theory." Unpublished Master's thesis, Georgetown University, 1959.

Territorial Claims in the Sino-Soviet Dispute: documents and analysis. Edited by Dennis J. Dooklin. Stanford, California: Stanford University press, 1965.

Wittfogel, Karl August. *Mao Tse-tung: liberator o destructor de los campesinos Chinos?* (Mao Tse-tung: a liberator or destroyer of the Chinese peasants?) New York: Comite de Sindicalismo Libre de la Federacion Americana del Trabajo, 1955.

Zabloski, J. *Sino-Soviet Rivalry: Implementation for U.S. Policy.* Princeton, N.J.: Princeton University press, 1962.

VIII. HANDBOOKS, DICTIONARIES AND ENCYCLOPEDIAS

Bol'shaya sovetskaya entsiklopediya (The great Soviet encyclopedia). 1st ed. Moskva: Aktsionernoe obshchestvo "sovetskaya entsiklopediya," 1927–47, 65 vols. 2nd ed. 1949–57, 50 vols. 3rd ed. 1970–
——. *Ezhegodnik* (Annual supplement), 1957–69.
Facts on File. New York: Facts on File Company. Current.
Handbook on Marxism. Edited by Emile Burns. New York: International publishers [n.d.]
Jen-min shou-ts'e (People's handbook). Peking: Tai-kung pao, 1957– Irregular.
Malaya sovetskaya entsiklopediya (The small Soviet encyclopedia). 1st ed. Moskva: Ogiz RSFSR gos. institut sovetskaya entsiklopediya, 1928–31, 11 vols. 2nd ed., 1933–40, 10 vols. 3rd ed., 1955–61, 11 vols.
Politicheskii slovar' (Political dictionary). Edited by E. Ponomarev. 2nd ed. Moskva: Gos. izd-vo polit. lit-ry, 1962. 1st ed. 1958.
Shih-chieh chih-shih nien-chieh (World encyclopedia). Peking: Shih-chieh chih-shih nien-chieh, 1958.
Shih-shih shou-ts'e (Current affairs handbook). Peking: Irregular.
Slovar' osnovnykh voennykh terminov (Dictionary of basic military terms), Moskva Voen. izd-vo, 1965.
Slovar' sovremennogo russkogo literaturnogo yazyka (Dictionary of modern Russian literature language). Moskva/Leningrad: Izd-vo "Nauka," 1948–65. 12 vols. This dictionary contains many military and political terms.

INDEX

Chao, Shin 7, 44
Chen, King C. 152
Chen-pao *see* Damanskii
Ch'en, Yi accusing Khrushchev 3, accusing
  U.S. 164, disarmament 113, divided
  West 36, 66, hatred of communism
  charged 44, nuclear war 159, peaceful
  coexistence 59, war and irrationality 36,
  Western powers' internal rivalry 66
Cheprakov,V. 170
Chi, Lung 120, 143
Chiang, Kai-shek 73, 164
China 3, 6, 20, 25, 29, 36, 72, 73, 74, 77,
  112, 116, 118, 148, 151, 154, 156, 166,
  167, 168, 176, 180, 181, 182, 183, 188
Chinese Communist Party *see* Communist
  Party of China
Chinese imperialism (Soviets charged) 174
Chinese militarism (Soviets charged) 177,
  178, 179
Chinese Nationalists *see* Taiwan
Chinese People's Republic *see* China
Chinese Revolution (1949) 54, 95, 103
Chou, En-lai 26, 29, 36, 56, 152, 173, 175
Chou, Mou-yang 57
Chrepanov, A. I. 2
Christendom 4
Chu, Hsin-min 126
Chu, Teh 3, 26, 32, 85
Chung, Hsin-ching 36, 42, 43, 60
Civil War in China 73
Civil War in Russia 23, 74
Class struggle and contradiction 8, 12, 13,
  16, 18, 21, 47, 48, 51, 53, 58, 68, 69, 85,
  86, 87, 95, 103, 108, 109, 117, 119, 120,
  132, 156, 184, 186
Clausewitz, Karl von 23, 63
Coexistence *see* Peaceful coexistence
Cold war 51, 107, 187 see also sub-entry
  under Stalin
Colonies and colonialism 51, 57, 63, 69, 113
  115, 116, 117, 117, 119, 120, 121, 122,
  123, 124, 125, 126, 127, 129, 130, 132,
  133, 134, 136, 137, 186, 187
Comintern 1
Communications *see* Diplomacy
Communism 4, 6, 7, 9, 18, 76, 79, 81 *see*
  also Socialism
Communist nations *see* the East
Communist parties and workers' parties
  68, 104, 134, 148, 151, 157, 180
Communist Party of Burma 155, of China
  1, 5, 27, 32, 61, 92, 97, 113, 126, 129,

130, 148, 152, 156, 157, 162, 166, 176,
177, 179, 180, of Chile 181, of France
149, 181, of India 1, of Indonesia 181,
182, of Italy 181, of Japan 182, of Preu
181, of the Soviet Union 1, 2, 3, 5, 7,
13, 14, 16, 19, 20, 24, 25, 26, 27, 67, 90,
103, 124, 129, 133, 142, 148, 150, 156,
161, 162, 163, 166, 172, 180, of the
United States 151
Conflict solution 31
Congo 129, 146
Correlation of forces 8, 14, 16, 18, 24, 25,
  26, 27, 33, 34, 48, 75, 76, 78, 79, 90, 106,
  185 *see* also International relations
Couls, Gardner 31, 50, 79, 81
Council for Mutual Economic Aid 172
Crankshaw, Edward 4, 89, 133
Crozier, Brian 6, 92, 121
Cuba 76, 119, 143
Cultural Revolution *see* Great Proletarian
  Cultural Revolution
Czechoslovakia 124, 134, 174, 175, 176

Dahomey 135
Damanskii 168, 176, 188
Davydov, L. 174
Declaration of the Ruling Communist
  Parties (1957) 5, 6, 17, 34, 61, 68, 88, 93,
  99, 104, 131, 148
Dedjer, Vladimir 110
de Gaulle, Charles 35, 187
Democratic centralism 179
Detente 2, 4, 7, 29, 31, 34, 37, 39, 44, 51,
  52, 59, 127, 187, *see* also Peaceful co-
  existence, International relations
Dialectical materialism 11, 33, 52, 97, 98,
  104
Diplomacy 30, 31, 32, 34, 36, 37, 38, 50,
  51, 66, 68, 131, 132, 148, 153
Disarmament *see* Armament and disarma-
  ment
Djilas, M. 4
Dogmatism 49, 108, 132, 185
Duverger, Maurice 76
East, the 9, 21, 22, 26, 30, 33, 37, 38, 39,
  42, 45, 47, 52, 55, 65, 66, 67, 71, 106,
  109, 110, 113, 121, 130, 131, 139, 141,
  143, 145, 158, 159, 161, 175, 180, 187
Eden, Anthony 142
Economic determinism 11, 15, 52, 72, 74,
  75, 76, 94, 121, 130, 131, 139, 141, 143,
  145, 158, 159, 161, 175, 180, 187
Economy and war *see* War and capitalist

economy; Imperialism and imperialists
Egypt 133, 142
Eisenhower, Dwight D. 3, 7, 35, 37, 39, 138, 139
Engels, F. 24, 39, 46, 54, 91, 117, 124, 138, 160, 180
Epoch 2, 10, 47, 49, 51, 56, 57, 109, 111, 112, 132, 185
Ethiopia 72
Eurasia 164, 181
Europe 164, 166 *see* also Western Europe
European Common Market 138

Farrell, Robert 4
Fedenko, P. 24
Fedorov, G. 140
Fedoseev, A. A. 180
Feinsod, Merle 5
Fetov, V. 179
Feudalism 79, 115
France 36, 66, 73, 116, 127, 144, 156, 187
Frantsev, Iu. 13, 18, 26, 38, 53, 63, 64, 85, 107, 121, 131
French Revolution (1789) 95
Frunze, M. V. 10, 24, 116, 160
Fu, Chung 29

Garthoff, Raymond 107
Gavrilov, I. 176, 177
Genghis Khan 55
Genoa Conference (1922) 160, 167
Germany 16, 22, 28, 45, 60, 66, 165
Ghana 135
Gittings, John 1, 3, 4, 19, 74, 113, 143, 145
Gladkov, J. A. 14
Gorbach, V. I. 173
Gorev, V. I. 12, 53
Great Britain 36, 39, 66, 73, 99, 116, 141
Great Patriotic War 77
Great Proletarian Cultural Revolution 169, 177, 178, 180
Grechko, A. 175
Griffith, William 7, 37, 125
Grigor'ev, K. 27
Gromyko, A. 175
Guesde, Jules 120

Halperin, Ernst 133, 134
Halpern, A. M. 74, 131
Harriman, W. Averrel 152
Harrington, Michael 31
Harris, Richard 1, 74
Herter, Ch. 37
Heyst, Alex 9, 114

Hilferding, Rudolf 14, 120
Hilsman, R. 31, 76, 125, 143
Hinton, Harold C. 29, 45, 54, 134
Historical determinism *see* Economic determinism
Hitler 43, 75
Ho, Chi-minh 150, 151, 166
Hobson, John 14, 120
Hong Kong 151, 177
Hook, Sidney 97
Hot-line 45
Howard, R. 88
Hsiao, Hua 108
Hsieh, Sheng-wen 159
Hsiu, Lieh-chün 136
Hsiu, Pan-han 142
Huang, Chan-pen 136
Hudson, George F. 2
Hugh, Richard 4
Hung, Tsin-ta 170
Hungarian Revolt (1956) 134
Hungary 74

Il'ichev, L. F. 161
Imperialism and imperialists 8, 9, 12, 14, 15, 17, 18, 19, 20, 21, 22, 23, 30, 32, 38, 41, 42, 43, 44, 48, 49, 51, 52, 55, 56, 59, 60, 61, 62, 66, 70, 75, 76, 77, 83, 88, 102, 107, 109, 110, 111, 113, 115, 116, 117, 118, 120, 121, 122, 123, 124, 125, 126, 128, 129, 130, 132, 133, 137, 138, 141, 149, 151, 153, 155, 156, 157, 174, 176, 180, 184, 186, 187, 188
Imperialist camp *see* the West; the West, decline of
Imperialist-capitalism *see* Capitalism
India 3, 113, 114, 116, 133, 173, 174
Indochina 142, 154, 157, 181
Indonesia 3, 135, 174
Industry 25, 27, 38, 70
Inozemtsev, N. 160
Inter-bloc war *see* War, world
International relations 9, 14, 29, 64 *see* also Detente, Correlation of forces
International war *see* War, world
Iran 116
Iraq 85, 142, 144
Ireland 116
Isaacs, Harold 2
Islam 4
Italo-Ethiopian War 72
Iur'ev, M. F. 2
Ivory Coast 135